Heroes for All Time

Heroes for All Time

Connecticut Civil War Soldiers Tell Their Stories

Dione Longley and Buck Zaidel

Wesleyan University Press

Middletown, Connecticut

Wesleyan University Press

Middletown CT 06459

www.wesleyan.edu/wespress

© 2015 Dione Longley and Peter A. Zaidel

Manufactured in China

Designed by David Wolfram

Typeset in Palatino, ITC Stone Sans, and OPTI York

The Driftless Connecticut Series is funded by the
Beatrice Fox Auerbach Foundation Fund
at the Hartford Foundation for Public Giving.

Library of Congress Cataloging-in-Publication Data

Longley, Dione.

Heroes for all time : Connecticut Civil War soldiers tell their stories/
Dione Longley and Buck Zaidel.

pages cm. — (A Driftless Connecticut series book)

Includes bibliographical references and index.

ISBN 978-0-8195-7116-8 (cloth : alk. paper) —

ISBN 978-0-8195-7117-5 (ebook)

1. Connecticut—History—Civil War, 1861–1865. 2. Connecticut—
History—Civil War, 1861–1865—Personal narratives.
3. Soldiers—Connecticut—History—19th century. 4. United States—
History—Civil War, 1861–1865. 5. United States—History—
Civil War, 1861–1865—Personal narratives. 6. United States—History—
Civil War, 1861–1865—Campaigns. I. Zaidel, Buck. II. Title.

E499.L66 2014

973.7'446—dc23   2014022334

5 4 3 2 1

Contents

PREFACE

This is a book of stories.

Every Civil War soldier had a story. The stories were as varied as the men and boys who enlisted. And over 50,000 of them came from Connecticut.

In this book you will hear the voices of those Connecticut soldiers—not the interpretations of modern Civil War scholars, but the words of the men who actually fought the war.

Many were eager to share their war experiences in letters home, often finding relief in pouring out their feelings. "That night after the battle I never shall forget the groans and sreiks of the wounded," a shaken soldier reported to his mother.[1] Others kept diaries, recording dramatic events and snippets of daily life. "Thanksgiving. Snow Storm. Shoes full of holes, think of home," wrote a woebegone teenager from Gales Ferry.[2] And in the years after the war, some veterans felt the need to preserve their stories in memoirs. A Suffield cigar maker hoped his reminiscences would "awaken in my Children a deep love of the Government that their Father shouldered his musket to defend."[3]

Some soldiers wrote eloquently, like Henry Camp, a Yale graduate and infantry officer: "We were to storm the fort. Our hearts beat high and fast . . . The feeling was not of doubt or shrinking, but of curiosity mingled with firm resolve."[4] Just as moving were the words of men like Lucien Dunham of Warehouse Point, who mused about the Confederates and the war: "it dident sean like they wear enmeys to us   if they would let the soilders come together they would settle this prutey quick."[5]

While some soldiers used the written word, many men chose to document their history in a different medium: photography. The camera caught their proud expressions as they posed in their new uniforms; or their weathered, philosophical faces transformed by hard service and the appalling scenes they had witnessed. In some images, a man's intensity of gaze conveyed his resolve more clearly than any letter could.

Soldiers often brought home artifacts that held important memories. Levi Jewett carefully preserved his felt hat, marked with a bloodstained gash from a shell fragment that wounded him. George Stannard's family treasured the bone ring he carved on the battlefield at Antietam. Such personal mementoes are vehicles to the past, connecting us to a soldier's story with surprising immediacy.

Together, the individual stories of Connecticut soldiers create an astonishing whole that lays out the war before us. We offer this book so that, as one old soldier put it, "our children's children may see with their eyes, as we saw with our eyes, the scenes and places of the great War for the Union. Lest we and they forget."[6]

ACKNOWLEDGMENTS

A great many kind people went out of their way to help us. Dean Nelson, Museum Administrator of the Museum of Connecticut History, made the museum's collection available to us time and again. Dean provided twenty-five years of Civil War tutelage, along with some memorable lines like "Right as rain" and "If you're going to buy a fake, make it a good one." Andy deCusati gave us his insights and advice. Bill McFarland graciously allowed the Wadhams brothers to be reunited. John Giammatteo, with camera, skill, and patience, was always there when we needed him.

At historical societies and museums in Connecticut and elsewhere, staff people were infinitely helpful. In particular we thank Deborah D. Shapiro at the Middlesex County Historical Society; Rich Malley, Diana McCain, Nancy Finlay, Judy Johnson, Sierra Dixon, and Karen DePauw of the Connecticut Historical Society; Gail Kruppa at the Torrington Historical Society; and Don McCue of the Lincoln Memorial Shrine.

We are also indebted to the New Haven Museum, Litchfield Historical Society, Deep River Historical Society, the Gunn Memorial Museum of Washington, Connecticut, Stamford Historical Society, the Cheshire Historical Society, Danbury Historical Society, Mansfield Historical Society, the New England Civil War Museum, the United States Army Military History Institute, the Virginia Historical Society, the Montana Historical Society, the National Museum of American History at the Smithsonian, and the Harriet Beecher Stowe Center. Ted Alexander at Antietam National Battlefield, National Park Service, and Eric Leonard at Andersonville National Historic Site, National Park Service, also gave us their help.

We were fortunate to have the help of professionals at libraries and archives at colleges and universities, as well as public and private libraries. Our thanks go to Suzy Taraba and Leith Johnson of Special Collections and Archives at Wesleyan University, Peter J. Blodgett of the Huntington Library, Kate Collins and Valerie Gillispie of Duke University Archives, Tom Mullusky of Gilder Lehrman Institute of American History, Mary Witkowski at the Bridgeport History Center, the Southington Library and Barnes Museum, Edith B. Nettleton Historical Room at the Guilford Free Library, the Pearce Museum at Navarro College, the Beinecke Library at Yale University, the State Archives at the Connecticut State Library, and of course the Library of Congress and National Archives.

Many generous people kindly allowed us to use images and manuscripts from their collections: Linda L. Goodyear, Lawrence S. Matthew, the family of Horace Purdy, Don Troiani, C. Paul Loane, Joyce Werkman, Cathy Branch Stebbins, Mary Rounsavall, Toddy Turrentine, Chris and Louise Wilkinson, Jeff Kowalis, Mike McAfee, Thomas Harris, Nancy George, Diane Ulbrich, Ken and Jean Owings, Scott Hann, Bruce Rebman, Gary O'Neil, Ron Coddington, Calvin Goddard Zon, Ernie Barker, the family of Evelyn E. Packard, Soldierstories.org, Cal Packard at

MuseumQualityAmericana.com, Cowan's Auctions, as well as several private owners who chose to remain anonymous.

To those who helped us with research and advice, we extend our warmest thanks: Nick Picerno, Frederick W. Chesson, Dale E. Call of the 17th Connecticut Volunteer Infantry website (www.17thcvi.org); Peter Drummey at the Massachusetts Historical Society; and Phil Devlin, Walt Powell, David Bingham, Michael Diamond, Jacques F. Peters, Geraldine and Bill Caughman. Mike McAfee and Roger Hunt answered countless questions over the years.

Our grateful thanks go to the ever-patient and supportive Suzanna Tamminen at Wesleyan University Press, as well as Leslie Starr, and Parker Smathers. Kudos to editors Cannon Labrie and the amazing E. Ann Brash. We offer our admiration to Dave Wolfram, who manages to be both a brilliant designer and a guy that we really like to be around.

To all those who helped us along the way—especially those whose names we've forgotten to include—we offer our gratitude. We each extend personal thanks as well.

Dione:

I'd like to blame my sister, Lois Thibault, for starting me down this path. At age seventeen, I felt the first magical shiver when Lois brought me to the Wilderness, where I stood in a hollow dug by soldiers in 1864, and imagined flames overtaking the wounded.

That first tentative interest in the Civil War was fostered years later by a dentist on his lunch hour, who showed up at the historical society where I worked and asked if we had any Civil War artifacts. Buck Zaidel's enthusiasm was contagious, even to someone who didn't know a haversack from a havelock. I quickly came to share his reverence for Civil War soldiers and Abraham Lincoln. After years of discussing history and playing hockey together, we hatched the idea for this book. Buck brought a highly trained eye and an unshakeable determination to the project, and remained patient and encouraging when I faltered. His dedication to honoring those who fought in the war continually inspires me.

Meredith Roberts, my sister, helped make this book a reality by keeping our household running smoothly while simultaneously cracking her metaphorical whip to keep me on task. Thank you, Meme. I'm also thankful for Kate Knopp's thoughtful editing, Sarah Leavitt's fine research, and Avery Schmitz's curiosity.

My most heartfelt thanks go to Chris Diamond, always my cheerleader, who encouraged me at every step of this book. He read chapters, made suggestions, and somehow never looked bored when listening to my endless anecdotes about my "dead guys." Our daughters Lilly Diamond and Meredith Diamond cheerfully traveled to battlefields, planted flowers on soldiers' graves, and understood why I couldn't be with them when I was researching and writing. Their three names should be on this book as surely as mine should.

Buck:

I thank Mom and Pop for the 1965 trip to Gettysburg, and the set of toy Civil War soldiers, which proved to be the seeds of a lifelong interest in history. Your enthusiastic and enduring support, encouragement, and occasional funding was and is most appreciated. Pop in particular would have loved to see this book and passion come to fruition. No folks ever did more for a number one son.

To S.P., Peter, and K.K.: thanks for the photo log, typing, transcriptions, and the annual trips to Gettysburg. Thank you for patiently listening to another story about some new little sepia-toned photo that's neater than the last one. Peter said it best as a four-year-old at Civil War Day, when asked why we were there: "To remember the soldier men."

Many thanks to Mr. and Mrs. Ramisk for many good newspaper clips on Lincoln and the Civil War, plus years of support for the C.W.R.A.F. Thanks to Unkie Mike for his insightful collecting philosophy: "I like what I like."

I will always appreciate the late Bernie Rogers, whose stories of the early days of collecting could fill a ten-hour car ride (with no radio), and who always had a kid's enthusiasm for what we would find at the next show. I thank Tom Harris for his keen artist's eye that made me search for the fine line where art and history meet.

What Bobby Orr was to hockey, Di Longley is to Civil War research—always looking for stories of sacrifice, duty, courage, and humor buried in libraries, museums, graveyards, or webpages. And thank God for beer drinking after Panthers hockey games, or this book might never have been written.

CHAPTER ONE

Men of Connecticut!

WAR BEGINS, SPRING 1861

"Men of Connecticut! TO ARMS!!" thundered the *Hartford Daily Courant* on April 13, 1861.[1]

Splashed across the newspaper was the shocking news: The day before, the Confederate military had opened fire on Fort Sumter in Charleston harbor. Forty-three Confederate guns and mortars pounded Sumter until the Union commander surrendered the fort to the Southerners. With undeniable certainty, civil war had arrived.

Suddenly the Land of Steady Habits was anything but. Agitated and confused, people drew together to discuss the astounding events.

"Large groups were congregated upon the streets, and . . . the war was the all absorbing theme . . . In the conversation, heated and passionate, in which the crowds participated, there was but little to be heard except indignation at the outrage of the Southern Rebels. It was deep and earnest."[2]

In the quiet town of Winchester, it wasn't much different. "The bombardment of Fort Sumter flew over the telegraph wires on Saturday, April 14, 1861, and electrified the country," wrote resident John Boyd. The *Winsted Herald* declared grimly, "Northern blood is up, and history, faster than the pen can write, is making."[3]

But not everyone was astonished by the South's attack. For months, Governor William Buckingham had vigilantly followed each development in the national conflict. After Abraham Lincoln's election on November 6, 1860, South Carolina had moved to secede. Six other states had quickly followed. When Southerners fired upon an unarmed ship bringing troops and supplies to Fort Sumter on January 9, 1861, Buckingham had quietly directed his state quartermaster to order equipment for 5,000 troops, and advised militia units around the state to fill their ranks and stand ready.

Right: Just days before Fort Sumter fell, members of the Governor's Foot Guard assembled at the state armory. Before long, many of the men—like George Haskell—would lay aside their ceremonial Foot Guard uniforms to don the utilitarian blue wool of the Union army.

Far right: An impassioned early broadside proclaimed, "Your country is in danger!" and urged Connecticut men to *"drill, drill* with such muskets as are at hand" in preparation for war.

Gw. H. Haskell.

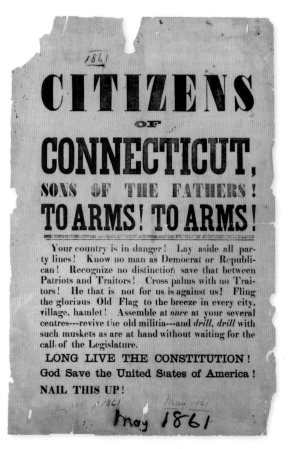

Buckingham's forethought was providential: on April 15, President Lincoln called for 75,000 troops to suppress the rebellion. The governor turned to his citizens and asked for a regiment of volunteers. Would Connecticut respond?

FOR OR AGAINST

"You must be counted for or against the government: which shall it be?" the *Hartford Daily Courant* demanded. "Descendants of those who marched under the banner of George Washington, which shall it be? . . . Sons of the old Charter Oak State, on which side do you enlist?"[4]

The answer came swiftly, from virtually every community in the state. Men crowded into hastily called meetings in town halls, assembly rooms, and churches. In Hartford, "men of all parties met, buried in a common grave all differences of opinion, and stood up as one man, brave, earnest, and steady for the contest. There was no faltering voice."[5]

Men gave passionate speeches, calling for volunteers to defend the nation. George Burnham, a clerk, "said that if he had been so mean and despicable as to hesitate about his duty to his country's flag, he could not have hesitated longer after seeing the brave, determined men before him . . . what he could *do,* he *would* do, and with his whole heart."[6]

The dispute between North and South, and between Republicans and Democrats, was many years in the making. In 1859, John Brown, a deeply religious native of Torrington, Connecticut, brought the situation to a boiling point. A radical abolitionist, Brown advocated violence against slaveholders. He and twenty-one followers tried to initiate a slave rebellion, seizing a Federal arsenal in Harpers Ferry, Virginia, with the aim of arming slaves and abolitionists to fight for freedom. The plan failed. Captured and convicted of treason, an unrepentant Brown was executed on December 2, 1859. Brown's plot outraged and frightened Southerners, and fueled the antagonism of Democrats everywhere. Slavery was now *the* issue dividing the nation, and the Republicans and Democrats squared off.

Farmers, teachers, factory workers and college students jumped to their feet and cried, "I'll go!" At a meeting in Brooklyn, Connecticut, a town of perhaps 2,000 people, 60 men enlisted in the space of half an hour.[7] John Boyd, the secretary of the state, enrolled in the 3rd Regiment —at the age of sixty-two.

"O! Pa. you do not know what enthusiasm, what patriotism, there is here among all classes," a New Haven woman wrote excitedly to her father. "Party distinctions are not named, every body is for our country and the right. Not only the American born but the Irish and the Germans [immigrants] are ready to take up arms in our common defense."[8]

WIDE AWAKE

The spirited support for the Union had emerged in Connecticut more than a year earlier, in February of 1860, sparked by the enthusiasm of a group of young Republican men in Hartford.

A group of Northerners had formed the Republican Party in 1854 to fight the spread of slavery into the nation's western territories. Steadily, the Republicans gained support in the Northern states and began to challenge the long-established Democratic Party, which supported the extension of slavery.

In early 1860, Connecticut's gubernatorial race was in full swing. Thomas H. Seymour, a pro-South Democrat, faced Republican governor William Buckingham, who strongly opposed the expansion of slavery. Connecticut's election for governor was viewed as a bellwether for the upcoming presidential election.

"It is the commencement of the contest BETWEEN FREE AND SLAVE LABOR," announced the *Hartford Daily Courant*, adding that "a vote this spring in Connecticut for Thomas H. Seymour, is a vote for slave labor in the territories. Laboring men—young men of enterprise and muscle—you are interested in this decision! . . . Shall the territories become plantation of negroes?—or shall they be the homes of . . . every man following his own plow, on his own soil, working for his own family?"[9]

The young men that the *Courant* addressed were not asleep. Daniel Francis, twenty-four, and Edgar Yergason, nineteen, were clerks in a dry-goods store in Hartford. In February of 1860, the two attended a meeting of Hartford Republicans, which closed with an enthusiastic torchlight parade. Several hundred men lined up and lit kerosene torches, only to find that many were leaking. Just a few steps away was the store where Francis and Yergason worked; they hurried in and emerged with lengths of inexpensive black fabric which they and a few others tied around their necks like capes to protect their clothing from the kerosene. The capes gave the men a military look, and the procession's organizer put them at the head of parade.

A few days later, Dan Francis, Ed Yergason, and thirty-four other young working men formed a Republican club. The group would promote the election of Republican candidates, beginning with William Buckingham. The members decided their organization would assume a military air: they would wear dark capes and caps as they escorted Republican speakers, kept order at political rallies, and generated enthusiasm for the upcoming elections. Francis, Yergason, and the others might as well have slapped the Democrats in the face with their gloves—the challenge was clear.[10]

Several weeks earlier, the Republican state convention's chairman had spoken of the party's "wide-awake spirit."[11] Now the young men took up the phrase for their club: they became the Wide Awakes. For decades, political questions had been decided by older, established men; now, suddenly, the young men found they had a voice.

THE RAIL-SPLITTER ARRIVES

The club's inception could not have come at a better time. Just a week before, Abraham Lincoln had come east. In New York, 1,500 people came to hear what the ungainly Illinois lawyer had to say about the issue facing the nation. Deftly, Lincoln showed that America's founders had *expected* to regulate slavery. President Washington had signed a bill modifying slavery, and a majority of the signers of the Constitution voted in Congress to limit slavery.

Members of Hartford's Wide Awakes, with their distinctive capes and swinging lanterns, posed for a historic portrait in 1860. In just a few short months, the group of young Republican men from Connecticut would create an astonishing impact on the presidential election.

As he drew to a close after more than an hour, he urged quietly, "Let us have faith that right makes might, and in that faith, let us, to the end, dare to do our duty as we understand it."[12] The audience exploded into cheers.

The next day Lincoln's speech graced the front page of the *New York Times*, and suddenly his name was everywhere. Republican leaders in Connecticut invited him to speak. On March 5, he faced a large and curious audience at Hartford's City Hall. Lincoln got right to the point: "Whether we will have it so or not, the slave question is the prevailing question before the nation."

As he often did, Lincoln drew his listeners in with stories and metaphors.

Suppose, he said, he found a rattlesnake out in the field. "I take a stake and kill him. Everybody would applaud the act and say I did right. But suppose the snake was in a bed where children were sleeping. Would I do right to strike him there? I might hurt the children; or I might not kill, but only arouse and exasperate the snake, and he might bite the children . . . Slavery is like this." Getting rid of the rattlesnake, he cautioned, took careful preparation.[13]

In New Haven the following evening, Lincoln met with "the wildest scene of enthusiasm and excitement."[14] But his next appearance was to be the blockbuster. In spite of rain, sleet, and the resulting mud, the streets of Meriden were thronged with people. When Lincoln's train arrived, the crush at the station included Wide Awakes, several bands, and thousands of citizens who marched along with the speaker's carriage to the hall. As an estimated 3,000 people crammed in, with hundreds more standing outside the open doors, Lincoln held the crowd spellbound.[15]

Lincoln's visit left Connecticut Republicans primed for the turbulent campaigns. Around the state, young men immediately launched more Wide Awake chapters. As the gubernatorial election approached, the Wide Awakes rallied for Republican William Buckingham. The Democrats, just as tenacious, assailed Republican rallies and parades, hurling derision and rocks. On April 2, over 88,000 Connecticut voters cast their ballots. Buckingham won by 541 votes. The Wide Awakes breathed a collective sigh of relief.

WIDE AWAKE FOR LINCOLN

Six weeks later, the nation's Republican convention chose Abraham Lincoln as its presidential nominee. "Momentum" can't begin to describe the energy that the Wide Awakes now spread. All over the North and West, from Maine to California, hundreds of Wide Awake chapters sprang up and filled with members. In bigger cities, Wide Awakes filled car after car on special trains that brought them to rallies with other clubs.

Getting Lincoln into office promised to be a vicious battle. "Wherever the fight is hottest, there is their post of duty, and there the Wide Awakes are found," declared the Hartford group in a circular it sent to other chapters.[16]

The day after Lincoln's victory, the *Hartford Times*—a Democratic newspaper—predicted that the states that allowed slavery would "form a separate confederacy, and retire peaceably from the Union . . . We can never *force* sovereign States to remain in the Union when they desire to go out, without bringing upon our country the shocking evils of civil war, under which the Republic could not, of course, long exist."[17]

Democrats were bitter. Many would nurse their resentment against Lincoln, the Republicans, and abolitionists for years.

The Evening Press.
PUBLISHED BY
J. R. HAWLEY & CO.

No. 66 State Street.
(BETWEEN HARTFORD AND EXCHANGE BANKS.)
Terms—Subscription price.....$5.00 per annum
Paid in advance.............$4.00

Hartford Evening Press.

VOL. V., No. 265.   HARTFORD, CONN., WEDNESDAY, NOVEMBER 7, 1860.   WHOLE No. 1449.

The Connecticut Press.
PUBLISHED BY
J. R. HAWLEY & CO.

Office No. 66 State Street,—between the Hartford and Exchange Banks.
Terms—$2.00 per annum, PAYABLE IN ADVANCE.
Advertising, per square, of twenty lines, one insertion, 75 cents—every subsequent, 25 cents per week.

LET THE EAGLE SCREAM!

A REPUBLICAN PRESIDENT!

ABRAHAM LINCOLN

OF ILLINOIS.

A REPUBLICAN VICE PRESIDENT!

HANNIBAL HAMLIN

OF MAINE.

Glorious Triumph OF REPUBLICAN PRINCIPLES!

The Hartford Evening Press, November 7, 1860.

The Wide Awakes, exultant in Lincoln's victory, had little left to do. Their role in the presidential campaign had very possibly changed history.

It would be just a few months before Dan Francis and Ed Yergason put away their capes, donned the blue wool uniforms of Union infantry, and faced bullets instead of rocks as the fight moved from the political arena to the battlefield.

Help from All Quarters

Now that war had arrived, those who couldn't enlist found other ways to help. Factory owners promised to continue the salaries of employees who enlisted. Towns pledged to support their soldiers' families: at a single meeting, Norwich citizens donated over $14,000.[18] In Middletown, Dr. Baker proposed to treat soldiers' families at no cost, and the photography team of Bundy and Williams promised free pictures of all the volunteers.[19]

Henry Schulze, a Hartford tailor, offered to cut out uniforms; other tailors throughout the state did the same. Thousands of Connecticut women joined them, sewing uniforms and haversacks in shifts, day and night.

Everywhere, Connecticut citizens showed their support for the Union. William North Rice, a Wesleyan student, described the scene in Middletown: "The war spirit is rampant here. About half the people one meets in the street wear union badges—cockades, neck-ties, pins, buttons, etc. . . . Flags are hung out from many of the houses."[20]

"Already the national flag had come to have a new and strange significance," asserted one Connecticut writer. "When the stars and stripes went down at Sumter, they went up in every county of our State."[21]

EVERYTHING IS WARLIKE

As Connecticut scrambled to organize troops, Massachusetts' 6th Regiment had already filled its ranks and was on its way south. When their train pulled into the Hartford station on April 18, the Massachusetts boys found 2,500 Connecticut people waiting—at two o'clock in the morning—with enthusiastic speeches, food, and rousing cheers.[22]

Dr. George Clary portrayed the mood in Hartford: "Everything is warlike, the streets, the dress of people, the papers, etc. The air resounds with the din of war and nothing else can be thought or talked of."[23]

CONNECTICUT VOLUNTEERS

A Charter Oak insignia marked the militia uniform of an unidentified Connecticut man. Militia units from New Haven, Middletown, Danbury, Waterbury, and a host of other communities enlisted in Connecticut's first three Civil War regiments in April and May of 1861 and made up the core of early officers.

Now Connecticut moved forward, rapidly filling three regiments during April and May of 1861. A regiment (usually 800 to 1,000 men) was composed of about ten companies, each assigned a letter.

Horace Purdy joined Company E of the 1st Regiment. A twenty-six-year-old hatter, Horace was a member of the Wooster Guard, a volunteer militia unit in Danbury. As events unfolded, the Wooster Guard gathered with a sense of rising urgency. Horace jotted the proceedings in his diary: "*Wednesday April 17th* . . . Attended a special meeting of the Guards at our Hall in the eve at which we volunteered our services to the Governor (Buckingham) as volunteers in the U States service in answer to the Presidents call for 75,000 troops. There were a large number of spectators at the room and when we with one voice offered our services, a long loud shout went up from the people."[24]

Across the state, other militia units did the same, each acting as the nucleus of a company of 75 to 100 soldiers. Most community militias had drilled together and marched in parades, but few had serious military training. As the *Hartford Daily Courant* put it, "The Hartford City Guard was not organized for the purpose of performing military duty . . . But the time has come when men are wanted to protect the government, and the Hartford City Guard have overthrown their character as holiday troops, and are putting themselves in condition for acceptance as volunteers."[25]

Soldiers of the 1st, 2nd, and 3rd regiments enlisted for only three months—a term so brief that it was hardly an impediment to the mostly young men who in a surge of patriotism had stepped forward to volunteer. Gustavus Dana, a toolmaker who enlisted in the 1st Regiment, noted: "the general opinion was that the trouble would be ended and that we would be home at the end of the three months."[26]

While the governor appointed the colonels who would lead the regiments, the captaincy of each company was usually awarded to the man who had actively recruited most of its soldiers. Daniel Klein, the son of a German immigrant, became a captain in the 3rd Regiment after he enlisted scores of men from New Haven's German community, with names like Gustav Voltz, Caspar Zimmerman, and Otto Frankel.

As each company filled, its soldiers left for training camp: New Haven, for the 1st and 2nd Regiments; Hartford, for the 3rd Regiment. As they left their hometowns, the soldiers found themselves surrounded by well-wishers. A young tinworker from Middletown described his departure:

In the early weeks of the war, stores around Connecticut could barely keep up with the demand for American flags, cockades, flag pins, and red, white, and blue ties. Other hot sellers were firearms and blankets for the soldiers, and military tactics manuals.

> As our company were taking the [railroad] cars to Hartford, the rendezvous of the Third regiment, a good, honest farmer, from the village in which I had been living, came along . . . There was a large crowd around the cars, so that he could not get to the door, but he edged his way up to my window, and reaching up his hand, said, "Pull me up, I want to see you." . . . He hung onto the car window for half a minute, wishing me the best of luck and good wishes generally, and then shook hands with me and left. As he shook hands, he left a five dollar bill in my hand . . . there was something in this man's style that showed he was sincere in what he said; that his heart was with his country in the hour of trouble, and that his heart and sympathies were with those that were going to fight for the country's honor. He might have made a patriotic speech two hours long, and it would not have impressed me as favorably as that five dollar bill did.[27]

George Branch, a harness maker in Hartford, enlisted in Connecticut's 1st Regiment on April 16. On the evening of April 19 he got married; the next morning, his regiment departed for camp.

Military fever struck the children as well, and boys like this one contributed to "the din of war," many forming their own drum corps. This young drummer wore an improvised uniform based on the colorful Zouave style—baggy red pants, short jacket, and a fez or turban on the head—adapted from the uniform of the French Zouaves in the Crimean War, and popularized in America by Col. Elmer Ellsworth, whose Zouave drill team had toured and electrified the country in 1860.

Sgt. Andrew Knox, a housepainter in the 1st Regiment, left behind his nineteen-year-old bride, Sarah. In a letter from training camp, he tried to explain why: "it was as much as I could do to tear myself away from you but my country called and I must obey my duty. For the first time the proud flag of my country has been insulted and disgraced it must be avenged at any cost and now my dear wife be true to me and I may soon [be] back but if I fall on the field of battle remember . . . that I die in [a] good cause the cause which our fathers fought for and died for."[28]

THE BEGINNING OF SOLDIER LIFE

Once in camp, training began in earnest. Most men found it difficult, if not impossible, to adjust immediately to army life. "Discontent amounting almost to mutiny in our Co on account of our rations," noted a private in the New Haven training camp of the 1st Connecticut.[29] A number of men ran the guard and headed into downtown New Haven for breakfast, earning a stern reprimand from their colonel.

But time was short. The Confederates could attack Washington at any time. Connecticut's green troops had to rush to learn drills, tactics, and the army's daily routine. Many volunteers had never handled a musket. Now they struggled to learn "load in nine times," the intricate nine-step process to load and fire a single cartridge.

Many officers were as inexperienced as the enlisted men, and had to learn as they went along. They consulted their new copies of *Rifle and Light Infantry Tactics for the Exercise and Manoeuvres of Troops When Acting as Light Infantry or Riflemen*, more commonly called *Hardee's Tactics*. The men of the 2nd Regiment, quartered in New Haven, swallowed their pride as boys at William Huntington Russell's military academy taught them their drills.[30]

Boys at the Collegiate and Commercial Institute in New Haven—like this young drummer—had been learning military drills for years before the war began. Students there put the new soldiers of the 2nd Regiment through their paces, drumbeats keeping the marching soldiers in step. Some 300 of the Institute's former students would go on to become commissioned officers in the Union army.

Connecticut issued 700 of these nonregulation blue-painted canteens to men in the 1st Regiment. The state quartermaster's report described them as "canteen-ration boxes." The upper half contained two compartments for liquids with brass spout caps marked "patent April 2 1861" by Meriden inventor James Breckenridge. A swinging latch hook held the top and bottom compartments together. (Patent and quartermaster information courtesy of Dean Nelson, Museum Administrator, Museum of Connecticut History, Hartford.)

But being a soldier had its advantages, too: they hadn't yet left for the war, and they were already heroes. "O, it was a glorious thing to be a soldier in those days!" recalled one volunteer.

> [F]or those seventy-five thousand soldiers that had enlisted and were actually going to the war there was nothing too good. During the few weeks of preparation for the seat of war while they were at their rendezvous in their native states, they were petted and feasted, and grasped warmly by the hand with a fervent "God bless you" by the older people; smiled upon and urged to accept all kinds of presents, such as needle cases, pin-cushions, handkerchiefs, havelocks, pictorial newspapers, tracts and bibles, by beautiful ladies and bright-eyed girls, or invited into hotels and saloons and "treated" by some of their old chums who hadn't quite courage enough to go for soldiers themselves, but heartily admired those who had; admitted to theaters and other places of amusement with no other ticket than enough of their soldier's uniform on to show who they were.[31]

When they'd finished their brief training, the time came to depart for Washington. A great many had never been outside of the state. Opening ahead of them was a world they knew nothing about. Each man wondered what the future would bring for *him*.

Connecticut's Lyon

Nearly 1,000 miles from his home in Connecticut, Capt. Nathaniel Lyon, a West Point graduate and a twenty-year veteran of the regular army, recognized the strategic importance of the arsenal at St. Louis, Missouri. Outfoxing the Rebel opposition in April of 1861, he secured most of the arms in the arsenal, thereby preventing thousands of guns from falling into Confederate hands.

Hoping to avoid fighting within Missouri, conservatives from the state called a meeting between its Southern-leaning militias and officers of federal forces. When Confederate sympathizers proposed that each side should disband its military units and keep troops of both armies out of the state, the red-headed Lyon spat: "Rather than concede to the State of Missouri for one single instant the right to dictate to my Government in any matter . . . I would see you . . . and every man, woman, and child in the State, dead and buried. This means War."[32]

He meant it. After driving Confederate forces to the outskirts of Missouri, an outnumbered Lyon—now promoted to general—launched a bold attack at the Battle of Wilson's Creek on June 11. The assault worked initially, but fizzled after Lyon, waving his hat to encourage his men, was shot through the heart.

Known for his red hair and equally fiery personality, Nathaniel Lyon was the first general to give his life for the Union. As the procession carrying his coffin made its way through the night to his hometown of Easton, hundreds of citizens lined its route, lighting the way with candles, lanterns, and torches. Thousands of people (estimates range from 10,000 to 20,000) attended General Lyon's funeral.

Joe Hawley, a thirty-four-year-old newspaper editor in Hartford, enlisted as soon as Governor Buckingham issued the call. He and two friends immediately began recruiting soldiers. Just twenty-six hours later, they had signed up an entire company (eighty-four men), with more waiting. Joe's wife Harriet was as fiercely patriotic as her husband. Over and over she expressed her frustration at not being able to serve as the soldiers did. "I envy him," she wrote of her husband. "I ain't sure but that I wish I was his brother instead of his wife—or him instead of myself." The Hawleys fervently opposed slavery, and their devotion to the Union cause was unshakeable. In the next four years, both of them were to offer their lives for it repeatedly. (Letter from Harriet Foote Hawley, June 18, 1864, Connecticut Historical Society, Hartford.)

In Meriden, an eager twenty-one-year-old clerk in a dry-goods store took off his apron and signed his enlistment papers. Charles Upham began as a sergeant in Connecticut's 3rd Regiment. By war's end, he would wear a colonel's silver eagles on his shoulder straps. He would also bear the marks of personal tragedy and a battle wound that would never heal.

In April 1861, Col. Joseph Mansfield waited tensely at his home in Middletown. A career army officer, the fifty-seven-year-old colonel had more than an inkling of what lay ahead.

His courage in battle during the Mexican War had earned him advances, but Mansfield was also highly respected for his skill and experience as an army engineer. He had supervised the construction of military forts across the West and the South—and at the same time, observed the nation's gathering storm. Now orders summoned him to Washington: the capital lay open to attack. Thorough and methodical, Mansfield could be trusted to direct the city's defenses. President Lincoln promoted him to brigadier general, commanding the Department of Washington. General Mansfield went to work immediately, creating a ring of forts that would protect the capital from every direction—but in his heart, he longed to lead troops into battle.

Leaving Home

For the Nutmeggers just finishing their training, the adventure was about to begin. Each regiment, before leaving the state, received its regimental colors in a solemn ceremony. On May 8, former lieutenant governor Julius Catlin spoke movingly to the 1st Regiment as he presented it with an American flag and a hand-painted silk regimental flag. "Take this flag to be your standard in the battle," Catlin declared, "where blows fall thickest and the fight rages hottest, there may it float, and beneath it strike the strong arms and brave hearts of Connecticut. Remember whose children you are—whose honor you inherit."[33]

With proud, jaunty airs, the men fell in behind the spotless flags. Onlookers cheered and bands played. Three months later, the flags would return bullet-ridden; the men beaten and shocked. The war, which that day looked to be brief and glorious, would drag on for years and affect every single person in Connecticut.

CHAPTER TWO

No One Dreamed of Anything but Victory

BULL RUN, SUMMER 1861

The officers didn't know what they were doing. A bookkeeper, a hatter, a few machinists, some store clerks, a carpenter—what did they know about war?

Yet here they were in the nation's capital, with the Confederate army just a few miles away. Thousands of men were looking to them for direction. The generals, who were used to experienced soldiers from the regular army, had all kinds of demands. Desperately, the new captains and lieutenants pored over their tactics manuals.

It was hard enough putting the men through squad drill, dress parade, and regimental inspection, never mind memorizing what their manuals called "By the rear of column, left or right, into line, wheel" or "To form square by double column, marching."

A private in the 3rd Connecticut wrote sarcastically:

> The most remarkable thing we did is drill; and we did do some drilling during those five or six weeks that we stayed at Washington. For instance, we would take an hour's drill before breakfast; that was to give us an appetite. After breakfast we would take an hour and a half drill; that was to settle our breakfast. After the breakfast settler came guard mounting. After guard mounting came the regular forenoon drill, which ended about dinner time.

> An hour or so allowed for dinner, then we went out and drilled some. Then the regular afternoon drill lasting until late in the afternoon. Then we were

dismissed for fifteen or twenty minutes to get ready for dress parade . . .
it began to grow a little monotonous; we wanted a change of some kind . . .
If the rebels could only have quietly surrounded us some night and have
taken us all prisoners, we should doubtless have hailed the circumstance with
delight, for it would probably take our officers two or three days to get us
paroled and exchanged so that we might go to drilling again.[1]

A Connecticut soldier described their new routines in
Washington: "for every drill we are called out & back by tap of
drum." (Letter of Wolcott P. Marsh to his wife, May 19, 1861, in
*Letters to a Civil War Bride: The Civil War Letters of Captain Wolcott
Pascal Marsh*, compiled by Sandra Marsh Mercer and Jerry Mercer
[Westminster, MD: Heritage Books, 2006], p. 11.)

Between drills, a photographer captured an image of a
company of the 3rd Connecticut Infantry in Camp Douglass in
June of 1861. At left knelt the drummer who rousted the men

to duty, while the captain and two lieutenants—with sashes
and swords—struck confident poses in front. Behind stood the
enlisted men, muskets at the ready.

For several weeks the men camped here in a grove of trees
just north of the city. In the brief periods they were off duty,
some soldiers walked into Washington to see the sights. Grand
government buildings like the White House and the unfinished
Capitol awed many of the boys who had never been outside of
Connecticut.

Joe Hawley, the newspaper editor now captain in the 1st Connecticut, was not so cavalier. "You can have no idea of the intense application, the perfect absorption of my mind and body in the duties before me," he wrote to a friend. "The great cause, the honor of the state—of our regiment, our company, the lives and health of my boys—you can see what considerations press upon me every instant and demand that I, five weeks ago a greenhorn in military matters, should exert myself to the utmost."[2]

Turning volunteers into soldiers was a long, difficult process. Drilling was just a fraction of that process. The men had to learn unquestioning obedience to officers who just weeks earlier had been merely neighbors or cousins. They had to march long distances, and accept being deprived of sleep and food. They had to learn to mend their uniforms and make coffee over a fire.

The Union's general-in-chief was Winfield Scott, nearly seventy-five years old and so obese he could no longer ride a horse. Commanding the troops in the field was Gen. Irvin McDowell. A career army officer, McDowell could see that weeks of drilling had not prepared his volunteer troops for battle. But he felt constant pressure from Washington, and it was obvious that if the Union army were to annihilate the Confederacy, he would have to act before his troops' ninety-day enlistments elapsed and they all went home.

A month after arriving in Washington, the Connecticut soldiers found themselves crossing the Potomac River and marching into Virginia. This was enemy territory, and each man realized that here a Confederate attack could come at any second.

PICKET DUTY

"I don't think I shall ever forget my first night on picket," an anxious Connecticut soldier confessed later. He stood picket in the woods overnight, at some distance from camp.

WHO GOES THERE!

Elnathan B. Tyler of the 3rd Connecticut met the enemy— or was it a friend?—in an illustration from his 1872 book, "Wooden Nutmegs" at Bull Run, A Humorous Account of Some of the Exploits and Experiences of the Three Months Connecticut Brigade and the Part They Played in the National Stampede.

> Hour after hour rolled on. 'Twas midnight . . . Thought it very reasonable to suppose that if the rebels intended to make an attack they would avoid the regular road and go through the woods . . . somewhere near where I was posted . . . I heard, or fancied I heard a slight disturbance in a clump of bushes near by . . . Had the rebels appeared? . . .
>
> Army regulations require a sentinel to challenge an approaching party . . . I proceeded to address myself to the mysterious clump of bushes. Opened my mouth and went through all the motions of saying something . . . A sound issued from my mouth; but such a sound!
>
> Just then a dark form seemed to be moving out from the bushes. It looked like a man crawling along on his hands and knees . . . Then the dark object spoke! It spoke in a language that had been familiar to my ear since my boyhood days. It was the grunt of a hog! . . . Was delighted to see that hog . . . Felt like twining my arms around its neck and shedding a few tears of joy . . .[3]

Hogs or no hogs, the boys soon got undeniable proof that the enemy was real and nearby. On the 17th of June, the 1st and 2nd Connecticut regiments rushed to the aid of Ohio troops that had been ambushed by the enemy at Vienna, Virginia. "We found the Ohio boys near the track," wrote a shaken private. "By the aid of campfires and a lantern they were burying their dead, amputating the limbs of the wounded and caring for others who were badly wounded . . . It looked hard to see the long row of wounded dying and the dead."[4]

Besides fear and inexperience, the new soldiers had to contend with bureaucratic incompetence. John C. Comstock, a Hartford printer who served as captain in Connecticut's 1st Regiment, complained "We are yet suffering for lack of shoes and pantaloons . . . Many of the men are absolutely shoeless, and have not trowsers enough to cover their legs."[5]

Gus Dana, a private in the same regiment, groused about "insufficient and very poor" rations. One lot of hardtack was impossible to eat; Dana and his buddies bored holes through them and hung them around their necks in protest. When their colonel cursed them, "we revenged [ourselves] by skyving our tin plates at his tent while we stood in line waiting for supper."[6]

Still, in spite of the difficulties, most soldiers felt confident that the Union would put down the rebellion quickly and easily. Eli Walter Osborn, a captain in the 2nd Connecticut, confided to his family, "between you and me, I do not think we shall be required to fight much. The other side is too much frightened."[7]

By mid-July, many regiments had only days left on their ninety-day enlistments. General McDowell had to act. "We have orders to prepare for a long march," Andrew Knox wrote excitedly to his wife. "All that we are to carry is our blankets and three days provisions . . . you can expect by far the largest battle or the most inglorious retreat the coming week."[8]

With the Confederates massing near Manassas Junction, McDowell ordered his officers to push the Union troops forward rapidly. He planned a surprise attack on the Confederate troops commanded by General Beauregard, his old classmate from West Point. It was imperative to strike before Confederate general Johnston could arrive with reinforcements.

"General Tyler, a Connecticut man, was in command of the first and largest division of the army [about 30,000 men]," explained a Middletown private, "and the Connecticut Brigade, consisting of the [1st, 2nd, and 3rd] Connecticut regiments and the Second Maine, formed the first brigade of that division, and were thus, in regular formation, the advance of the entire force. On the afternoon of the 16th of July General Tyler put his division in motion, the Connecticut men in the advance."[9]

Hoping to move swiftly, McDowell was disgusted to find he could not. "The men were not used to marching; they stopped every moment to pick blackberries or to get water. They would not keep in the ranks, order as much as you pleased. When they came where water was fresh they would pour the old water out of their canteens and fill them with fresh water; they were not used to denying themselves much."[10] For the next three days, McDowell fumed over continuous delays.

Gus Dana described the march from the enlisted man's view:

> About noon of the 17th we came in sight of Fairfax Court House and could plainly see the enemys gun barrels glisten: the officers who had glasses said they were in rapid retreat . . . We were halted and ordered to lie down while a [Union] battery fired over our heads; we only scooched though, because great

luscious ripe blackberries were in abundance within our reach. We would occasionally hear Maj Speidel yell at us "Keep your intervals damn you" when an especially fine bush had caused several men to group together. But we had to fill up on something.[11]

Confederate troops fled before the First Division's advance. When the Union soldiers halted to rest, they were not far behind the enemy. "We found campfires burning which the Rebels had left in their hasty retreat," wrote Horace Purdy of Danbury. "Also some provisions Ham, Whisky & Tents—Drums—shoes, clothing were also found. We had some sport at this place, some of the men dressing themselves in secession clothing and such rigs as some of them were, it was enough to make ones sides ache with laughter."[12]

At daylight, three days before the Battle of Bull Run would take place, the advance resumed.

[We] followed the rebels through Germantown trying to head them off but the trees they had felled across the road during their retreat delayed the artillery and we had to . . . chop the obstructions away. We bivouacked that night about four miles west of Centerville, nearly famished for food and water . . . our stomachs ached with emptiness . . . finding an old cow, one of our boys killed it and cut it up, each one that could get near enough cutting off a gob and then frizzling it over a little fire of leaves and twigs. Nat Middletown had half a hard tack & I had a piece of beef the size of the palm of my hand, so we divided and *banquetted*."[13]

With the 3rd Connecticut Regiment marched Sgt. Charles Upham, a quiet twenty-two-year-old imbued with a strong sense of duty. In his pocket, Charlie carried a roll book in which he'd written the names of each man in his company, and recorded assignments such as guard posting. Charlie knew many of the men well; most came from Meriden, where he lived and worked as a dry-goods clerk.

In the days ahead, Sergeant Upham would lead and encourage these young soldiers as they faced the enemy for the first time. At times like this, a soldier's thoughts shifted inexorably to home. Setting aside his roll book, Charlie could reflect on a small memento he carried: a lock of fine brown hair encircled by a silk ribbon. The lock was folded into a slip of paper inscribed "Evening. May 18, 1861"—presumably when Charlie had received it from eighteen-year-old Emma Clark as he departed for war.

Blackburn's Ford

General Tyler had left the Connecticut men of the 1st Brigade with their colonel, fifty-one-year-old Erasmus Keyes, and pushed ahead with other units to determine the position of the Confederate flank. At Blackburn's Ford, a crossing of Bull Run, Tyler suddenly met a Confederate force that pulled him into a sharp skirmish.

The brief engagement "had a disheartening effect upon our soldiers," mused Elnathan Tyler of Middletown, "especially those who thought the rebels would not fight, or at most would only fight a few minutes and then run away . . . As our dead and wounded soldiers lay in the shady door yard of an old house in Centreville we had a chance for the first time to see some of the horrors of war. To many of us who had seemed to think the whole thing was a grand military picnic, those dead and dying soldiers was a dispiriting reality, and our enthusiasm which had been at the boiling point, was chilled by a doubt."[14]

It was now July 20, the day before the fight at Bull Run was to take place. Few of the soldiers got any sleep that night. Quartermasters hurriedly issued rations, and the Connecticut regiments' brigade pulled out shortly after 2:00 a.m., leading the advance.

One of the chaplains with the 2nd Connecticut was forty-eight-year-old Hiram Eddy, a Presbyterian minister of imposing physique. Eddy had left his pulpit in Winsted, as well as his wife and five children, to volunteer. His diary preserved his impressions from the historic morning when 30,000 Union troops prepared for battle: "The grandeur of the army. All parts of the nation, representatives passing by from Main[e] to Minnesota and Iowa—All in good cheer & thousand 'buly for yous' rang out as the regiments & brigades went past. Every body was hopeful. No one dreamed of anything but victory."[15]

News of the attack on Fort Sumter reached Winsted, Connecticut, on a Sunday morning. Rev. Hiram Eddy, minister of the town's Second Congregational Church, immediately rewrote the sermon he was to give that day. According to a parishioner, Eddy's fiery new sermon, emphasizing devotion to the Union, "electrified his hearers, and raised them to the plane of his own patriot ardor." At forty-eight years old, Reverend Eddy was twice the age of most soldiers, but he asked his church for a leave of absence and joined the state's 2nd Regiment as chaplain. (John Boyd, *Annals and Family Records of Winchester, Connecticut*, p. 462).

"We had heard the artillery of both sides for some time, and as we went rapidly forward for the last mile or two before reaching the scene of action, the increased roar warned us that we might soon feel as well as hear. We soon emerged from the last piece of woods between us and the battle-field . . . the perspiration streaming down our faces . . . panting, and puffing, and trying to catch our breath," wrote Elnathan Tyler.[16]

Just before ten in the morning, the Connecticut soldiers approached the stream called Bull Run. Gus Dana described the 1st Connecticut's movements: "We inclined to the right to cross an open field & ford the stream . . . half way across this field the rebels opened on us with shot and shell, one plowing a furrow at the feet of Maj Rodman and turning him a somerset unhurt. Orders to doublequick soon brought us to the bank of Bull Run; the stream itself was insignificant but the banks very precipitous . . . On nearing the run an officer on a grey or white horse on the high bank on the further side, shouted

The men of the 1st Connecticut pounded onto the battlefield with their regimental flag held aloft by the color-bearer. Two months earlier, Julius Catlin, Connecticut's lieutenant governor, had presented the national flag to the regiment with these words: "Take the flag, and, when it presses closest on the foe in some hard-set contest, will some brave boy among you strike one true blow for freedom for an old man at home, whose heart and prayers go with these colors to the field?" (W. A. Croffut and John M. Morris, *The Military and Civil History of Connecticut during the War of 1861–65*, p. 67).

'What regiment is that,' 'First Conn' we shouted and Gen. W. T. Sherman, as it proved to be, said 'Bully for the First Conn, here's work for you up here.'"[17]

"We followed Gen Sherman . . . through the woods and half way down the valley that separated us from Beauregard's command," went on Gus Dana. "Orders to fire were given and afterwards we learned that we drove off a force of rebel Inf and Cav but I could only see the white gate posts I was ordered to aim at. I fired 22 rounds, kneeling down, while the rear rank fired over us . . . One of my comrades from East Hartford, the next to me in the front rank kneeling to fire . . . said 'Ain't this glorious Gus, I'm going to re-enlist.'"[18]

The 2nd and 3rd Connecticut regiments, along with the 2nd Maine, had diverted into the woods to avoid artillery fire before reaching the stream. A soldier from the 3rd recalled: "We found General Tyler there awaiting us . . . As we came up in good order and on the double quick, the General greeted us with 'Ha! Ha! Here comes my Connecticut boys!' and then he ordered one of the bands . . . to stop there and strike up 'Yankee Doodle' while we pressed forward and crossed the Run."[19]

"At 11 or 12 the contest was at its height & the spectacle was grand & awful," wrote Chaplain Eddy.

> The cannonade—The musketry—The working of the great Parrot gun planted in the corner of the woods. The discharge & the bursting a mile & a half away. It seemed like a tuft of cloud bursting out . . . then the runing of the soldiers away from beneath it to avoid the contents of the shell. And finally, about two o'clock we co'd distinctly see the rebels leave the place on double quick. From the commencement there was not a doubt but that the day wo'd be ours. Among the large number of spectators there was not the least appearance of fear . . . And at this time there was no doubt the enemy was in our hands. They had been driven from all the positions which they occupied in the morning.[20]

Gen. Daniel Tyler, commanding the 1st Division (approximately 5,000 troops) opened the Battle of Bull Run on July 21, 1861. Born in the village of Brooklyn, Connecticut, Tyler was nearly sixty-two years old. He was a graduate of West Point but had left the military nearly thirty years earlier to become a manufacturer.

From the crest of a hill, a Confederate battery was shelling Union forces. About two in the afternoon, General Tyler ordered Colonel Keyes to capture the battery.

A twenty-two-year-old tinworker in the 3rd Connecticut recounted: "Keyes took the Second Maine and our regiment and pressed forward up the hill at double quick. We went up that hill shouting and yelling as if two thousand demons had suddenly been let loose from Pandemonium . . . We pressed forward towards the top of the hill. Here we found ourselves under the fire of infantry as well as artillery."[21]

Colonel Keyes reported, "Colonel Jameson of the Second Maine, and Colonel Chatfield of the Third Connecticut Volunteers, pressed forward their regiments up the base of the slope about one hundred yards, when I ordered them to lie down, at a point offering a small protection, and load. I then ordered them to advance again . . . As we moved forward we came under the fire of other large bodies of the enemy posted behind breastworks, and on reaching the summit of the hill the firing became so hot that an exposure to it of five minutes would have annihilated my whole line."[22]

"We fell back a few rods and lay down on the Warrenton road, where by lying close to the ground we were somewhat protected from the enemy's guns," wrote one of the men. "General Tyler, who had followed us up the hill, was now seen talking anxiously with Keyes and some of the other officers, as well as taking a general survey of the situation himself. The old General evidently wanted us to try the bayonet. But the other officers tried to discourage him." Tyler now appealed to the men, asking if they could take the battery at the point of the bayonet; "but you see we wasn't that kind of heroes, so we just said, 'No sir! We can't take it, and there ain't no use of trying.'"[23]

In the 2nd Connecticut, Captain Eli Walter Osborn led a company formed of the New Haven Grays militia. His boys, he wrote, "stood fire like bricks it was a hard matter to keep them back, we were ordered to charge one of their batteries, and then the order was countermanded by Col Keyes if we had gone there would not have been a dozen of us left to tell the tale, but the boys wanted to try it, and could not see why they could not." (Letter from E. Walter Osborn to his brother, July 27, 1861, typescript in private collection.)

For hours, the Union forced the Confederates back. But between three and four in the afternoon, the Rebels launched a strong counterattack and the tide began to turn. "[The Confederates] had their choice of the ground and had a strong position but notwithstanding this we whipped them and the Battle was ours up to 3 oclock when they were reinforced by Gen Johnston and we were obliged to retreat," wrote Horace Purdy of the 1st Connecticut.[24]

"At 4 P.M. I heard [Colonel] Keyes tell another officer, with the tears running down his cheeks, 'My God, the whole day is lost; we have been ordered to fall back!' We supposed till then we were victorious for every move to the front we had made, the rebels had fallen back."[25]

Chaplain Eddy had been bringing water to the field hospital when he saw Union troops moving away from the battlefield "so quietly as to suggest nothing special . . . while there I heard the cry 'They come. They come.' Then followed the discharge of arms & the flying of the multitude into the woods back of the hospital. All was consternation, each one runing for his life & I with the multitude."[26]

As the Connecticut regiments began to retreat, the Confederate cavalry formed for a charge.

> General Tyler, seeing the rebel cavalry meant mischief, ordered us to halt and face to the rear. A few, but at first a very few, obeyed the order promptly. The old general's ire was up in a moment; galloping his horse through the retreating mass, at the imminent risk of riding over the men, his form erect, his eyes flashing, and with an energy we little dreamed was in the old man, he fairly yelled, "Halt! Come back here! Come back, you cowards, and face this cavalry!"

> . . . Cowards we might be, but we wasn't going to have it thrown in our faces in that way; so while some still pressed on, many more halted and resolutely turned our faces to the foe again . . . Several times we were obliged to turn and face them . . . but a few shots from us seemed to cool their ardor.[27]

As regiment after regiment joined the retreat, the withdrawal devolved into pandemonium. A Connecticut soldier wrote:

> the road before us was the greatest scene of excitement that I ever witnessed. The lots were full of men, the roads crowded with artillery wagons, their horses on a dead run, colliding with freight wagons, and smashing hacks containing gentlemen spectators. I cannot begin to describe the confusion . . . Everything that we had on, which had the least tendency to stop our progress, was thrown away . . .

> . . . I took to the woods, threw off my haversack, which contained a number of eatables, writing materials, and many other things I would liked to have saved, next my belt, cartridge box, etc.; then went my blankets. It was hard to do it; but we were scattered, and running for dear life.[28]

While Chaplain Eddy of the 2nd Regiment hurried along with thousands of retreating Union troops, he saw a familiar face: Captain Joseph Hawley of the 1st Regiment.

> I now determined to move along with Capt. Holley's [Hawley's] company. The men were not in line but they might be said to be in company as birds are in a flock. Capt. Holley took a gun from one of his men & requested me to take it & go to the rear & endeavor to keep the men in line. This I did for some time as well as I co'd but I have seen geece march in better order. Nevertheless I worked at my task, but all the men seemed safer near Capt. Holley, & I confess [I] myself did when I heard his calm voice & saw his steady steps.

> But soon there came another sharp crash of musketry a short distance behind us, followed by a universal runing for the woods. I still hear the Capt.'s voice calm as ever 'Steady, men. Steady, men. Steady.' But all in vain. The men scattered like patridges in the woods & the Capt with the rest & your humble

servant was among those who scaled the fence, after which every man was for himself. I ran again until my right lung gave out, & seeing a clump of bushes with a close curtaine of leaves on all sides, I determined to try my chances in it. I dropped in.[29]

Gus Dana, who marched on for miles with his exhausted comrades, finally approached the town of Centerville and noted with relief: "we found a line of troops, Blenkers Reserve, sent out from Washington . . . our tired and hungry army passed behind them and laid down supperless to sleep."[30]

"As we lay down on the same ground that we had left about eighteen hours before," Elnathan Tyler continued, "it seemed as if we had never been so tired, so disheartened, so thoroughly disgusted with everybody and every thing as we were then. But even the most weary soldier had hardly got asleep, when the order came again to fall in and continue our weary march to the rear. The officers concluded it was not safe to stay there, even through the night; we might all be prisoners by morning."[31]

A correspondent of *The New York World* reported:

> Though so wearied that one officer of the [3rd Connecticut] regiment says that $10,000 and a colonelcy at Vienna would not have induced him to march there for it, they were pushed right along by orders, and reached their old camp at Falls Church after daylight on Monday morning.
>
> Here they found the Ohio camps, at which the First and Second Ohio had refused to pause in their retreat. Tents, stores and munitions were here all abandoned—property amounting in value to $200,000—and Col. Chatfield ordered his men to take hold and save it. Sending to Alexandria for a special train, they worked all day loading it with the deserted Ohio property, sent it off, and marched away themselves, just in time to escape the vanguard of the pursuing enemy.[32]

The *New York Times* added, "This service was performed in thirty-six hours, during which time they were entirely without food, and drenched in the tremendous rain that raged without intermission."[33]

Word of the rout traveled north, reaching Connecticut before the soldiers did. Everywhere, shock greeted the news. "Our defeat at the battle of Bull Run corrected, as nothing else could have done, an extravagant estimate of our own strength . . . it swept away our 'ninety days' optimism, and showed us that what we had mistaken for an April shower was to be a long storm, and a hard one."[34]

The dazed soldiers made their way back home. Elnathan Tyler described the 3rd Regiment's homecoming: "as the good citizens of Connecticut had assembled only a few months before to bid us good bye and wish us success in our defence of the old flag, so now they assembled to bid us welcome home again. Although our success on the whole must have fallen far short of what they desired . . . they listened patiently to our stories of hardships in the camp and field; inquired just how we felt when we first came under fire on the battle-field; asked if all the rest of the Northern soldiers did as well as we did, if we didn't think we would have won the battle, and finally if we were going again."[35]

In fact, Private Tyler did go again, enlisting for three years in the state's hardest-fighting regiment, the 14th Connecticut. Many of the "Three Month Men" did the same, joining the rapidly forming regiments that answered the Union's call for troops.

But not everyone reenlisted. Some veterans had had enough; others had obligations to family or work. And some men didn't return with their regiments after Bull Run: Chaplain Hiram Eddy, who had hidden in a clump of bushes during the rout, was captured by the Rebels some days later and remained a prisoner of war for a year.

David Case of Norwich never returned; during the battle, the twenty-six-year-old was hit by a cannonball and died an hour later. Yet the day after his death, David's brother Joseph Case enlisted in Connecticut's 5th Regiment, putting into action exactly what Reverend Horace Bushnell preached to his Hartford congregation a week after the Union defeat: "Let us . . . thank God for what is already made clear—that our spirit as a people is not quelled, but that we find ourselves beginning at once to meet our adversity with a steady and stout resolve, pushing forward new regiments and preparing to double the army already raised . . . the fire of duty burns only the more intensely, and the determination of sacrifice is as much more firmly set as it is more rationally made."[36]

And so, Bull Run became a catalyst. "The wonderful uprising which followed the fall of Sumter was repeated after our bewildered volunteers surged back upon Washington," wrote the authors of the 1868 *Military and Civil History of Connecticut During the War of 1861–65.* "If the second rally was less ardent than the first, it was more deliberate and determined. Instead of a brief military recreation, men felt it to be a struggle for life; and every town in the State renewed its patriotic resolution, and every neighborhood responded to the recruiting drum."[37]

Charles Pelton, a twenty-one-year-old druggist's clerk, wore this wool jacket in Middletown's militia unit, the Mansfield Guard. When war broke out, Pelton enlisted with scores of others from the guard, forming Company A of Connecticut's 2nd Regiment. Until Bull Run, Corporal Pelton's militia jacket, with its tails and gold trim, had seen only parades and drills. Its owner was equally inexperienced in warfare. Pelton came safely through Bull Run and returned to Middletown. Though his army had taken a beating, the young corporal was proud of his role in the conflict. He carefully preserved his sweat-stained battle jacket, and labeled his canteen so that all would know the part he had played: "Bull Run July 21, 1861 / Co A 2d Regt Conn Vols."

CHAPTER THREE

The Voice of Duty

A LONG WAR AHEAD, AUTUMN 1861 TO SUMMER 1862

After the rout at Bull Run, Joe Hawley, a captain in the 1st Regiment, sought out Col. Alfred Terry of Connecticut's 2nd Regiment.

> "Colonel," said the captain, "This makes me feel that the whole North is humiliated; what effect do you think it will have on future enlistments?"
>
> "How does it make you feel, like backing out?"
>
> "No! I feel if possible more like seeing the thing through than before."
>
> "Well, I think that will be the effect all through the North; I, for one, am determined to commence recruiting a regiment for the war as soon as this farce of three months' regiments is played out."[1]

Despite the humiliating defeat at Bull Run, roughly half of the Connecticut soldiers who fought there reenlisted. Joining the veterans were thousands of new soldiers, flushed with a desire to avenge the Union's early loss. Horace Garrigus, seventeen, joined the 8th Connecticut. The Waterbury teenager reported to training camp in Hartford along with his brother, and wrote a hurried letter to their father in New Jersey. "I am going to war. I have enlisted in the U.S. Army and will fight till the last. The Regiment will leave in a week I think. Dear Father think not hard that I have not let you know before . . . I cannot come to Morristown. It is too late to think of that. We must save the Union!"[2]

This time, the soldiers were not three-months' men. The day after Bull Run, Congress had authorized President Lincoln to call for 500,000 troops to enlist for three-year terms. Three days

(*Hartford Daily Courant*, August 20, 1861.)

"Now is your Time," proclaimed a recruiting poster for the 21st Connecticut Regiment.

The small print listed multiple bounties for those who enlisted. A married man with two children landed a hefty $652, in addition to his army pay of $13 per month.

later, Lincoln called for an additional half million men.

Within a month, two Connecticut regiments had left for the south, another was nearly ready, and a fourth was training. When enlistments slackened in the summer of 1862, President Lincoln asked for 300,000 more men to enlist. Connecticut's share was 7,145 soldiers. Governor Buckingham sent an impassioned entreaty to his people: "Close your manufactories and workshops—turn aside from your farms and your business—leave for a while your families and your homes—meet face to face the enemies of your liberties."[3]

Rallies in almost every city and town spread "intense patriotic enthusiasm and fervor. The effect of the Governor's appeal and the influence of these meetings were electrical. From one end of the state to the other, the stirring scenes of April, 1861, were reenacted. Young men flocked to the recruiting offices eager and earnest to enlist in the service of their country."[4]

In Guilford, nearly 40 men enlisted in Connecticut's 1st Light Battery. A local man described their departure from their hometown:

The whole population turned out to see them off. A drum corps, . . . acted as escort, and as the contingent marched out of the Music Hall, one hundred of the "Fathers of Guilford," (old militiamen) were drawn up in line to join in the march . . . Grand old men were those "Fathers of Guilford"! They represented a century of patriotism. Closely allied to the veterans of the revolution, of the war of 1812, and the Mexican war, they again testified their devotion to their country by encouraging their sons and grandsons. Too old to volunteer, they could bid the younger ones do their duty, and though they kept a brave face as their sons and grandsons marched to the war, it could be seen that they inwardly realized that the parting with some would be until the Archangel's trump shall sound . . .

One young Guilford man thought it his duty to enlist—in fact he heard the girls say that they would never speak to a boy who was afraid to go to the front—so he put down his name. His minister had told him it was his duty, but his father and mother urged him to stay at home. Enthusiasm won, and he marched with the boys to the camp. His parents cried; they knew he would never return; their lack of Spartan courage was demoralizing the crowd, every one of which had some relative in the army . . . A sturdy veteran, with not a tear in his eye, walked up to the agonized parents and exclaimed: "For God's sake, dont send the boys away from us like that."

There was a loud cheer for the man, for they knew that all his sons had left him to go and fight.

In speaking of that march to the depot, Edward Griswold, thirty years after, wrote: "We can never forget those old patriots, their erect forms, firm step and patriotic spirit. How they marched, how we felt, the road lined with people, the flags waving, the 'God bless you' of the ladies, the way we were sent off made us feel that we could have whipped the whole rebel army that morning. We wondered if we were dreaming, if we were really going to war and to participate in such scenes of war as had been told us around the fireside by our patriotic grandsires."[5]

When the *New York Evening Post* published a poem called, "We Are Coming, Father Abraham, Three Hundred Thousand More," composer Stephen Foster set the words to a jaunty melody. By the end of the summer of 1862, it seemed no one in the North could stop singing it.

THE ENEMY AT HOME

Did all of Connecticut's people back the Union? By no means.

When Confederate troops first attacked Fort Sumter, plenty of Democrats aligned themselves with the Union cause, but *thousands* of Connecticut residents remained strongly opposed to the war and the Union.

In July of 1861, when the telegraph carried to Connecticut the distressing news of the Union loss at Bull Run, Nathan Morse smiled smugly. The thirty-two-year-old editor of the *Bridgeport Advertiser and Farmer* newspaper could hardly wait to set the type for his editorial. "The 'grand army' marched on the 17th . . . It also ran back on the 21st," he sneered. For abolitionists, he declared contemptuously, the defeat "blasted prospects of their fanaticism." Of the Confederates, he wrote glowingly, "Like our Revolutionary fathers, they are fighting for their just rights."[6]

Nathan Morse was not alone. Across the state, and especially in western Connecticut, throngs of protesters arose. In Darien, a farmer named Stephen Raymond fired a cannon to celebrate the Confederate victory at Bull Run. (Union supporters replied by dumping the cannon in a river.)[7]

The *Hartford Times*, a Democratic paper, had reported sightings of white flags, often adorned with the word "Peace," as early as May of 1861. "Peace Democrats," as the war protesters called themselves, had raised their banners in Ridgefield, Windsor, West Hartford, and Goshen.[8] Union supporters ripped them down and raised the American flag in their stead.

But the loss at Bull Run gave the Peace Democrats more confidence. Three days after the battle, a group of about thirty young women from

An upside-down flag symbolizes distress—perhaps the message sent by a Connecticut Democrat in this unusual wartime image taken in Hartford.

Danbury, accompanied by a band of musicians, paraded to the hickory pole in their town, where they took down the American flag and raised a white "peace banner." At the *Farmer*, Nathan Morse crowed over the incident, running the story under the headline: "A Proud People Beginning to Move."[9]

"Peace meetings" took place in scattered communities, where participants raised their flags and gave speeches. But once the veterans of Bull Run returned to Connecticut, the stage was set for a showdown between Union supporters and Peace Democrats.

> A peace-meeting was called at Stepney [in Monroe], for Aug. 24, to declare against the war. The three months' soldiers, just mustered out of service, were in no mood to tolerate what they regarded as incipient treason, and resolved to disperse this assemblage. On the morning of the appointed day, two or three omnibus-loads of Capt. Frye's company, Third Regiment, armed with revolvers, made their way out of Bridgeport, accompanied by a long procession of citizens. There was an immense gathering of peace-men at Stepney. Families had come from all the towns around to "stop the unrighteous war." A very tall hickory pole was raised [flying] the pale emblem of their patriotism, bearing the word "peace" . . . a multitude of armed peace-men rallied around the strange bunting, and swore to defend it . . .[10]

Men on both sides were knocked down, and threats exchanged. In the end, the Union men tore down the peace flag and raised the American flag, while the Peace Democrats dispersed. The New Haven *Palladium* newspaper carried the story of what happened next:

> Upon the arrival home of the Bridgeport party, with the white flag as a trophy, an excited concourse of people surrounded them . . . rending the air with shouts, and apparently ready for any desperate enterprise . . . when voices in the crowd shouted "To the *Farmer* office."

A rare photograph taken soon after the riot at the *Bridgeport Advertiser and Farmer* showed the aftermath of the chaos.

> A body of four or five hundred persons, followed by thousands of spectators, immediately moved down the street . . . Once within the walls [of the *Bridgeport Advertiser and Farmer* newspaper], a scene of destruction occurred that almost passes description . . . Type, job presses, ink, paper, books, all the paraphernalia of a printing establishment were thrown into the street, and two presses, too large to get through the windows, were broken in pieces by aid of a large and heavy lever. The crowd even ascended to the roof, and tore off such of the signs as they could reach. The appearance of the building on Sunday morning, windowless and rifled, was dreary in the extreme . . .[11]

The Peace Democrats, later known derisively as "Copperheads," never gave up. Their voices were to rise again and again for the duration of the war, especially when Union morale was low.

TRAINING CAMP

Once a man had enlisted in a regiment, he was examined by a doctor. "We had to strip naked and be pounded in the back, punched in the ribs, lungs and heart sounded and we were put through certain motions and antics to show our strength and endurance," said James Sawyer of Woodstock when he joined the 18th Connecticut.[12]

At training camp, the brand-new soldiers received their uniforms and equipment. Sawyer listed his new gear:

1 dark blue blouse	2 pr drawers
1 pr of pants, sky blue	1 knapsack
1 overcoat, sky blue	1 canteen
1 forage cap	1 haversack
1 pr coarse wide shoes	cartridge box with shoulder belt
2 pr socks	waist belt with bayonet scabbard attached
2 shirts	

While James Sawyer left a detailed list of his army gear, this unidentified soldier, his blanket rolled snugly atop his knapsack, had a photographer record his transformation from civilian to soldier.

"There was a good deal of changing about after we got our clothes," Sawyer added; "they were handed out regardless of size so that but few received clothes that fitted. The long slim man got a short fat man's suit and vice versa. I had lots of trouble in getting fitted in pants, and did not get suited till . . . mother cut the bottoms off."[13]

Wearing their forage caps and blue uniforms, the men must have been pleased with their military appearances—but scarcely any of them were prepared for what came next. One soldier described the rude awakening they faced at training camp:

> The enthusiasm awakened by public meetings and the enlistment fever . . . passes away; while the frequent call of the drum to various duties, the command of superior officers and the rigid regulations of the camp, combine to impress upon him the serious change that has come in to his hitherto peaceful experience . . .
>
> Soon it dawns upon him that he is no longer his own master. The oath to support the Constitution of the United States is as yet a theoretical pledge in which he glories, but the obligation to obey the officers appointed over him he finds a practical thing and sometimes very difficult.[14]

It wasn't always easy to make a man obey when a few days earlier he had been a private citizen who made his own decisions.

> "Guard duty" at Camp Lyon when first established was something to be remembered . . . Capt. Smith was the first officer to mount a guard, and it is related that for the first few days it took all of his men to watch Capt. Bassett's company, and vice versa. Only a few old State muskets were in use about headquarters and the "gate." Corporal Griffin recounts how he paced the lonely rounds of his beat armed with only a fence picket. Many of the boys carried nothing whatever, but if a comrade sought to "run the guard" chased him and if able, collared and marched him back to headquarters.[15]

Many of the men were less concerned with learning military drills than with enjoying themselves before they left for the war. And whether they'd enlisted for patriotic or other reasons, they found their new regulations eye-opening. Michael Kelly described an incident in the 19th Connecticut's early days in camp:

> At about 11 AM we were all amazed at the sight of a tall and portly man equiped from his spurs to his shoulder straps. I[t] was our Lieutenant Colonel Elisha S. Kellogg . . . [We] were drilling quiet [quite] awhile when Lt. Col. Kellogg came along & shouts like a tiger at a soldier named Burns who was smoking. "Take that pipe out of your mouth, Sir, and attend to your drill." Poor Burns trembled like a leaf. He [Col. Kellogg] caught the pipe & threw it with such [force] he never knew to this day where the pipe gone.[16]

Years later, soldiers looked back on their training with a laugh at how "green" they'd been. Jim Sawyer of the 18th Regiment allowed that at Camp Aiken in Norwich, "Our rations seemed pretty coarse, and of course there was a great deal of complaint about it. We hadn't yet become very well educated in privation. We saw the time afterward when the rations we had in Camp Aiken would have seemed luxurious."[17]

When a New Haven newspaper hyped the bulletproof vests made by Atwater Armor Company on Chapel Street, Connecticut soldiers rushed to acquire them. William G. Ely, colonel of the 18th Regiment,

> found a man in the camp dispensing to the soldiers "bullet-proof vests." To be "iron clad" when the bullets should fly as thick as hail! what more could a soldier ask? But Col. Ely, who had often smelt powder in dangerous proximity to bullets, was incredulous of the statement made by the dispenser of the steel vests. He took one of the garments from the dealer, and setting it up as a target for his revolver put several holes through it. He then ordered the arrest of the vender, made him refund to each soldier the amount which he had received in exchange for the worthless armor, and gave him opportunity for reflection in the regimental guard-house.[18]

The green soldiers of the 15th Regiment were not so lucky. They shelled out the money for the "iron-clad life preservers," and struggled under the extra weight when they went off to war.

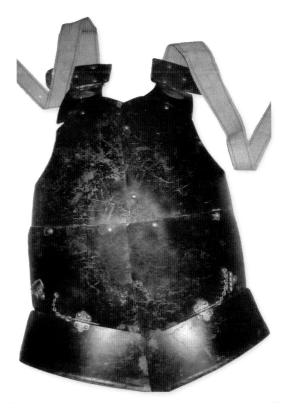

"It is said that at least fifty per cent of the regiment first wore away and then swore away this device. The track of the command from Washington to Arlington Heights was marked by these abandoned 'armor plates,' the largest quantity being hurled from Long Bridge into the Potomac . . . The balance of the lot, after being rudely perforated with bullets at 'Camp Chase,' was ignominiously kicked aside, and the skeletons probably repose there to this day." (Sheldon Brainerd Thorpe, *The History of the Fifteenth Connecticut Volunteers in the War for the Defense of the Union, 1861–1865*, p. 15.)

In their new roles as conquering heroes, men often posed with muskets or swords, showing they meant business. Standing with the flag of his country or regiment also gave a soldier's portrait a patriotic message. But occasionally a soldier's choice of "props" leaves the viewer wondering.

George Parmelee, a farm laborer in Woodbury, sat beside a winsome boy who might have been his little brother. George enlisted in the 7th Regiment in August of 1861. Were the flowers a gesture for his wife Sarah before he departed for war? If so, it was a prescient choice: Sarah died at the end of September.

For some, training camp had its perks. Connecticut's 19th Regiment, largely composed of Litchfield County residents, trained at Camp Dutton, about a mile from the town of Litchfield—close enough to the soldiers' homes that they often had visitors. "Camp Dutton was a beautiful spot," joked the adjutant, Theodore Vaill, "but no place for a regiment to learn its hard and ugly trade. Fond mothers and aunts raked the position with a galling and incessant fire of doughnuts, apples, butter, pies, cheese, honey, and other dainties not conducive to the suppression of the rebellion."[19]

Before their regiments left the state, many soldiers opted to have their likenesses taken. "The Moore Bro's, photographers, always first in the field, are building a large wooden house on the grounds of the 16th Regiment for the purpose of taking soldiers' pictures," reported the *Hartford Daily Courant*. "Now the girls will have a chance to have their lovers taken before they go to war."[20]

The Moore Brothers cranked out hundreds of portraits for the new soldiers. In fact, Nelson Augustus Moore, a Kensington native, had begun as a painter, known for his Hudson River landscapes. But in 1854, he and his brother Roswell had adopted the new medium, photography. Nelson's artistry was apparent in the backdrops of many of their images.

The Moore Brothers photographed this unidentified soldier of the 16th Connecticut standing stiffly before a backdrop of a camp scene, as if on guard duty. A cast iron headstand (its base visible beside this soldier's shoes) held the head stationary over a long exposure time, making the subject's posture look unnaturally rigid.

Using the same backdrop but a different pose, the Moore Brothers produced a soldier portrait radically different from the one on the left. Here it's easy to see a connection between the old art form—painting—and the new one—photography. With shading and hand coloring, the Moores' backdrop took on depth and perspective. Though this picture is only a few inches high, it manages to evoke the formal painted portraits of earlier decades.

Before the final departure, some soldiers made a last visit home to say goodbye. "I shall never forget the scene of my parting with mother and the girls," recalled Jim Sawyer. "About the last words I heard her say were, 'O, Jimmie, how can I let you go?' Father took me to the depot. A great crowd was there for most soldiers had friends with them who came to see them off . . . There were many affecting scenes. Father shook my hand with tears running down his face, and I know they were running down mine."[21]

The final ceremony before leaving the state was the presentation of the colors. Each regiment would carry an American flag and a state flag, usually painted with the seal of Connecticut, then customized with the name of the regiment. At the presentations, speakers urged the troops to protect their flags with their lives. "Bear it bravely up above the storm of war," said Hartford mayor Henry C. Deming, "follow it to the death in the crisis of battle, and return it to our midst emblazoned with triumphs nobly won, or leave it behind in a soldier's honorable grave."[22]

The flags would become sacred to the men. In battle, color-bearers carried the two silk banners, each over six feet by six feet, waving from staffs that stood nearly ten feet high. Their large size made them visible in the chaos and smoke of combat when the soldiers most needed them. A regiment's flag didn't just mark battle position for the troops; it became a physical symbol that actually inspired the men's courage and recharged their passion.

Before the 25th Regiment left Hartford for the South, privates Lucien Royce (*left*) and Aaron Cook visited Wilson Brothers Photographers on Main Street. The new soldiers displayed all their military gear: at center stage was a black canvas knapsack painted with "25 CV" (for 25th Regiment Connecticut Volunteers). Royce wore a four-button blouse while Cook had a nine-button frock coat, both common to Union infantrymen. Cook also wore his Union overcoat. They slung their canteens over their shoulders, and rested their forage caps atop the knapsack, while Cook prominently displayed a piece of cloth in his left hand. Was it a handkerchief made by an admirer?

In the center of Litchfield, surrounded by well-wishers, the men of Connecticut's 19th Regiment stood at attention to receive their colors on September 10, 1862.

The colors were a special target for the enemy, so color-bearers were often the first to fall. Then the next man in the supporting color guard would snatch up the flag and continue until he was hit. "All but one of the color guards were shot & the colors were down several times but up they would go again," wrote Capt. Charles M. Coit of the 8th Connecticut after his regiment saw battle.[23]

But in these early days, the new soldiers didn't yet know what the flag would come to mean to them. For most, the flag presentation was just part of the excitement of departure day. An officer of the 14th Connecticut remembered departing from Hartford, "which was all alive with flags and the waving of handkerchiefs in the hands of her fair daughters, whose eyes filled with tears as our magnificent band . . . played 'The girl I left behind me,' leading us to sob, some, for the girls we had left, others, because we hadn't any girls to leave behind."[24]

The 14th's steamboat headed from Hartford down the Connecticut River, pausing at Middletown where many of the regiment lived. Their assistant surgeon, Levi Jewett, wrote:

"When we reached Middletown it seemed as if the whole city had turned out to meet us. The dock and all the space about was black with people. Many came to the boats with baskets of fruit and food, which were greatly appreciated by 'the boys.' At Cobalt a great gun on the hill gave us a roaring 'God-speed'. . ."[25]

Many soldiers—especially officers—brought along small flasks as they went to war. Few could equal the fine style of the flask owned by Charles Upham of Meriden.

This soldier of Connecticut's 1st Light Battery went south by steamboat, along with his regiment's soldiers, horses, and artillery. It wasn't an easy voyage, as one of the men recalled: "The most of my time was taken up in throwing dead horses and the contents of my stomach overboard." (Herbert W. Beecher, *History of the First Light Battery Connecticut Volunteers, 1861–1865*, vol. 1, p. 78.)

Lt. Henry P. Goddard recalled, "As we passed out of the Connecticut that night, I remember standing with Johnny Broatch on the after deck of the boat, for a last look at the dear old state, whose good health we drank, emptying a half pint flask that a worthy relative had filled, telling me that unless I was badly wounded it ought to last me through the war."[26]

But the trip south was definitely not all hope and glory. "Our boys on their way to the field slept on the dirty decks of a steamer, lying together as thick as rows of pins on a paper," wrote Samuel Fiske of the 14th Regiment. Later they "were packed in dirty, close [railroad] cars like sheep in a pen."[27]

And while citizens had showered the troops with cakes, fruit, and other tidbits along the way, soldiers found a slightly different diet awaited them in Washington.

> Here was a long building, having painted in large letters upon it "The Soldiers' Rest." In this we found long wooden tables, and on them the usual fare, boiled corned beef and hard bread, with potatoes boiled in their jackets. The tables were not very clean and flies were much in evidence, but we were too hungry to mind such little things. Along the tables here and there were placed camp kettles filled with coffee.

> One of the boys took his plate, knife and fork from his haversack, laid the plate on the table and laid on it an attractive hunk of beef. On cutting it open two or three fat maggots rolled out. He emptied his plate on the dish and reached for a hard tack. This broke easy. The reason was shown, as several lively skippers trickled down on his plate. "I Yum!" said he, "I'll drink my coffee with my eyes shut," and he did.[28]

From the very beginning, one Connecticut regiment—the 14th—showed it had more than enough bravado to go around. Cpl. Albert Crittenden looked back on the green regiment's spunk as it marched in a formal review of troops just after reaching Washington:

I recall the reviewing stand where President Lincoln, General Scott, Secretary Stanton and other dignitaries stood while we passed in review. Our staff-officers and captains entered the reviewing stand and were in turn introduced to the President and his staff of officials. When the head of B Company, the left of the regiment, reached the stand, President Lincoln was so busy we felt we were not to be noticed, so with one accord, we struck up loudly singing, "We are coming, Father Abraham, three hundred thousand more." At once he faced us, straightened up his tall form, doffed his high silk hat and bowed and bowed until we were by.[29]

In Dixie

When the Nutmeg troops arrived in the vicinity of Washington, many found a new general waiting to lead them. George B. McClellan commanded the newly formed Army of the Potomac. "Young Napoleon," as the papers dubbed him, set about transforming the gawky farmers, bank clerks, and factory workers into a professional fighting force.

That meant more drilling, and here the learning curve rose far more sharply than it had back in training camp in the Land of Steady Habits. The volunteer officers especially struggled with

When an officer from the regular army took command of the 4th Connecticut, "He found the regiment . . . an uneducated and undisciplined body of men. It was his task to make soldiers out of them." Though the troops lacked uniform coats and shoes, Colonel Tyler required rigid military order. He punished the loafers and praised those who adopted a military bearing; Here, the 4th soldiers marched smartly to the parade ground for drill in Arlington, Virginia, in the fall of 1861.

their responsibilities: it wasn't so easy "to take the Company of one hundred men and so discipline them that each shall observe his position so that the whole body may move as one perfect machine, keeping step in the march—observing a perfect line in company front—march without crowding—break up into platoons and re-form with no confusion—to accomplish all this is no little task."[30]

Charles Coit, the 8th Regiment's adjutant, wrote to his parents: "am studying harder than I have before for a long time. I am so deficient in the 'Tactics' I make a good many blunders at Battalion Drills."[31]

Plenty of officers got lost in the tangled wording of the tactics manuals, and no wonder; directions for "By Platoon, right wheel" included:

> At the command *march*, the right front rank man of each platoon will face to the right, the covering sergeant standing fast; the chief of each platoon will move quickly by the shortest line, a little beyond the point at which the marching flank will rest when the wheel shall be completed, face to the late rear, and place himself so that the line which he forms with the man on the right (who had faced), shall be perpendicular to that occupied by the company in line of battle; each platoon will wheel according to the principles prescribed for the wheel on a fixed pivot.[32]

The army ordered regimental commanders to send their officers to school. "All the non-commissioned officers in our Reg. are obliged hereafter to meet twice a week in the Captains quarters to recite lessons in Military Tactics," wrote Fred Lucas of the 19th Connecticut. "We met last night for the first time. Not a man knew his lessons in our Co. We had considerable sport during the recitation. All the Field & Staff officers recite to Col. Kellogg twice a week."[33]

If their school sessions didn't teach the officers, their colonel could always resort to swearing,

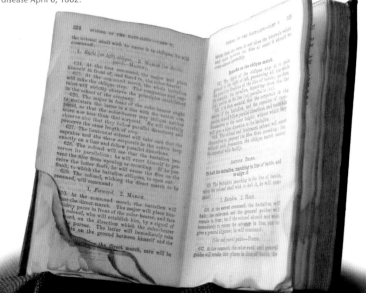

Concentrating intently on his tactics reading, William H. Johnson apparently didn't notice how close his book was to his candle, resulting in charred pages in his *Casey's Infantry Tactics*. A second lieutenant in the 8th Connecticut, Johnson died of disease April 6, 1862.

as Michael Kelly described in his diary in 1862: "Col. Kellogg went for Capts. Gold, Peck, Sperry & Williams [during drill]. Gold made a mistake in the movements. Col. shouted, Capt., ask any of your privates &c., and he told Capt. Sperry he would drill his Co. ('I') from hell to breakfast, and Peck he called an old woman, & Williams, Turkey Cock. On the whole it was an excitable regimental drill or battallion drill. I tell you the Capts. trembled."[34]

Along with continual drilling came the introduction to forced marches. In the months ahead, marching twenty or even thirty miles a day would become commonplace for the Nutmeggers, but right now they were definitely still tenderfeet. The 14th Regiment was scarcely two weeks out of Connecticut when Frederick Burr Hawley noted in his diary, "Tuesday, Sept 9th, 1862. Drilled 2½ hours loading and firing. 12:00 march 5 miles and camp in a lot. One man belonging to Co. K marched to death."[35] The soldier who collapsed and died was James McVay, a Norwich man with two sons in the same company.

On the flip side of the coin was the early experience of Connecticut's 4th Regiment (later to become the 1st Heavy Artillery). Chaplain Edward Walker described the regiment's camp in the Maryland fairgrounds in the summer of 1861:

> In this beautiful spot we . . . made ourselves thoroughly at home. A number of buildings on the premises, which had been erected for the accommodation of the county fair, were refitted by the men for various uses. The largest served as an evening lectureroom, and as a church in rainy weather; in another were held our daily prayer-meetings, glee-clubs, rehearsals, etc.; another was occupied as a guard-house; another was used for forage, while excellent stalls were furnished for our horses.
>
> In addition to these comforts, the men put up swings and bars for gymnastic exercises, so that we were abundantly provided with means of recreation, as well as with all the necessities of life. I think I never saw an equal number of men more happy, contented, and good-natured, than ours were at Camp Abercrombie. Our life there was like that of a summer picnic; and the men, though keen for fighting and prompt to perform all their military duties, had the air of a party of summer excursionists.[36]

The picnic ended abruptly when the regiment's lenient colonel resigned, replaced by a colonel from the regular army who "saw at a glance that rigid discipline was needed."[37] Military procedures immediately replaced glee clubs and gymnastics.

John DeForest, an officer in the 12th Regiment, described the daily grind that most volunteer troops followed:

> we get up at sunrise. Then the *reveille* beats; the men turn out under arms; the three commissioned officers look on while the first sergeant calls the roll; the muskets are stacked and the men break ranks. At half past six we breakfast; from seven to eight there is company drill; from half past nine to half past ten, more company drill; at twelve, dinner, which means soup and hardtack; from four to six, battalion drill; at half past six, hardtack, pork and coffee; at nine, another roll call; at a quarter past nine, lights out.
>
> It is a healthy, monotonous, stupid life, and makes one long to go somewhere, even at the risk of being shot.[38]

ON THE MOVE

Connecticut's regiments didn't remain long in Washington. The objectives of two generals had them moving all over the South in two early attempts to snuff out the Confederacy.

SCOTT'S GREAT SNAKE.

General Scott's proposal became known as the Anaconda Plan for its resemblance to the constricting snake. By tightening the cord around the Confederacy, Scott hoped to cut off supplies to the Rebels, hinder their movements, and force their surrender.

General-in-chief Winfield Scott felt that reuniting the nation would be easier if little blood was shed. Instead of masterminding battles, Scott proposed to "envelop" the South with a blockade by sea, and a fleet of gunboats supported by soldiers along the Mississippi River.

Meanwhile, Union supporters in the North were impatient for battle. "Here we have spent some hundreds of millions of dollars; some six months of time; a vast amount of patience in collecting, and equipping, and drilling our forces, and have got together some three hundred thousand men, and now we begin to hear talk of 'going into winter quarters,'" complained the *Hartford Daily Courant*. "The public will be disgusted! We have nothing but the bitter mortification of the Bull Run affair to chew upon . . . nothing but a good smart, ringing victory . . . will do . . . Gross disheartenment will settle down on the Union cause, unless more vigor is shown in taking the offensive."[39]

In November of 1861, Scott retired, and George B. McClellan sprang into his position. Little Mac responded to the North's clamor, planning the Peninsula Campaign, which called for the Union army and navy to capture Richmond, the capital of the Confederacy. The winter gave McClellan time to further train his green troops while he polished his "On to Richmond" scheme for the spring of 1862.

Connecticut soldiers found themselves ordered throughout the South to prosecute the strategies created by Generals Scott and McClellan. The 5th Regiment, on picket duty outside of Washington, kept Stonewall Jackson's troops from the Potomac River, the railroad, and the Chesapeake and Ohio Canal. Charles Squires of Roxbury groused about not going into combat, writing to his sister, "I think that you have more fighting at home than we have down here."[40] (Squires would see action soon enough; in the Spring of 1862, the 5th would scuffle with Jackson's troops around Winchester, Virginia, and in the Shenandoah Valley.)

Meanwhile, the men of Connecticut's 6th and 7th Regiments boarded steamers for an expedition to the coast of South Carolina under Gen. William T. Sherman and the navy's admiral DuPont. On November 7, Union ships bombarded the Confederate-held Fort Walker in Hilton Head, and Fort Beauregard across the sound, forcing their submission. The 6th and 7th Connecticut were the first infantry to land, prepared for hand-to-hand fighting if the Confederates resisted. As the boats approached land, the men of the 7th jumped out and splashed ashore at Hilton Head. Marching into Fort Walker unopposed, they had the honor of planting their regiment's flags on the battlements—the first Union colors to wave over South Carolina since its secession.

Connecticut's 8th, 10th, and 11th Regiments also took part in Gen. Ambrose Burnside's expedition to establish control of the North Carolina coast. At Roanoke Island, the 10th Regiment advanced on a Confederate battery under heavy fire, taking the battery but losing their colonel, Charles Russell, to a gunshot wound at the outset of their first fight. In the port of New Berne, the

Camp near Llamston Md. "Gen. Banks' division"
5th Conn. Vols. On Muddy Branch

8th and 11th Connecticut successfully fought the Rebels to gain control of the Neuse River. "Gen Burnside came along up side our Regt and order us to charge on them," wrote Cyrus Harrington of the 8th, "in which we did in double quick time in which they fired upon us killing 8 wounding several. It was a bold attempt but we won the victory driving the rebels in every direction."[41]

"The order to charge was given," wrote the 11th's lieutenant Joseph Converse, "up sprang thousands of blue-coats,—a glittering wave of steel flashing in front,—and rushed forward with loud huzzas, an invincible line."[42] The Confederates fled their works.

Back in Connecticut, the 9th Infantry (also known as the Irish Regiment) broke camp at New Haven, finally ending up at desolate Ship Island, Mississippi. Under Gen. Benjamin Butler, the men of the 9th Connecticut, along with their comrades in Connecticut's 12th and 13th Regiments, helped capture New Orleans.

The soldiers of Connecticut's 1st Cavalry were always on the move, galloping throughout Virginia, as they scouted and skirmished with the enemy around the countryside. In the narrow valleys among the Allegheny and Branch Mountains, "The winding roads and countless convenient hiding-places . . . swarmed with guerrillas. These partisans of slavery and rebellion gathered everywhere in small squads to persecute Union citizens, annoy our soldiers, capture our scouts and carriers, and shoot our pickets . . . To destroy these roving rascals was to be the task of our cavalry battalion."[43]

It was March of 1862 when General McClellan launched the Peninsula Campaign, his first foray to capture Richmond. He pushed thousands of troops up the Virginia Peninsula between the York and James Rivers. Among them was Connecticut's 1st Heavy Artillery, which had originated months before as the state's 4th Infantry Regiment. Now the regiment traveled with sixty-five enormous field pieces and more than four tons of ammunition over land that *seemed* solid and dry, but wasn't.

"Puncture the surface anywhere and water gushes forth," declared one of the 1st Heavies. "The tent pins drew water where we pitched our tents . . . as the heavy hundred-pounder [gun] moved slowly along the road, the wheels of the sling cart would sometimes pierce the upper crust,

"Perrine's New Military Map Illustrating the Seat of War," 1862

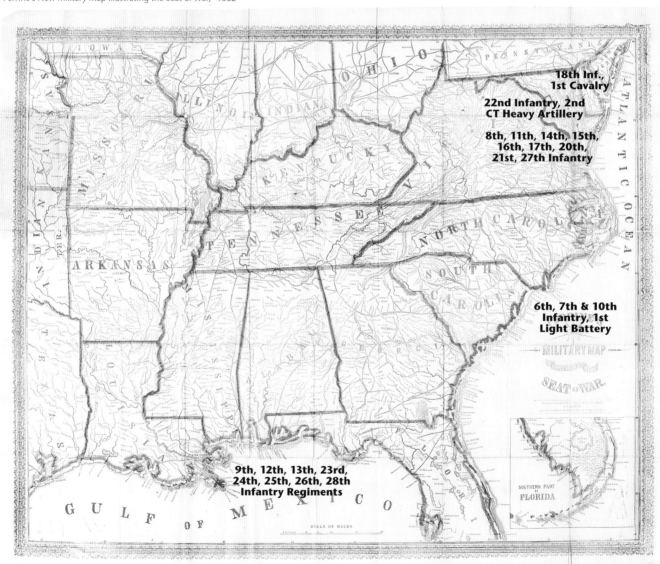

18th Inf.,
1st Cavalry

22nd Infantry, 2nd
CT Heavy Artillery

8th, 11th, 14th, 15th,
16th, 17th, 20th,
21st, 27th Infantry

6th, 7th & 10th
Infantry, 1st
Light Battery

9th, 12th, 13th, 23rd,
24th, 25th, 26th, 28th
Infantry Regiments

and the monster gun would be almost hopelessly mired . . . it often happened that horses and mules would prove of no avail to draw them out. Then several hundred men would man the ropes; Major Kellogg would mount on the axle of the sling cart, give the word of command, and with a long pull all together the huge guns would be dragged out and drawn steadily along the road."[44] In many places, the men had to chop down small trees and saplings, laying the slender trunks across the path, one alongside the other, to make corduroy roads for their big guns to travel upon.

As the phrase "On to Richmond!" rang through the North, Union troops advanced ever so gradually toward the Confederate capital. They never reached it. After seven days of fighting, the Rebel forces (now under Robert E. Lee) repelled McClellan's troops, forcing them to retreat toward Washington.

When the summer of 1862 arrived, the Union army had little to crow about. It had succeeded in winning strategic positions along the eastern coast, but hadn't achieved its commanders' greater aims. The anniversary of the loss at Bull Run called up dismay throughout the North, while the Confederates felt that victory was within their reach.

INTO THE FIRE

On the eighth of August, Connecticut's 5th Regiment, along with a regiment from New York and another from Pennsylvania, encamped along a stream called Cedar Run near Culpeper, Virginia. Gen. John Pope had positioned their brigade to block a possible advance by Stonewall Jackson's Rebel troops until Union reinforcements could arrive. But on August 9, Union general Nathaniel Banks took the situation into his own hands. Believing that a delay would allow the Confederates to amass more troops, he decided to attack.

Just before five o'clock on the evening of August 9, Banks ordered his men to prepare to advance. Col. George D. Chapman, leading the Connecticut 5th, took his post behind the regiment's colors and spoke encouragingly to his soldiers, telling them "to remember their good name and to be sure to do credit to themselves and the state." One of the color sergeants saw that the colonel wasn't wearing a sidearm, and offered him his own revolver. "The Colonel refused it, telling the sergeant that his life was just as valuable."

Then the order came: "Fix bayonets and charge," "Charge, charge and yell"—and "the whole brigade sprang over the fence." As the troops moved swiftly forward into the stubble of a wheat field, they entered a storm of bullets from the Confederates hidden in the woods before them. "Color Sergeant Jones, carrying the stars and stripes, fell on his face, killed outright . . . Captain Corliss . . . caught up and bore on the flag, until he was brought to the ground with a bullet . . . Sergeant Luzerne A. Palmer took it from Captain Corliss and bore it to the front again, until he fell wounded."[45] According to one of its lieutenants, *seven* of the 5th Regiment's color-bearers gave their lives for the flag that day; two more fell wounded.

> Color Sergeant James Hewison, bearing the State colors, was wounded early in the charge, but kept along, bearing the colors till . . . he was again severely wounded and fell, unable to go further. Many were falling about him at the time, and his fall was unobserved till the line had passed on and he was left among the dead and dying with the flag in his possession.

After the first shock of his wound had passed and he had regained some strength he resolved that neither himself nor it should fall into the hands of the enemy if he could prevent it, and carefully tearing it from the staff, he wrapped it about his person beneath his uniform; then he crawled from the field on his hands and knees, as rapidly as his wounds would permit, and he was taken by comrades to a hospital, wearing the flag, and so he saved it.[46]

Through the galling fire the brigade came on, until the blue-clad Union soldiers entered the woods and were in the midst of the Rebels. A section of the Confederate line gave way quickly, the soldiers fleeing to the rear, which allowed the 5th Connecticut boys to break through "surging into the woods through this gap thus made and swinging to the left as they advanced . . . our ranks, which had now become a furious yelling line, sweeping right forward towards the rear of the enemy's line . . . From this point on, for the next fifteen minutes, it was a hand to hand encounter. There were few loaded guns on either side and very little chance to load them. Clubbed muskets and bayonets were the rule."[47]

Before leaving New Haven to join his regiment, Ned Blake faced the camera with the honest, open gaze that characterized him.

But in a matter of minutes, the tide turned. Stonewall Jackson galloped forward, waving a battle flag, and his brigade rallied to him, charging the Union line. The Rebels, already in retreat, turned and reformed, and A. P. Hill's troops rushed forward to reinforce them. The Confederates now outnumbered the Union troops two to one. The 5th Connecticut men and their comrades rallied, making a stand in the woods while they prayed for reinforcements to arrive.

The report of their brigade commander, General Crawford, described "vastly superior numbers of the enemy." Of his own troops, Crawford wrote: "Their field officers had all been killed, wounded, or taken prisoners, the support I looked for did not arrive, and my gallant men, broken, decimated by that fearful fire, that unequal contest, fell back again across the space, leaving most of their number upon the field. The slaughter was fearful."[48]

That night, the soldiers of the shattered regiment tried to regroup. Henry Daboll, twenty-eight, had been the regiment's eighth-ranked captain that morning. Now, with so many officers dead or wounded, Captain Daboll found himself in command of the 5th Connecticut—or what was left of it.[49]

As the battered men of 5th Connecticut stumbled in to their regiment after the battle, there was no sign of one of their most respected officers, Maj. Edward Blake.

The major, called Ned, came from a large and close New Haven family. As a student at Yale, he'd gained his classmates' esteem without trying. "Whoever knew Blake loved him," declared the Class Record; "nor was it difficult to know him, for he carried his heart in his hand. A man of fine physique and of the most exuberant spirits, he delighted and excelled in out-door sport."[50] A member of Yale's crew team, Ned had also joined the mysterious Skull and Bones society, proudly wearing a gold pin with the group's insignia.

When the war began, Ned was in law school and did not immediately enlist. After much reflection, he decided that the rebellion was "a war on which the most immense results for the whole world depended," a friend related.[51]

"Naturally of a mild gentle and peaceful disposition, a military career was the very last thing he would have selected if it had not been for the voice of duty sounding in his ears," said his brother.[52] The governor appointed Blake adjutant of Connecticut's 5th Regiment; three days later, Ned left Connecticut for Maryland.

It was a hard winter for the 5th Regiment, full of exhausting marches. Maj. Henry B. Stone described one of the most grueling:

> When I tell you that the snow was driving all day, and ankle-deep; that the men had just marched one hundred and thirty miles with scarcely two days' rest; that their feet were sore and blistered, many of them without shoes, and using handkerchiefs and old rags to tie up their feet and keep them out of the snow,—you may appreciate the march, and the indomitable perseverance of our men to accomplish it. Some of the boys were compelled to fall out from exhaustion; and the poor fellows wept bitterly because they were unable to stand up longer.[53]

That spring, the 5th Regiment's brigade drove Stonewall Jackson's troops out of Winchester, Virginia, only to find the tables turned less than three months later. With their brigade cut off from the rest of the army and in imminent danger of capture, the men of the 5th made a forced march of *forty-three miles*, reaching the Potomac River near midnight. Instead of riding a horse as officers usually did, Ned Blake marched with his men.[54]

Weeks later, Blake received a promotion to major. In early August, his regiment went into battle at Cedar Mountain with him on horseback, leading his troops in the charge. Forced to dismount when his horse was wounded, Major Blake fought on foot with his men. Then the flow of battle changed; Union troops were forced to retreat, and the 5th Connecticut became divided. It was impossible to know who had been wounded, killed, or captured.

The next day both sides began to bury their dead. With the temperature nearly 100 degrees, bloating and decomposition quickly made many of the young men's bodies unrecognizable. In addition, many bodies had been pillaged of their clothing and personal effects.

No one had come across Major Blake. He wasn't among the Union prisoners, nor with the wounded. Yet no one had found his body on the field, either.

In the weeks that followed, Ned's parents and siblings suffered in excruciating uncertainty. Telegrams and letters flew back and forth between the family and Ned's regiment. Then an officer in the same brigade, who'd been wounded and taken prisoner, "stated that the body of a major, near where he lay, was rifled by an enemy officer, who showed him among other things a gold pin (skull and crossbones) which he had appropriated."[55]

Two months after the battle, one of Ned's friends wrote that he had located a soldier who had seen the major fall:

> He tells me that in the second wood Major Blake told him they were falling back. He looked around & they two were almost the only ones of the regiment in sight. They went back to the fence & found Col. Chapman with a prisoner. They all started to go back across the wheat field and when half way across Col. C fainted (he had not been well) and Major Blake was struck, fell, and did not stir afterward.
>
> Major told him in the wood he had been wounded twice. He did not know where he was wounded or where the last shot struck him but regarded his death as instantaneous from the fact of his making no motion afterward.[56]

Still, some of Ned's family clung to the belief that he could have been merely unconscious. His body was never found.

A year and a half after the Battle of Cedar Mountain, an envelope addressed to Ned arrived at the Blake home in New Haven. It was an invitation to the wedding of a Yale classmate. Ned's brother George wrote to the groom, explaining that Ned had fallen in battle. "For weeks, and agonizing months, we could not believe him dead, and eagerly clung to the hope that he might have been taken prisoner, but nearly two long years have long since blotted out that hope and we now know that he [has] bravely fulfilled his mission and fallen a martyr to his Country," wrote George sadly.[57]

ANOTHER BULL RUN

Three weeks after Union general John Pope suffered the Cedar Mountain defeat at the hands of Stonewall Jackson, he faced him again at the Second Battle of Bull Run. Commanding the Army of Virginia, Pope aimed to protect Washington and the Shenandoah Valley, and distract the Rebels from General McClellan's Army of the Potomac, which was still licking its wounds on the Virginia Peninsula.

None of the Union commanders had reckoned on the skills of Gen. Robert E. Lee, who saw a way to take the conflict away from Richmond, toward Washington. Lee ordered Stonewall Jackson's troops to cut around Pope's forces, and capture the Orange and Alexandria Railroad, thereby cutting off Pope's communication with Washington.

Jackson's forces tangled with Pope over several days in engagements along the Rappahannock River. On August 26, the rebels flanked Pope's troops and took the railroad, then marched on to capture a Union supply depot. The Confederate troops went on to take up position on the old battlefield at Bull Run. Stonewall Jackson knew that Confederate general James G. Longstreet was nearby; sure of reinforcements, Jackson goaded Pope into an attack.

For his part, Pope felt he had Stonewall Jackson cornered. He assumed that Jackson's troops were retreating, and planned a series of attacks that he thought would crush the Rebels. During two days of battle, both sides suffered heavy casualties. On August 30, Pope watched as Confederate artillery decimated his troops; then, as Longstreet sent forward his force of over 25,000 Rebel troops, the Union once again fled Bull Run.

Pope's two defeats—Cedar Mountain and Second Bull Run—left the Union army demoralized, while the Confederates, buoyed by their victories and Robert E. Lee's leadership, proceeded confidently with their plans.

No Time to Lose

In September of 1862, Lee's Army of Northern Virginia crossed the Potomac into Maryland, and McClellan hurried his troops north to block the Rebels' access to Washington.

By now, Connecticut had numerous regiments in the south, among them the 14th, 15th, and 16th Regiments. Several of the green regiments were quickly gathered into McClellan's command. "Here it was," wrote a soldier in the 14th Connecticut, "that the torn and tattered veterans of the army of the Potomac, fresh from the swamps and battles of the Peninsula campaign, excited our wondering interest as they marched by on their way to the front. But how they repaid our deprecatory looks at the condition of their clothes and accoutrements with their jeering 'Hulloa children! Poor boys, dark blue pants, soft bread three times a week, three hundred miles from home and ain't got but one mother a piece.'"[58]

The Union army had to move fast. Men who days ago had been bank clerks, painters, barbers, and pastry chefs had to be soldiers. Instantly. Connecticut's 8th, 11th, 14th, and 16th Regiments joined the thousands of troops hurrying north toward Frederick, Maryland. The 14th and 16th Regiments were still unaccustomed to their new rifle muskets, which they'd received just days earlier.

The men and boys of the 14th Connecticut—those who had impulsively burst into song before President Lincoln—swung along the road eagerly. "The boys were in the best of spirits and sang with a will 'John Brown's Body' etc. . . . As they passed an old engine-house in which were a number of Confederate prisoners, one called out 'What regiment is that?' 'The 14th Wooden Nutmeg' was the reply, to which the audacious prisoner answered 'You will soon get your heads grated.'"[59]

But even the most gung-ho soldiers began to sober up as their inexperienced eyes took in the sights of real war. "Step by step they saw the desolation and waste of war-ruined homes, dismantled gun-carriages, piles of muskets and the putrefying bodies of horses and mules."[60] In the dark, the regiment reached South Mountain, where a bloody battle between the troops of McClellan and Lee had left thousands dead and wounded. The next morning, the 14th men looked around them in horror.

"I awoke about five o'clock on the battle-field of yesterday," wrote Benjamin Hirst, "and went out to see what war was without romance. I cannot describe my feelings, but I hope to God never to see the like again."[61]

Nelson Bailey, nineteen, saw the bloody, broken bodies and swallowed hard. "We were in the enemy's front yard," Nelson realized, "and he was there with his lawn-mowers."[62]

War by Citizen Soldiers

THE MAKINGS OF AN ARMY

In Connecticut's 26th Regiment, the men of Company I took their orders from Captain Bentley, an ice dealer. A bookbinder, assisted by a train conductor, commanded the 25th Regiment's Company K. In the 2nd Heavy Artillery, men in their forties answered to an eighteen-year-old student, Lt. Augustus Fenn. In the ranks were lace weavers, oystermen, bartenders, and factory workers. How in the world could Abraham Lincoln hope to win a war with an army like this?

Just a few weeks after the war began, a Hartford doctor named George Clary had observed: "all sorts and conditions of men are enlisting here . . . A company is this moment marching by my windows. Some of the recruits are stout, hardy farmer boys from the country and then there are clerks from the counter, young lawyers, and Gentlemen's sons forming companies by themselves and then foreigners of all descriptions—some thirsting for fame, some for whiskey, and some for nothing but $11.00 per month."[1]

Would this odd jumble—hundreds of thousands of untrained men led by a tiny percentage of West Point professionals—fight? "'War,' said a great statesman, 'can only be successfully prosecuted when the army is well seasoned . . . the raw recruits who have responded to President Lincoln's call will only hasten the downfall of the Republic by their inefficiency on the field.'"[2]

Untrained, yes; but Lincoln's raw recruits were for the most part united in the cause and willing to give their lives for their country. A New Haven bookkeeper-turned-soldier put it simply: "The experiment was to be tried of . . . a war by citizen soldiers who left the desk, the farm and the workshop in answer to their country's call."[3]

Smooth-cheeked boys marched beside white-bearded grandfathers. A soldier in the 21st Connecticut wrote of their oldest member: "the boys wondered why the Army had sent them a

The 2nd Heavy Artillery's "most unpromising officer," wrote one of the men, "was First Lieutenant Augustus H. Fenn. He was but eighteen years old, of freckled face and awkward gait, and was regarded with surly contempt by windy and consequential brother officers. Every private soldier, too, had his fling at him. It was considered very impudent in him to be an officer, at all; but he had recruited his forty men, and there he was, with a commission in his pocket from Governor Buckingham." (Theodore F. Vaill, *History of the Second Connecticut Volunteer Heavy Artillery. Originally the Nineteenth Connecticut Vols.*, p. 334.)

Fenn's company contained the men rejected by the officers of the other nine companies. But though young and inexperienced, Fenn was not a quitter. The regiment's adjutant wrote that "Lieutenant Fenn grew in the estimation . . . of all who knew him . . . He proved himself one of the best drill masters and disciplinarians in the regiment, and one of the most competent officers in every position." His company of disdained soldiers became "one of the best, most faithful, trusted Companies that ever went into the service." (Ibid., p. 334.)

At the Battle of Cedar Creek, Fenn (then a captain) was wounded in the arm. Surgeons amputated it at the shoulder, and arranged for the young officer to be discharged from the army. Indignant, Fenn appealed to his colonel who allowed him to stay in the regiment. Less than seven weeks after his amputation, Captain Fenn returned to his troops at the front. By war's end, Augustus Fenn, no longer the "most unpromising officer," had been brevetted colonel. One-armed, he returned to his home in Plymouth, Connecticut. He went on to attend Harvard Law School, later becoming a respected judge in Connecticut.

Chaplain who was three times as old as most of them, 64. He could never in the world, they thought, stand the rigors of camp life, much less the stress of battle."[4]

But the 21st soldiers soon grew to love their chaplain, Rev. Thomas G. Brown of Chatham. He was a quiet, unpretentious man, "doing all that was possible for the physical, as well as the spiritual, well being of even the most humble man in the regiment."[5]

In May of 1864, when the regiment went into battle at Drewry's Bluff, its chaplain went in with them.

> Our sturdy old chaplain, anxious to render practical aid, armed himself with an axe and found a short method of opening ammunition boxes, from which he distributed cartridges . . . Death was thinning our ranks and anon the good Chaplain . . . was beckoned to the side of a dying soldier . . .
>
> And down on bended knees by the dying man's side sank the fearless minister, and with bared head, looking up to Heaven, lifted his soul in prayer

An unknown photographer captured the likenesses of two boys in Connecticut's 2nd Heavy Artillery, who posed in their musicians' uniforms. Dick Butler (*left*) was about thirteen and Henry VanDeusen about fifteen when they enlisted in December of 1863. For such youngsters, it must have seemed like a dream come true to join the army. Camping in tents, foregoing school and church, and being free from a parent's oversight—what could be better? But along with adventure and freedom came responsibilities, deprivation, and danger. The drummer boys grew up fast—if they lived to grow up at all. Dick Butler and Henry VanDeusen survived the war.

In battle, musicians didn't usually bear arms, but they still came under fire while working as stretcher-bearers for the wounded. The 2nd Heavies' adjutant described what happened to one of their drummer boys at the Battle of Cold Harbor: "two men were carried to the rear, on stretchers, apparently in such a state of exhaustion that they could not stand . . . they were carried by some of the musicians,—whose duty it was to perform such work when fighting was going on—and placed in a ravine, about a mile to the rear; they had just arrived there when a rebel shell burst near the spot, taking off the foot of a drummer boy of Company E, named Frederick D. Painter." (Vaill, *History of the Second Connecticut Volunteer Heavy Artillery*, p. 324.) The son of an itinerant minister, Frederick "Frank" Painter came from a large family. He was about fourteen when he enlisted. The shell at Cold Harbor killed him, and he was buried on the field. At the Battle of Winchester, another drummer in his regiment, James VanBuren, met the same fate.

that God would receive the departing spirit. Meanwhile the air was alive with leaden hail, and the roar at times drowned the firmly spoken words of him that prayed.[6]

"He was our father, we his boys," wrote one of the 21st soldiers.[7]

At the other end of the spectrum from Chaplain Brown were the boy soldiers—and there were many. Fourteen- and fifteen-year-old boys (who claimed to be eighteen) enlisted throughout Connecticut. An old story claimed that boys often placed in one of their shoes a scrap of paper with the numeral eighteen written on it. When asked their age, they would reply truthfully that they were "over eighteen." The doctors who examined the new soldiers often knew or suspected their deceptions, but were willing to look the other way.

Drummer boys were often a regiment's youngest members. In the 2nd Heavy Artillery, Theodore Vaill mentioned "eight or ten boys, not more than thirteen or fifteen years of age, who had enlisted and come to the regiment with the rest of the recruits, as drummer boys."[8] At such a young age, the drummers probably didn't enlist out of patriotic or moral sentiments, but from a yearning for adventure, or an innocent desire to be a soldier.

In between the young drummers and the old men were thousands and thousands of soldiers whose ages spanned decades. Some Connecticut families sent more than one generation: in Salisbury, fifteen-year-old Charlie Ball fought for the 2nd Heavy Artillery, while his father *and* his grandfather enlisted the 28th Regiment.

Elihu Moulthrop and his son Evelyn were among many father-son combinations in the Union army. Elihu was forty-four and Evelyn twenty-one when they enlisted in Connecticut's 20th Regiment. In August of 1864, Evelyn was killed at Turner's Ford, Georgia—not in battle, but in a peculiar mishap in camp. Evelyn had just come in off picket duty when a neighbor from Derby, Scott Baker, asked for his help. Baker had a musket ball stuck in his gun. Using a ball screw on the end of his ramrod, Baker had screwed it into the jammed bullet. He asked to borrow the strap from Evelyn's knapsack to fasten to the ramrod. Baker said he intended to attach the strap's other end to a tree, but Evelyn said "that he would pull out the ball, and he took hold of the strap, and I hold of the breech of the gun, and he gave a sudden pull, and by some unaccountable cause the powder exploded, and the ramrod entered one side of his body, passing through it, and could not be removed from his body except by being filed in two." (Statement of Scott Baker of Derby, Connecticut, October 30, 1872, in pension file of Evelyn Moulthrop, 20th Connecticut Volunteers, National Archives.)

Evelyn lived only until the next night. At war's end, his father returned to Connecticut alone; "for ten years he was the worse for Liquor," wrote his daughter Antoinette. (Statement of Mrs. R. Y. Stevenson of Ansonia, January 21, 1886, in pension file of Evelyn Moulthrop, 20th Connecticut Volunteers, National Archives.)

The majority of Connecticut soldiers were able to read and write, thanks to an 1838 state law that had improved public education. Their schooling ensured that most could write letters home, and record events in their diaries, preserving their thoughts and experiences.

College-educated men were not unusual, especially among the officers, some of whom were quite cultured and literary. Captain John Griswold, a Yale graduate, recited a Horace poem in ancient Greek as he lay dying from his wounds at Antietam.[9]

In the ranks, though, few men could claim such lofty scholarship. A small percentage of Connecticut soldiers (some of them immigrants, some native Nutmeggers) were actually illiterate, or nearly so. Still, the fact that a well digger couldn't speak eloquently about duty and honor did not make his devotion to his country any less than Captain Griswold's. "Some were scholars; some were farmers; some were artisans or laborers—plain men who had never heard of Thermopylae or Sempach, but in whose breasts burned the fire of Leonidas at the pass," said Captain Henry Jones of his brothers-in-arms in the 8th Regiment.[10]

With America on its way to becoming a melting pot, the Union army reflected the country's increasing ethnic diversity. Lt. William Cogswell,[11] a Native American from Cornwall, fought in the 2nd Heavy Artillery, while a Hawaiian named Friday Kanaka enlisted in Connecticut's 30th Regiment. Lt. Augustus Rodrigues of the 15th Connecticut came from Puerto Rico. A company of men in the 27th Regiment had names like Frederick Buchholz, Peter Schmidt, and Jacob Herman; nearly all of them born in Germany, or the children of German immigrants.

In fact, immigrants made up one-third of the Union army. In Connecticut's 9th Regiment, which drew most of its soldiers from Irish families, the regimental flag bore an Irish harp beside the stars and stripes. Other regiments contained men born in a host of other nations—England, Poland, Italy, Spain—who risked, and often gave, their lives for their adopted country.

MOTIVATIONS

As the soldiers' backgrounds varied, so did their reasons for fighting. At the beginning of the war, many men and boys enlisted in the wave of fervor sweeping the state. Joining the army in the Civil War—as now—also appealed to many young men who wanted to see something of the world beyond their hometown.

But thousands of men decided to fight out of true patriotism. Having endured nearly three years of war, Lt. Benjamin Wright of the 10th Regiment wrote to his wife in Greenwich: "there has got to be some hard fighting, a good many lives must be sacrificed, but I feel that the cause is worth all that it has or will cost. We shall be a better Nation for the ordeal through which we have passed. It will be settled so that we need have no fears that our children will have to settle it again. If we lay down our lives in such a cause we can have the satisfaction of knowing they were sacrificed in a good cause and for the good of the country."[12]

Of course, among Connecticut's thousands of soldiers, opinion varied hugely.

"We are all tired of the war the whole army we never shall whip them I believe," wrote Henry Thompson, an East Haven oysterman in the 15th Regiment. "I look at it as a great slaughter of lives."[13]

William Walter VanDeursen's father had been a captain in the War of 1812, and his grandfather had served in the Revolution. His forebears may have been patriots, but Willy joined the Union army for one reason: money.

William VanDeursen of Middletown had the blood of patriots flowing in his veins, but he was clear about his own motivation: "Money was all I enlisted for, to get enough to pay of[f] some of our debts."[14]

Besides his monthly pay, every man who enlisted received healthy enlistment bonuses from the state of Connecticut and the federal government. In addition, each city and town offered as high a bounty as possible in an effort to entice men to enlist from their town—and thus meet the quota of soldiers that the state had assigned it. Middletown began by offering $100 and increased it to $150 later in the war. Individual regiments and companies sometimes offered inducements as well.

While commissioned staff officers received much more than enlisted men, they had additional expenses; they had to buy their own food, and pay for their horses' forage.

Union Army, White Soldiers' Monthly Pay, 1862

Private	$13	1st Lieut.	$110.50
Corporal	$14	Captain	$120.50
Sergeant	$17	Major	$179
Sgt. Major	$21	Lt. Colonel	$198
2nd Lieut.	$105.50	Colonel	$222[15]

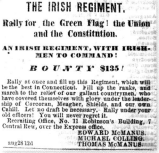

The Hartford Daily Times, September 1, 1862

THE DRAFT

When bounties didn't bring in enough men to win the war, the government moved to a draft. On March 3, 1863, Congress passed the Enrollment and Conscription Act, requiring males between the ages of twenty and forty-five to register for the draft. The act applied to both American citizens and immigrants who intended to become citizens. The threat of a draft brought plenty of opposition.

As the day of the draft approached, hundreds of men applied for medical exemptions. "The halt, the blind, the diseased, swelled to a fabulous number. Some surgeons seemed, from excessive good nature, or for the sake of popularity, or for the paltry twenty-five cents received for each certificate, inclined to grant almost every application."[16]

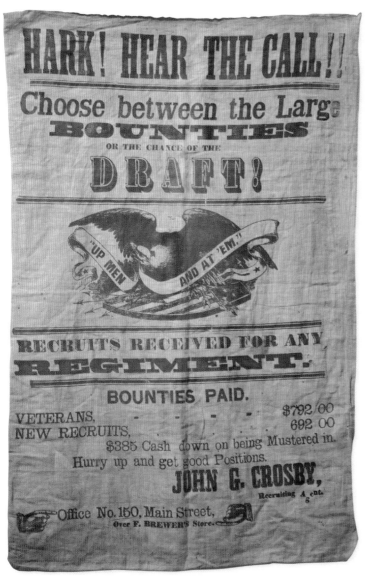

In Middletown, a recruiting poster advised men to "Choose between the Large bounties or the chance of the draft!" Veteran soldiers—more valuable since they'd already been trained—could rake in $792 in bounties, while new recruits received $692 for enlisting.

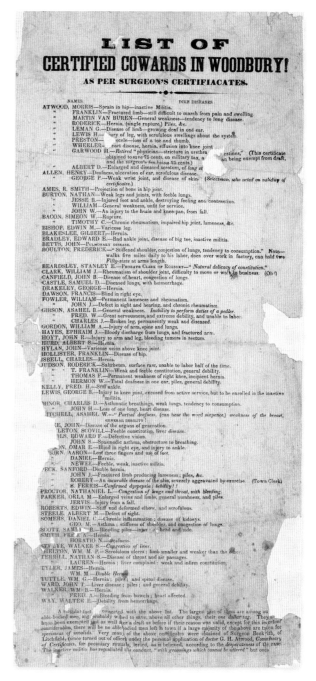

It was possible for men who did get drafted to avoid their military service if they had enough money. A drafted man (called a "conscript") could pay $300 to the government, or hire a substitute soldier to go in his place.

Many substitutes used aliases, and after claiming their fee, deserted at the first opportunity. "A <u>sweet</u> lot of substitutes they send us," wrote a disgusted Harry Goddard of the 14th

CONNECTICUT
UNION
VOLUNTEER & SUBSTITUTE ASSOCIATION.

HEAD-QUARTERS, - - HARTFORD, CONN.

RECRUITS AND SUBSTITUTES furnished Individuals and Town Authorities upon the most favorable terms. Application can be made by letter, or in person, at

THE OFFICE, No. 14 GROVE ST,
Post-Office Building.

E. B. STRONG.   S. R. PERKINS.   G. H. OLMSTED.

Soon after the war began, businesses that supplied substitute soldiers opened in many cities. For a fee, the firms provided alternates for those who couldn't or wouldn't serve in the military. Some patriotic women, like sisters Elizabeth and Augusta Greene of Norwich, hired substitutes for themselves for the length of the war.

Drafted men reported to this conscript camp in Grapevine Point, New Haven (now the site of Criscuolo Park). Here veteran officers did their best to turn them into fighting men. Most conscripts were reluctant soldiers at best; many were bounty jumpers, intent on escaping so they could enlist elsewhere for the bounty money. To prevent desertions, security at the conscript camp was tight, but that didn't stop the most determined conscripts. In January of 1865, an officer reported that "the denizens of the guard-house had tunnelled out during the night, and all who cared to go, twenty-six in number, had left for parts unknown." (George B. Peck, Jr., *Camp & Hospital*, pp. 16–17.)

Connecticut. "All New York roughs. Of the 380 who reached us, 92 have deserted, four have been shot, and I almost wish they would send them with or in their coffins."[17]

Over 200,000 Union soldiers deserted during the war. Gilbert Smith of the 6th Connecticut described the ambivalence he and many others felt at deserters' executions: "There was 2 men shot for desertion yesterday but I did not go to see them it is something I have a great dislike for but yet I think it serves them right."[18]

MANY WAYS TO SERVE

Connecticut provided the Union with over a score of Union generals, including Daniel Tyler, J. K. F. Mansfield, Alfred Terry, John Sedgwick, Alpheus Williams, Horatio Wright, Alexander Shaler, and Nathaniel Lyon.

Beneath these lofty leaders, Connecticut men filled a huge range of positions that included clerks, commissaries, wagoners, musicians, hospital stewards, and chaplains, each with its own vital function. Soldiers who weren't fighting men were still crucial to the cause. When a regiment marched eighty miles in three days, it needed a competent commissary who would have rations waiting for the hungry soldiers. Without that commissary, everything broke down.

MIGHTIER THAN THE SWORD

"Fighting" men were often contemptuous of the soldiers who wielded pens rather than muskets. Clerks usually avoided combat, but their duties were demanding. Eddie Brewer, a clerk in the 14th Connecticut, wrote: "Out of seventeen days we have been at Harper's Ferry, there have been but five when I could find time to cook my regular meals, and I have often been under the necessity of getting along with one meal, and several times have written until after eleven o'clock at night."[19]

TRUE MORAL COURAGE

A post in the Ambulance Corps was also considered a soft job by other soldiers. "I think I would go [into the Ambulance Corps] if I could get a chance to in a moment," wrote Lucius Bidwell of Middletown; "the dutys are not so hard for thay have no drilling nor fighting to trouble them."[20]

Eddie Brewer (left), a bank clerk in Middletown, enlisted in the 14th Connecticut along with his best friend, Amos Fairchild. Close as brothers, the two young men were comrades until Eddie was pulled from the ranks and assigned to be a clerk at Gen. French's headquarters. While Eddie wrote orders, his friend Amos went into battle with the regiment. Though being a clerk was considered a safe position by those in combat, Eddie and Amos met exactly the same fate: they died of disease in the army.

For the army clerk, the writing never stopped. Among the constant forms he filled out was the daily countersign, which soldiers needed in order to pass the picket line. Eddie Brewer noted that he made seven copies of the document each day. In September of 1863, Colonel Upham of the 15th Regiment opened this document, folded in a neat triangle, to learn the day's password: "Petersburg."

But John G. Pelton vehemently refuted Bidwell's impression of the Ambulance Corps. Like Bidwell, John Pelton had joined the 14th Connecticut in 1862. In the months that followed, his regiment would fight in one major battle after another. ("How I have escaped being killed . . . is a mystery to me," Pelton wrote to his brother.)[21]

But Pelton's familiarity with battle would prove invaluable. In April of 1864 he became ambulance chief for the Army of the Potomac's 2nd Corps. Three weeks later, Pelton had his baptism by fire: the battles of May 1864 resulted in over 36,000 Union casualties.

Pelton demanded courage, competence, and sympathy from the hundreds of stretcher-bearers and ambulance drivers he commanded. One of his officers, John Harpster, described the duties that Pelton laid out for his men during battle:

> We were to keep in the rear of the Army, but, as he significantly pointed out, not too far in the rear! The stretcher bearers were to be allowed to take shelter, provided they did not have to hunt too far from the line for it; otherwise they were to take what came, just as the men on the front line had to; for they were in error, he said, if they thought their office was to carry with it any special immunity from danger . . . The wounded were to be removed beyond the line of fire as quickly and as carefully as possible, put into the ambulances and removed to the field hospital . . .
>
> The drivers, during battle . . . were to keep the two water kegs in their ambulances constantly replenished, and were to be ready to move the instant a wounded man was delivered to their charge. They were to drive carefully, taking every precaution against causing the wounded unnecessary suffering, and, having delivered their charge at the field hospital, were to return to the front as rapidly as possible.[22]

John Graves Pelton was twenty-four when he enlisted for the Union. An intelligent man with a good sense of humor, Pelton quickly became adept at running the ambulance corps. In the spring of 1864, with battle an almost daily occurrence, Pelton smoothly transferred ambulances and personnel from battlefield to battlefield, providing wounded soldiers with swifter, more humane care.

Pelton was proud of his men, writing that "it requires more true moral courage to advance up to a line of Battle unarmed and unsupported than it does to charge in line nerved by the presence of officers and the excitement of battle."[23] His official reports listed scores of ambulance drivers and stretcher-bearers who were killed, wounded, or captured while performing their duties.

Harpster added that "There is another test of the stuff a man is made of to which the ambulance men are put . . . to take a train load of mangled and mutilated men back to the field hospital and, having delivered your charge, stand a while watching the surgeons cutting and sawing at human bodies, and see the holes dug at the foot of the amputating tables gradually filling up with dissevered arms and legs, and then, with the horror of it all before your eyes . . . approach again that fatal line of fire . . . this, I say, will be conceded to be a pretty stiff test of the amount of iron that is in the blood of a man."[24]

Once a battle was over, Pelton's men were not allowed to rest, of course. They were searching the battlefields for wounded, then hurrying their ambulances along clogged roads to reach field hospitals. They often spent all night tending to the wounded; then turned to the care of their horses and mules before they could sleep.

A Duty to Inspire

In a fight to the death, there was even a place for ministers. For Henry Clay Trumbull, chaplain of Connecticut's 10th Regiment, that place was on the battle line.

A chaplain's job was what he made of it: some limited themselves to holding Sunday services and passing out religious tracts to the soldiers. For his part, Trumbull saw with clarity that a successful chaplain had to be willing to risk his life alongside the men.

> Every soldier must be ready to meet danger or death, and, if he failed in that supreme test of a soldier in time of war, he was every way a failure. A chaplain had a duty to inspire men for their service for their country. If he was himself a coward, or deemed unready to face a soldier's perils, no words from him could have weight with his men. If, on the other hand, their chaplain shared their dangers bravely, his men gave him more than full credit for his courage and fidelity, and were the readier to do their duty under his direct appeals.[25]

In combat, Trumbull took charge of his regiment's wounded, supervising their removal to field hospitals and making certain they were cared for. His calm attention as the bullets flew gave the soldiers confidence.

In August of 1864, the 10th Connecticut found itself in a desperate fight in Deep Bottom, Virginia. Trumbull's friend and comrade, Henry Ward Camp, painted a droll image of the chaplain's composure under fire:

> the ground held by our advance was swept by a cross-fire against which no ordinary cover afforded security. Word came from the skirmish-line that Captain White was wounded seriously, it was feared mortally. Henry saw to his being carried back to the hospital . . . In a short time Henry returned . . . With thoughtful kindness, he brought for us a huge watermelon. It was speedily cut and divided; General Foster very glad to get his share. What could have been more refreshing under fire? Before it was finished, orders were given for our regiment to swing around, fronting the left, and covering the flank, upon which an attack was momentarily expected. It was comical enough to see officers forming their men, enforcing their orders with brandished slices of melon, and taking a bite between each command.[26]

Musicians assigned to be stretcher-bearers in battle wore strips of green cloth on their hats to identify their jobs. "The green band around their caps," John Pelton told them, "would secure them against being laid hold of for other duty . . . but the green band and the white feather [traditionally symbolizing cowardice], they must understand, must by no means be construed as meaning the same thing." (Capt. J. H. Harpster, "The Ambulance Officer's Story," in *The Story of Our Regiment: A History of the 148th Pennsylvania Volunteers*, edited by Joseph Wendell Muffly, p. 290.)

A Fighting Force

As the war progressed, most of the Connecticut troops—whether they started as ministers, farmers, or pastry chefs—developed into competent soldiers, each filling a role. The citizen soldiers who had never held a gun or marched a mile would become a fighting force that left a record of honor on battlefields throughout the South.

CHAPTER FIVE

I Never Knew What War Meant till Today

ANTIETAM, SEPTEMBER 1862

The battle was coming; the men knew it. All day, off and on, they'd heard the boom of distant artillery. They had made camp in the rolling hills of western Maryland, just outside the town of Sharpsburg, and more and more troops kept arriving. Officers strode back and forth, looking tense; clerks were hunched over field desks, rapidly writing orders.

Connecticut's raw 16th Regiment came into camp toward the end of the day, joining the other regiments in their brigade. Furtively, the 16th's soldiers studied the dusty veterans who lounged around trading battle stories and smoking their pipes. The 16th had left Hartford just nineteen days earlier. They'd had almost no training. "It was little more than a crowd of earnest Connecticut boys, " wrote one soldier.[1] But there was no time left.

The day's march had been a hard one, and the boys were hungry. The supply wagons hadn't caught up with them yet, so some of them stripped a nearby cornfield, roasting the ears over fires built from fence rails. They'd hardly finished eating when they were hustled into ranks: their brigade was moving to the front.

They marched through the gathering darkness "into a meadow which lay between two hills," wrote Lt. B. G. Blakeslee. "While getting into this position we could plainly see the rebel gunners load and fire, some of the shells coming quite near us . . . we were within a few rods of the enemy, and orders were given in a whisper; we were ordered to make no noise and to rest on our arms; for thirty minutes the utmost quiet prevailed. A musket was accidentally discharged; in a second

On the day he turned
sixteen, Wells Bingham (*left*)
enlisted in Connecticut's
16th Regiment, along with
his seventeen-year-old
brother John (*right*). Less than
three weeks after leaving
Connecticut, the woefully
inexperienced soldiers found
themselves hurled into
the chaos of battle near a
meandering creek in western
Maryland.

the troops were on their feet, with arms at a 'ready,' and as they stood peering into the darkness ahead you could hear both lines of battle spring to arms for miles."[2]

"[W]hat a queer sound it was," wrote Pvt. William Relyea, "that rising of the hosts. Like the rushing of a strong wind that preceeds the storm, welling in fierceness and receeding in the distance . . . What a peculiar sensation it left upon our hearts, a dread and a fear of you knew not what . . . every nerve as you bend forward peering into the darkness before you, is strained to the utmost, and the heart beats loudly at the mystery of it all, yet we stood up manfully with the rest, though our blanching faces were kindly hidden by the darkness."[3]

For Relyea and the other rookies of the 16th Connecticut, sleep was virtually impossible that night. But even with their minds running wild with anxiety, none of them could have imagined what tomorrow's battle would bring. Those who survived would never look at life in the same way again.

SEPTEMBER 17, 1862, SHARPSBURG, MARYLAND

Minutes after sunrise, men were dying. In a pastoral landscape of cornfields, apple orchards, farmhouses, and woodlots, the bloodiest day in American history had begun. It would end with over 22,000 Americans dead, wounded, or missing.

Robert E. Lee had had the audacity to march his Rebels north into Maryland. He felt, mistakenly, that Maryland would support the Southern cause, and expected men there to flock to his army. From here, the Confederates posed a real threat to Washington. McClellan had to hurry his Union troops north to block them.

Lee had massed his Rebel troops—about 36,000 soldiers—on the west side of Antietam Creek, with the Potomac River at their backs. Meanwhile, McClellan had been gathering his Union troops on the east side of the creek.

The day before the battle, McClellan sent some 8,600 Union soldiers across the creek with Maj. Gen. Joseph Hooker, who maneuvered them to the north of Stonewall Jackson's position. That night in the rain more Union troops, under Gen. J. K. F. Mansfield, followed Hooker across the creek.

At dawn, Union artillery opened on the Rebels, slicing into Stonewall Jackson's forces. "Fighting Joe" Hooker marched his infantry south toward the Confederate line, pulling up before a great cornfield from which bayonets protruded. Union artillery raked the field, and Hooker reported: "In the time I am writing every stalk of corn in the northern and greater part of the field was cut as closely as could have been done with a knife, and the slain lay in rows precisely as they stood in their ranks a few moments before."[4]

The blue-coated infantry moved forward again, pushing Jackson's Rebels back. Lee hustled reinforcements forward, and a little after seven o'clock, Hooker called for support. General Mansfield, waiting in the rear with his 12th Corps, swiftly advanced to reinforce the wavering Union forces.

The white-bearded Mansfield, fifty-eight, projected an air of alertness and experience to the roughly 8,000 men he commanded. Fifteen years earlier, in the Mexican War, Mansfield had been severely wounded and brevetted three separate times for his actions in battle. One of his Mexican War subordinates, John Pope, said that Mansfield "pervaded all places of danger, and everywhere put himself in the forefront of the battle . . . I never yet have seen a man so regardless of his personal safety or so eager to imperil it."[5]

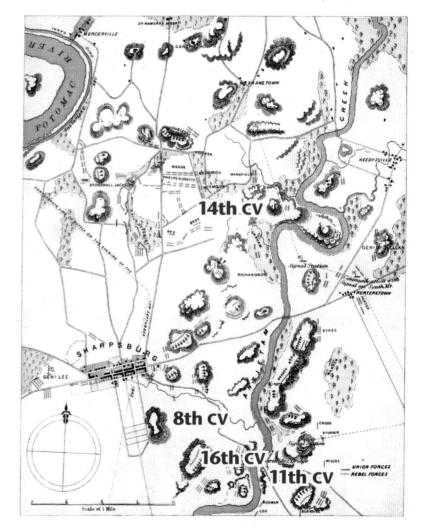

Antietam, Sharpsburg and Vicinity Constructed and Engraved to Illustrate "The War with the South," by Charles Sholl, 1864.

Today was no different. "The General was moving around the field continually," wrote one of his men. "He seemed to be everywhere."[6] Mansfield rode rapidly back and forth, positioning his troops, then watching from the high ground the overall movement of the battle.

One of his regiments, the 10th Maine, was now firing into a wooded area where Confederates were using trees and woodpiles as cover. Mansfield had received a report that Hooker's troops held the woods; when he saw the 10th Maine loading and firing,

> Mansfield at once came galloping down the hill and passed through the scattered men of the right companies, shouting "Cease firing, you are firing into our own men!" He rode very rapidly . . .
>
> Captain Jordan now ran forward . . . and insisted that Gen. Mansfield should "Look and see." He and Sergt. Burnham pointed out particular men of the enemy, who were not 50 yards away, that were then aiming their rifles at us and at him . . . he was convinced, and remarked, "Yes, you are right."[7]

Mansfield had ridden into "a most perilous position—where the bullets and missiles were flying like hail, and where no one upon a horse could survive. It seemed as if the very depths of Pandemonia had sent her furies," wrote Surgeon P. H. Flood of the 107th New York.[8] A conspicuous target, the general immediately drew the fire of Confederates in the woods before him. One of the 10th Maine soldiers watched as his commander moved off: "He then turned his horse and . . . attempted to go through [a broken fence], but the horse, which . . . appeared to be wounded, refused to step into the traplike mass of rails and rubbish, or to jump over. The General thereupon promptly dismounted and led the horse . . . as he dismounted his coat blew open, and I saw that blood was streaming down the right side of his vest."[9] A minié ball had pierced Mansfield's lung. As blood soaked his chest, soldiers slung him in a blanket and carried him to the rear. He would die the following morning.

While General Mansfield was borne to the rear, the fight continued to rage back and forth, with first the Federal, then the Confederate forces dominating. Both sides suffered appalling casualties. By nine in the morning, a lull had set in at the northern end of the battlefield, while the battle had ignited farther south.

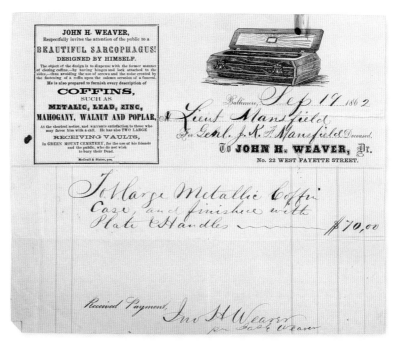

THE 14TH CONNECTICUT
I never prayed more fervently for darkness.

About eight o'clock that morning, Cornwall native general John Sedgwick had forded Antietam Creek with about 5,500 troops. At the center of Sedgwick's line marched the men of Connecticut's 14th Regiment, who had left Hartford less than a month before. How green were they? Frederick Burr Hawley of Bridgeport wrote peevishly in his journal, "Immediately after crossing [Antietam Creek], we come into a ploughed lot, our feet being wet, get covered with mud, some gets in my shoes & chafes my feet."[10]

Minutes later, Hawley and his 14th comrades had more than chafed feet to worry about. Sedgwick rapidly moved his forces toward the center of the battlefield, and into the East Woods.

> The order was given to form line of battle, shells were bursting about them, tearing off huge branches of trees while shot were cutting the air with their sharp shriek.
>
> This order to form line of battle was perhaps the supreme moment of their experience, as there shot through the minds of the men the thought of the loved ones at home; the terrible possibilities of the engagement made vivid by the ghastly scenes through which they had already passed at South Mountain; some indeed would be wounded, some slain outright; there must inevitably be suffering and death: and as they looked at the familiar faces of their comrades, they wondered who it would be.[11]

Capt Willard on the field of Antietam, Sept. 16, 1862.

"These may be my last words," Samuel Willard wrote to his wife; "if so, they are these: I have full faith in Jesus Christ, my Savior; I do not regret that I have fallen in defence of my country; I have loved you truly and know that you have loved me . . . If my body should ever reach home, let there be no ceremony; I ask no higher honor than to die for my country." (Samuel Willard, as quoted in Samuel Irenaeus Prime, *The Power of Prayer*, pp. 408–11.)

"I cannot sing the old songs. Or, the late Home of a Union Soldier," ran the title of a touching print published in 1868. A downcast woman standing at the piano wiped away a tear. Over her shoulder lingered a faint image of her lost soldier husband.

When the 14th Regiment had left Connecticut for the South, Madison's Samuel Willard, a captain in Company G, carried a small diary in his pocket. Here the thirty-two-year-old penciled thoughts and experiences that he later copied into letters to his wife Margaret. Now, about to enter battle, the realization struck him that he might meet death at any moment.

In the midst of the booming of Union and Confederate artillery, as the 14th Regiment prepared to advance, he added, "The battle has commenced, one man killed within 20 rods of me, by a shell . . . God save my men, God save me, God save the United States of America. God bless you my own dear wife, and may we meet at last in heaven where there will be no war."[12]

Captain Willard fell in battle that day, shot through the head. His brother-in-law, Pvt. John Bradley, stayed with him while he died on the field.

Long after the Civil War, a Connecticut woman described a scene from her childhood. One day, in the early twentieth century, she was playing the piano for her grandmother in her home in Madison. When she performed an old Civil War song called "Tenting on the Old Camp Grounds," her grandmother "threw her apron over her face and broke into shuddering sobs. It wasn't until she cried and asked me never to play that song again, that I realized what the war had done to her," said Margaret Shepard.[13] Her grandmother was Margaret Willard, widow of Captain Samuel Willard. Some four decades earlier, the war had taken her husband and two of her three brothers.

The 14th soldiers now moved forward on the double- quick, scrambling over fences and leaping ditches amid the shriek of artillery shells and the whiz of musket balls. Raw as they were, the 14th men were bold-spirited, plucky. As the regiment advanced through fields and farms, Company A made its way through an apple orchard, and a couple of daredevils stopped—under fire—to pick apples. (One, a young Bridgeport sergeant named William B. Hincks, would later win the Medal of Honor for his intrepid actions in battle.)[14]

Meanwhile, at the other end of the 14th Regiment's line, Company B had to skirt several obstacles in its way, which caused it to split off from the rest of the regiment. Their captain, thirty-year-old Elijah Gibbons, was no greenhorn, having previously served in Connecticut's 4th Infantry. Seeing his company veering away, Gibbons quickly adjusted its position, leading the men between a farmhouse and barn on the Roulette farm. Sheltered by the buildings there, Confederate sharpshooters had been peppering the regiment with musket fire.

"Captain Gibbons . . . finding the farm-house occupied by a large force of the enemy, ordered his company to advance and fire, scattering them and driving a portion of them into the cellar, where, by closing the door, a large number of them were captured."[15] Just minutes into its first battle, the 14th Connecticut already had a tidy package of Rebel prisoners to its credit.

Reunited, the regiment advanced into a cornfield "where the musket Balls & Cannon Balls are whizzing & tearing dreadfully," wrote Frederick Burr Hawley in his journal. Tall stalks of corn hid the 14th soldiers from the enemy's view but also made it impossible for them to see. "Our men fire in confusion & keep up a fire for a short time amid cries from Officers to 'Stop that' 'there is a Delaware Reg in front of us.'"[16]

In front of the 14th Connecticut was the 1st Delaware Regiment; beyond that, a ravine and then another cornfield, filled with Confederates. It was about 9:30 a.m. Sgt. Benjamin Hirst of Rockville described his view of the chaos:

> [A] voley tore through our ranks killing and wounding quite a number. The Regiment was thrown in some confusion and most of the Boys fell on their Bellies, firing indiscrimately and i am sorry to think wounding some of our men . . . i saw the whole of this at a glance and roard like a mad Bull for our men to cease firing until they could see the rebs. They finally crawled back a few yards and staid there . . .
>
> i carried Wilkie [James Wilkie, wounded] from the front to the rear. i then came back to the front, and got a splendid view of the Rebels in a piece of corn opposite to ours. there was just 4 of our own Company and a few men of a Delaware Regiment giving them fits and i was just in the humour to join in, until i fired 13 rounds into their midst . . . seeing our colours falling further back we backed out to our Company, who were all lying on their faces expecting the Rebels were going to charge on us.[17]

From the edge of the cornfield, the 14th men fired across at the Confederates, while the Delaware regiment pressed ahead toward an old road that farm wagons had worn down until it was sunken into the ground. This sunken road, later known as Bloody Lane, now sheltered enemy soldiers who, in their first musket volley, took down about a third of the Delaware regiment. The Delaware line "seemed to melt under the enemy's fire and breaking many of the men ran through the ranks of the Fourteenth toward the rear," wrote one of the Nutmeggers.[18] The fleeing soldiers unnerved the Connecticut boys; a few joined the rout, and their lieutenant colonel had all he could do to rally the rest.

Then it was the 14th's turn to advance toward the Rebels waiting in the sunken road. "Forward!" came the order, and the jumpy men emerged from the cornfield and into "a smashing fire full in the face."[19] The vicious fire quickly drove them back. "We advance & fall back, without doing much if any good," wrote a frustrated Fred Hawley; "we see men hit all around us & some are reported killed we remain flat on our faces on the ground for 1½ hours."[20]

Near noon, the 14th fell back and reformed. Sgt. Benjamin Hirst recalled:

> we were then moved further to the left in front to support one of our Batterys, in getting to which position, we as a Regiment were complimented for the coolness displayed in marching under fire. we were then Faced behind a stone wall just as the Rebels broke through the place lately occupied by us, but the 2nd line of Batle soon settled them, and we were again moved further to the front, during which a shell dropt in our midst killing 3 and wounding four of our Company.
>
> I had just told the men to close up, and had got a couple of files ahead when it came to us with a whiz and the job was done, Sam Burrows, and Gross were covered with blood, and Albert Towne had his Haversack shot away without hurting him . . . we closed up like Veterans and moved on as if nothing had happened. we came under the shelter of a hill behind which the 81st pa were lying, in their front was one of our Batterys with every horse killed. they stood up and gave us 3 cheers as we took position along side of them.[21]

Robert Hubbard

✵ ✵ ✵

Reconciling a soldier's death was—is—never easy. In the Civil War, the most difficult losses to accept were those like Robert Hubbard's.

Hubbard, thirty-one, was the eldest son in a Middletown farming family. In the summer of 1862, Robert wrote to his younger brother, Josiah, who had moved west to settle Kansas with a group of Connecticut abolitionists determined to keep the new territory from becoming a slave state. Robert asked his brother to return to Connecticut to care for their elderly parents—their father was seventy-seven years old—and their younger sisters.

Robert himself was joining Connecticut's 14th Regiment. "I feel as if I could never forgive myself if this government should be overthrown and I had no weapon in its defense," Robert explained to Josiah.[22] Coincidentally, Josiah had sent a similar letter to Robert, announcing that he had joined a Kansas cavalry unit. The brothers' letters crossed in the mail.

In the early afternoon of September 17, 1862, the 14th Connecticut moved from the cornfield near Bloody Lane through Roulette's farm to a battery it was to guard. With Rebel artillery shells flying overhead, the 14th troops rapidly obeyed an order to lie down in the plowed field

The 14th Connecticut passed through William Roulette's farm twice. To farmers like Robert Hubbard, the bucolic surroundings would have held a sense of familiarity, but the screaming shells, smoke, and corpses of soldiers and horses transformed the tranquil farm scene into something horrific. The farmhouse became a bloody field hospital where surgeons cut and bandaged. Later, hundreds of bodies were buried on the Roulette grounds.

where they were positioned. Fred Hawley wrote: "we lay close to the ground the shell & cannon balls flying all around us often wounding and killing some one. These missels as they fly near us have a most hateful spiteful sing to them. They sound as if they meant evil."[23]

Flattened into the dirt, the 14th men waited for their next orders. Then above the shriek of the shells came an officer's voice: they were moving. As the men rose from the field, "a rifle in Co. B was accidentally discharged, and we saw one of our members, one of the best men in the company, Robert Hubbard lying upon the ground writhing in the agony of a mortal wound."[24]

Their captain directed some of his men to carry Robert to the rear. Hubbard died while the battle continued. His friends buried him beside the corncrib on Roulette's farm.

On the day the 14th Regiment left Connecticut for the South, Hubbard had written to his mother, "If I should never return, my short life may have been of greater service to my family, my country and the cause of freedom than a life spent at home devoted to self."[25] In December of 1862, Robert's sister wrote to William Roulette, who owned the farm where her brother was buried. The Maryland farmer had a coffin made for the Connecticut farmer, and sent Robert's remains north. In a graveyard near their farm, the Hubbards laid him to rest.

Robert's brother Josiah would survive the war and return to the farm in Middletown. Here, five years after the Battle of Antietam, Josiah's first son, Robert, would be born.

✯ ✯ ✯

Day's End

It was a baffling afternoon for the men of the 14th Connecticut: they seemed to be marching all around the battlefield—shells exploding everywhere, bullets whizzing by—yet their own guns were quiet. Leaving the battery they'd been sent to guard, the Nutmeggers took up a new position, when the order came once again to *lie down*: "the enemy had seen us and at once commenced shelling us. It was very trying to have to lie inactive under fire and listen to the hideous howling of the shell varied only by their crash in exploding and occasionally the shriek of some one who was struck. I lay closer to the ground than ever before in my life, although it was a plowed field and an exceedingly dirty place, and I never prayed more fervently for darkness than then."[26]

Nightfall brought a blessed end to the shelling. "As most of us threw away our Coats & Blankets which were in the way when we first entered the fight we are now without any covering & are compelled to sleep on the damp cold ground," wrote Fred Hawley. He seemed unable to take in the enormity of what he had just passed through. "We feel very tired & hungry having ate nothing since morning & many threw away their Haversacks so Hard tack is scarce." Exhausted, scared, and hungry, the boys of the 14th lay down on the ground to sleep.[27]

Sleep didn't come easily. Henry Stevens, the 14th's chaplain, wrote: "All that night through and the following day and night they heard the dreadful groans and cries of the wounded and dying wretches in Bloody Lane just over the hill calling for water or help, or to have taken off others who, dead, were lying across or upon their tortured and helpless bodies, or for death to release them from their anguish . . . but they were powerless to render the assistance their hearts longed to give."[28]

George E. Stannard was the youngest child of widow Roxanna Stannard of Clinton. He was about twenty-three when he wrote this letter to his mother:[29]

Keatyville MD
September 20, 1862

Dear Mother

I take great pleasure in writing to you once more   we have had a battle and a hard one but I am all right but our rgmt was badly cut up we formed a line of battle and charged through the corn on double quick   the boys behaved like heros

a good many of our boys went down   Pendleton was shot through the breast and arm Luit. Sherman in the arm John Parks through the leg he will die   John Hurd in the arm twice   George Doane in the knee   Lewellin Dibble in the foot and a good many more not so bad and after we came out of the corn we were marched up through a narrow lane onto a hill between 2 cross fires and there our loved capt [Samuel Willard] fell with a shot through the brain   he never spoke   his body was sent home today   Horace Stevens is missing but I think he is dead for the men that buried the dead in that part of the field say that they buried one of Co. G's men and he is the only one not accounted for   I don't know how many men our rgmt lost altogether but it was enough

after the capt was killed we charged across the hill to the left and were ordered to report to Col Brooks and he ordered us to support the left wing   we drove across the field amid such a storm of shot and shell, grape and canister and rifle balls as I never want to see again   we marched on to the left of the Irish Brigade they received us with such cheers and yells as only an Irishman can give they told us afterwards that they thought we were the regulars we came up in such style after we had succeded in turning the devils we had a very easy time most too much so we were ordered to lie down flat on our faces and not move and we did not feel much inclinde to move I tell you for the shell from thier baterrys were flying all around us . . . after a minute a Liut was lying about ten feet from me and he stuck up his head to speak to his Capt and a shell came along and took the top of his head off I went to him and three of his Co helped carry him off the field as we were getting over a fence a round shot came and saved us the trouble for it knocked it all down

just as we got back an orderly came along and said that Gen Richardson was killed Gen Morris sung out who will go and bring him off and four of us started and it was a race but we got him he was not dead but badly wounded in the breast we carried him to the hospital

after that we laid 36 hours on the plowed ground behind a little knoll but that night after the battle I never shall forget the groans and sreiks of the wounded curces and shell mixed up promiscous it was awful I can assure you but I cant write any more for we are going to move some where I am all right only hit once and that was with a spent ball in the leg it stung a little

GES

The battle's final stage would begin at the southern end of the battlefield with the command of Maj. Gen. Ambrose E. Burnside. Among the roughly 8,500 Union soldiers in Burnside's 9th Corps were three Connecticut regiments: the 8th, 11th, and 16th Connecticut Volunteers.

The 11th's colonel, Henry Walter Kingsbury, was just twenty-five years old. A West Point graduate, Kingsbury would need all of his training for the assault on the bridge. His 440 men had to move down a slope and across an open field exposed to Confederate artillery fire and a hail of bullets from two Georgian infantry regiments sheltered behind trees and stone walls on the far side of the creek.

11TH CONNECTICUT REGIMENT
I can speak of time no more.[30]

That morning, General Burnside separated the 11th Connecticut from the rest of the 9th Corps. Burnside was friendly with the 11th's colonel, twenty-five-year-old Henry Walter Kingsbury; years earlier, he had been young Kingsbury's guardian. So when McClellan ordered Burnside to send his troops across Antietam Creek to attack Lee's right flank, Burnside turned to Kingsbury to help him gain control of a stone bridge spanning the stream. Across this bridge, just twelve feet wide, Burnside intended to march his troops—but first he had to clear out the Confederates who held it.

Nathan Mayer, the 11th's assistant surgeon, dismounted from his horse and took off his sword, canteen, haversack, and blanket. Taking his pocket surgical kit, he directed the stretcher-bearers to follow him, and fell in behind the soldiers.

Colonel Kingsbury had ordered Companies A and B to deploy as skirmishers, under Capt. John Griswold. While the remainder of the regiment was to storm the bridge, Griswold's men would scramble down the banks on either side of the bridge and wade the fifty feet across Antietam Creek. Holding their muskets over

Captain John Griswold, twenty-five, came from an old Connecticut family of some prominence. Both his grandfather and great-grandfather had served as governors of Connecticut. John, the baby of his family, had been just two when his father died, but he hadn't grown up coddled and protected in his wealthy home in Lyme. As a boy he went off to boarding school, then on to Yale where he studied civil engineering as well as the classics. Instead of becoming a lawyer or merchant as did many of the Griswold men, John became a surveyor in Kansas, where bloody conflicts raged continually between abolitionists and pro-slavery settlers. Adventure and fortune soon lured him even farther from home: in 1860 "he sailed from New London for Honolulu, to engage in business [and] remained for six months, with a single Kanaka companion, on a Guano island in the Pacific, of which it was important to claim possession. He was at length taken off by a company of Chinamen and carried to San Francisco. At the outbreak of the rebellion, he hastened home and entered the national service." (*Obituary Record of Graduates of Yale College Deceased from July, 1859, to July, 1870*, pp. 106–7.)

their heads and pushing through chest-deep water, the skirmishers would move straight into a hurricane of bullets from the two Georgia regiments hidden on the opposite side of the creek. It was no wonder they hesitated. Then Captain John Griswold leaped into the stream at the head of his men.

Within the regiment, Surgeon Mayer observed, Captain Griswold gained the admiration of many. "He was a great-hearted gentleman, well born, liberally educated, and wonderfully retentive of all the studies in ancient and modern literature . . . but, more than this, his character was trained, and his heart disciplined." As the 11th Regiment traveled through the South, recounted Mayer, "We quoted Horace, and discussed questions of moral philosophy." No matter the hardships they endured—hunger, exhaustion, cold or heat—John Griswold "would preserve the same cheerfulness of demeanor, and never forget the least of those courtesies which make life in refined circles run in such an even course . . . whoever approached him felt that he had entered a circle of refinement. Nor was this intended for equals alone. He was particular in extending the same courtesies to the soldiers under his command."[31]

Now as bullets flew around him, John Griswold splashed through the Antietam Creek toward the enemy. Mayer wrote:

> In the middle of the creek a ball penetrated his body. He reached the opposite side and lay down to die. Meanwhile we had reached the bridge and formed. The 12th Ohio was on our left and lay behind the rail fence firing at the wooded steep [bank] opposite, from which a brisk fire was returned. Hither I hastened with four men and a stretcher and in the face of both fires climbed over the fence, forded the creek and bore off the body.[32]

> We took him into a low shed near the bank, and laid him on the straw . . . he was ashy pale, so much had he suffered.

> "Doctor," he said, "pardon the trouble I give you; but I am mortally wounded, I believe." I examined. The bullet had passed through the body in the region of the stomach. "You are, captain," I replied. "Then let me die quickly, and without pain, if you can," he rejoined . . .

Seeing through the door of the shed the blue water flash in the sunshine, he repeated the first lines of one of those gems of Horace we had so often admired:—

O Fons Bandusiae, splendidior vitro,
Dulci digno mero, non sine floribus.

[O spring of Bandusia, clearer than glass,
Worthy of sweet wine and flowers, too] . . .

The end came soon. Gen. Burnside called. The sufferer told him . . . "I am happy, general . . . I die as I have ever wished to die,—for my country."

"Tell my mother," he said to a comrade, "that I died at the head of my company." Tears rolled down Burnside's cheeks, as, delicately trying to suppress all symptoms of his pain, the philosophic and heroic spirit calmly passed away.[33]

John's family brought his body home to Old Lyme and buried him in the Griswolds' peaceful family cemetery with his famous ancestors. Rising from his grave is an elegant stone obelisk carved with John's last words and a laurel wreath encircling a soldier's cap. In the distance the sun flashes off the Black Hall River that flows alongside the burying ground.

Griswold's last words were inscribed on his monument: "Tell my Mother that I died at the head of my Company," and "I die, as I have ever wished to die, for my country." A writer for the *Hartford Daily Courant* declared, "We have never seen a monument more strikingly beautiful; more earnestly expressive." (*Hartford Daily Courant*, August 5, 1863.)

In fifteen minutes' fighting near the bridge, the 11th Connecticut had suffered over 130 casualties. "Col. Kingsbury was active, inciting his soldiers to the charge by his gallant bearing and the inspiration of his voice. Many men fell. The colonel was a special mark; and he was soon shot in the foot, and immediately thereafter in the leg; when he was at last prevailed upon to leave the field . . . The men were still fighting; now falling back, and again charging on the bridge."[34]

Dr. Mayer "worked at dressing wounds and amputations until my head ached . . . men with the most frightful hurts were brought, carried, and dragged into the garden of the farm house" that was acting as a field hospital.[35]

Colonel Kingsbury would not survive. While his men carried him from the field, one ball in his foot and another in his leg, he took a bullet in the shoulder and then a fourth in the abdomen, a mortal wound. At the field hospital, a surgeon gave him morphine, and General Burnside came to his side. Kingsbury held on through the night and into the following day. "The colonel has opened his eyes, and given me the sweetest smile, and then closed them forever," wrote Dr. Nathan Mayer. "He made us all better and nobler."[36]

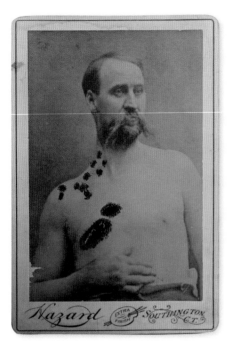

Among the scores of wounded at Antietam was nineteen-year-old Alonzo Maynard of Stafford, shot again and again and again. Nearly twenty-five years after the battle, Maynard would describe what he had gone through that humid September day in 1862 as his regiment tried to take Burnside's Bridge. "At Antietam I was shot through the right lung and shoulder with four balls, splintering the ribs in front, breaking collar-bone twice, destroying shoulder-joint, passing through lung, striking the spine and knocking off four ribs, breaking shoulder-blade in three or four pieces, splintering spine badly and breaking one vertebra. Thirteen pieces of bone came out of the wounds. My right lung is gone—torn in pieces and came out of wounds. There are 16 separate wounds through right breast and shoulder. Some of them were as large as a silver half dollar. I was confined to my bed five years. When I was wounded the doctors said there was no help for me, and it was several days before they dressed my wounds. I had a strong constitution and Yankee grit." (*National Tribune*, May 27, 1886.) Yankee grit. And a New Englander's gift for understatement.

This image from long after the war was used by the Committee on Invalid Pensions as part of a bill in the House of Representatives to increase Maynard's pension. (Retouching in red emphasized the scars and sores.) The committee declared, "The evidence in this case discloses that the man has suffered terribly . . . Large burrowing abscesses frequently form upon the chest." (Report of the Committee on Invalid Pensions, to whom was referred the bill [H.R. 3478] to increase the pension of Alonzo Maynard.) Despite his wounds, Alonzo Maynard married, had a son, and lived for more than four decades after the Battle of Antietam.

Hours later, other units were able to secure the bridge, and Union troops finally crossed the Antietam to attack the Rebels. While the battle ignited on the west side of the creek, the men of the 11th searched for their wounded friends, and began to bury their dead.

8TH CONNECTICUT REGIMENT
The men fought like Tigeres.

While the 11th Regiment battled it out at the bridge, the other units in their brigade—the 8th Connecticut, 16th Connecticut, and 4th Rhode Island—were doing what soldiers always do: they were waiting.

"[W]e were in line ready for work before sunrise," wrote a lieutenant in the 8th; "the shot & shell flew around us like fun but there was not much fun about it as we soon found out it struck in our ranks & took one file completely out killing both of the men composing that file & a Sergeant of another Company who was in the rear & badly wounding another."[37]

The fallen sergeant was a Hartford silversmith named George Marsh. "He was ill, but determined to be at his post," wrote a comrade, "and there he died."[38]

Once the enemy battery had the range on them, the Union soldiers were sitting ducks. The shells "came thick & fast but . . . there was no reply from our side we wondered at this thus it went on they using their artillery on us continually . . . Yet not a man in regit. stirred excepting ambulance corps who attended to wounded."[39]

The 8th's colonel, Edward Harland, who was commanding the brigade, directed the troops to move to a safer position. As the three regiments moved off, the Rebel artillery again tried to find their range. "[O]ur men would instinctively stoop and hesitate when the shells burst around

The Charge across the Burnside Bridge
Antietam. 1 PM. Sept 17th 1862. E Forbes.

them," said Jacob Eaton. "Our Chaplain, the Rev. Mr. Morris, . . . passed up and down the lines, exclaiming after each explosion, 'Never mind, boys! Come on; no one is hurt.'"[40]

Finally the troops reached comparative safety. To the north, Rebel fire made the stone bridge still impassable. How would Burnside get his troops to the other side of the creek? Colonel Harland sent two companies south to search for a place to ford Antietam Creek. Leading them was a trusted officer, Captain Charles Upham of the 8th Connecticut.

Six months before Antietam, Charlie Upham had taken a bullet in the shoulder in the Battle of Newbern, North Carolina. The wound never healed, but he refused to let it stop him. Now Upham, twenty-three, led his own company and another down the steep banks of the winding Antietam Creek, until they found a fording place.

The troops would face a sharp, slippery ascent up the far banks. While a Union battery, supported by the 8th Connecticut, distracted the Rebel artillery on the other side, Harland began to send his troops splashing across Antietam Creek. It was about one in the afternoon. A mile or so

An eighteen-year-old sergeant in the 8th Connecticut, Forrest Spofford was wounded in the left arm at Antietam. After a surgeon amputated, Spofford returned to his regiment, serving another two years. Later in the war, Spofford suffered a battle wound to his other arm, but again survived. After the war, he would serve as a one-armed librarian in Norwich.

north of them, Union soldiers finally broke through Rebel fire to cross the stone bridge. Burnside's troops, by bridge and by ford, were across; now they could come together for a united attack on the rebels.

But troops to the north needed ammunition, and each brigade had to move into position. The Georgian infantry regiments that had defended the bridge continued to harass the Union troops. Confederate artillery shelled Harland's brigade again, but "We lay down & let them work," remembered Wolcott Marsh.[41]

Finally, at about four o'clock, the order came to advance on the enemy. The delay would prove devastating.

The hiatus had allowed the Confederates to bring up forces from other parts of the battlefield, and re-form their lines in anticipation of Burnside's attack. It also brought the arrival of over 2,000 Rebel soldiers under A. P. Hill. That humid day Hill's men had rapidly marched the seventeen miles from Harper's Ferry, many falling out from exhaustion. Now those who remained came down the road at the double-quick, just in time to turn the tide for the South.

The 1st Brigade of the Union's 9th Corps advanced up the hill into a barrage of artillery and musketry, and then Colonel Harland ordered his own brigade forward. At the head of the 8th Regiment was Lt. Col. Hiram Appelman.

Col. Appelman led the Eighth forward in steady step up the hill. Nearly the whole corps was now charging, and the advancing line stretched far away to the right. As they reached the crest, the rebel troops were but a few rods in front. The Union line halted, and poured in a telling volley, and again leaped forward; and the enemy broke and fled, halting and firing as they could. A storm of shot, shell, and musketry, was sweeping through the ranks of the Eighth, now on the extreme Union left . . .

Steadily forward moves the line, now marking every yard of advance with blood of fallen men. The rebels still fall back. The 1st Brigade wavers, and slowly retires in disorder. Wilcox's division, too, is giving way farther to the right. Forward presses the Eighth, until the men can see the road whereby Lee must retreat. "The position is ours" they shout; and a "Hurrah" goes down the line.

But already many have observed an immense force moving straight up on the left flank. "Re-inforcements," say some: but Gen. Harland knows better; and he rides rapidly to the rear to hurry forward regiments to meet

this new rebel move . . . The Eighth is now alone clinging to the crest. Three batteries are turned on them, and the enemy's infantry close in around . . .

No re-inforcements come. Twenty men are falling every minute. Col. Appelman is borne to the rear. John McCall falls bleeding. Eaton totters, wounded, down the hill. Wait, bullet-riddled, staggers a few rods, and sinks. Ripley stands with a shattered arm. Russell lies white and still. Morgan and Maine have fallen. Whitney Wilcox is dead. Men grow frantic. The wounded prop themselves behind the rude stone fence, and hurl leaden vengeance at the foe. Even the chaplain snatches the rifle and cartridge-box of a dead man, and fights for life.[42]

✳ ✳ ✳

Early in the fall of 1861, a Norwich teenager named Marvin Wait left Union College, where he was a student, to join Connecticut's 8th Regiment. An intelligent, dedicated young man, he learned quickly; less than six months after enlisting, Private Wait of Company D had become 1st Lieutenant Wait.

Wait received orders to report to the Signal Corps in Burnside's division, where he rapidly learned the use of signal flags. Using a spyglass and flags at the Battle of Roanoke Island, Wait had been able to transmit messages from General Burnside's gunboat to his officers. At the Siege of Fort Macon, North Carolina, Marvin Wait and another officer, Lieutenant Andrews, took a position where they could see the Union shells as the artillerymen attempted to bombard the Confederate-held fort. Andrews' official report explained:

> The ten-inch shell were falling almost without exception more than three hundred yards beyond the Fort. Lieutenant Wait and myself continued to signal to the officer in charge until the correct range was obtained. The eight-inch shell were falling short—we signaled to the officer in charge of that battery with the same effect . . .

From the position of our batteries, it was impossible for the officers in charge to *see* how their shots fell, but owing to the observations made by Lieutenant Wait and myself, and signaled to them from time to time, an accurate range was obtained by all the batteries . . . *After 12 m.. every shot fired from our batteries fell in or on the Fort.* At 4 o'clock, P.M., a white flag appeared on the Fort.[43]

The head of the Signal Corps presented a battle flag to Lieutenant Wait in recognition of his meritorious conduct that day.

Wait returned to the 8th Regiment a month before it marched with McClellan to Sharpsburg, Maryland. On the morning of the Battle of Antietam, it was just after seven when a Confederate cannonball bounded through the ranks of Company D. Three men were killed outright; a fourth wounded. Wait was so close that he was covered with dirt and blood.

As the 8th Regiment moved into line of battle later that day, one of the officers noticed the "determined fire of his eye" as nineteen-year-old Marvin Wait moved forward with his men.[44] As he raised his sword high in the advance, a bullet shattered his right arm, but Wait would not leave his troops. Shifting his sword to his left hand, he continued. "If Lieutenant Wait had only left the battle of his own accord when first hit in the arm, all would have been well, but he bravely stood to encourage his men still further by his own example," wrote Captain Charles Coit.[45]

Young Marvin Wait of Norwich (*left*) would not leave the field after being wounded. Hit by multiple bullets, he finally fell. Chaplain John M. Morris (*right*) carefully tucked the bleeding Wait into a sheltered spot behind a stone wall, and hurried off to find an ambulance for him.

In the minutes that followed, Wait was hit in the left arm, the abdomen, and the leg. He staggered, and went down. An enlisted man ran to his young lieutenant and began helping him to the rear, when the regiment's chaplain appeared and took over.

Men were falling everywhere, and Major Ward was begging his soldiers to fall back, *fall back* before the regiment was annihilated. Lieutenant Wait died of his wounds before he reached a surgeon.

"A braver man than Marvin Wait never confronted a foe; a more generous heart never beat: a more unselfish patriot never fell," wrote Lt. Jacob Eaton sadly.[46]

The Waits had their only son's body brought home, and they buried him in Yantic Cemetery in Norwich. Over his grave they set a white monument carved with spy glass and signal flags, and engraved "He died with his young fame about him for a shroud."

✯ ✯ ✯

Somehow, two regiments—the 16th Connecticut and 4th Rhode Island—hadn't received (or understood) the order to advance. General Rodman, commanding the division, directed Colonel Harland to continue on with the 8th, while Rodman himself would race back to hurry on the other two regiments. But the two missing regiments never came up, and the 8th Connecticut found itself alone as it moved through a hurricane of bullets and shells coming from three sides. The men didn't flinch for a moment.

Captain Wolcott Marsh, twenty-three, led the men of Company F, many of them farmers from rural communities like Plainfield, Canterbury, and Brooklyn. Writing to his wife just after the battle, Marsh wonderingly recorded their grit:

> the order came for us to go forward which we did on a double quick as we came to the brow of hill & over it a terrible fire was concentrated upon our little band but on we pushed down the hill & up the top of next bullets came in terrible showers & from all sides of us
>
> We now returned their fire & the men went to their work as cooly as if on drill. But we were in trapped on our left flank was a large corn field & it was full of rebels on our right was a high hill where they were pouring in a gauling [fire] upon us & all this beside those in our front. Where was our support . . . Where was the 16th [Connecticut] & 4th [Rhode Island regiments] who were on left & were to engage the rebels in corn field . . .
>
> It was death to remain in this advanced position longer. The Lt. Colonel was wounded & taken to rear 6 out of my little company of 39 men lay dead at my feet & some 15 had been wounded . . . Capt. Hoyts company was as bad off & on right they were suffering terribly but not a man faltered a steady & continual fire was returned against 6 times or more of our numbers but a few minutes had gone & it seemed as if the regit. must be entirely annihilated.
>
> The Major seeing that it was more than folly to remain ordered us to fall back. But many of the men seemed determined not to leave & would yell to each

other "Boys Lets Never Retreat. No Never." The major yelled at top of his voice in a pleading tone "Boys will you follow your colors" rally around them & follow me["] the Word "Colors" brought the men to their senses & the devoted little band rallied around them down the hill we came the men continually facing about and firing.[47]

In an indefensible position, against frightening numbers, the men of the 8th refused to retreat. Major Ward turned to the flags to lead them off the field.

A regiment's flags were sacred, and the post of color-bearer brought both great honor and great responsibility. Leading the regiment under fire took no small courage. And the color bearer, holding aloft the regiment's huge silk banner, was a conspicuous target for the enemy. That day at Antietam, the 8th Connecticut lost every single man in the color guard.

Captain Charlie Upham's company of Meriden men took on a daring mission, described by their lieutenant, Roger Ford:

After serving with the 1st Connecticut early in the war, Roger M. Ford of Meriden joined the 8th Regiment in August of 1861. Ford became lieutenant and then captain, making it through over three years of fighting before being wounded at Petersburg in 1864. Discharged because of his wound, Captain Ford went home to Connecticut to recover. Four months later, he reenlisted as a private in the same company he had left—and once more rose to a captaincy. After the war, Captain Ford became Chief Ford in Meriden's police force.

as we got to the top of the hill or most to the top there was a man came & told Major Lyon that there was a battery of 3 guns on the hill abandoned. my comp was then detached to take the battery   we started with a cheer   we got within 6 or 7 rods of the battery when we saw the Rebs were lying down behind their guns. we opened on them before they had time to open on us . . . we played on them untill we heard a yelling on our left & there came up a Rebel Brigade. we then commenced on them   we were firing brisk when we heard them shout we were surrounded on three sides. still the men fought bravely.

the Captain finally ordered us back [to] the Regt. they had been deployed into line. they were cutting us right & left & also in the front but with all to discourage them the men fought like Tigeres . . . all the while the men were falling around us but thank God I am safe thus far . . . the order was to change front to rear . . . we then gave it to them again   we gave as well as they but our position was terrible   we now had orders to fall back we done so but we halted & formed & commenced on them gave them lead & we sent some of them to their homes. we were ordered to move back again   we done so & rallied the third time & the men were as fast for fighting as they were at first.[48]

"Major Ward rallies the thinning ranks, and looks for re-inforcements," wrote 2nd Lt. Henry R. Jones. "We must fall back. And down the hill, in stern, unwilling column, march a hundred men where four times that number charged bravely up the slope."[49] Jones himself was left wounded on the field, where Rebels captured him. Early in the battle a shell fragment had hit him, then he'd taken a minié ball in the shoulder. The ball remained embedded in his collarbone.[50]

Lieutenant Marsh described for his wife the 8th Regiment's stubborn retreat:

> in a little distance we came to a board fence over which we climbed & there halted exchanged shots with them again for 20 or 25 minutes keeping the rebels back . . . So we marched along down hill to kind of ravine which screened us from rebels behind us when halted & blazed away at them again for while till it seemed as if there was no one left . . . We now kept on to rear of some hay stacks all this time remember exposed not only to an awful fire of musketry but grape & canister . . . I had but 7 men left of my company (4 having gone with Lt. Maine.) & so it was through regit . . . we marched down to creek, it was now night dark, our rations were on opposite side & . . . we crossed & encamped or bivouacked near. A sad exhausted little company.[51]

"Night closed the contest," wrote Henry Jones, "but Oh! the appalling scenes after the battle, the agonies of the wounded and the dying, the unspeakably mournful tasks of the surgeons and the survivors who all that night and the next day buried their dead. Near the point where they made their gallant charge, side by side, were laid the dead of the Eighth, with rude pine head-boards marking the graves."[52]

THE 16TH CONNECTICUT
We were murdered.

Before dawn, the rookie soldiers of the 16th Connecticut filed into ranks. Just twenty days after leaving home, the regiment stuck out like a sore thumb among the veteran units. Dr. Mayer, who'd encountered them the previous evening, called them "fresh, cheery boys, clean and well uniformed."[53]

They stood, shouldering their muskets, "a thousand men full of life facing in all the pride of their young manhood, the enemies of their country," as one of them put it. "Having no realizing sense of the dread carnage of war the regiment went into this fiery vortex with calm serenity of purpose."[54]

The serenity ended abruptly. Sgt. Austin Thompson of Bristol wrote:

> at early dawn the rebels began to fire their shells at us killing and wounding quite a number. it seemed to me like being in rather of a critical situation, the shells began to come thicker and faster and more of them, and were exploding all around us, when the orders came for us to retreat into a small piece of woods, which stood near by. as we retreated each one of us were blidged [obliged] to pass directly under a heavy fire. as I passed a shell burst within about a rod or two of me, a small piece of it lodged on my overcoat. you may as well believe that I did not stop.[55]

An hour or so later, the 16th followed the 8th Regiment, marching away from the action at the bridge. "[A]ll this while the artillery was playing loud and fast on both sides," said Austin Thompson; "we were now in a large piece of corn advancing as fast as we could to the top of a hill. we jumped over ditches and fences going as fast as we possibly could. we soon arrived at the top of the hill. we had a good view of the battle that was now going on."[56]

While the soldiers excitedly exchanged ideas on where they were headed, the surgeons held a sick call. William Relyea was derisive of his comrades in the 16th who suddenly claimed to be "the subjects of fits, colic and sudden faintness . . . heart disease, shortness of breath, diahoreah . . . what made it laughable was that most all of these . . . skulks we[re] those same brave chaps that wanted a chance to 'Draw a bead on Old Jeff D[avis].' Some of these heroes in their fright got to running so fast that they could not stop."[57]

With the sun now high overhead, the troops moved on to Antietam Creek. Relyea said:

> It now dawned on us what was heretofore a puzzle . . . we were flanking the enemy at the bridge and our delay . . . was caused by not knowing where the ford was . . . In we plunged, putting our guns and equipments above our heads we waded the stream . . . as we ascended the bank the booming of cannon and sharp volleys of musketry told us of the bloody work going on at the bridge. We were hurried up an incline toward the rear of the enemy but before we reached the top of the hill the noise of battle had ceased at the bridge. We were to late to intercept the enemy who had withdrawn and left the bridge in our possesion . . . we had become the extreme left of our whole line . . . The Rebs discovered us, these were the troops driven from the bridge and they opened on us with artillery, one shot passing the front of Co. D, taking out three men. It was a singular shot not one of the men were touched but the ball came so close that the displaced air knocked them senseless.
>
> An aid of McClellans that was conducting our flanking movement and known to us as Old Hat saw the shot as he sat on his horse near by, rode up to us and quietly remarked in broken English, "Poys does rebs is tam-med sassy. If dey don't stop dat, we'll go offer dere und dake dat pattery eh!" the coolness of the aid lent itself to the men and they steadied up instantly . . .
>
> We had crossed the Antietam about 1 p.m. . . . The fact that we had crossed the creek made it untenable for the enemy to stay [at the bridge] as we were getting well in their rear. This made the forcing of the bridge easier for our folks.[58]

As the 16th's brigade advanced, Confederate artillerymen threw everything they had at them; the thunder of the cannon and shrieking of shells was deafening. "Hundreds of cannon were now aimed at us," wrote Bernard F. Blakeslee, then a nineteen-year-old corporal; "grape and cannister, marbles and railroad iron were showered down like rain. The crest of the hill was a great protection to the Sixteenth."[59]

Col. Frank Beach ordered his men to move out. Some of the 16th men witnessed a Union battery near them "whirled back in less than five minutes, losing every officer, seven men, and five

Capt. Henry L. Beach (*left*) and Corporal Jasper S. Harris fell wounded as "the regiment melted away." Beach, the colonel's younger brother, would resign his commission within a year, but young Harris—wounded in the side and elbow, and taken prisoner by the Rebels— recovered and rejoined the regiment.

horses. To see those men stand there and be shot down till they received orders to retire was a fearful sight," Bernard Blakeslee wrote feelingly.[60]

It was close to four o'clock. While the 8th Connecticut had advanced well ahead toward the enemy, the commanders of the 16th Connecticut and 4th Rhode Island had misunderstood or missed their orders. They moved their troops into a cornfield and ordered the soldiers to lie down so the rebel shells would pass overhead. "In the meanwhile the Division of A. P. Hill, which had arrived from Harper's Ferry, and joined Lee's army, were coming into this cornfield from the opposite side, unobserved."[61] The men could hear the cornstalks rustling.

"While we were lying here," says the diary of Lt. B. F. Blakeslee, "we were suddenly ordered to 'Attention!' when a terrible volley was fired into us from behind a stone wall about five rods in front of us. We were ordered to fix bayonets and advance. In a moment we were riddled with shot . . .orders were given which were not understood. Neither the line-officers nor the men had any knowledge of regimental movements."[62]

Colonel Beach "undertook to face half of the regiment in a new direction . . . in order to meet the enemy and protect our flank which was in the air," explained Relyea. "This was difficult for us to do undrilled as we were, and some trouble occurred by neither officers or men being able to understand the orders given. One officer cried out, 'Tell us what you want us to do and we'll try to obey you.' The Colonel replied 'I want my men to face the enemy.' All this time the regiment had been receiving a terrible fire from a stone fence fronting the right wing and just when the left wing was in the midst of its movement the 4th R.I. [Regiment] broke to the rear . . . plunging through the moving companies throwing them into great disorder. At the same time terrible volleys were

Robert Kellogg, an eighteen-year-old private from Wethersfield, reported angrily to his father, "We were *murdered*. A green Regt. placed unsupported in a cornfield in the immediate vicinity of a cunning foe—and as it were left to take care of itself." (Letter of Robert H. Kellogg to his father, September 20, 1862, Robert H. Kellogg Papers, Connecticut Historical Society, Hartford.)

being poured into them from our front and flank and the regiment melted away like a mist before the sun."[63]

"[T]hree captains, a lieutenant, and forty enlisted men were already dead. Men were falling on every hand. The survivors at last extricated themselves from the fatal field, and fled, broken and decimated."[64]

In short, the inexperienced 16th men broke and ran.

"There was some pretty tall running in the 16th and I guess that I made myself scarce rather fast," admitted William Drake of Company B.[65]

"The bullets flying thick and fast, men falling all around. I turned with the rest and made for the fence over which I climed," Elizur Belden wrote in his diary.[66]

John Cuzner was blunt in his shame. "As for myself, I am a big coward," he confessed in a letter to his fiancée.[67]

"You may call the feeling fear or anything you choose," John Burnham, the regiment's adjutant wrote. "I don't deny that I trembled and wished we were well out of it. I tried to do my duty and am satisfied. I came off the field side by side with Col. Beach. Afterward we led the remnants of our own regiment and the 11th [Regiment] on to the field again through as hot a fire as I saw any time during the day. So far as my experience goes, I should not be sorry to see the war ended tomorrow without firing another shot, and yet I am a little eager to see one more battle. Not from any reckless desire for the excitement, but I have a little practical knowledge now and I think I should be more at home next time and perhaps do better. I should be considerable cooler, I have not doubt."[68]

"I have no special tales of heroism to tell," said William Relyea simply, "for all who went into that battle were heroes." He went on, "Pure gold were those who withstood the ordeal, and living or dead are honored as brave men." Relyea then named twenty-four soldiers of the 16th Regiment who "deserted during the day."[69]

An officer of the 8th Connecticut, writing about the 16th men, allowed: "I think myself they did as well as any green troops would have done but if they had been old troops this conduct would have been shameful. But the time is coming when they will be a splendid regiment . . . the regt is composed of good men to make soldiers of."[70]

"Col. Beach was obliged to report to Col. Harland that his regiment had never had a battalion-drill, and only one dress-parade, and hardly knew how to form in line of battle."[71]

✵ ✵ ✵

Newton Spaulding Manross: his name sounded like what he was—a scholar. It was a long road that led the thirty-seven-year-old college professor to the hard-luck 16th Connecticut. Newton Manross grew up in Bristol, the son of a clockmaker. From his boyhood, Newton had a mechanical bent, and was forever inventing things in his father's workshop. But his intellect ranged further, to chemistry, botany, and geology.

As a teenager in boarding school, he loved exploring nature, bringing back bugs, rocks, and flowers from his hikes. A school friend recalled that "With his fellow students Manross was a great favorite. His great good sense, his inexhaustible stores of information, his uniform cheerfulness, his imperturbable good nature, and his ready wit, made his companionship a rich prize." He had "a reputation for quickness in scholarship, for preeminence in athletic games and sports, and for a genius in roguery."

At Yale, Manross "towered head and shoulders above the Class" in the natural sciences. After earning his doctorate in Germany, Manross worked as a mineralogist for mining companies that sent him to South America, Mexico, and Panama. Returning to Bristol, he married and settled down, inventing machines and experimenting in his laboratory. In the fall of 1861 he became a professor at Amherst College in Massachusetts.

Manross was home in Bristol in the summer of 1862 when he attended a war rally. The professor rose and made an impassioned speech to the young men gathered there, urging them to enlist for the Union. The young men assured him they would join if he became their captain. "You can better afford to have a country without a husband, than a husband without a country," Newton told his wife Charlotte.

Three weeks later, Captain Manross brought Company K into the 16th Connecticut's camp in Hartford. He was offered the position of major in a Massachusetts unit, but refused it to honor his promise to his Bristol boys. As the regiment steamed south, Manross told a friend, "If I can only bring out what I know is in my men, I want no different shoulder-straps from these."[72] His men loved him fiercely.

At Antietam, Manross was leading Company K forward in the cornfield when a cannon ball hit him in the left side. Pvt. Lester Taylor said, "When I first saw him, he was trying to get up," so he and another soldier helped their captain to the corner of a fence, where they gently laid him down. "I could look down inside of him and see his heart beat, his left shoulder all shot off," Taylor wrote.[73]

He was carried to a field hospital where he soon became unconscious. A friend bending over him heard him murmur, "O, my poor wife; my poor wife!"[74]

The men of Company K sent their captain's body home to Connecticut. Hundreds came to his funeral, "and he sleeps there in the family burial ground at Forestville, his strong arm nerveless, and his great heart cold and still. O, fortunate he to die for such a country, and still more fortunate country to have such as he to die in her defence." His soldiers as well as his college friends erected there a stone monument to the man they loved.

"His successor in command, after his death, once said to the colonel of the regiment, 'Those boys care more for Manross' old shoes than they do for the best man in the regiment.'"[75]

The 16th's helter-skelter retreat at Antietam echoed the Union army's panicked race from the field at Bull Run: troops under fire for the first time, with inexperienced officers, and little knowledge of military movements. And not every man of the 16th Connecticut fell victim to the panic.

Newton S. Manross, a thirty-seven-year-old geologist and professor, possessed a curious mind and a courageous heart. A cannonball would end his life on the field at Antietam.

Bill Relyea recorded his withdrawal from the field:

> We were ordered to fix bayonetts and the next moment we were ordered to aim and fire this was our first and only volley. I had loaded and was going to fire [again] when happening to look around I saw only dead men laying where they fell, I very quickly decided it was no place for me. I went out of the cornfield at the same place we entered it. I saw a man laying up against a fence, frenzied by a wound and cursing terribly saying "don't run boys, don't run, don't you see the—rebs up there" pointing to our right. It was a useless exhortation to me I could not run if I tried so I stopped, took a piece of my coat and with a splinter of a rail tried to stop the flow of blood from a wound near his thigh, but it was no use I found him dead where I left him, three days after . . . he belonged to the 8th C.V.
>
> I tried to run but could not and I said to myself Bill you wont get out of this alive and you may as well die walking as running "oh it was hot" I went up the hill on which our battery was trying to do its best. the ground being newly ploughed made it hard footing as I went on I saw a man down on his hands and knees as if looking for something when I got to him, I saw he had fallen forward up the hill and . . . had been telescoped by a cannon shot. I stopped and found the man's name pinned it on his coat, he proved to be Corporal Grace of Co. D.
>
> I then went on up the hill amid a terrible fire from the enemy who were shelling the battery . . . I passed between the guns and found myself in front of the 13th N.H . . . .an officer of this regiment who had been watching me fuss with the dead corporal on the side hill said, as I asked permission to pass through his ranks, "You're a damned cool cuss anyhow" I might have been cool, if I was I did'nt know it for I kept saying You'll never get out alive, your wife's a widow . . . the Johnnies kept ploughing up dirt around me so thick that it kept me spitting mud and rubbing it out of my eyes so much that I got angry and turning shook my fist at them in impotent rage.[76]

At last Relyea made it over the bridge, "and getting beyond the reach of hostile muskets lay down to rest from sheer exhaustion and falling asleep . . . did not wake until daylight next morning."[77]

Bernard Blakeslee found rest harder to come by. "Of all gloomy nights, this was the saddest we ever experienced," he wrote miserably. "The cries and groans of the wounded that lay on the battle-field could be heard distinctly, and the occasional report of artillery sounded solemn and death-like."[78]

Many surgeons didn't sleep at all on the night of the battle, but remained on their feet trying to save the unending stream of wounded brought in on stretchers and in the jolting, horse-drawn ambulances. A corporal in the 16th described one scene: "In a room about 12 × 20 a bloody table stood and around it were five surgeons. A wounded man was laid on the table and it took but a few seconds for them to decide what to do, and but a few minutes to do it. The amputated limbs

were thrown out of a window. In forty-eight hours there were as many as two cart loads of amputated legs, feet, arms, and hands in the pile."[79]

Dr. Mayer, assistant surgeon of the 8th Connecticut, was astonished to find that

> All the wounded came in, exalted in spirit, full of patriotic fire, anxious for the battle, the defeat of the rebs, and complaining hardly of their own injury . . . Whether the whiskey that was given to a wounded man at once—and needed in the collapse of serious gunshot wounds, contributed to this exaltation I know not. But I have still in mind some badly wounded boys that fiercely demanded the fate of the battle before they cared about themselves, and the beautiful resignation with which others awaited their certain death. This is not romance. I saw it and it is realism.[80]

The Aftermath

"On the morning of the 18th the remnants of the [16th Connecticut] regiment were gathered together. It was a pitiable sight. When we were again formed in regimental line and awaiting for orders each man was craneing his neck, peering about him in every direction to see who of his comrades was missing. A roll call was made and the men were told to answer for their absent comrades. It was indeed a sorrowful calling of names to many who had to answer 'dead' 'wounded' 'missing' 'prisoner' 'left on the field.'"[81]

In Company H, sixteen-year-old Wells Bingham mourned for his brother John, shot dead on the field beside him. Back in East Haddam, their family would erect a stone obelisk for seventeen-year-old John, engraved: "A Hero in whose bosom Freedom brightly burned."

Harry Barnett of Suffield had marched into the cornfield the day before, singing "You shant have any of my peanuts when your peanuts are gone." His body had been left on the battlefield.[82]

Henry Bugbee, wounded in three places, lay all night on the field before a Confederate surgeon tended to him.

Skilled at carving, George Stannard of the 14th Regiment turned a piece of bone into a patriotic ring, and carved several tiny baskets from peach pits. Despite the fact that his regiment was under fire, and the soldiers could not raise their heads from the ground, George somehow managed to keep at his carving on the battlefield. He sent one of the baskets home for his nephew, writing: "Tell Claude that I send him the enclosed little basket that I whittled out when there was some mighty quare music playing. Tell him that was whittled out on the battle field of Antietam by his uncle George." (Letter of George E. Stannard to his sister, October 12, 1862; Buck Zaidel collection.)

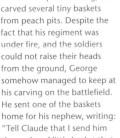

Hundreds of 16th men had fallen. In the cornfield of John Otto's farm, blood drenched the patch where the men of Company I had fought: thirty-four of them had been killed or wounded in a matter of minutes.

"Genl Burnside came riding along and when on inquiry of who we were, he was told, 'that is all of the 16th Conn that we know of,' tears filled his eyes and ran down his cheek as he tried to cheer us by saying, 'Well never mind boys, we will whip them to day so keep up your courage and pay them back with interest.' Torn as we were, we were ready to enter the fight again, and we verily expected to."[83]

But no attack was ordered. "Genl Caution who ruled McClellan controlled events that day," Relyea wrote sarcastically. "It seemed very queer to us, that after losing so many men to gain a bridge in order to cross over and fight the rebels, that we should be kept standing still and not . . . go over it to have the fight."[84]

Though even Burnside assumed that McClellan would order his army to engage Lee and finish the job of yesterday, the ever-cautious "Young Napoleon" convinced himself that the Confederates' numbers were far greater than his own. (In fact, Union troops well outnumbered their enemy at Antietam.) Bill Relyea was disgusted; McClellan had "insufficient brains to accomplish anything," he wrote later.[85]

The soldiers of the 14th Connecticut lay in a muddy field, pinned down by rebel sharpshooters. Rascals that they were, the 14th boys still found "some food for mirth even in the shadow of impending death . . . Lt. Galpin, then Orderly Sergeant of Co. B, complain[ed] that the confederates sent their bullets so close to his head . . . that he couldn't make out his morning report with any comfort or precision."[86]

The 16th Connecticut was posted at Burnside's Bridge in case the Confederates tried to cross. "All that long afternoon and throughout the night that followed we kept vigil," wrote Bill Relyea. "It rained terribly and as we were not allowed to have any fires, we remained in rain soaked discomfort until daylight of the 19th then it was discovered that the enemy had folded his tents and silently stole away."[87]

Alexander Gardner's photograph captured the field two days after the battle.

Two days after the battle, the Union troops could finally go back to the field to help their wounded and bury their dead. "It was to me a sad scene, the most so that I ever saw in my life or ever imagined," wrote a heartsick Austin Thompson.[88]

Writing to his wife a week later, Bill Relyea still could not shake the horror of it. "When my mind goes back to that bloody field of Antietam, that wreck of human flesh, my blood curdles in my veins . . . Piles of heads, arms, legs and fragments of other portions of humanity all thrown together promiscuously . . . I am detailed to bury the dead, sickening, sorrowful task. I wish there was no War."[89]

On September 20, a Connecticut soldier whose unit hadn't taken part in the battle crossed the battlefield. "[W]e marched through that part of the field where the right wing fought," wrote Charles Greenleaf. "I have been in the service a year but I never knew what war meant till to day. All along both sides of the road for two miles dead rebels lay piled up like cord wood. They have lain there two days in the sun and are all bloated . . . I was also up to one of the hospitals and saw over a hundred arms and legs in the yard."[90]

The Battle of Antietam claimed over 22,000 casualties in one day. Though the Union held a technical victory, McClellan's refusal to finish off Lee's army the following day left the outcome nearly pointless. Lee withdrew uncontested. A few weeks later, President Lincoln removed McClellan from command.

But the battle had unexpected benefits. William Relyea, 16th Connecticut, pointed out one: "Up to this time there had been but little sympathy shown toward one another among the members of the regt . . . but that one day of bloody carnage opened the fountain of brotherly love to the very depths and from our hearts flowed a stream of comradeship for every man of us that has never been diminished . . . officers understood their men better, men respected their officers more. They had all been proved in the firey furnace of war."[91]

For the nation as a whole, the battle was a catalyst for historic change. President Lincoln announced it on September 22, 1862.

Years later, Relyea remembered: "for the six months following[,] everything I eat [ate] drank or smelled had an odor of dead men in it and the memory of the scene and the place and the four trees that stood in the field to mark the place of burrial will never be effaced." (Manuscript of William Relyea, pp. 54–55, Connecticut Historical Society, Hartford.)

CHAPTER SIX

Emancipation Is a Mighty Word

FREEDOM ARRIVES

Five days after the Battle of Antietam, Abraham Lincoln came forward to speak to his country. "I, Abraham Lincoln, President of the United States of America, and Commander-in-chief of the Army and Navy thereof, do hereby proclaim and declare that . . . on the first day of January . . . one thousand eight hundred and sixty-three, all persons held as slaves within any state, or designated part of a state, the people whereof shall then be in rebellion against the United States shall be then, thenceforward, and forever free."[1]

"[W]hen the proclamation of freedom was proclaimed; it sent a thrill of joy through every avenue of my soul," exulted James Lindsay Smith, a Norwich man who had escaped a Virginia slave master years earlier.[2] Now a shoemaker and minister instead of a slave, Smith reveled in his city's celebration: all over Norwich, bells rang out for a full hour following a 100-gun salute to President Lincoln's proclamation.

Morally opposed to slavery, Lincoln had campaigned on a platform that prohibited its spread to new states without promising to *abolish* slavery. But now, as a war president, Lincoln saw that the Union could gain a significant strategic advantage if he could weaken the South's economy, and cripple its ability to arm, supply, and feed the Confederate army.

"Stand up a man!" decreed an 1860s print extolling the Emancipation Proclamation. An African American man, bearing the vicious marks of an overseer's whip, knelt to kiss the American flag, while a white Union soldier bade him rise.

"My paramount object in this struggle is to save the Union, and is not either to save or to destroy slavery," he had explained to Horace Greeley on August 22, 1862. "If I could save the Union without freeing any slave I would do it, and if I could save it by freeing all the slaves I would do it; and if I could save it by freeing some and leaving others alone I would also do that. What I do about slavery, and the colored race, I do because I believe it helps to save the Union."[3]

Lincoln had not come to his decision hastily. Gideon Welles, a native of Glastonbury, Connecticut, was Lincoln's secretary of the navy. Back on July 13, 1862, Welles had noted in his diary that he had gone for a carriage ride with the president, who spoke "of emancipating the slaves by proclamation in case the Rebels did not cease to persist in their war on the Government and the Union . . . He dwelt earnestly on the gravity, importance, and delicacy of the movement, said he had given it much thought and had about come to the conclusion that it was a military necessity absolutely essential for the salvation of the Union, that we must free the slaves or be ourselves subdued."[4]

In fact, the Emancipation Proclamation *did* free some slaves, and leave others alone, as Lincoln had put it to Greeley. The document did not liberate enslaved African Americans in the so-called border states of Delaware, Maryland, Missouri, and Kentucky, since those states had not joined the Confederacy. Lincoln didn't want to alienate the people of the border states, for fear they would join the rebellion.

✵ ✵ ✵

On the day the Emancipation Proclamation became law, Hartford residents Harriet and Joe Hawley witnessed something they would never forget. Joe, colonel of the 7th Connecticut, was stationed in South Carolina with his regiment. His wife Harriet was visiting.

On January 1, 1863, the 1st Regiment South Carolina Volunteers, an early unit of African American soldiers, held a celebration of the Emancipation Proclamation near Beaufort, South Carolina. The soldiers of the "First South" had been enslaved; now, under their colonel, white abolitionist Thomas Wentworth Higginson, they stood ready to fight and kill Confederate slaveholders. That day they commemorated the historic change the Emancipation Proclamation brought. Between two and three thousand people, black and white, had gathered for the celebration. The Hawleys were among them.

In a letter she wrote that night, Harriet Hawley tried to convey her emotions to her family of Connecticut Yankees:

> If you at the north had half as happy a New Year's day as we in the Southern Department you enjoyed a great deal. I dare say that many of you remembered that it was Emancipation Day—but we saw and felt it with every breath we drew . . .

The African American soldiers who stood at attention before the great live oak might have been the First South Carolina on Emancipation Day, or Connecticut's first black regiment, the 29th Connecticut Infantry, at a later date.

. . . [T]he [1st South Carolina] regiment was drawn up to receive us and we were most kindly greeted by Col. Higginson and the other officers—the grand live oaks standing out clear against the southern sky, in the fore-ground the black soldiers in their bright red trousers and nearer the water groups of negroes of all ages, all styles of costume, their queer made "dug-outs" and flatboats crowded with them . . .

. . . [T]he President's Proclamation was read . . . A beautiful stand of colors was then presented to the regiment . . . and as Col. Higginson received the unfurled banner in his hand and turned to reply, a single quavering voice, evidently that of an aged negro, burst out into the song "America:"

> My Country, 'tis of thee
> Sweet Land of Liberty.

Instantly other voices among them joined in,—the audience on the platform, much moved, would have joined also, but waving his hand and saying "leave them to themselves," Col. Higginson silenced us and the song went on

"'Emancipation Day in South Carolina' The color sergeant of the 1st South Carolina (Colored) Volunteers addressing the regiment, after having been presented with the Stars and Stripes." (*Frank Leslie's Illustrated Newspaper*, January 24, 1863.)

swelling louder and fuller till the whole regiment had joined and all the great crowd also. Tears filled many eyes around me—for myself I could hardly check the sobs, as I thought, for the first time now they have a country; it is to them now a Land of Liberty.[5]

✳ ✳ ✳

Back in Connecticut, reaction to the Emancipation Proclamation was split. African Americans and abolitionists were exhilarated, while stalwart Democrats were enraged. Those in between—the bulk of the state's population—seemed to have had mixed feelings.

As for Connecticut's white soldiers, many had immediate negative reactions. Living in a deeply prejudiced culture, their ordinary state was one of bigotry. "It has got to be an abolition war now and I don't like the idea of suffering and risking my life for niggers," complained Sgt. Charles Greenleaf of Hartford a few weeks after the Emancipation Proclamation became law.[6]

Bill Relyea of the 16th Connecticut confirmed "there are very few men who will say they are satisfied, their common remark being, 'We did not come out here to fight for Niggers, we came to fight for the Union . . . ' This is not the remark of here and there one individual, but it is universal in the army here."[7]

Widespread, but not universal. Soldiers who actually witnessed slavery's agonies and injustices often found themselves thinking twice about what they'd always believed. "I never was half an abolitionist until I came here and saw slavery in its full bloom," wrote an unidentified soldier in Connecticut's 7th Regiment in 1861. "If the government dares not put an end to it now, it will be no government and not worth fighting for."[8]

Soldiers learned bits of truth about slavery from the African Americans who fled to the Union lines for refuge. The army termed them "contrabands," and as Confederate property, they didn't have to be returned. Long before the Emancipation Proclamation, Union troops had been harboring refugees. Homer Sprague, a captain in the 13th Connecticut, wrote of the former slaves his regiment encountered:

> Some of these chattels had their backs shockingly lacerated by whipping; others had huge freshly burned marks of the branding iron. Many had chains on their wrists, ankles and necks. A few wore great iron collars with long projecting

prongs, like the spokes of a wheel. More than once did the writer of this history work till past midnight filing off these collars. "I used to think," said Captain McCord, "that the stories about cruel treatment of slaves were exaggerated; but the reality is fully equal to the worst description."[9]

Of course, some soldiers had been abolitionists all along. One of the most tenacious was Harriet Hawley's cousin, Uriah Parmelee. A native of Guilford, the nineteen-year-old Parmelee had left Yale in his junior year to enlist as a private in a New York cavalry unit. He was an unswerving abolitionist; for him, the war was not about preserving the Union, but eradicating slavery. Months before Lincoln introduced the Emancipation Proclamation, Uriah wrote to his brother Sam, "if I had money enough to raise a few hundred contrabands and arm them I'd get up an insurrection among the slaves—told Capt. I'd desert to do it." In the spring of 1862, he was indignant that as the war stood, the Union might win, but "the great heart wound, Slavery, will not be reached."[10]

Just two weeks before Lincoln announced his proclamation, Uriah wrote in frustration, "I thought that the progress of events must surely bring about universal Emancipation, this either as an indirect result of our subduing the rebels, or a direct result of the light which would dawn on men's minds."[11]

Once the Emancipation Proclamation took effect, Uriah threw himself into winning the war. "I do not intend to shirk now there is really something to fight for—I mean *Freedom*. Since the First of January it has become more & more evident to my mind that the war is henceforth to be conducted upon a different basis . . . So then I am willing to remain & endure whatever may fall to my share."[12]

What fell to Uriah's share in the fight for freedom were scores of engagements, including Antietam, Fredericksburg, Chancellorsville, and Gettysburg. In battle, he was conspicuous for his courage; his commander, Gen. John C. Caldwell,

Wilson Chinn's forehead bore the brand "VBM"—the initials of Louisiana sugar planter Volsey B. Marmillion. (From C. C. Leigh, "White and Colored Slaves," *Harper's Weekly*, January 30, 1864, p. 71.) About sixty years old, Chinn wore a spoked collar and leg irons, with other instruments of cruelty at his feet, in this photograph taken by New York photographer Myron H. Kimball.

"I am fighting for Liberty, for the slave and the white man alike," affirmed Uriah Parmelee. (Letter of Uriah Parmelee to his mother, April 18, 1862, David M. Rubenstein Rare Book & Manuscript Library, Duke University.)

Kept in East Haddam for nearly 150 years, this portrait of an anonymous young man in uniform likely showed one of the thousands of "contrabands"—former slaves—who sought shelter within Union lines. Many became servants to the soldiers in blue, cooking meals, washing clothes, cutting wood, and tending to gear. At war's end, some soldiers brought their attendants north with them, bolstering Connecticut's small African American population.

said "he had never seen a braver soldier."[13] It was Uriah Parmelee's courage that ultimately would bring about his death just days before the South surrendered.

Parmelee's passion for freedom was unusual among Connecticut soldiers. Nearly all of them had grown up in a society that considered racism normal. When they joined the army, these men had volunteered because they wanted to save the Union, not end slavery.

But gradually, many Connecticut men experienced a shift in their attitudes. For most, emancipation never became their primary aim in fighting against the Confederacy; still, many began to think of freedom as an honorable and just goal.

Some eight months after Lincoln's proclamation, an officer in the 9th Connecticut asserted: "The regiment to which I belong came South Democrats—that you know—and, on my honor as a man, they are this day abolitionists, almost every one of them, and why? Because they have seen slavery in its naked deformity, in its every guise . . . We shall have gained everything in this contest if we gain a free country."[14]

Charles A. Boyle, a young painter from New Haven, put it simply, "Who does not feel that a noble work is going on in the liberation of thousands of Slaves?"[15]

Once word of the Emancipation Proclamation had spread among African Americans, more and more left the plantations where they had been enslaved and sought protection with the Yankee soldiers. "Many negro men, women and children are following the army, their dresses all muddy and the little children hungry and weary. I pity them. But they seem cheerful and happy and bear up with fortitude and courage, so great is their love of freedom," wrote Horatio Chapman, an East Hampton man in Connecticut's 20th Regiment.[16]

Fred Lucas of Goshen, serving in Connecticut's 2nd Heavy Artillery, had a different view. "Negroes are roaming all over this region—free and too ignorant to make proper use of freedom, they are become a pest & a nuisance to the army and their former masters," he complained. Nevertheless, Lucas was willing to use the "pests" and "nuisances" for his own ends: "Each of us has a good servant who tends to all rations, does all cooking, cleaning, & washing & tends the fires."[17]

Captain Andrew Upson of the 20th Connecticut was curious about the man who worked as his servant.

> He goes by the name of George Washington & was until a month since a "chattel"—He ran away from "Massa" when Sherman's troops came through Alabama recently, joined the Yankees & now turns up a waiter & cook for your correspondent . . . Night before last he asked me to get him a book—that is so he could learn to read . . . You can soon see the scope of their thoughts & how the condition of their lives has bound them in darkness . . .

> The desire to be free is the deep, absorbing passion . . . the cherished wish of these down trodden people to put themselves where they can call their children & wives their own . . . Emancipation is a mighty word.[18]

Robert W. Morton

In the army camps, African American women worked as laundresses to the troops, while men chopped firewood, tended livestock, and acted as servants. Among the white soldiers, unfortunately, there were always bigots ready to abuse African Americans. Charles Boyle, writing of African Americans who'd taken refuge with the Union army, declared, "I know that they suffer such wrongs from the hands of their pretended benefactors, as would sicken your hearts to see."[19]

Strong motivations drove those who had spent their lives enslaved until now. In the face of countless difficulties, they persevered. The chaplain of the 10th Connecticut, Henry Clay Trumbull, described the men who worked as servants in his regiment: "In some way they had obtained two spelling books, or small readers, and these were in constant use among them. Not only in the intervals of active work during the day, but all through the night . . . As I lay in my tent at night, and waked from time to time, I would hear low negro voices, back of the tent . . . 'The hen is in the yard. The dog barks at the hen . . . This boy is James. He drives a hoop.'"[20]

In Connecticut's 15th Regiment, Pvt. Enoch E. Rogers got permission to open an evening school for African Americans in Kinston, North Carolina. Other soldiers in the regiment volunteered as well.

> The school opened May 1st, in one of the churches, with an attendance of about forty. Rogers became enthusiastic in his work, and the work correspondingly prospered. On May 3d, the school numbered one hundred ninety-two members . . . and by the first of June something over three hundred names had been enrolled, of all ages from five years to seventy years and over. Not

This winsome boy, proudly wearing a uniform that he wouldn't grow into for years, was Robert Morton. Young Morton went to work as a servant for Robert Potter (*center*) of Plymouth, a captain in Connecticut's 2nd Heavy Artillery. As with most of the African American people who hired themselves out to Union soldiers, little is known of his life. But Morton must have been a favorite among the troops: he posed for photographs at least twice.

content with this, Rogers, by permission of his officers, started a day school May 22d, also for the colored people, with an average attendance of upward of two hundred. Five sessions per week were held and the eagerness manifested to learn, as well as the progress made, was most surprising.[21]

In many cases, Union soldiers found that the teenagers and men they'd hired as servants took on more important roles, sometimes even accompanying the troops into battle.

"Among the men in subordinate positions connected with the 20th [Connecticut Regiment]," says Capt. Beardsley, "I know of none that I take more pleasure in making especial mention of, for bravery, than of my faithful colored servant, William Manning. Though he was simply a body servant, whose duties were those only of a non-combatant, yet, whenever the regiment was going into a fight, he always asked permission to go with the boys, and do his part of the fighting. In the charge at Ressaca he was among the first to reach the Confederate lines, and was wounded in the breast while upon the Rebel works . . . [S]urely his name should be enrolled upon its list of honored veterans."[22]

Yet as soldiers, men of color faced an inordinate amount of antagonism from white troops. Even before the Emancipation Proclamation, Union general John W. Phelps had begun organizing men who were fugitive slaves into a regiment. When Phelps found that his superiors would allow his black troops only to dig ditches and handle other physical labor, he offered his resignation. His commander, General Butler, refused it, and Phelps's men received their muskets.

Lt. Solomon R. Hinsdale, of Connecticut's 12th Regiment, wrote indignantly:

there is considerable hard feeling among our soldiers and officers in regard to Gen Phelps . . . [recruiting] the Negroes . . . Gen Phelps is determined to arm them They are now drilling, learning the military movement and you cannot imagine the feelings that exist between our officers and soldiers. They say that if the North has come so long and think . . . that it is right to bring them down to the level with the Negroes, they will not fight and if possible return home.

I must say that if they arm the Negroes, I cannot stay in the service that cannot furnish white soldiers enough to do their fighting, for I cannot, as yet, bring myself to think that is right and just.[23]

Some white soldiers could see the sense in accepting black troops, but far more white soldiers were unconditionally hostile. They especially resented that some of the early African American units had black officers.

"Last Saturday there was a Regiment of Nigger soldiers arrived here," wrote Lt. John G. Crosby of Middletown to his wife. "Nigger Captains and Lieutenants &c; it made me a little mad to see the dam'd monkeys dressed up in clothes like white men, but I said nothing. Capts Parker and Addis thought twas all right, and that if they could do any good, they would be willing to mix right in with them, but some . . . officers met a couple of the nigger officers in town in the evening and they tore their uniforms off them and broke their swords."[24]

For men of color, joining the Union army meant fighting two separate sets of enemies: the Confederates, and the bigots in their own army. Thousands enlisted anyway.

Menominee L. Maimi, a resident of Middletown and West Hartford, had African American, Native American, and perhaps white roots. He'd enlisted in the 12th Connecticut, a white regiment, and remained with the unit for months, encountering plenty of racism from his comrades before he was transferred to the Colored 54th Massachusetts. In a letter to his wife Fanny, Menominee envisioned how black soldiers would punish southern slaveholders:

> They tried to convince the world that the black man sprang from . . . the loins of monkeys and apes . . . and it was but right to buy and steal the children of apes or monkeys and to enslave them . . . They shall see these gentle monkeys, that they thought they had so fast in chains and fetters, coming on a long visit to them, with rifle, saber, and all the terrible trappings of war. Not one at a time, cringing like whipped hounds as we were, but by thousands, and if that doesn't suffice, by millions.[25]

Menominee was one of a handful of men of color who managed to enlist in white regiments. By the time Connecticut's African Americans could *legally* enlist in a regiment of their own state, two and half years of war had passed.

Chaplain Asher and the 6th U.S. Colored Troops

Reverend Jeremiah Asher

In the village of North Branford, Connecticut, a boy named Jeremiah Asher had grown up listening to the stories that his grandfather, Gad Asher, told of his life. Born in Africa, Gad had been a child of four when white slavers forced him aboard a ship that carried him to Connecticut. Year after year, Gad worked as the slave of a white family there. When soldiers were needed to fight the British in the Revolutionary War, Gad Asher took the place of his white master in the army, serving until war's end. Though his master had promised Gad his freedom in exchange for his military service, he required the veteran soldier to pay him his purchase price.[26]

Jeremiah, Gad's grandson, was born free in 1812. He took great pride in his grandfather's Revolutionary service, and his determination to attain freedom from slavery. When Jeremiah's father decided that his son should become a shoemaker, the boy refused, taking his own path, which eventually led to the ministry.

On a large piece of dark blue silk, Philadelphia artist David Bustill Bowser, an African American, painted the regimental flag of the 6th U.S. Colored Troops. A fierce spread eagle dominated one side; on the other side, Bowser depicted an African American soldier beside a classical figure representing Liberty. Above the two figures floated the inscription "Freedom for All." Philadelphia's black citizens presented the flag to the 6th U.S. Colored Infantry on August 31, 1863, before the regiment headed south.

Thirteen months later, rebel bullets would fell the men of the 6th's color guard in the Battle of Chaffin's Farm, Virginia. That day, *three* members of the regiment would earn the Medal of Honor for their "extraordinary heroism" in saving their flags after the color guard had been shot down. Many years later, the 6th's regimental flag was discarded accidentally. These rare wartime images bear witness to the artist's skill in creating a noble symbol for the men to follow.

In 1849, Reverend Asher moved his family to Philadelphia, where he would lead the Shiloh Baptist Church. While traveling in England to raise money for his church, he found many people interested in his experiences. He wrote *Incidents in the Life of the Rev. J. Asher,* published in 1850 in England.[27]

Back in Philadelphia, Asher remained a strong voice for abolition. In 1863, when black men finally gained the right to join the Union army, Reverend Asher and others endorsed the admission of black chaplains.

In the summer of 1863, the 6th Regiment U.S. Colored Troops began enlisting men in Pennsylvania. Reverend Asher, grandson of a soldier who fought for George Washington, became its chaplain.

The men of the 6th U.S.C.T. fought in engagements around Virginia and North Carolina, and served in the trenches at the Siege of Petersburg. More than 200 of them gave their lives.

In 1865, the regiment helped capture the city of Wilmington, North Carolina, and remained on duty there. Thousands of sick prisoners of war were released to Wilmington, and they brought deadly diseases with them. Within days, disease was running unchecked through the city, claiming victims everywhere. Doctors and nurses were scarce, and army chaplains—including Reverend Asher—volunteered to tend soldiers in the makeshift hospitals. While caring for the sick and dying, Jeremiah Asher fell sick with typhoid fever. He was fifty-two when he died.

Some Body Has Got to Do Something

In March of 1863, Congress passed the Conscription Act, which established that "all able-bodied male citizens of the United States"—including African Americans—were eligible for the draft.[28]

Massachusetts and Rhode Island formed black units and began enlisting. But Connecticut stalled, many of its legislators refusing to consider the idea of African American soldiers, despite the fact that thousands had fought alongside whites in the Revolutionary War, and that the U.S. Navy included black sailors, and had for decades.

A dozen or so Connecticut men traveled north to enlist in the 54th Massachusetts Regiment, the first African American unit in the Northern states. On July 18, 1863, the men of the 54th Massachusetts led the assault on Fort Wagner in South Carolina, persevering through a hurricane of bullets and artillery. The 54th succeeded in planting the American flag on the Confederates' parapet before being driven back, with casualties near 50 percent.

The bravery of the 54th Massachusetts clearly demonstrated what black men could, and would, do for their country. Still, Connecticut did not act.

But when the government actually began drafting citizens in July of 1863, waves of hostility and violence resulted. In New York City, thousands of workingmen, who didn't have the $300 needed to hire substitute soldiers, rioted. They attacked the draft office, overcame police, and murdered countless African Americans whom they labeled as the reason for the war.

The draft brought another outcome as well. For white men who didn't want to be conscripted into the Union army, it suddenly made sense to create regiments of black men who would contribute to the state's quota of soldiers so that fewer whites would need to.

In November of 1863 Connecticut's legislature finally took up a bill "providing for the raising of colored troops." It met aggressive opposition from many of the state's legislators. Henry Mitchell, a senator from Bristol, called the bill "the greatest monstrosity ever." William W. Eaton of Hartford exclaimed, "don't let the State of Connecticut go back upon civilization . . . You will let loose upon every household south of Mason and Dixon's line a band of ferocious men who will spread lust and rapine all over that land . . . The African cannot be controlled, possessing, as he does, all the elements of a brutal civilization."[29]

President Lincoln had something to say to Americans who opposed emancipation and the enlistment of African Americans. "You say you will not fight to free negroes. Some of them seem willing to fight for you," he wrote. Lincoln predicted that when the war ended "there will be some black men who can remember that, with silent tongue, and clenched teeth, and steady eye, and well-poised bayonet, they have helped mankind on to this great consummation; while, I fear, there will be some white ones, unable to forget that, with malignant heart, and deceitful speech, they strove to hinder it."[30]

The opponents of Connecticut's bill to enlist soldiers of color did all they could to crush the proposal, but they were in the minority. Governor Buckingham signed it into law, and established Connecticut's 29th Regiment. Though the Federal government paid black soldiers less than white soldiers, the state of Connecticut pledged to make up the difference. Nevertheless, African Americans were drastically limited in their service: they could not rise above the position of sergeant, and all their commissioned officers were white.

In spite of the system's injustices, black men from all over Connecticut stepped forward. "It is war times now and Some Body has got to do some thing For their Country," wrote Joseph Cross. A farm laborer from Griswold, Cross left his wife and four small children to join the 29th Regiment.[31]

While patriotism was a strong catalyst for enlistment, black men had other reasons driving them as well. "I confess that I had a burning desire to eke out some vengeance which for years

Sergeant Alexander H. Newton (*left*) was born in New Bern, North Carolina in 1837, to a free mother and an enslaved father. In the 1850s, Newton worked on the Underground Railroad, helping refugees find their way North to unfettered lives. Newton enlisted as a private in Connecticut's 29th Regiment in 1863, rising to commissary sergeant some months later. While in the trenches at Petersburg, a shell exploded beside him, killing the man next to him. The explosion permanently injured Newton's sight. After the war, Newton became a minister, and in his later years, wrote a book about his life and experiences, entitled *Out of the Briars*.

had been pent up in my nature," admitted Alexander Herritage Newton, whose father had been enslaved in North Carolina.[32] As a Union soldier, Newton would take a measure of revenge on southern slaveholders.

Hundreds of African Americans from outside the state enlisted in Connecticut's regiment as well. Many had been enslaved in the South; others came from places that had no black units. When the ranks of the 29th Connecticut had filled, men of color spilled over into the next African American unit, the 30th Regiment. Connecticut welcomed the out-of-staters, as the draft required a quota of soldiers from each city and town. Thus the city of Norwich claimed a New Jersey carpenter named Rodman Dutton as one of its number, while Hartford counted Friday Kanaka, a Hawaiian, in its quota.

The troops of the 29th Regiment trained in a Fair Haven camp in the early weeks of 1864. After the flag presentation, the colonel marched his men through the streets of New Haven to the wharf where their vessel waited. "Cheer after cheer broke from the lips of these colored men, as they beheld the banners of the patriotic citizens along the route floating to the breeze in honor of them," a newspaper reporter wrote. "Occasionally expressions like these would be heard as they marched along: 'We'll show you that we can fight;' 'We'll show you that we are men;' and they meant it."[33]

Isaac J. Hill, a thirty-seven-year-old minister from Pennsylvania, was touched by the crowd's kindheartedness. "White and colored ladies and gentlemen grasped me by the hand, with tears streaming down their cheeks, and bid me good bye, expressing the hope that we might have a safe return. My heart felt the sobbing impulse for the first time, and although I had no mother, no wife, and no sisters there to greet me, yet strangers ministered unto me, and never shall I forget their kind attentions to me."[34]

When the 29th reached Maryland, the men finally received muskets before sailing to Beaufort, South Carolina. Wearing a Union uniform and carrying a musket, "I was in full realization of what it meant to be again in the South, not a cringing black man, but a proud American soldier," wrote Sgt. Alexander Newton, who'd been born in North Carolina.[35]

Here the 29th soldiers encountered both measured respect and brazen derision from the Union's white troops. Pvt. Abner Mitchell, a white farmer from Washington, Connecticut, explained to his parents: "There is a general feeling here among the better class that the negroes are not well used by the Officers, the government, by anyone, the Government dont pay them as it ought, their Officers are very tyrannical and the white Soldiers are willing they should fight but want them to do all their work and fight as well or better than themselves besides."[36]

From the very beginning, the 29th Regiment had been exploited. At enlistment, the men had been promised a $75 bounty from their counties. They never received the money.[37] And when the paymaster finally arrived with the regiment's first pay, it wasn't the $13 per month that had been promised; instead the soldiers got just $7. Their officers advised the men to take the lesser amount, and all but one did so. The colonel's orderly, I. J. Hill, refused to accept less than he deserved.

A few days later, Hill and the others were gratified by a visit from Gen. Rufus Saxton, who had formed and commanded the First South Carolina Regiment of former slaves. Saxton told them:

Few images survive of the 29th Connecticut's soldiers. This unidentified private with the steady gaze left a photographic legacy that included hand tinting and gilding to his brass belt plate and buttons, but his name and fate will probably never be known.

> Boys, I have come to greet you with an order I have received that you are to be considered soldiers of the United States and receive your pay as white soldiers, and I hope you will consider yourselves men. Although your skins are dark, you have the same muscle as white men, and the same courage to fight. It is for you to get the same skill by strictly attending to your duty, not from fear of punishment, but because you are soldiers . . . Boys, if you ever want to make good soldiers you must look a white man straight in the face, and let him know that you are a man.[38]

It was hard enough to be a soldier in the Civil War. Being a *black* soldier meant facing overwhelming obstacles at every turn. As African American regiments continued to demonstrate their courage and steadfastness, many white soldiers who had disparaged black troops gradually changed their views. Theodore F. Vaill described an encounter that his white regiment, Connecticut's 2nd Heavy Artillery, had with soldiers of color:

> Many of them were men of fine physique, and soldierly bearing; and as we contemplated their stacks of muskets, and then surveyed the rebel lines just ahead, (which we knew somebody must take,) there was not a man of the "superior Anglo-Saxon race" in all the division, with brains enough to put two ideas together, who would have deemed "niggers" unfit for soldiers.

> "Well, you colored fellows have had a pretty rough job, I reckon," said one of our men, in a tone of respectful and neighborly inquiry; for observe, when white soldiers stand side by side with black ones, facing rebel breastworks, they never "damn the niggers," nor insult them in any way . . . "Yes, we have," was the reply, "as rough as we care for. We have to die for eight dollars a month, while you get thirteen for the same business."[39]

In Connecticut's 29th regiment, Alexander Newton was clear about the task that stood before his unit and the rest of the Colored Troops. "While it had always been said that this was a white man's country, we were determined that the black man should share in this honor of ownership. And the best way that this ownership could be established was through the loyalty of the black man on the battlefield. For surely it will be conceded that when a man has bought his adopted country by his blood, it is his own."[40]

CHAPTER SEVEN

No Men on Earth Can Be Braver

FREDERICKSBURG, DECEMBER 1862

Looking to the west, Frederick Burr Hawley was uneasy. It was December 12, 1862. That morning, the twenty-four-year-old lieutenant had arrived in Fredericksburg, Virginia, with his regiment, the 14th Connecticut. On top of a hill called Marye's Heights, he could plainly see thousands and thousands of entrenched Confederate troops. Ranged across the crest, the rebels had a hundred threatening artillery pieces, their muzzles pointing down the slope.

Three months earlier, Hawley and the other survivors of the 14th Regiment had limped away from Antietam with their muskets and not much else. Since then, deadly typhoid and dysentery had swept through their ranks. Ten days after they left Antietam, Hawley had written: "Some 200 men sick . . . most every one trouble with the Diarrhea and some sick with Dysentery."[1] Before Antietam, their gear had gone missing, leaving them without blankets or overcoats in freezing temperatures. They went long periods without enough food. Their regiment had left Hartford with 1,008 men; now, four months later, only about 325 were fit for duty.

And battle was imminent.

Hawley looked from the rebels' propitious position on the high ground, to the thousands of Union troops milling about the town. He was perplexed. "It appeared to us we were in a poor situation . . . directly under & at the mercy of the enemy's cannon & a river behind us to cut off our retreat," he wrote. "We could not help but feel that a great blunder had been made. Yet we comforted ourselves by the reflection that our great Gen[eral]s must know better than to make a move that any private could see was foolish."[2]

Frederick Burr Hawley of Bridgeport enlisted in the 14th Connecticut along with his younger brother in the summer of 1862. The day his regiment left Connecticut, Fred began a journal of his life as a soldier. He often jotted down unusual details. After racing into battle at Antietam, Fred had noted that mud in his shoes had chafed his feet—a singular observation when describing his first battle experience. At Fredericksburg, Hawley recorded what he ate for breakfast—boiled pork and hardtack—before the battle. Wounded a few hours later, he wrote matter-of-factly: "In the side of my shoe was a hole where the ball had entered from which the red blood was flowing." (Frederick Burr Hawley journal, Buck Zaidel collection.)

In fact, the general in charge, Ambrose Burnside, was in a bind. Back in the beginning of November, Burnside had reluctantly taken command of the Army of the Potomac after a frustrated Abraham Lincoln had removed Gen. George McClellan. Lincoln hoped he could rely on Burnside more than the stubbornly overcautious Little Mac.

Though Burnside felt himself unqualified to command, he came up with an excellent strategy to take Richmond, the Confederate capital. He planned to mass troops at Warrenton, Virginia, feigning advances on nearby towns. Once Robert E. Lee summoned his forces to defend the area, Burnside's troops would steal away, dashing southeast to cross the Rappahannock River into Fredericksburg, then rushing south to attack Richmond. To succeed, his army would need to act swiftly.

At first, Burnside's plan looked extremely promising. By November 17, his forces had given Lee the slip and were gathering near Falmouth, ready

Engraving of Fredericksburg, looking west toward Marye's Heights. (From a sketch by Alfred R. Waud, *Harper's Weekly*, January 3, 1863.)

to cross the Rappahannock River into Fredericksburg. But the rebels had destroyed the bridges, and the pontoon bridges Burnside had ordered hadn't arrived.

On Thanksgiving Day, Benjamin Hirst, a thirty-four-year-old sergeant in the 14th Connecticut, complained to his wife: "everything in the fighting line seems to have come to a stand still . . . when our division arrived opposite Fredericksburg we might have walked in the City without much trouble but to day it would be a big job for our whole Army to do it, and in my humble opinion the longer it is put off, the more difficult it will be."[3]

Days stretched into weeks. While thousands of Union soldiers waited on the northeast side of the river, Robert E. Lee swung his troops down to the river's southwest side, in Fredericksburg.

Had he chosen the location himself, Lee couldn't have found a landscape better suited to a Confederate victory. One of the Connecticut soldiers described it: "Fredericksburg is situated in a large amphitheatre, admirably adapted for defence. Directly in the rear of the town is a smooth field with a slightly ascending grade, extending back a little less than half a mile to the telegraph road, which is flanked by a stone wall, beyond which rises a ridge some what abruptly from a hundred to a hundred and fifty feet high."[4]

Burnside snuck his troops away from Lee at Warrenton (*upper left*), racing south. He planned to cross the Rappahannock River, sweep through Fredericksburg, and rush on to take Richmond. (*Seat of War in America*, Bacon & Co., 1863.)

The rebels quickly secured the high ground, dug in, and established their artillery. In the town below, their sharpshooters took up positions, while Stonewall Jackson's infantry prepared defenses south of the town.

More Confederate troops arrived every day, and still, Burnside waited. At last the pontoon bridges arrived, but Burnside's element of surprise had been lost. Instead of sweeping through Fredericksburg unhindered, he now faced an enemy with a virtually impregnable battle position. But if Burnside decided to abandon his plan, if he pulled back his army and instead went into winter quarters, wouldn't Lincoln—and perhaps the rest of the Union—think he was just like McClellan?

Finally Burnside decided to go ahead. He would throw across three pontoon bridges and send his troops to assault Lee.

On December 10, a feeling of expectancy spread rapidly through the Union lines. The men of the 27th Connecticut, a fresh nine-months' regiment, assembled for an inspection by their brigade commander, Col. Samuel K. Zook. The 27th soldiers knew they were at a disadvantage: not only were they were untested in combat, but their weapons were unreliable—"Austrian rifles of such an inferior order that no regular inspector would have passed them. Scarcely one of these weapons was without defects in the most essential particulars." Examining their guns, Zook pronounced them "unfit for service. One of his staff . . . remarked: 'Boys, if you can't discharge them, you can use the bayonet.'"[5] No doubt the men found this advice comforting.

Zook's aide-de-camp, Lt. Josiah Favill, went to work drilling the 27th Connecticut, which he found "wholly inexperienced."[6] Among the regiment's green soldiers was Henry Wing, a twenty-three-year-old from Goshen. He looked to the battle ahead with a sense of solemn duty: "I was chosen as one of the twelve boys in the color guard. We took it awfully serious. We swore we would die before our flag should be taken. You haven't any idea what a holy thing it was to us. I guess I felt about that flag like father seemed to feel about the family Bible. He always handled it gently, and I have seen him kiss it."[7]

Waiting along with the 14th and 27th Connecticut regiments were the state's 8th, 11th, 15th, 16th, and 21st Infantry Regiments, and a portion of Connecticut's 1st Heavy Artillery. Some of the boys had been killing time here for over three weeks, watching as their enemies across the river built fortifications.

At three in the morning on December 11, Union engineers began constructing the floating roads in the darkness. Dawn arrived with a providential fog that hid them from the Confederates' view, but at midmorning, the mist lifted "and a sheet of flame bursts from houses on the opposite bank, where hundreds of sharp-shooters lie concealed," wrote Winthrop Sheldon, a private in the 27th Connecticut.[8] The fire drove off the engineers, leaving the bridge unfinished.

Burnside's artillery units sent hundreds of shells hurtling across the river, temporarily silencing the rebel sharpshooters. But when the engineers resumed their work on the bridges, the snipers drove them off again. Later that day, a Michigan regiment crossed the river in boats under fire. Building by building, the Michigan men cleared out the Confederate sharpshooters, so that Burnside could begin the long process of crossing his troops—about 118,000 of them—along with horses, supply wagons, and artillery.

On the morning of December 12, fog and smoke from Fredericksburg's burning buildings created a cloud over the city, and shrouded the western rise held by the Confederates. The poor visibility prevented the Rebel artillery from decimating the Army of the Potomac as it crossed the bridges.

As the Fighting 14th marched into Fredericksburg, its band struck up "Dixie." The boys reacted gleefully.

But in the afternoon, the smoke and fog cleared off and the 14th men got an unobscured view of their surroundings. "The feeling of joy and exaltation in reaching Fredericksburg and finding it practically abandoned . . . gradually wore away and there came over the regiment a gloomy and solemn frame of mind. There was something unnatural in the quiet of the enemy . . . The range of hills back of the town had a grim and threatening appearance."[9] Fred Hawley and the others scrutinized the rebel guns at the top and realized that the 14th would not be singing "Dixie" the next day.

Over with the 27th Connecticut, which had also crossed into the city, Colonel Zook's aide noted: "we all felt shaky about coming events and there was very little hilarity."[10] From time to time, the Confederate artillery fired into the town. When a shell burst amid the ranks of the 27th, it killed several men and "almost paralyzed" the rest with fear.[11]

Downtown Fredericksburg had taken a terrible beating, first from the Union artillery barrages the day before, and then from the Union soldiers who were even now busy looting. "The city was thoroughly pillaged that day in a manner beyond description," wrote Henry Perkins Goddard of the 14th. "Every house and store in the city bears the marks of our terrific bombardment . . . Dead and wounded rebs lay all everywhere, and every house and store has been ransacked. The boys are all eating pickles, preserves, hams, flour cakes, etc., out of silver, glass and china, smoking 10 cent cigars . . . stuffing their pockets with chewing tobacco . . . and reclining on sofas, reading from private libraries."[12]

But while they were feasting on pickles, and smoking cigars, the soldiers found their gazes returning to the western heights. Henry Wing of the 27th Connecticut had never experienced battle, but he knew that "those bluffs were stuck full of Confederate cannons and rifle pits, and that if they ever opened fire a chicken couldn't live on the field." Still, Wing recalled, "when [General] Hancock came around . . . and told us we were to be ready to go out in the morning, we cheered and cheered him."[13]

That night, some soldiers wrapped themselves in their blankets and slept in the streets, shivering. Harry Goddard, a twenty-year-old lieutenant in the 14th Connecticut, was lucky to spend the night in one of the damaged houses, along with his captain, Elijah Gibbons, and 2nd Lt. David Canfield. The impending battle overlaid a sense of solemnity on them all.

> Never shall I forget the scene as Captain Gibbons read us from an old Bible found in the house, till the flickering fire-light by which he read died out, and bidding us each good-night, he retired. Gibbons was in his sweetest mood that night, and Canfield made many anxious inquiries as to his views of life and death, and announcing his willingness to face the grim conqueror for the sake of his country and God, relapsed into silence. That was our last night together.[14]

The Fighting 14th

Before dawn, the men of the 14th Connecticut were roused and ordered to eat breakfast and be ready to fall in at any moment. Frederick Burr Hawley, a Bridgeport native, had enlisted in Company A along with other local boys, but today as 2nd lieutenant he would lead a different company. He worried about being separated from his younger brother and their friends.

> I called on the boys in Co A, all had serious faces & seemed to think that very unpleasant & serious business was before us. I bid my boys good bye & told them not to expose themselves needlessly & to look out for one another. I was in command of Co K & should probably not see much of them during the day . . .
>
> Formed line by 6 o'c and ordered farther forward (2 or 3 streets higher up) . . . Shells & Solid shot from the enemy often striking very near us . . . The enemy could . . . plainly see our troops near with our colors flying. They fired low   2 of the balls went through the lower windows in the church. One of them so low as to cut (nearly) off the legs of a poor fellow. His awful cries of pain, as they bore him past us was heart rending to hear.
>
> At 11 o'c we were ordered to 'Fix Bayonetts' & cap pieces & Forward March.[15]

Maj. Gen. William H. French, a beefy man with pale blue eyes and a thick, drooping moustache, was leading the 14th Regiment's division. French halted in front of the corps commander, Gen. Darius Couch, who gave him his orders. "French did not like the orders," wrote Harry Goddard. "I heard him expostulate with Couch but to no avail."[16]

French could see as well as anyone that the orders were ludicrous: charge uphill across an open plain, under heavy artillery and infantry fire, and take the enemy's entrenchments at point of bayonet.

The rebel artillery kept up a relentless fire as French moved his troops out of town and across the railroad tracks, the men moving at the double-quick. Fred Hawley wrote in horror:

> The pale faces of the dead & wounded were thick in our path   the most frightful mutilations the human body can suffer—Packs, arms, clothes etc scattered in the ground. Men could be seen dropping all around us under the deadly fire. The shells & cannon balls screamed & crashed through the brick buildings & bounded about us like marbles in front of us . . .
>
> . . . The man on my right was cut in two by a cannon ball. Without a word he dropped On every side are the dead & the wounded—many of the wounded crying for help, but we can take no notice of them. The enemy have a fine position. On a hill ½ a mile back of the city.[17]

What lay ahead? "In rear of the town is a broken plain, traversed about midway by a canal or ditch, running from right to left . . . impassable, except at the bridges," reported General Couch. "A little beyond it the ground rises, forming a cover, behind which the troops were able to deploy . . . The intermediate ground was obstructed here and there by houses and garden fences."[18]

Leaving the safety of the town, where buildings had shielded them from the enemy's sight, Union troops had to cross an open plain with a slight rise. Confederate artillery hammered them with shells while the blue coats moved at the double-quick. As they waited their turns to cross a plank spanning a small canal, the soldiers knew they were sitting ducks for the Rebel gunners.

Then the ground gradually sloped up to a substantial stone wall. Behind that wall rose the bluffs called Marye's Heights; atop them, the enemy's artillery stood ensconced behind sturdy breastworks. The Rebels had cunningly arranged their big guns in a crescent shape that curved down the hill on either side—requiring the Union troops to walk into a "grand semicircle of death," as one Connecticut soldier put it.[19] The curve allowed the Confederates to fire at the Union soldiers from three sides at once.

And behind the stone wall at the base of the bluffs, crouched hundreds of Rebel infantrymen. Waiting.

The soldiers of the 14th could see what awaited them. As the moment of battle drew near, some of the men found ways to evade it: they feigned illness, or hid in sheltered areas when their regiment advanced into the fight. But mostly, the men and boys marched forward into the inevitable. Why?

Their reasons were as diverse as they were. Some men acted out of a sense of honor, or love for their country. Many were afraid they'd seem cowardly—to their comrades or themselves. Some soldiers were responding to the simple instinct to defeat their enemy. And by now the men realized that their charge was part of a larger plan that depended on each unit doing its share, each soldier doing his duty.

Frederick Burr Hawley had been a lieutenant for only a month. Shepherding the thirty-odd men in his company, he advanced through the storm of artillery fire coming from three directions.

> When about $1/3$ of the distance to the Rebel batteries we were ordered to pros-
> trate ourselves. Every man hugged the ground for dear life. The Rebs had us

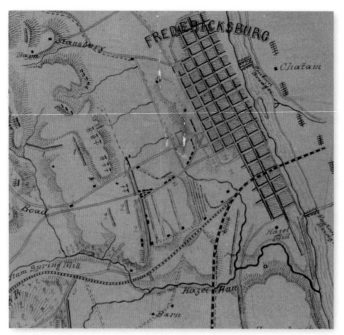

This small section of a map of the Battle of Fredericksburg shows in *red* the Confederate artillery along the crest of the hill. The *blue* lines of Union troops moving up the hill included the 14th and 27th Connecticut, heading directly at the Rebel infantry dug in behind a four-foot high stone wall. Map by William W. Blackford, circa 1866.

in good range and the balls & shells whizzed & burst all around us often striking in our ranks throwing dirt in our faces & killing & wounding our men Many times, for an instant we would think we were hit so very near our heads the balls came . . .

We lay in this position 15 minutes losing men every moment without being able to do anything Word was sent to Col Palmer who was commanding the Brigade asking what was to be done We could not remain here & be slaughtered without lifting a hand. He replied he did not know what to do. That he had no orders, we fell back 15 or 20 paces thinking that we would not be so much exposed. But it made little difference . . .[20]

A short distance away, in Company D, nineteen-year-old Cpl. Charles Lyman flattened himself to the ground beside his buddies. "Symonds and Dart and I were lying side by side," wrote Lyman; "[John] Symonds on the right, [Oliver] Dart next, and I next, with a fence-post about four inches square between Dart's head and mine . . . A shell from the battery on our right burst near us, and an irregularly shaped fragment, probably about three inches long and two inches wide, struck the ground in front of Symonds, throwing sand in his eyes and permanently destroying his sight; lifting from its contact with the ground it tore away part of Dart's upper jaw and nose and struck the post directly opposite my head."[21]

"Poor Oliver Dart," said his comrade, Benjamin Hirst. "As he rolled over he looked as though his whole face was shot away."[22]

For the regiment to remain where it lay was ludicrous. But the 14th was about to pass from the frying pan into the fire. "The order finally came from our Col. Perkins 'Forward 14th Every man up and forward like men,'" wrote Frederick Hawley. "Quickly the men rose up and formed our line & onward we pressed into the hotter fire of musketry."

While the Federals had remained in the distance, Confederate artillery sent long-range shells and cannonballs spinning toward them. But as the blue coats got closer, the rebel gunners added canister, a casing stuffed with dozens of marble-sized iron balls that sprayed in a huge swath when the casing split apart. The projectiles raked the oncoming men, and screams could be heard above the noise of the guns. The 14th still came on.

Hawley wrote:

we came up with the Brigade in front. They were lying close to the ground & firing. Our men followed their example. We could plainly see where the fire came from but could not get much of a chance at them because they were under cover. The order came again to "Forward" & while advancing at a rapid pace I felt a sharp sting & a numb feeling in my foot & at the same time fell wounded. In the side of my shoe was a hole where the ball had entered from which the red blood was flowing.

I got up & limped a short distance to the rear . . . tied my handkerchief tight around my leg just above the ankle . . .[23]

For Lieutenant Hawley, the battle was finished. But it was just beginning for young Henry Goddard of Company B, who was following his captain, Elijah Gibbons, into the chaos:

We started up and away—over the hill, over fences, over ditches, up to the extreme front where rebel bullets falling like hail were sounding the death rattle of many (ah! So many) noble Union soldiers. Here we halted and poured forth volley after volley at the infernal cowards hidden in their breastworks. The grape and canister were mowing our men down in swaths. Shells actually crushed the bones of men like glass. After ten minutes or a little more, I observed that my company had melted away, not a man of them to be found. Capt. Gibbons was no where near and I looked round to see our color bearers running back and all the troops just starting to leave.

Left: Lt. Henry ("Harry") Goddard was just twenty years old when he charged forward with the 14th Connecticut at Fredericksburg. Wounded slightly, he was still able to help his bleeding colonel off the field. In a letter to his mother, he called it "The proudest day in Harry Goddard's life." (Letter of Henry P. Goddard, December 14, 1862, courtesy of Calvin Goddard Zon.)

Right: Lt. Col. Sanford Perkins commanded Connecticut's 14th Regiment at Fredericksburg. Though some of his men considered him fussy and difficult, Perkins proved to be a gutsy leader under fire, falling with a bullet in the neck while advancing with raised sword.

I hesitated a moment, but saw Col. Perkins wave his sword and cry "Fall in," "Form in order," "Don't go back!" I swung my sword up and shouted "Form" . . . But could see none of our regiment save three or four . . . The whole army had commenced to run like blazes. I turned again to the Colonel to see him struck in the neck and to catch him as he fell.

I grasped and waved my sword, shouted and screamed "For God's sake, come back 14th, come and save your Colonel." Three of Co. B came and that was all the regiment left there. The Colonel begged us to carry him off the field, when we pledged our lives to save him, or die, or be taken with him.[24]

The 14th's colonel was gone, as were its major and three captains. Command suddenly fell to Capt. Samuel H. Davis, twenty-three years old and the regimental scamp.[25] Known more for his insubordination than his leadership, Davis failed to rally the 14th men who were left.

Without a leader, the regiment's charge faltered. The chaplain wrote: "On pressed the rest . . . reaching to within one hundred and fifty yards or less of the wall, when, hopeless of success, most dropped beside the huge fence posts or into little hollows for slight protection and to use their guns as best they might . . . "[26] Here they stayed until darkness, when they could fall back to the town.

✳ ✳ ✳

George Foote

In battle, each soldier had to make a choice: risk death, or run. For men like George Foote, a devotion to honor and duty left just one path.

Foote had left his Guilford farm to enlist for the Union as soon as the war began, fighting with the 3rd Connecticut at Bull Run before reenlisting as sergeant in the 14th Connecticut.

Soon after the Battle of Antietam, Sergeant Foote got sick. Shivering and weak with fever, he insisted on reporting for duty. He marched mile after mile in the ranks until he finally fainted and was carried to a wagon.

George Augustus Foote Jr. came from a Guilford family steeped in duty and determination. His older sister, Harriet Hawley, longed to fight alongside Union soldiers. His cousin Uriah Parmelee gave his life for the cause of emancipation.

At Fredericksburg, he was still so sick that his captain directed him to sit out the battle. "He replied, 'there are skulks enough without me,' and he . . . 'went in,' [to battle] as cheerful and cool as if it were a breakfast at home."[27]

His cousin recounted that as Foote's regiment advanced across the battlefield, "A bit of shell took away the bottom of his cartridge box letting all his cartridges fall on the ground, but he coolly picked them up and put them in his pocket, just then a bullet pierced his canteen; seeing the water running out he put his mouth to the hole which the bullet had made, remarking he would have 'one more drink.'"[28]

Minutes later, George was hit in the leg and fell. One of his comrades wrote:

After lying on the field a short time, he tried to rise, but was instantly fired upon again by the rebels, wounding him slightly in the head and the hip. All the rest of that awful day, he lay still where he had fallen. Three times our men charged over him, of course trampling on his wounded leg, while he, half delirious, begged them to kill him to end his sufferings. But no one had time then to attend to one poor wounded fellow.

That night, he managed to crawl off to a little hut near the field, where some other wounded men had hung out a yellow flag. Here they lay with a little hard tack, and still less water, till the third day after the fight, when they were visited by a rebel officer, with a few men. He spoke roughly to them, asking, "what they were here for?" and two or three began whining, and saying, they "did not want to fight the South, . . ." when Foote cooly lifted his head and said, "I came to fight rebels, and I have found them, and if ever I get well, I will come back and fight them again." "Bully for you," said the officer, "you are a boy that I like," and at once gave him some water out of his own canteen, sent one of his men for more water, washed his leg and foot, and bound it up as well as he could, paroled him, and helped him across the river to the Lacy-house hospital. In fact, he and his men gave him a blanket, and cheered him as the wagon drove off.

Foote said, afterward, "I did not know but he would blow my brains out on the spot, but I did not mean he should think we were all sneaks." He was soon removed from the Lacy-house to Armory-square hospital, where his leg (which had been hastily amputated at the Lacy-house) was again operated upon, Dr. Bliss finding it necessary to cut the bone still shorter. His sufferings were thus protracted and very terrible, although, he had the constant care of a devoted brother, who left home to find him the moment he heard that he was "missing," as he was at first reported.[29]

The survival rate for such amputations was about 50 percent—George was one of the lucky ones. Months later, his brother Christopher was able to bring him home to Nut Plains, their Guilford neighborhood. It was a long and painful trip. George slowly gained strength but never recovered. He turned again to farming, but found it was beyond him. Over the next six years, his family watched as he grew weak and frail, finally dying in 1869 at the age of thirty-four.

Years later, an officer from the 14th described George with deep respect: "An unusually strong and healthy man, attached to life, to his friends, to his chosen pursuit, farming, and to his dear old home at 'Nut Plains,' he yet never regretted for a moment that he had given himself for his country, but said to his mother, even in his last days, that 'he would do it all over again, for the same cause.'"[30]

✳ ✳ ✳

The 27th Connecticut

Though the 14th had arrived in Fredericksburg with reduced numbers, its men had already experienced battle. The same couldn't be said of Connecticut's 27th Regiment, whose men had been nearly frozen with terror the day before, when a shell exploded in their midst.[31]

On the morning of the battle, the regiment massed in the streets of Fredericksburg. "At this moment," one of the men remembered, "General Hancock rides up to the Twenty-seventh, and leaning forward in his saddle, with his right arm upraised, briefly addresses them: 'You are the only Connecticut regiment in my division. Bring no dishonor upon the State you represent.'"[32]

At the command to advance, the jumpy soldiers moved ahead into deafening chaos: "the incessant rattle of the rifles, rising at times to a continued roar, the shouts of the charging columns, the spiteful crack of the light batteries, the screaming missiles in the air, and over all the terrible thunder of the heavy guns upon either heights," as one man described it.[33] The regiment passed out of the town, crossed the canal, and moved up the sloping plain, passing the prostrate troops of the 14th Connecticut.

Lieutenant Favill, advancing with the 27th, wrote: "in full line of battle, we marched directly forward . . . the rebel guns plowing great furrows in our ranks at every step; all we could do was to close up the gaps and press forward. When within some 300 yards of the rebel works, the men burst into a cheer and charged for the heights."[34]

"We were mighty proud of ourselves for a minute," said Henry Wing of the 27th's color guard.[35]

But in an instant, everything changed. As the blue-coated soldiers rushed up the hill toward the long stone wall, from behind it hundreds of rebel infantrymen rose as one and fired. "Immediately the hill in front was hid from view by a continuous sheet of flame from base to summit," wrote Lieutenant Favill in awe. "The rebel infantry poured in a murderous fire while their guns from every available point fired shot and shell and canister."[36]

The 27th Connecticut "went down like wheat does under a scythe, hardly a head standing," Wing said dismally.[37]

"They were brave men," wrote a Confederate infantryman, "and it looked like a pity to kill them."[38]

Henry Wing remembered:

> I was hit pretty quick in the leg, and I guess I didn't know much for a time. When I came to I raised up and looked for the flag. I could see it going down—coming up—going down—coming up . . .
>
> I could not see the flag any more and I began to worry about it. I just had to be sure that our boys still had it, and I started to crawl to where I thought it might be, and then I got hit in the hand. After a little, I crawled on again, and then I found the flag. And I found some more of our boys dead; there were ten killed there.[39]

"The losses were so tremendous that before we knew it our momentum was gone, and the charge was a failure," Favill declared. Dropping down, the survivors flattened themselves to the earth, some hundred yards from the stone wall. Prone, the men would load their weapons and get off a quick shot from time to time.

And "many were the men who stood to fire and fell back wounded or a corpse," wrote Sam Waldron, then a sixteen-year-old in Company A. For the Confederate infantrymen behind the wall, it was just a matter of waiting until one of the Union soldiers rose, an easy mark.

In Waldron's company of New Haven boys, eighteen-year-old Cpl. Billy Goodwin, "the life of the Company," insisted on rising to fire at the enemy. Sam related: "He had loaded and fired several times until admonished by his comrade that it was a foolish exposure of his person and did no good but again he loaded and rose on one knee to give them just one more shot and while bending his head and in the act of cocking his piece was struck by a bullet just over the forehead which passed completely through his head killing him instantly. A bright light was extinguished. A brave heart at rest."[40]

For hours, the rookies of the 27th remained pinned down on the slope, watching while "line after line of fresh troops, like ocean waves, followed each other in rapid succession."[41] Lying prostrate with his 27th comrades, Win Sheldon witnessed the soldiers' advance:

> How splendidly they charge! with what a perfect line! We can look into the faces of the men as they come on. Nothing apparently can withstand their onset. They come steadily to within a few paces of where we lie. Then bursts forth from the rebel works an iron tempest . . . Showers of bullets went whistling by or struck the ground in every direction, while pieces of shell, bits of old iron, grape and canister, rained down . . . Arrested in its course, the line wavers, fires a few volleys, then scatters.[42]

Not a single Union soldier would reach the stone wall. Lieutenant Favill wrote painfully:

> Looking over the field in rear, from where I lay, the plain seemed swarming with men, but it was easy to see that the attack was a failure, and that nothing that could henceforth be done would amount to anything . . . I wondered while I lay there how it all came about that these thousands of men in broad daylight were trying their best to kill each other. Just then there was no romance, no glorious pomp, nothing but disgust for the genius who planned so frightful a slaughter.[43]

Doomed

The assault on Marye's Heights had been doomed from the beginning. Henry Goddard later noted: "a London Times correspondent, who sat by Gen. Lee's side and watched the charges of the 2d corps, wrote that 'no men on earth can be braver than those who thrice essayed to carry Marye's Heights.'"[44]

As the early darkness fell, the Union troops trapped on the hill began their retreat. The 14th Regiment's Frederick Burr Hawley, shot through the foot, had managed to limp down the hill into town a few hours earlier. There was no sign of his regiment, so he and two other wounded soldiers made their way into the basement of a house near the river.

Though Corporal Billy Goodwin struck a solemn pose for his photograph, the eighteen-year-old had the reputation of being the life of his company. The oldest of his parents' six sons, Billy had been a clerk in New Haven before enlisting.

We found here 2 poor white women and some small children & an old Negro man . . . Early in the evening . . . 4 more soldiers came in . . . They went out & got some pieces of fence & built a fire in the fireplace. & soon each one had a cup of coffee. Those that had anything to eat shared with others who had none—without knowing where or when they would get more.

We stretched out on the floor . . . the sharp rattle of musketry was often heard during the night. It sounded as if it were in the next street above us . . . We did not know the result of the battle. Thought as likely as not that we would be made prisoners by morning.[45]

Outside, the city of Fredericksburg was in tumult. "Lines of troops were under arms in the streets, ready to meet the enemy should they attempt to follow up their advantage and drive the army across the river," wrote one Connecticut man. "Crowds of soldiers, all excited by the events of the day, moved rapidly along the sidewalks. Processions of stretcher bearers tenderly conveyed their mangled freight to the hospitals. The eloquent red [hospital] flag waved from almost every house, suggesting that the surgeons were diligently at work, while the glare of candles from the windows added to the wildness of the scene without."[46]

For the surgeons, the next seventy-two hours would be one long nightmare. Overwhelmed, exhausted, and undersupplied, the doctors would attempt to treat thousands of wounded, extracting musket balls, amputating limbs, and bandaging lacerations.

Dr. T. Morton Hills, assistant surgeon to the 27th Connecticut, gave his wife a glimpse of their ordeal, writing: "Two other Surgeons & myself operating Saturday all day & till 1 oclock [Sunday] morning. I laid down on the bare floor without even any pillow—pulled my overcoat over me

Thomas Morton Hills was only twenty-three years old, and hadn't graduated from medical school when he became the 27th Regiment's assistant surgeon. Hills used this surgical kit to saw off shattered legs and arms, and extract bullets.

(wounded man had my blanket) & slept till morning. Yesterday we operated all day till late & all today . . . I have amputated . . . quite a number of times a dozen I should think I have not counted them up—have taken out any quantity of balls—I have been operating all the time for 3 days."[47]

A young corporal from the 14th Connecticut remembered a scene at his division's field hospital. "Well towards midnight a man was put upon the rude operating table under a big buttonball tree in the yard . . . for an amputation of the leg above the knee and I called to assist. My function was to sit on a cracker box opposite the surgeon with a candle in each hand, and by the light of these two candles the amputation was made."[48]

"The city is filled with the pieces of brave men who went whole into the conflict," said Samuel Fiske of the 14th. "Every basement and floor is covered with pools of blood. Limbs, in many houses, lie in heaps; and surgeons are exhausted."[49]

And hundreds of wounded had been left on the battlefield. Charles Lyman told the story of Jerry Grady, his comrade in the 14th Regiment. As Charles retreated after the battle, he found Jerry, "a large muscular Irishman" in his late forties, crawling along. He'd been shot in the foot, the bullet entering his heel, traveling through the length of his foot and out between his toes. "The wound was a severe one, the bones of the foot being badly broken and crushed. I bound it up with his handkerchief as well as I could, and at his request filled his clay pipe with plug tobacco and lighted it for him," wrote Lyman.

Lyman, Jerry Grady, and perhaps a hundred other wounded soldiers took shelter in an unfinished icehouse or cellar dug into a hill. Only nineteen years old, Charles did his best to bandage the men's wounds, using handkerchiefs and strips ripped from blankets or shirts—anything to stop the bleeding.

> As the night came on and the fighting ceased, I determined to get Jerry Grady to a hospital . . . got him on my back, with his arms around my neck, taking a leg under each of my arms . . . By the time I had reached the hay-stacks, I was so nearly exhausted that I was sure I would not be able to get him into town without help, and as there was no help to be had, decided to get up as near to a hay-stack as possible, placing it between us and the enemy, and make the night of it there.
>
> On reaching the place I found the ground literally covered with corpses, with not a space among them large enough to accommodate two men, so I laid Jerry down and went within fifteen or twenty feet of the first stack and moved several bodies, making a clear space about six feet square, then went back on the field and picked up several blankets any number of which could be found scattered about, and made as comfortable a bed as possible in the space I had cleared. Into this bed I put Jerry, and then lay down beside him. Here we spent the night, and both slept some, I, more than he, because I was without pain, while he suffered intensely.
>
> Early in the morning I started for town . . . to get help, and as there was yet no truce for burying the dead, the sharp-shooters of the enemy gave me a pretty warm reception . . .

I first applied for help at a temporary hospital, located in a wagon shop, just in the edge of the town, but found no one there willing to go back on the field with me . . . I finally found a man who was willing to take the risks involved and go with me. I felt then that this man had the true spirit of a soldier and comrade, and told him so, and thanked him as warmly as I could for his willingness to render a service of humanity, which involved real danger from the sharp-shooters' fire . . . we went to the haystack and returned with our burden without harm, though many bullets came uncomfortably near us.

We left Jerry in the wagon shop where I had first gone for help, and after he had been made as comfortable as possible, I started off in search of my regiment . . . and was welcomed as one come back from the dead.[50]

The same morning, Frederick Burr Hawley awoke in the cellar where he had taken shelter, to find he could no longer raise his foot.

Two friends volunteered to carry me to a hospital so I placed an arm around each of their necks they joined hands making a seat on which I rode to the hospital about a ¼ of a mile distant . . .

The building used as a hospital to which I was taken was a fine house . . . filled full of wounded as thick as they could lye. The halls & portico likewise every foot of room in the yard were a number waiting their chance to have amputations performed. 4 or 5 surgeons were around with their knifes like butchers ready to cut up the human beef—poor victims few of them thought they would ever come to this.

I got a seat on a bench in the yard. I sat here about 3 hours. Had some coffee, tea & pork steak given me   the nurses seemed to be doing all they could for the comfort of the wounded. A little while after I arrived Dr. Rockwell came to me & dressed my foot with a bandage wet with cold water.[51]

Stretcher-bearers continued to bring wounded off the battlefield. Among the dead and wounded of the 27th Connecticut's color guard, they found Henry Wing, wounded in the leg and the hand. After lying on the field overnight, Wing regained consciousness in one of the Union's improvised hospitals in a Fredericksburg house.

The next thing I knew I was lying on top of a piano. There were doctors beside me, and they had made a mark around my leg and another around my arm; and when I saw that they meant to cut off my leg and my arm it made me mad, and I began to curse them. They just took me off the piano and threw me out on the grass. You couldn't blame them. There were twelve doctors for fifteen hundred wounded men, and they couldn't have patients fighting them. They didn't think I would live anyway.[52]

At length, Wing was transported to Hammond Hospital.

> The doctor came around and looked at me and went by—didn't say anything. Then a Sister of Charity [a Catholic nurse] came and asked me if she should get me a priest . . . "Does that mean you think I am going to die?" "Yes," she said, "You cannot live overnight."
>
> "I am not going to die," I said. "Before I left home my mother read from the ninety-first Psalm: 'A thousand shall fall at thy side, and ten thousand at thy right hand; but it shall not come nigh thee. You are coming back, Henry,' she said. You don't suppose that I am going to die after that do you?"[53]

Henry E. Wing of Goshen, a private in the 27th Connecticut, faced double amputation after Fredericksburg. Improbably, Wing went on to an important (and dangerous) career as a war correspondent, and had a personal connection to President Lincoln. (From Henry E. Wing, *When Lincoln Kissed Me.*)

Wing had the attention of a young, pretty sister who first used scissors to cut off his two shattered fingers, and then spent a week flushing his wounds day and night. Three months later, Henry Wing left on crutches for his home in Connecticut. He didn't have Sister Mary—whom he'd wanted to marry—but he did have his arm and leg.

Henry Wing, Frederick Burr Hawley, and Jerry Grady all survived.[54] Scores of Connecticut men did not. The 14th's esteemed captain, Elijah Gibbons, had fallen on the field, his left femur shattered. Lt. David Canfield bent over him—and gave his life, killed by a shot in the head. Under fire, Captain Gibbons had been "picked up by the men who loved him so dearly, and conveyed to the Falmouth side of the river, where he lingered in great suffering but sweet resignation for six days until the 19th of December—when he died," wrote Harry Goddard.[55] "Captain Gibbons was buried on a pleasant hillside looking toward the rising sun, just beyond the outskirts of the camp," wrote the regiment's historian. "The men moving slowly with reversed arms behind the coffin, the weird and mournful dirge from the band and the volley of musketry over the grave, all were different from the ceremonies the men were familiar with at home and yet seemed not inappropriate."[56]

AFTER THE FIGHTING

The day after the battle, Union troops milled around nervously in Fredericksburg. "A disagreeable uncertainty hung over every moment of the day,"

The 14th Connecticut had existed just four months when it entered the Battle of Fredericksburg. In that short time, Capt. Elijah Gibbons had earned his men's deep respect and devotion. After his death at age thirty-one, "his company and his fellow-officers missed his influence and example sadly," wrote Harry Goddard; "at our regimental re-unions, years after his death, we somehow feel as if we needed him with us." (Henry P. Goddard, *Memorial of Deceased Officers of the 14th Regiment Connecticut Volunteers*, pp. 12–13.)

remembered a soldier of the 27th Connecticut.[57] Would the Confederates attack? Would Burnside order another assault?

But there was no assault. Instead, the Union troops looked for their wounded and buried their dead. The two Connecticut regiments that had seen battle were decimated: the 14th Regiment had 118 casualties, while the green 27th lost 114.

Even the commanders were shaken by their men's useless sacrifice. Colonel Zook wrote to a friend:

> I walked over the field, close under the enemy's picket line, last night about 3 o'clock. The ground was strewn thickly with corpses of the hero's who perished there on Saturday. I never realized before what war was. I never before felt so horribly since I was born. To see men dashed to pieces by shot & torn into shreds by shells during the heat and crash of battle is bad enough God knows, but to walk alone amongst slaughtered brave in the "still small hours" of the night would make the bravest man living "blue." God grant I may never have to repeat my last night's experience.[58]

After the battle, "Scores of our wounded from the fight passed by," wrote Fred Lucas of the 2nd Heavy Artillery. "One squad were new recruits. Nearly every man had some trophy of the battlefield. One with his left arm broken had 3 muskets on his back. He took them from the hands of dead rebels on the field. Another with his scalp nearly torn from his head, himself streched in an ambulance, and still clung with the greatest tenacity to an officers broken sword. Nearly all had some traitors weapon as a memento of the 'Battle of Fredericksburg.'"[59]

Wilbur D. Fiske of the 14th had perhaps the most personal souvenir of Fredericksburg. After a surgeon dug a rebel bullet out of a "frightful wound" in Fiske's chest, the twenty-one-year-old sergeant preserved the lead projectile which had nearly taken his life. (Charles D. Page, *History of the Fourteenth Regiment, Connecticut Volunteer Infantry* [Meriden, CT: Horton Printing Co., 1906], p. 86.) Despite the seriousness of his wound, Sergeant Fiske returned to his regiment. Before a year had passed, he was wounded in battle again, this time at Bristoe Station, Virginia. After his discharge, Fiske had the Fredericksburg bullet encased in an engraved gold watch fob, an ever-present reminder of his close escape.

* * *

Connecticut's 8th Regiment, which had avoided battle, waited with the other troops in the city. Many of the men were ill with dysentery, but not John Q. Thayer, nineteen, who found himself hankering for pancakes:

> It was learned that somewhere at the north end of Main street some flour had been discovered. An occasional arrival of a haversack full of it in our neighborhood suggested the thought to Sergeant Irwin and myself that if we had some

of it, we could make some pancakes that would faintly resemble those we had in early boyhood with maple syrup on them, in far away Connecticut.

Irwin assured me that he understood the process of making pancakes . . . if I would get the flour he would do the mixing and cooking, so after having prepared to cook them, by hammering the rivets out of a length of old stove pipe and flattening it; providing a few bricks to lay it upon, and gathering some fence pickets for fuel, I started up street in search of flour. I was occasionally encouraged in my expedition by meeting some of the boys with their haversack filled with the precious stuff, and was told by them an abundance of it was left in an old brick warehouse . . . I entered and found a large number of barrels therein . . . hastily filled my haversack and returned.

Irwin as was myself was delighted . . . He procured some water from the river in a basin he had borrowed from a comrade, and without yeast, and with salt and water only, mixed and tried to make flour pancakes—with plaster of paris.[60]

✳ ✳ ✳

The troops grew more and more jittery staying in Fredericksburg while Lee's triumphant troops overlooked their every move. "It was plain that something must be done, and that very soon," wrote one soldier. "The army must fight, or evacuate the city. Every few minutes during the day we were ordered to fall in. The expectation was universal that we were again to be led to the attack."[61]

The night of December 15 came dark and foggy. Sam Waldron of the 27th wrote: "At midnight and without a whisper the 27th moved quickly down the street to the Pontoon Bridge past soldiers who stood like spectres ready to loosen the moorings which held the Pontoons to the bank. A brief halt and of the 27th which had crossed the bridges four days before one third were killed or wounded and the rest of the little band left the slaughter pen behind them and stood on what seemed to them safety and home."[62]

An image of slain captain Bernard Schweizer marks this letter written by his brother-in-arms, Capt. R. P. Cowles of Connecticut's 27th Regiment. Months after the battle, Cowles wrote asking permission to cross into Fredericksburg to recover the remains of Schweizer, who'd been killed by Confederate artillery early in the battle while their regiment formed near Caroline Street. Cowles noted that Captain Schweizer "was interred alone in a rough Box." Cowles and his comrades hoped to send the body to New Haven, where Schweizer's widow and two small sons lived. Confederate authorities denied the request. Schweizer had led a company of about 100 men of German birth or descent. Though he himself was an immigrant, Schweizer "went to the field purely from a sense of duty," wrote one of the men in his regiment. (Winthrop D. Sheldon, *The Twenty-Seventh: A Regimental History*, p. 34.)

Once across the Rappahannock, the Union troops felt safe. But now—now they had time to reflect on the battle. "OH! my heart is sick and sad," wrote Samuel Fiske of the 14th. "Another tremendous, terrible, murderous butchery of brave men."[63]

"Is there one who witnessed that Roll Call on the 16th Dec. that can readily forget it," asked Sam Waldron forlornly. "Sergt Blair and Wilmot did not answer to their names. We missed the merry 'Aye' of Corporal Goodwin, the answer of Corporal Cornwall, the hearty 'here' of Frank Johnson and the quiet response of Hilliard and Fairchild. As the names were called of the wounded we thought 'Will he die'—of the dead—'At peace.'"[64]

"The army is pretty demoralized now," Harry Goddard wrote grimly, "and all of us say a good many hard things of our commanders."[65]

Over 12,000 Union soldiers fell at Fredericksburg. The Confederates' casualties totaled less than half that number.

"In these dark moments when the tension of the heart strings was so intense as to be nearly breaking," wrote the 14th Regiment's historian, the men "felt that their lives were being made the playthings of the high officers in command. That they were sacrificed . . . and thrown against the impregnable intrenchments that skirted Marye's Heights by obstinate stupidity."[66] Their duty to their country, their determination to fight the good fight—what did they matter?

A soldier of the 15th, which had seen little action, was able to paint a more cheerful picture of the situation as the two armies faced each other across the river, and Christmas approached.

On the 21st [of December], the regiment was on picket on the Rappahannock, in front of the city [Fredericksburg]. The citizens had returned to their homes, and the Confederate lines were brought again to the waters edge. Considerable chaffing and some trading in coffee and tobacco were done across the stream . . .

Christmas came warm and serene, a surprise even to the citizens of that latitude. Many private boxes reached the camp in season, and these, with a special issue of fresh beef and vegetables, made the occasion an enjoyable one. The night was clear and the moon at its full. It was no hour for strife or bitterness. Where but a few days before the hot muzzles of a hundred and more cannon on each side had hurled death across the narrow valley, now stood

"Tobacco sent across the Rappahannock by the rebel pickets to the Union Soldiers sending [news]papers in return," wrote the 15th Connecticut's William H. Catlin of the souvenir he sent home to Meriden. "It was sent on a board fitted with a sail and rudder." It wasn't unusual for Union and Confederate soldiers to interact soon after they'd been fighting to the death. Lucien R. Dunham, a Connecticut native serving in the 13th New Hampshire, wrote to his brother in February of 1863 from Falmouth about trading and talking with Confederates across the Rappahannock: "it dident sean like they wear enmeys to us if they would let the soilders come together they would settel this prutey quick." (Letter of Lucien R. Dunham, February 3, 1863, Connecticut Historical Society, Hartford.)

various military bands playing the old time tunes of the Union to the listening thousands of soldiers. As the night wore along, the musical selections on both sides shaded off to "The Girl I Left Behind Me," and finally as if by a common impulse, the strains of "Home, Sweet Home" broke out right, left and centre from friend and foe, till the air was tremulous with melody.[67]

As 1862 drew to a close, soldiers on both sides became contemplative. The war would soon enter its third year.

On New Year's Eve, Pvt. George Hubbard of the 14th Connecticut sat beside the campfire, along with six of his brothers-in-arms. Nearly ninety percent of their regiment was gone—sick, wounded, or dead. Scratching out a letter to a friend back in Connecticut, Hubbard admitted to feeling ambivalent: "Here we sit over fire tonight, the 7 of us, but little do we know how soon some one of us may be separated from the rest. We are living at present chiefly upon Hard-Tack, Salt Pork and Faith," he finished, philosophically, "the last article being our chief subsistence."[68]

In Washington, President Lincoln, reflecting on the useless sacrifice, said quietly, "If there is a worse place than Hell, I am in it."

CHAPTER EIGHT

Who Wouldn't Be a Soldier?

LIFE IN CAMP

Winter was coming on hard in Virginia. Already the ground was starting to freeze up, making it harder for the 14th Connecticut men who were trying to dig a double grave on the outskirts of their camp.

The two Hollister brothers in Company K had gone weeks without blankets, overcoats, or tents. The regiment's gear had been collected before Antietam, and that was the last the men saw of it. Some had been lucky enough to scrounge coats or blankets from the battlefields, but not the Hollisters. As typhus fever enveloped the regiment, twenty-year-old Francis and eighteen-year-old Frederick had to "crouch scantily clad all night long over a smoky camp-fire," shaking with cold and fever. Typhus victims endured blinding headaches, coughs, severe muscle pain, high fevers, and delirium. Toward the end of December, the brothers died, a half hour apart. The 14th could only muster about 100 men fit for duty by then; a few picked up shovels and began their sad task. Frank and Fred, who had probably shared the same bed for most of their lives, now shared a soldiers' grave.[1]

Burials were constant in the Army of the Potomac as more and more men succumbed to typhus or wounds from Fredericksburg. In their camp near Falmouth, Virginia, the soldiers tried to get warm and somehow find enough to eat while they waited for Burnside's next move.

Many men were sleeping on the frozen ground under flimsy shelter tents—or as one soldier put it, "*so called* shelters. What gave them that name I can't imagine. We pitch them by uniting two of them at the top and stretching over a pole where they are supposed to afford 'Shelter' for two. When we lay down (and we can't get into them without laying down) either our heads or our feet protrude outside."[2]

In winter, shelter tents promised nothing but misery. Theodore Vaill described the experience of his regiment: "The storm continued all night, and many a man waked up next morning to find his legs firmly packed in new-fallen snow . . . At daylight orders came to pack up and be ready to move at once; which was a difficult order to execute, on account of many things, especially the shelter tents;—for they were as rigid as sheet-iron, and yet had to be rolled up and strapped on the knapsacks."[3]

Being crammed into a shelter tent was a special hell for those who were sick—and for their tent mates. A soldier in the 1st Heavy Artillery wrote about his brother-in-arms, Roswell Douglas:

> after a hard day's fight at Fredericksburg, Douglass was very sick, and ought to have been in hospital, but he was bound to stick as long as there was any fighting. It was December and bitter cold, and we used to double up in order to have more blankets. Douglass lay on the ground, with his back to his companion, in order to relieve his constant stomach sickness without offense. Unfortunately, he got turned over . . . and . . . pour[ed] his bile into his companion's face.[4]

The Union army provided an assortment of tents for its troops: wall tents, Sibleys, "A" tents—all had their shortcomings. Augustus Bronson wrote that in the 17th Connecticut "we have more styles of tent than even Josephs coat has colors."[5]

Adjutant Theodore Vaill had a few choice words to describe the "A" tents of his regiment:

> The A tents were of linen, woven about as compactly as a sieve, and were intended for just five men, and no more; and woe to the squad that contained a fat man, or one over six feet long—for somebody, or at least some part of somebody, must sleep out of doors. "Spoon-fashion" was the only possible fashion: no man could make a personal revolution on his own axis without compelling a similar movement on the part of each of his tent-mates, and a world of complaint besides . . . the chill of night would penetrate the bones of the soldiers, and cause them to turn over and over from midnight until dawn, when each Company, without waiting for Reveille, would rally in a huddle on the long sheet-iron cookstove at the foot of the street, and endeavor to burn the pain out of their marrows, while toasting their bread.[6]

A student at Wesleyan University when war broke out, twenty-one-year-old Roswell Douglass wrote his uncle and guardian a series of letters asking permission to enlist. Roswell and many other Wesleyan men had already begun military drilling. He closed his argument to his uncle, saying "it will be a time of need and then I ought and want to go." (Letter of Roswell Douglass to his uncle, April 26, 1861, Buck Zaidel collection.)

MUD MARCH

Winter weather made moving an army impracticable. In the Virginia theatre, troops usually went into winter quarters by January, hunkering down until spring. But Burnside seemed resistant to the idea of settling into camp. Since he'd taken command, everything had gone wrong. The pontoon bridges had been late, ruining his chance to cross the river and sweep on into Richmond. Lee's forces had crushed the Union troops at Fredericksburg. Morale was terrible. Was there some way Burnside could redeem himself?

"Jan. 20th, general orders were read . . . announcing an immediate movement of the Army of the Potomac," wrote a soldier in Connecticut's 15th Regiment.[7] Again, Burnside planned to throw pontoon bridges over the Rappahannock, then quickly cross his artillery and infantry to catch Lee by surprise.

"The two succeeding days, rain fell incessantly, but notwithstanding this, Burnside began his second attempt to cross the river and troops were moving aimlessly in all directions."[8]

"It rained all day and all night until the little rivulets became brooks and the brooks became rivers, and the road for miles was choked with supply wagons, fast in the mud," wrote the 14th's historian.[9] Union artillery pieces sank deep into the mud, along with cavalry horses, and thousands of infantry soldiers.

> As the advance reached the brink of the river, they were met by the rebels on the opposite side with mock politeness, who offered to assist them in building the bridge and not to open fire upon them until they were fairly across, but as the artillery, pontoons, ammunition and supply trains were back stuck in the mud, they were obliged to decline the hospitable invitation, whereupon the Confederates jeered at them and erected a large sign with the inscription "Burnside stuck in the mud."[10]

This time, Burnside recognized the signs of impending disaster and threw in the towel. Many of the soldiers, picturing a replay of Fredericksburg, were grateful for the terrible conditions. "It was mud that checked the movement, mud that saved thousands of lives, and mud that spared the Army of the Potomac another crushing defeat," pronounced a relieved private in the 15th Regiment.[11]

There would be no more serious action until the spring. The Army of the Potomac settled into winter camp.

With the flag they loved behind them, two soldiers posed for an image that perfectly expressed their devotion to their country and each other.

A SOLDIER'S HOME

The shared experience of battle forged strong bonds between soldiers. Living together in camp created different connections, often just as strong. Though the men thought of themselves first as warriors, they averaged about seven weeks in camp for each day in battle.

In camp, a soldier's largest community was his regiment, then his company. But his most important bond was to those who shared his hut or tent. The four to six soldiers who commonly bunked together were called a squad or a "mess" since they frequently cooked and ate as a group. Messmates often came from the same community; some had known each other their whole lives. For many soldiers, their mess became a surrogate family.

Captain Fred Doten described the camaraderie he felt in camp with the 14th: "we soldiers live side by side eating, sleeping, riding, with joys and sorrows and sympathies in common. Sympathies that are felt by each but rarely spoken. A look or a slight word is sufficient. And I know that I have friends here that are true friends."[12]

The troops' first order of business in camp was building their quarters. In the 18th Connecticut, Cpl. James Sawyer, an artist from Woodstock, described in words and sketches the construction process.

> The regiment was divided into messes of from four to six men. Each mess . . . cut down a suitable tree, and employed the regimental teams to haul them to the mill and saw them into boards.
>
> Sam Spaulding, Geo Heath, Geo Baker and I formed a mess. We got a big log down to the mill and in due time our load of green oak boards and a few pieces of scantling was delivered on . . . the site of our winter residence. Our house was 10 feet long, 6 wide and about four feet high from the ground to the eaves. It was high enough to stand up in the middle and to sit down in around the edges.
>
> The roof was covered with the shelter tents of the occupants . . . all buttoned together and thrown over the rafters . . . Rather thin as we could see the moon through it, nevertheless, it shed the thickest of the rain. We made two bunks in the end opposite the door; the lower about 18 inches from the ground and the other as high up as it could be put. Heath and Spaulding took the lower and Sawyer and Baker the upper. A little sheet iron stove, some boxes for rations, some stools to sit on and a shelf along one side to eat on, comp[l]eted our list of furnishings. Altogether it made quite a comfortable shanty.[13]

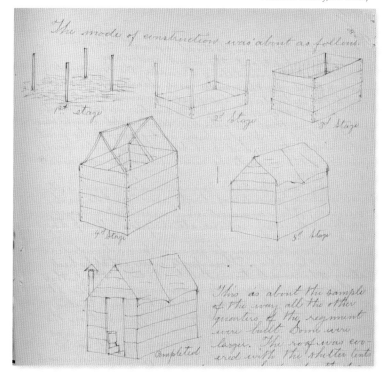

James H. Sawyer sketched the construction of his hut in the camp of the 18th Connecticut. (Connecticut Historical Society, Hartford.)

Troops that didn't have the luxury of stoves to heat their quarters searched for flat stones and built fireplaces, cemented with mud. "Over the fire-place a mantle was generally located, containing a confused collection of tin plates and cups, knives and forks . . . The man whose fire-place is adorned with an iron frying-pan, is an object of envy to all his comrades . . . However, the halves of old canteens, fitted with handles, answer very well in its place."[14]

Win Sheldon of the 27th Regiment spoke affectionately of "our little regimental village" in Falmouth. Looking around at their homes, "with no little satisfaction we surveyed their rough architecture, pork-barrel chimneys, and cracker-box doors, feeling that though the winds might blow, and the rainy season pour down its floods, we were prepared to endure it patiently."[15]

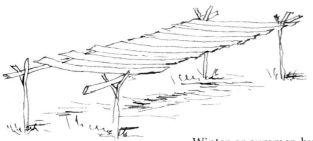

In winter huts, soldiers could attach wooden bunks to a wall; in tents, it was the ground or an improvised cot. "Dear Emma," wrote Charles Upham from the camp of the 8th Connecticut to his sweetheart in Meriden, "I have just taken a nap [in] my rustic bed (composed of four crotches, two poles lengthwise, and barrel staves laid across)."[16]

James H. Sawyer sketched a soldier's cot, just as Charlie Upham described it. (Connecticut Historical Society, Hartford.)

Winter or summer, huts or tents, the men did their best to make their quarters homelike. In November of 1863, Capt. Andrew Upson described his digs for his wife:

In the corner below the bunk is the cupboard, another hard tack box with two shelves—There our kitchen ware is set away & whatever provisions we may have on hand . . . A few bits of hard bread, with corners a good deal rounded because long carried & a little tea told the whole story of our commissariat—But today we have made a purchase & you could be entertained with tea & sugar . . .

Looking like its inhabitants had just stepped outside, this sketch of a hut interior revealed how soldiers lived. Lt. George Elton of the 27th Connecticut sketched laundry drying on a line over his cot; below it his valise (marked with his name) rested on the cot above another soldier's bed made up on the ground. An overcoat lay on the cot at left, with a knapsack and two haversacks hanging behind it. Beside a bucket of water stood two stools probably made from hardtack crates. In the fireplace a pot was boiling; a shelf above held tin cups and beside it, three canteens hung over a stack of firewood.

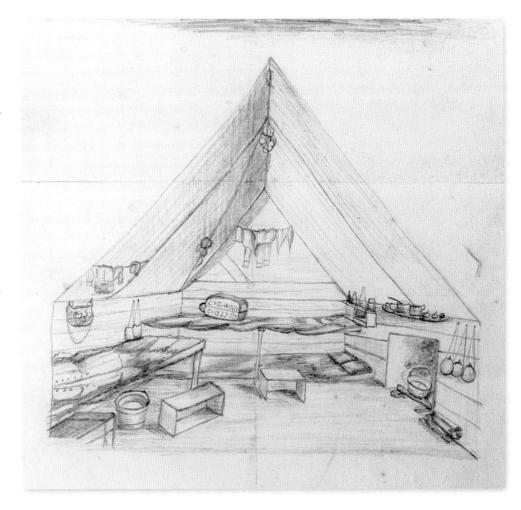

The fire place is the main thing just now & that sends out such genial warmth that we can't help being happy—Now don't you wish you could sit down beside our glowing fire & see how soldiers live when they are comfortable.[17]

The men grew attached to their camp communities. "We have something of a home feeling for our poor little mud-built cities," wrote Samuel Fiske of the 14th Connecticut. "Our streets are not Broadways, but a part of our life has grown round these little log huts and chimneys of plastered sticks."[18]

COMRADES

As the weeks passed, a soldier's connection to his "family" in camp might increase. Cpl. Titus Moss of the 20th Connecticut wrote from Virginia to his wife in Cheshire, about two of his mess mates, Samuel (Titus's brother) and Franklin:

> It is a wintry day here the ground is covered with snow about four inches in depth and the wind is blowing quite hard . . . S & F have gone out this morning [on picket] . . . I cooked their breakfast for them this morning. Every thing was

A photographer who visited the Louisiana camp of the 26th Connecticut was able to capture this relaxed image of eight comrades taking their ease in their "home away from home." The private seated at right added a touch of refinement, holding a bouquet of flowers in his tin cup.

covered with snow so that the cook was not like to have breakfast in time for the picket so I took some of the chicken pie and turkey with some meal and a little potato we had save of our yesterday dinner and warmed it in a small pan that I have so that they had a good breakfast to start on.[19]

Two weeks later, Titus reported on another comrade: "Henry is sick tonight, has a bad bowel complaint. I have been to see the surgeon and have some medicine for him. I shall take as good care of him as I can, hope he will be better in the morning."[20]

Writing in his diary in January of 1864, Pvt. Levi Whittaker described an instance of kindness between comrades in the 11th Connecticut, "Willard goes on guard for Curtice he being shoeless."[21]

In a song that became a favorite at veterans' reunions, one soldier wrote

> We've shared our blankets and tents together,
> And marched and fought in all kinds of weather,
> And hungry and full we've been;
> Had days of battle and days of rest,
> But this memory I cling to and love the best:
> We've drunk from the same canteen. . . . .
>
> There's never a bond, old friend, like this:
> We have drunk from the same canteen![22]

In the 14th Regiment, camaraderie included good-humored tomfoolery, as William Hincks recalled.

> Chaplain Stevens was then, as now, exceedingly fond of sardines . . . and as the government was not in the habit of issuing these palatable little fishes for rations, he had taken a supply of them with him when he started from old Connecticut. By the time that he arrived at our quarters, however, only a single box remained and this happened to be incautiously left in plain sight upon the top of his pile of luggage while its owner was absent in another part of camp . . .
>
> Imagine . . . the deep pathos of the scene when upon Mr. Stevens' return he found that Commissary Sergeant Dibble and Adjutant Doten had coolly opened the box and were just finishing the contents. "Why, gentlemen, how is this?" he asked. "Those sardines were mine. Didn't you see my initials scratched upon the box?" "Your initials" said Dibble, "where are they?" "Why here,"

"What gay pictures might I not draw of our life at Falmouth!" wrote a soldier in the 11th Regiment. "We had chimneys of mud and barrels. Whenever we were cozily ensconced, with a good fire burning, the guard, by a series of savage howls, would inform us that our barrel chimney was ablaze. We rushed forth, anxious to save our tent; and with liberal pails of water extinguished both chimney and fire." (*The Connecticut War Record*, February 1865, p. 358.)

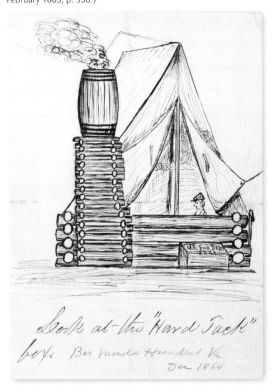

Look at the "Hard Tack" box. Bermuda Hundred Va. Dec 1864

replied the Chaplain. "Don't you see upon the lid 'H. S. S.,' Henry S. Stevens?" "Really then, Chaplain, I must ask your pardon," replied Dibble. "I noticed the letters, indeed, but entirely misunderstood their meaning. Both Adjutant Doten and myself supposed that H S. S. instead of meaning Henry S. Stevens stood for Have Some Sardines, and accordingly we gratefully availed ourselves of your polite invitation."[23]

Reese Gwillim, a schoolteacher from Hartford, enlisted in Connecticut's earliest nine-month unit, the 22nd Regiment. In November of 1862, as his inexperienced regiment camped outside of Washington, Gwillim sought his bunkmates' feelings about the war. He recorded in his journal an intimate portrait of five brothers-in-arms sharing their thoughts.

> Our mess were alone in our tent as the rain pattered down on the linen roof, and I sat thinking of going into battle. Baker was writing on his box. Goodale sat on his knapsack on my one side while Mason sat on the other, both talking about the march to Babcock. I looked up from a letter I had just finished, . . . and said I "Boys how do you feel at the prospect of going into battle? Goodale what do you think of it?"
>
> "Well," said he in a thoughtful way his eyes falling to the ground in seeming effort to analyse his feelings, "I feel ready to go wherever it is my duty. I feel that I can trust God. I am weak; I own it, and I may possibly run, but I do not intend to. I shall do the best I can."
>
> "Well, Mason, what are your feelings?" said I.
>
> Mason in his quiet way said, as he fixes his eyes on the corner of his box, "I suppose I came out here to do anything that was required [of] me. I am ready to go onto the battle field if I am called there   I hope I am ready for it. I feel a trust in God."
>
> "How is it with you Babcock," said I turning to him next.
>
> "Oh! I ain't very anxious about going. I should rather stay here. However, I suppose I must go if they want me. I wont back out."
>
> There was too much of Yankee ambiguity in his reply to suit the occasion. Baker, meanwhile had sat, writing but little, hearing all the replies made. I knew he only wanted a chance to express his up & down, straight forward opinion of going into battle. I well knew how he felt about it, but to complete the round, I asked him.
>
> "Well," said he "I look forward to the battle field without any feelings of dread. If my poor life will help in sustain[ing] this glorious government, I willingly offer it up on my Countrys altar. I came down here to fight for that noble old flag, and I am ready to do it. I do not expect to go back. I expect to fall on the battle-field."[24]

CAMP DUTIES

"When a great army is doing nothing, how is it employed?" asked the 14th's Samuel Fiske, writing to the *Republican* newspaper in Springfield, Massachusetts. "[E]very officer and soldier has to take his turn as eye for the regiment or camp about once in three or four days. It keeps its long arms stretched out in all directions, feeling for danger and avoiding surprise."[25]

Daniel Dewey, a nineteen-year-old Trinity student in the 25th Connecticut, sent his family a detailed description of picket duty:

> we take our sleeping arrangements and rations and march out to the picket post, generally one or two miles from the main camp—we go in the morning and remain twenty-four hours. The main company is posted as a reserve, usually at some deserted house or sheltered spot. Advance post, or the real pickets are then posted some distance in advance, two or three together, the posts being in calling distance of each other.
>
> One of these pickets must be always awake and watching. Half of the reserve have also to be on their feet; in case of an attack these pickets fall back to the reserve and the reserve to the camp, keeping the enemy in check till the line of battle can be formed. So you see what it means when you read that the pickets were driven in.[26]

"Just in off picket. 48 hour tour" reads the inscription on this image of two tired soldiers, who stopped at the photographer's to pose just as they were, with their equipment and overcoats still on, blankets and muskets slung, and likely thoughts of a long nap in their heads.

Standing picket in driving snow, ice, or rain was no picnic. After enduring a snowstorm near Stafford Courthouse, Virginia, Titus Moss of Cheshire wrote:

> Brooks and I put up our rubber blankets for a shelter   made a fire in front and sat under our shelter feeling quite comfortable. It stopt snowing at noon but continued damp and rained all the time after midnight covering the bushes with ice . . . it is so dark that you cannot see anything only to look up towards the sky and just discern the tree tops. I ran into a stream of water that I was trying to walk by the side of . . .
>
> Our dinner answered for dinner and supper   it was hard bread, beef and sauce with coffee. Brooks had a few dried apples that came from home. The same for breakfast minus the sauce in addition five small potatoes that I took out. I sometimes think of the quiet nights at home when I am blundering among the stumps and mud or brush at night.[27]

The men of Connecticut's 27th Regiment found picket duty to be something of a surprise. Just across the Rappahannock, they faced Confederate soldiers with the same duty. "By mutual agreement, the custom of picket firing . . . was discontinued, and friendly intercourse was no uncommon event . . . Frequently the rebels launched out on the river their diminutive craft, laden with tobacco and the latest Richmond papers, and bearing a note to 'Gentlemen of the United States' requesting an interchange of commodities."[28]

Sometimes soldiers relished picket duty for the freedom it brought them. Horatio Chapman, on picket for the 20th Connecticut, noted:

> All quiet on the picket line and we are enjoying ourselves hugely and hope it may continue. I went to a house this morning about one-half mile from here and bought some milk and paid fifteen cents for a pint, and had a good meal of hard-tack and milk. Went again this evening and bought some more.
>
> The family were poor and ignorant, living in a log house, the father, mother and six children, with only one room in the house. There were two beds which took one-half the space. I asked the largest girl how old she was. She did not know. I asked her father. Eight or ten he guessed, and turning to his wife asked if he was right, and she said she was right smart on to eleven she reckoned. They were quite pretty and clean, but poorly clothed.[29]

For those regiments—like Connecticut's 6th—lucky enough to be stationed in the coastal Carolina area, picket duty could be downright glorious.

Manton Upson of New Britain, a member of Connecticut's 1st Cavalry, sent two of his pictures home. "One is how I look in camp, the other how I look in the field," he explained.

His field portrait showed the fully equipped Union cavalryman, ready to set out for picket duty or scouting, with his Smith carbine, holstered revolver, and cavalry saber.

Each regiment took its turn at the ten days picket service, which duty called them out to some fine plantations in the suburbs of the town. Here we enjoyed the life of the soldier . . . The fields were filled with sweet potatoes and corn, together with the orange and fig trees which abounded near the houses, made our visits on this picket duty desirable. Our lines skirted the banks of the rivers and streams, with an occasional raid upon the main land in search of the Johnnies. These raids sometimes resulted in great captures, not of the rebs themselves but of their fowls.[30]

Picket was just one of the soldiers' many duties in camp. Firewood and water had to be fetched, often from long distances. "These cold storms make the life of a soldier a bitter one," noted Charles Lynch, of the 18th Connecticut, in his diary on January 31, 1864. "Wood must be brought to camp, trees cut down, then worked up into fire-wood. Must go out about five miles from camp for the wood. All must take a hand at the axe. Teams and wood-choppers must be kept well guarded."[31]

And some officers drilled their men continually. Frederick Lucas explained the daily routine in Connecticut's 2nd Heavy Artillery:

Col Kellogg gives the boys two battalion drills a day, morning & afternoon with the usual dress parade at night. This keeps them straight as ever and out of mischief. He says if he dont keep them busy with drill, the Devil will find something for them to do. This is true. Idleness in camp is but the mother of every kind of vice. You cannot place a body of men together, such as compose

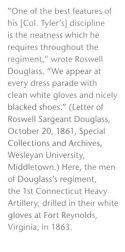

"One of the best features of his [Col. Tyler's] discipline is the neatness which he requires throughout the regiment," wrote Roswell Douglass. "We appear at every dress parade with clean white gloves and nicely blacked shoes." (Letter of Roswell Sargeant Douglass, October 20, 1861, Special Collections and Archives, Wesleyan University, Middletown.) Here, the men of Douglass's regiment, the 1st Connecticut Heavy Artillery, drilled in their white gloves at Fort Reynolds, Virginia, in 1863.

a Reg.[;] young boys ready for any kind of fun or mischief, with a good sprinkling of vile & unprincipled men. Place them away from all the influences and restraint of home & unless you keep them busy with active duty they will very soon fall into the practice of all kinds of wickedness.[32]

"[W]e are constantly on duty of some kind," complained a soldier in the 20th Connecticut. "It is inspection or roll-call or dress parade or picket or fatigue duty or clean camp or something or other all the time and I had rather be in front facing the enemy than be in camp where there is so much red tape."[33]

Scouting sometimes brought a welcome change of scenery and maybe a little excitement. Nineteen-year-old Alfred Hanks, from the village of Mansfield, recorded a comical scouting expedition with his regiment, the 21st Connecticut, in February of 1864:

Men from Connecticut's 22nd Regiment showed off their new digs. The group included at least one joker (*upper left*). (Connecticut Historical Society, Hartford.)

> . . . our company was deployed across a road just after dark as it was expected a squadron of Rebel Cavalry might come along . . . can plainly recall how Capt. Long cautioned us to make not the least noise, also how mad he got when someone broke wind and while he was trying to find out who   another would do the same away from the first . . . the boys could not keep from laughing to see the captain getting madder all the time at not being able to find out who was the guilty ones.[34]

VITTLES

"I have just been to dinner   had stued beans with hard bread in them   the hard bread we get here now is so old that it is full of bugs and worms   if I take a couple of them at a time lay one down while I eat the other when I look for the [first one,] find it walking off at the rate of ten knots an hour," Pvt. Abner Smith wrote sarcastically in the fall of 1862.[35] Cooking together, eating

Drawing from the journal of James H. Sawyer. (Connecticut Historical Society, Hartford.) The lowly cook, often disparaged by the men he served, could make important contributions. In the 19th Regiment, Pvt. Lewis Bissell reported the kindness of their company cook: "When any of the men are sick George Bradley fixes them some toast and makes tea and does all he can for them." (Letter of Lewis Bissell to his mother, November 3, 1862, in *The Civil War Letters of Lewis Bissell,* by Mark Olcott with David Lear [Washington, DC: The Field School Educational Foundation Press, 1981], p. 26.) Charles J. Osborn of the 24th Connecticut was willing to put in the extra effort to cheer his comrades with an unexpected treat: "We are agoing to have . . . some cakes for supper if we can get the flour in time," he wrote. (Diary of Charles J. Osborn; Courtesy of the Middlesex County Historical Society.)

together, and complaining together about their food were social experiences for the soldiers. Once a regiment had settled into camp, each company usually built a kitchen or cookhouse. The company cook then faced the daunting task of preparing palatable meals from army food. Most of the men learned to cook on their own as well, since they often had to prepare meals for themselves or their mess.

The government supplied a monotonous, unappetizing diet mainly consisting of hardtack, salt pork, and coffee. The soldiers loved their coffee, but salt pork and hardtack were another story. Hardtack was an impossibly hard and dry biscuit—"harder than the teeth nature has furnished us to crack it with," said Charles Dudley of Guilford.[36] Soldiers moistened hardtack with water, coffee, or grease to make it soft enough to eat.

"Before leaving Gainsville we received rations of raw salt pork and coffee," wrote Sgt. Augustus Bronson of the 17th Connecticut. "The wagons went off with the cooking utensils so my mess converted the wash basin into a stew pan, cooked our pork and boiled our coffee, caught a rabbit and made rabbit soup, then confiscated

With a piece of hardtack in one hand and his rifle musket in the other, Pvt. George Meech of Ledyard displayed the two things essential to the soldier's existence. Meech made sure his photograph would show the folks at home all the details of his new life as a soldier, even displaying the stitched "U.S." of his army blanket.

Hats off to those at home— or the white-aproned cook— as seven members of the 22nd Connecticut Volunteers gathered together to enjoy a meal in the field.

some apples and stewed them. How would you have fancied boarding at our hotel? Don't you think it was gay? Who wouldn't be a soldier?"[37]

A Goshen boy informed his mother that after years of the soldier's life, "We have various ways of mixing corn, apples, hard tack & meats with seasoning and making first rate dishes."[38]

"Oh! Mother! We are to have soft bread tonight if nothing prevents," wrote a hopeful Frederick Lucas from Virginia. "It is on the way to us. Will be only two days old they say & Oh! What a luxury for us."[39]

Soldiers who were heartily sick of army rations—and who wasn't?—could purchase food from their camp sutler. Civilian merchants, sutlers stocked provisions and luxuries which they sold from carts or tents, often charging hefty prices to soldiers desperate for something tasty or just edible. What could a man get from the sutler? Canned sardines, fresh bread, bologna and ham, tea, condensed milk, sugar, canned fruit, cigars, gingerbread, pies, liquor, and more.

With virtual monopolies, sutlers could not only charge what they wanted, they could also sell items of poor quality. When the 14th Connecticut soldiers finally got their pay—four months' worth—in February of 1863, Benjamin Hirst noted that "To-day army rations are not good enough for the boys, who are moving from one sutler's shop to another, buying wooden ginger cakes, brandy (vinegar) peaches, and castiron pies."[40]

Sutlers—"those noble patriots," as one soldier sneered—were generally viewed with contempt.[41] Most soldiers felt that while they were sacrificing everything for their country, sutlers made their fortunes by taking advantage of the troops' hardships. It wasn't unusual for frustrated soldiers to raid a sutler's supplies. One day the men of the 15th Connecticut had returned from duty to find that they were moving camp, and the commissary had already departed with all their rations.

"[I]n camp life, the inventive genius of the soldier is employed to make as good a provision as possible for his welfare," declared a soldier of the 21st Connecticut. (*The Story of the Twenty-first Connecticut Volunteer Infantry*, p. 39.) A hungry soldier could easily transform a tin can into a grater and use it on his tooth-breaking hardtack, or on a nutmeg that could supply some flavor to the army's lackluster rations.

The camp sutler had his effects all packed, but for some reason had not gotten away. The boys were hungry and the modest request was made that he unpack his stores and open up a temporary trade. To this he demurred, but alas for him the "demurrer" was not sustained.

No one assumes to know just how it happened, but when all was over there was a very mad sutler and a general wreck of his

Robert Kellogg (*right*) worked on his rations and Corporal Oscar Wiel enjoyed a smoke in a view that the two 16th Connecticut soldiers enacted for the camera in Hartford before leaving for the front in 1862. The image was an ironic contrast to the hellish future that awaited the 16th Regiment at Andersonville Prison, where starvation, exposure, disease, and death replaced this idyllic camp scene.

A group of hungry soldiers in the 1st Heavy Artillery delayed their dinner in quarters to pose for this image. The photographer peeled back sections of the canvas roof to illuminate the scene—a rare and intimate glimpse into soldier life. The camera captured a wealth of details: the young drummer at left, his drum beneath him, ready to exchange his drumsticks for a fork and knife; soldiers' forage caps hung on the walls behind them; the stove and pot in the foreground; and a cloth-covered table laden with pitchers, tin army cups, and platters heaped with the cook's fare.

"goods." This was called "Raid No. 1." The only person wounded was Adj. Brown, who was shot in the back with a ball of soft butter. This little episode was not without its lesson. It taught the sutlers to understand that they accompanied the regiment for its convenience as well as their own.[42]

Soldiers had another source for food as well: foraging from the farms and plantations around them. "We are beginning to get into a good country, and I find very hard work to keep my men within reasonable bounds in their foraging operations. In fact, the army are all becoming foragers," wrote Capt. Horace G. H. Tarr of the 20th Connecticut in 1864.[43]

Charles H. Lynch noted in his diary:

> Owing to our rations running very low some of the boys took the liberty to go foraging, going without a permit from the Generals headquarters. They were rounded up by cavalry scouts, placed under arrest, taken to headquarters, where they received a severe reprimand from General Hunter. All were punished. Non-commissioned officers reduced to the ranks. Privates made to carry a heavy fence rail over the shoulder and walk a beat for four hours. The

lack of rations and seeing the boys undergoing a severe punishment made a gloomy time for us. The life of a soldier in the field is no picnic. We can stand most anything but hunger. It did seem very strange to us that we could not forage in the enemy's country.[44]

But plenty of Union officers had a cavalier attitude toward foraging. In the 13th Regiment, Quartermaster Joseph B. Bromley took men with him on a foraging expedition, with these instructions: "I want my staff to be on the lookout for turkeys, geese, pigs, and sheep. Don't be the aggressor in any contest. Stand strictly on the defensive; but if you're attacked by any of these animals, show fight, and *don't forget to bring off the enemy's dead.*"[45]

The chaplain of the 18th Connecticut, William Walker, noted dryly that while his regiment was in camp, "Nothing of special interest occurred, except that another pig ran against the men's bayonets, and as a natural consequence they had fried pig."[46]

A soldier's experience in camp had much to do with the strictness or leniency of his regimental officers. "Lieut Bissell is a very strict and dignified officer when circumstance require," wrote Charles Boyle in 1863. "When he was Serg't Maj. of the reg't all the boys thought he was the very impersonation of military rigidity. All gave 'attention' when he said the word. But he can come down from that awful dignity, and make the meanest soldier in the ranks easy in conversation with himself; and our company are always much pleased to see him come into our street in his long calico dressing gown & slippers. He is ready then to talk on any subject, from bean soup to governmental policy."[47]

In Connecticut's 1st Heavy Artillery, a mild, permissive colonel was replaced by the disciplined and exacting Robert O. Tyler.

> He saw at a glance that rigid discipline was needed . . . Every morning at guardmounting he assisted, inspecting every musket, correcting faults in position, and trying to give to the men a soldierly bearing. True he had rather a motley set to begin with, there being no uniform coats and but few presentable pants in the regiment; but wherever an effort at neatness was made, the Colonel's eye perceived it and a compliment was sure to follow. Even the man that put a coat of blacking on his feet in lieu of shoes was thus rewarded for his pains, and, though destitute of pantaloons, marched off with the air of a major-general.[48]

To keep their uniforms presentable, soldiers relied on the needles and thread in their "housewives." Frederick Lucas of Goshen jokingly bemoaned his domestic skills:

> this morning, by some mishap I tore an awful rent in my pants, new ones too they were, and now I must hurry to get them repaired before some duty calls me out with them. What a life this is where men must do their own darning and mending, reinstate loose buttons, wash their clothing and wear it without ironing, do their own cooking, scour their own knives and

When Henry I. Clark of Old Saybrook enlisted in Connecticut's 24th Regiment, his cousin Eva Pratt made him this "housewife" containing needle and thread, "with the hope that it may prove useful when far away from the gentle fingers always so ready in the home circle."

forks and tin ware and wash their own dishes. I wonder if the girls are chuckling over these things, with the idea that they will marry a returned soldier, and be benefited by his knowledge of housewifery and culinary matters?[49]

The Sanitary Commission

Monday we each of us had a little piece of chockolate just enough for one cup given us by the Sanitary it seemed like a small present but when one looked round & saw the number of pieces there must be he saw it must take a good large pile to go round, & was thankful.[50]

A cup of hot chocolate. A warm quilt. Mittens, bandages, medicine. Hope.

Thanks to the United States Sanitary Commission, the lives of hundreds of thousands of Union soldiers changed for the better. The commission had its beginnings in New York not two weeks after the war began, when a group of women came together to determine how they could help the troops. Knitting socks wasn't what they had in mind: they were seeking more substantial and far-reaching ways to help. They sent an exploratory committee to Washington to find what was needed. Eight weeks later, President Lincoln signed legislation creating the United States Sanitary Commission.

"The object of the Sanitary Commission was to do what the government could not," wrote Mary Livermore, one of its agents.[51] While the government could feed soldiers with hardtack and salt pork, the Sanitary Commission could add pickles or the chocolate that Homer Sackett appreciated. When a cold snap hit Virginia, the Sanitary Commission sent woolen blankets and mittens for the men on picket duty in the snow. And almost before a battle had ended, the commission delivered bandages and anesthetics to the field hospitals.

How did it all work? Early in the war, commission workers had visited army camps, making lists of what the troops lacked. Next, the organization established its own warehouses in the large cities of the North; then it set out to fill them.

In towns throughout the North, women had formed soldiers' aid societies. Members knit socks, sewed flannel shirts, and rolled bandages to send to the troops. (In fact, on the day after Abraham Lincoln issued his first call for troops, a group of Bridgeport women gathered to "see what they could do" for the soldiers.[52] Their group grew into the Bridgeport Soldiers' Aid Society, the first such organization recorded in the North.)

Sanitary Commission administrators connected with the soldiers' aid societies in every city and town. Thousands upon thousands of women made up the aid societies, and soon they were sending what they'd made and collected to the nearest Sanitary Commission center, where volunteers labeled and organized them with like items in the warehouses. As soon as a need was anticipated, commission workers could quickly locate the proper supplies and send them off.

Even children did their part to help the soldiers. In Vernon, a twelve-year-old girl organized her friends to sew quilt squares, which her mother assembled into a patchwork quilt. One of the girls, Fannie Chester, tucked a note into the quilt's folds before the Patriotic Society of Vernon sent it off to the Sanitary Commission.

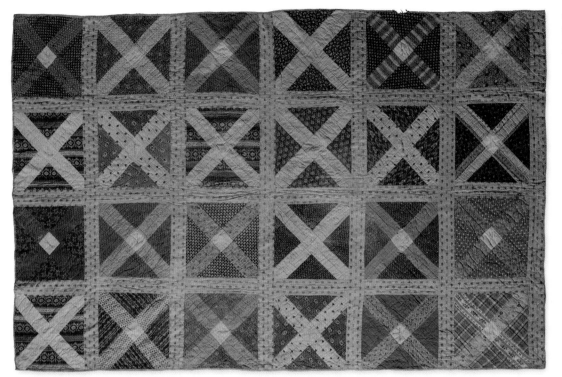

Quilt made in 1864 by the girls and women of the Patriotic Society of Vernon, and sent to Robert Fisk.

Elizabeth Chester

Robert Fisk

Eventually, the quilt reached a Union soldier in North Carolina. Capt. Robert E. Fisk, of the 132nd New York Infantry, finding Fannie's note, wrote a letter of thanks to the girl "and her fair companions," humbly declaring that the quilt was used by "a soldier who is not altogether unworthy of your sympathy . . . one whose only mistress is his country and whose patriotism has been tested on many battle fields." Fisk praised New England women as "the truest sweet hearts, the best wives, and most perfect mothers in the land."[53]

When Captain Fisk's letter reached Vernon, the women of the Patriotic League suggested that it was not proper for young Fannie to engage in correspondence with a soldier, so Fannie's older sister, Lizzie, responded to the captain's letter. Fisk replied, and soon the two were writing regularly, exchanging photographs, and—of course—falling in love.

At war's end, Robert Fisk came to Vernon and proposed. Lizzie married her soldier, and the couple moved to Montana, where they raised six children, and kept the quilt that brought them together.[54]

✳ ✳ ✳

Passing the Time

Chocolate and patchwork quilts might make camp feel more like home, but they couldn't alleviate the boredom. In the 14th Connecticut, Capt. Samuel Fiske, a newspaper correspondent, minister, and witty philosopher summed up the experience of camp life in two paragraphs:

> and so with guard and picket, inspections, parades and reviews, all the little and great necessary and unnecessary matters of camp life, rubbing up guns and distributing rations, writing letters and attending courts martial, bringing wood and water and plastering houses, reading newspapers and pitching quoits, we manage to fill up pretty easily all the waking hours of the twenty-four.

> A little time to read or study, a little time to chat, a little time to meditate, a little time to devote to the dear ones at home, and (it must be confessed) a good deal of time to sleeping and eating and lounging, and our day gets by from "reveille" to "tattoo," and through the night watches to morning roll-call again; a dull, monotonous, stupid, indifferent, make-shift of a life.[55]

Particularly in winter camp, with no marching or fighting on the horizon, "dull, monotonous, stupid" were fitting adjectives. But monotony was an enemy that could be conquered, and the intrepid colonel of Connecticut's 2nd Heavy Artillery, Elisha Kellogg, knew how to do it. One of his men wrote home in February of 1863 from Fort Worth, Virginia:

On any given day, a soldier might be surrounded by a scene like this, with men lounging in their tents, bringing water to camp, reading letters from home, eating and drinking, playing cards, and breaking the boredom with a friendly boxing match. Beside the barrel sat a young African American boy, probably one of the so-called "contrabands" that followed the Union troops and often acted as soldiers' servants.

We were marched outside the camp & formed in line of battle. Then the Col. Ordered the Commandants of the Co to him & informed them that he was going to have a sham fight with snowballs for weapons . . . the Col. Divided the Reg[iment], the right wing against the left & about six rods apart. He took command of the right wing & the Major of the left. Before the fight commenced he told the boys to "show their spunk & keep their tempers & have no ill feelings or quarrelling." Then he gave the command "load at will, load" and every man made his balls.

You would have been amused to have seen the two parties with three hundred men in each loaded & waiting for the signal "Fire." When the word came what a shower of snowballs & how the boys of the different Companies yelled. At the first fire, I received a black eye . . . But on we went & the blood flowed freely from the smashed noses & cut mouths.

Nearly every commissioned officer in the Reg received a bad bruise on the head or face. The snow was moist & of course the men made their balls effective. The Col. rushed in, fought like a perfect tiger. When he saw a portion of his wing giving away and losing ground he would yell like a fiend, rushing into the thickest part of the fray. When he left the field his eyes were both badly hurt & nearly closed, & the blood run from nose & mouth. He retired laughing & well satisfied with the results . . . When we were called in the snow on the ground where we fought was sprinkled with blood, and had the appearance of a battlefield.[56]

Less bloody, but still competitive, was baseball. With hundreds of men assembled in one place, desperate for something to do, the war proved the making of the young sport. "The boys are having a fine game of ball tonight," wrote Frederick Lucas to his mother. "There is great sport in playing ball here   if the thing gets a blow or bounds in the air it is sure to be caught by one or another of the regiment who are crowded around."[57]

When weather wasn't conducive to baseball, the boys found scores of other activities to pass the time. As in any community, there were people with different interests and talents.

James Sawyer described how his comrades in the 18th Connecticut amused themselves:

To pass away the evenings a debating society was organized. We had some pretty good talkers in the company . . . For a while these were carried on with spirit and many important questions were argued and settled . . . When this got worn, a mock trial was held and lots of sport was got out of it. When that palled, the boys took to dancing, and night after night for a long time the old building shook to the tread of heavy feet. Of course, the partners were of the same sex, but that made no difference. Albert Hibbard with his fiddle was the musician and Bill Handy usually called off.[58]

"Some of the boys got to making rings and other things of bone . . . Some sent for fine files and saws and produced some really fine work," wrote a soldier of the 18th Regiment. (Journal of James H. Sawyer, Connecticut Historical Society, Hartford.) A finely engraved image of an artillery piece ornaments the ring, left, of a member of Connecticut's 1st Light Battery; while a piece of beef or pork bone became a whimsical neckerchief ring, right, carved with a picture of what might have been the camp dog.

A rousing night of dancing among the 2nd Heavies came to life in Frederick Lucas's letter:

> I forgot to tell you of the christening we gave our quarters last evening. We had a fine old breakdown & money muss & cotillion several kinds of reels rush washer women etc. A good fiddle was kept in motion for our gratification & under the influence of the inspiring strains of catgut & rosin we soldier's "cut it down" beautifully. Of course our party was minus the fair faces of the fair sex & never a crinoline was present at our house warming banquet. And of course too we had no oyster supper or lemonade & champagne refreshments, where we might adjourn for a short season & chat over the dainties. O' no, none of these, but all soldiers dressed in the army blue, with a soldier blue fiddler too. Yet we were not a blue set after all but on the contrary a right jolly crew of boys.[59]

Connecticut's 1st Heavy Artillery kept two dogs, Sam and Bruno. Though Sam was old and rather hefty, "On all our marches he has followed us," wrote the chaplain. "At every dress-parade and grand review Sam has been in his place as file-closer."[60]

Of the "impetuous, audacious" Bruno, the chaplain recalled, "when I was reading prayers at dress parade, Bruno marched out in front of the battalion, stood up with his fore paws resting on my shoulders, and looked over the prayer book."[61]

The 9th Connecticut had a different kind of pet.

Sam the dog took his place as "file-closer" with Company A of Connecticut's 1st Heavy Artillery.

There was big Dennis and his educated pig . . . a stray, wild breed, with stripes . . . Dennis named the pig "Jeff Davis," taught him to stand on his hind legs, hold a pipe and perform various other evolutions. The pig became quite a pet in camp.

Gen. Phelps on going his rounds one day, noticed Dennis and the pig, and was invited to witness a "review." The General laughingly consented, and Dennis proceeded to put "Jeff Davis" through a regular "drill" with pipe and stick. Gen. Phelps was heartily amused by the performance. The pig went with Dennis to New Orleans and from thence was sent to New Haven by express.[62]

Four Danbury lads in the 1st Connecticut Heavy Artillery prominently displayed their pipes and tobacco as they lounged about in camp. Daniel Perkins Dewey of the 25th Regiment wrote: "tobacco is now one of the greatest comforts I have. I fill my pipe and lie down on my back and think of home and picture all dear faces in the smoke—and then too, on a cold night on picket duty away in the lonely woods without any fire, a pipe is a great companion." (Letter from Daniel Perkins Dewey, February 17, 1863, as quoted in *A Memorial of Lieutenant Daniel Perkins Dewey of the 25th Regiment of Connecticut Volunteers*, by Caroline Lloyd, p. 59.)

The vast downtime in camp had its advantages and disadvantages. Twenty-nine-year-old Charles Coit filled a stormy week in the spring of 1864 with "reading the April 'Atlantic,' whittling & playing chess with Capt. Roberts & Alf. Goddard."[63]

"What happy afternoons reading Hugo and Dickens!" reminisced a scholarly member of the 11th Regiment about time in camp after the Battle of Fredericksburg.[64]

Evenings, especially, were times to relax and bond with comrades. In a letter home, Frederick Lucas described the scene in his hut one winter night in Fort Worth, Virginia:

> We are very comfortably situated and really enjoy our selves in our quarters, let the snow fly & the wind blow ever so furiously. Dunbar lies at his ease on his bunk, amusing himself with a comic book, entitled, "Fun for Three Months." Seargeant Henry and Corporal David are busy at writing. Will has just been releived from Regimental guard & is warming himself over the fire. Woodruff is with the Cook. While my friend North & myself are dipping from the same ink bottle.[65]

Nelson Stowe, a Waterbury man in the 14th Regiment, painted a serene image of life in camp in January of 1865: "cooked up a Dish of Cod Fish Cakes for Supper, they were good too Beautiful

Two soldiers in Connecticut's 1st Heavy Artillery struck a sociable pose with their tin cups and a jug of refreshing beverage. Early in the war, the regiment's chaplain had held a temperance meeting where a number of soldiers pledged to abstain from alcohol. (Walker, *Our First Year of Army Life*, p. 39.) But as the war stretched on, many found it difficult to sustain their pledge, especially when a sutler could be persuaded to sell the men whiskey under the table. "A soldier's life is always gay," ran the words to a song popular among the troops. "Drink, drink my boys, drink, drink my boys, dream not of the morrow." ("The Maryland Cadets' Glee," by George F. Cole, 1839.)

Moonlight Evening   Brother Lines holding forth on the Violin, a tent full listening and telling Stories until 10 PM when we turned in for the Night."[66]

But boredom could lead soldiers into some nasty habits. Card playing was continual; gambling rampant—some soldiers gambled away three months' army pay in a day. Drinking was common among both officers and enlisted men: "staid in quarters the rest of the day   drank some . . . cider with Ducker . . . spent the evening playing gin," wrote Levi Whitaker of the 11th Regiment.[67]

"What a winter it was . . . in camp at Falmouth with no field officer," wrote a young lieutenant in the 14th. "Ah, what punches Fred Doten used to mix that winter, as we gathered in each other's Sibleys: 'When every officer seemed a friend, and every friend a brother.'"[68]

A disgusted Andrew Upson of the 20th Connecticut wrote to his wife of the officers who had sullied the honor of their positions: "That list of dismissed officers I have perused . . . visiting houses of amusements & fancy women is quite common—I know several in this camp who were caught in that situation . . . Whoring is far more common than I had imagined—Men sit down & coolly relate their experience with lewd women as though it was all proper—The revolutions of depravity in our men high & low lead me almost to tremble for the fate that await us as a nation."[69]

Chaplain Henry Clay Trumbull stood before the "rustic chapel" built by the 10th Connecticut men in their camp near Richmond. "A stockade of pine logs or posts formed side walls and gable ends. A large canvas tent-fly . . . stretched over ridge-pole and rafters . . . Spring pole benches provided easy seats for several hundred persons. An attractive . . . lectern was formed by setting a small tree trunk into the earthen floor, and surmounting it with a cracker-box cover, with a rustic border in fitting forms . . . A picture of President Lincoln in a rustic frame was on the central pillar." (Henry Clay Trumbull, *War Memories of An Army Chaplain*, pp. 35–36.)

A Chaplain's Power over Their Hearts

"Every soldier was human, and because he was human he welcomed human sympathy," wrote Henry Clay Trumbull, the insightful chaplain of the 10th Connecticut. "Away from home and friends, he was glad to have a chaplain show an interest in him and his dear ones . . . If the chaplain came to his tent, the soldier loved to show him his home photographs, and to tell him of his latest home letters."

Trumbull realized that constant interaction with the men developed a "chaplain's power over their hearts for good. The more he did for them wisely, the more he could do, and the more they loved and trusted him accordingly."[70]

A good chaplain could make a world of difference to the men of his regiment—but the job was what each chaplain chose to make of it. His position in the army was unique in that he could engage soldiers of all ranks, from the highest officers to the lowest enlisted men.

John B. Doolittle left divinity school at Yale in 1864 to become chaplain of the 15th Connecticut. He replaced an earlier chaplain who had never connected with his men. Doolittle, however, "sprang at once into favor." One of the soldiers described him as a "plain, unostentatious speaker, earnest, sympathetic and sincere." (Thorpe, *History of the Fifteenth*, p. 74.) A few months after he arrived, the men surprised their new chaplain with a Christmas gift. "After dress parade . . . Sergt. Reilly of Co. C, on behalf of his comrades, led into the enclosure a valuable horse and equipments and presented the same to Chaplain John B. Doolittle as an expression of the estimation in which he was held by the regiment. The Chaplain was completely surprised, and among things in expressing his thanks, said this: 'When I was a boy I used to tell mother that when I came to be a man there were two things that I was going to have, one was a horse and the other a wife. I am now nigh on to thirty years of age, and mother has been about discouraged as to my getting either, but I shall now write her that the horse is here, so she can take courage, and when this cruel war is over, perhaps—but we won't talk of that just now.'

"Chaplain Doolittle 'mustered out' his horse with himself at the close of the war and conveyed him to Connecticut. There he remained several years and when his work called him to Nebraska, took the faithful animal along with him. About 1890 the old fellow was still 'one of the family.'" (Thorpe, *History of the Fifteenth*, pp. 212–13.)

Chaplain Trumbull made a point of getting to know all the men in the 10th Regiment. Most evenings he walked through camp, stopping to speak with this one and that one. "He very soon could call every man by his right name," wrote Cpl. Van Buren Kinney. "He taught the men to depend upon him, and they, every man of them, took all of their troubles to him, almost the same as they would to their mother."[71]

Not every chaplain had the respect of his regiment. "Our chaplain is a little runt of a churchman whose principal business (begging his reverence's pardon) is to buy sutler's stores at N. Orleans and sell them to the officers at a small profit," griped Dr. George Clary of the 13th Connecticut. "I believe the General told him the other day that he must be either sutler or chaplain."[72]

About the chaplain of the 7th Connecticut, Col. Joseph R. Hawley wrote: "He would do well for a small country parrish where everybody is good & most of them old ladies."[73]

Soothing the Savage . . . Soldier

"Capt. Ford who occupies the next tent to mine commenced singing 'Heaven is my home' & I had to go in and join," wrote twenty-six-year-old Charles Coit in April of 1864. "Several others were with him he had been singing as usual all evening. We sang until tattoo . . . We performed all the old hymns we sing at home, in fact sang the soldier's hymn book through."[74]

Many a Union soldier would have agreed with Robert E. Lee when he mused, "I don't believe we can have an army without music." Lee wasn't just talking about the bugles that directed movements on the battlefield, nor the fifes and drums that enlivened long marches.

In camp, music was hugely important. After the 15th Connecticut had lost scores of men to yellow fever, one of its soldiers reflected, "Not the least inspiring agent to rouse their spirits was the return of the brigade band . . . the old familiar music served to relieve the terrible strain on many a soldier's mind."[75]

Composers churned out hundreds of songs for the war, from the upbeat "Battle Cry of Freedom" to the moving "Battle Hymn of the Republic"; from the plaintive "Just Before the Battle, Mother" to the jaunty "Marching through Georgia." Bands serenaded the troops in camp or on the

Leading the band of the 1st Connecticut Heavy Artillery was a young Danbury musician named George E. Ives (*far left*). His son, Charles Ives, would become a renowned American composer.

march, while soldiers playing their own fiddles or banjos brought the music alive for comrades who craved both entertainment and comfort in camp.

Best of all was singing. Capt. Isaac Bromley of Norwich described the melodies drifting through the camp of his regiment, the 18th Connecticut:

> From Capt. Bates' company's street, away out there on the left, a blended harmony, produced by the upper part of the street singing "Rock of ages," while the lower half are "putting in" with "Wait for the wagons," floats over me; next on their right, Lieut. Matthewson's company are singing "John Brown's body" by snatches, and "There'll be no more sorrow there," with energy. Capt. Bowen's boys add to the volume the touching strains of "Old dog Tray," mixed up with "Joyfully, joyfully" . . .

When George E. Ives started home for Danbury in 1865, he brought along Henry Anderson Brooks, a boy of about ten years old, who'd been enslaved in Virginia. In Danbury, George and his mother, Sarah Ives, took in young Henry and arranged for his schooling locally. Henry went on to enroll at the Hampton Normal and Agricultural Institute (later Hampton University) in Virginia. After graduating, he married and began his own business in Richmond. Henry remained connected to the Ives family for many years. When his first daughter was born, he named her Sarah Elizabeth Ives Brooks.

Fifers, drummers, and buglers summoned the boys to duty in camp, each tune having its own meaning. "Roast Beef" called them to dinner; other short melodies signified assembly, surgeon's call, or guard mounting. During drills and on the march, the fife and drum kept the troops energized and (hopefully) moving in rhythm with "Yankee Doodle," "Boston Quick Step," or similar tunes. James Capron of the 19th Connecticut (far left) posed in his musician's uniform with his fife, while an unidentified comrade showed off his drum, prominently displaying its regimental marking (which appeared backwards in this tintype photograph).

> From the extreme right wing comes the strains of "Marching along," sung by
> the Greeneville Glee Club, in Company A . . . while over all comes the shrill
> voice of the sentry on the sea-wall shouting . . . "Corporal of the guard number
> twenty-three"; and there is the bugle . . . with the officers call.[76]

Many regiments even boasted glee clubs. A singer from the 1st Connecticut Cavalry recalled "More than one of those mild evenings of early spring we would sing for hours in the open air the old songs with which all were familiar—'Oh the Home we love,' . . . and then . . . 'We may fall in the heat of battle' . . . Then, every little while we would stop singing to watch the signal lights of the enemy, just across the Rapidan, and wonder what they meant."[77]

Singing together comforted and nourished the boys. Hymns and patriotic songs could even strengthen the soldiers' resolve, confirming that their sacrifice for God and country was noble.

VISITORS

"Lieut. Fiske remarked at night he would like his wife's night cap with her in it. I second the motion," wrote R. Ward Benton of Guilford to his wife Hannah in 1862.[78]

For many officers (and a few lucky enlisted men) time in camp might bring a much-anticipated visit from their wives, who braved the long journey from Connecticut to spend a few days, weeks, or even months with their husbands in camp.

"That winter we spent in camp at the foot of Stony Mountain . . . all of us envied the happy married officers who had their wives in camp," wrote a wistful Henry Goddard of the 14th Connecticut.[79] Some couples were lucky enough to stay in houses; others made do with tents.

Occasionally a conjugal visit brought an awkward moment. While visiting her husband Henry, a lieutenant in the 14th Connecticut, Mary Wadhams learned firsthand how a wife's presence could compromise an officer's authority: "She was awakened one night by the groans of a prisoner, whom Capt. Rockwood, (officer of the day) had tied up for some offense; while peeping out of her tent to learn the cause of the sounds, she saw Mrs. Rockwood issue from her tent and untie the man. When the captain discovered her at it and demanded the reason, Mrs. R. replied, 'That man has been tied up long enough,' and Rockwood succumbed."[80]

THINK OF HOME

But most soldiers, especially the young unmarried men in the rank and file, never had a visit from a family member. The long days in camp could seem empty and unending. The men craved contact with their families.

"When the mail comes," wrote Frederick Lucas of Goshen, "we rush like mad . . . to see if there is anything for us & if there should be a letter, then how the long faces brighten and you might sometimes observe a soldier boy hiding behind a tent to read his letter and you might see the tears running down his cheeks . . . The roughest men we have are often seen in tears as they read from those they love."[81]

In a letter to his parents in Litchfield, Lewis Bissell wrote with feeling: "letters from home are like sunshine after storm."[82]

Spending holidays in camp emphasized the soldiers' separation from their families. Still, the men did their best to celebrate with gusto. Homer Sprague of the 13th Connecticut described their observance of Thanksgiving in 1862:

> The day was set apart to hilarity and enjoyment. There were horse-races, mule-races, and foot-races, games of ball, and numberless other amusing exercises. Colonel Birge temporarily abdicated his position, and allowed the regiment to choose a colonel for the holiday. They accordingly selected Sergeant Ezra M. Hull, company D, who immediately arrayed himself in the garb of an Indian chief, and issued a series of amusing orders, one of which was, that whosoever should do anything right during the day should be put in the guard-house! He appointed a suitable officer-of-the-day, who arrested all that were orderly and punished all that committed no offence. A great dinner was eaten.
>
> The whole of the festivities concluded with a sham dress-parade, in which the line officers in disguise

While the men of the 13th Regiment celebrated Thanksgiving with laughter and conviviality, many soldiers bore more likeness to this print of the period. In the 21st Regiment, a farm boy from Gales Ferry noted sadly in his diary: "Thanksgiving. Snow Storm. Shoes full of holes, think of home." (Diary of George Meech, Thanksgiving 1862; courtesy of the Middlesex County Historical Society, Middletown.)

HOMESICK

personated the band of music, and the whole regiment, attired in a style that would have broken even Falstaff's heart, obeyed the standing order to do nothing right. Such a Thanksgiving was never celebrated elsewhere.[83]

When Christmas rolled around, Austin Thompson of the 16th Connecticut described for his sweetheart in Connecticut his "celebration" of the day: "I had for Christmas dinner hard tack and coffee. I could not help from thinking where I was one yeare ago . . . I had the pleasure of carving a large fat turkey, but down here all that I get a chance to carve is hard tack."[84]

Camaraderie and community were good things, but they couldn't take the edge off a soldier's longing for home and family.

> In the First Connecticut Cavalry a custom was observed that became to the Regiment very dear. When a mail arrived our Chief Bugler, Voltz, came to Head Quarters, and with a skill which few knew so well as he, played "Home, Sweet Home." It was often a very strange sound, sometimes it came during a brief halt on a march; sometimes during the lull in a battle; sometimes on return from picket—always bringing as it rang through the regiment, memories and hopes which only a soldier can understand.

> During winter quarters at Winchester, Va, it was the last sound but one from the bugle at night[.] Many a tired boy lay down to rest humming as he fell asleep that sweet strain of Home, remembering it in his dreams, awaking at reveille to find home still far away, but hoping that hope which lightened all burdens, that one day the dream should be a fact.[85]

CHAPTER NINE

All This Heroism, and All This Appalling Carnage

FIGHTING IN VIRGINIA AND LOUISIANA, SPRING AND SUMMER 1863

It turned out Burnside had been right. From the beginning, he hadn't felt capable of commanding the Army of the Potomac. Now, after a disastrous battle at Fredericksburg, and the infamous Mud March, President Lincoln removed him and, on January 28, 1863, appointed Gen. Joseph Hooker in his place.

With his troops in winter quarters and no battle on the horizon, Hooker set to work to improve the soldiers' living conditions and to raise morale. The men of the 14th Connecticut "saw a great change in rations and clothing, with fresh bread every other day and plenty of fresh meat, potatoes, beans, peas and other vegetables . . . This had a marked influence on the spirit and good feeling of the boys."[1]

Fighting Joe now looked ahead, constructing a strategy for the spring of 1863 that he hoped would put the war on a new footing. Lee's 60,000 Confederates remained entrenched at Fredericksburg. Hooker planned to split his 130,000 troops into two wings. The majority would march north and west, cross the Rappahannock and Rapidan Rivers, and loop around behind the Confederates to hit Lee's left flank. The smaller force would cross the Rappahannock and attack the rebels' right flank.

"My plans are perfect," Hooker said smugly, "and when I start to carry them out may God have mercy on General Lee, for I will have none."

On April 27, the Army of the Potomac began to move. Speed was paramount, and when Union commanders found that the bridge spanning the Rapidan was gone, they couldn't wait. The men fixed bayonets, hung their cartridge boxes from them, and scrambled down the steep banks.

Holding their guns over their heads, they plunged in, singing "John Brown's Body" as the cold spring water reached their armpits.

Two days later, both of Hooker's wings were on Lee's side of the river and would soon close in on the Confederate entrenchments.

General Lee was looking into the lion's mouth. The obvious solution was to abandon Fredericksburg and flee south. Instead, Lee made the risky and astonishing decision to split his small force, leaving some 10,000 troops to defend Fredericksburg, while he took the remainder of his army through the snarled underbrush of the Wilderness to strike Hooker's troops head-on.

Hooker, sure that he had Lee's army at his mercy, moved ahead with his plan. By April 30, thousands of Union troops were massing near a hamlet called Chancellorsville, but instead of pushing on immediately, Hooker opted to wait for more of his troops to arrive.

The delay gave the Confederates a small window of opportunity—and with it came an incredible piece of good luck. Near midnight on April 30, Jeb Stuart brought Lee the news that the Union's right flank was unprotected. Gen. O. O. Howard, commanding the Union's 11th Corps, had failed to anchor his command (the far right of the Union line) against an obstacle that would protect it.

Lee and Stonewall Jackson rapidly drew up plans. On May 1, Jackson maneuvered his division through the tangled woods, aiming to come around behind Howard's troops on the Union right.

Union scouts spotted the rebel movements on May 2, but both Howard and Hooker, convinced that the enemy was in retreat, ignored the reports.

THE 11TH CORPS BREAKS

On the Union right, in General Howard's 11th Corps, the men of the 17th Connecticut were wondering what was going on. William Warren, twenty-one, was on picket duty on May 2. Around him the landscape was "low and swampy, and covered with patches of woods, with deep and thick underbrush, being almost impenetrable."[2] Warren and his comrades could hear—though not see—artillery passing by, yet their officers seemed unconcerned. Midafternoon, a new detail came on picket, relieving Warren and his fellows who returned to their regiment to cook dinner.

> It was while we were thus engaged—probably about 5 o'clock—that we were startled by a discharge of musketry. Immediately after we heard the order to "fall in!," and ran back to our position and our guns. When we got here the firing was rapidly increasing in volume . . . the shells skimming over the hill came close to our heads and caused us to hug the ground several times. The attack came on our right flank from the woods in which we had been on picket a short time before.[3]

The Rebels were nearly upon them. Between them and the Confederates was a low hill. "We could not see the enemy but we knew where they were," said William Warren, "and we could see some of the terrible effects of their fire." Shells screamed by, tearing up a barn, a fence, and one of the horses from the battery that the 17th Connecticut was supposed to be supporting. "Almost at the first fire the regiments on our right and our left fled from the scene, not even taking their guns with them . . . the [artillery] men cut their horses free from the guns and fled upon them."[4]

Wealthy and dignified, forty-nine-year-old William H. Noble commanded the 17th Connecticut. A Bridgeport lawyer and P. T. Barnum's business partner, Noble had been a conservative Democrat before the war—but when Sumter fell, Noble made clear his loyalty to the Union. In the regiment's early months, Noble was despised by the soldiers he led. "He did not understand the tactics. In fact he had not drilled the regiment since its organization. It was not believed he was capable of doing it," wrote one of his men. When all but two of the 17th's officers signed a petition to have him removed from command, Noble had them arrested. At Chancellorsville a few weeks later, "the colonel showed that for bravery he had no superior in the army, and the regiment became proud of the officer it had sought to remove." (William Warren, Article 9; Bridgeport History Center, Bridgeport Public Library.)

The 17th's colonel, William Noble, had galloped off to the right to find his pickets whom Stonewall Jackson's men had surprised. As Noble approached, his second-in-command, Lt. Col. Charles Walter, rose to his feet, only to be shot in the head a few moments later.

The remainder of the regiment, frantic with uncertainty, waited for orders on the left. "There we stood, with our guns in our hands, nobody to fire at, no one to tell us to go ahead or fall back," remembered Private Warren.[5] The sounds of musketry fire told the men that that at any second the enemy would crest the hill that protected them. The regiment's major, Allen Brady, was in command there, but he made no move.

One of the 17th's captains demanded that Brady act, but the major protested that he had no instructions from Colonel Noble. "I have no right to give orders."

"Thus we stood there, the metal hail becoming thicker and thicker. The captain again spoke: 'Major, if you don't give orders immediately, I will.' Then the major shouted: 'Break and run for the woods; every man for himself!'

"The instant the major's order was given we dashed across the road into the woods . . . The woods were full of fleeing patriots, each man bent on making the best possible time in widening the distance between us and the enemy."[6]

A Union officer watched the rout in wonder, exclaiming, "I have seen horses and cattle stampeded on the plains, blinded, apparently, by fright, rush over wagons, rocks, streams, any obstacle in the way; but never, before or since, saw I thousands of men actuated seemingly by the same unreasoning fear that takes possession of a herd of animals."[7]

As Colonel Noble attempted to lead his 17th Connecticut in an orderly withdrawal, a Confederate bullet sliced through an artery in his left arm. Bleeding profusely and nearing unconsciousness, Noble was unable to guide his wounded horse. Two of his soldiers rushed forward, and led him to a field hospital in the rear.[8]

Meanwhile, pandemonium reigned as the 11th Corps broke. Soldiers running for their lives, cavalry horses galloping in terror, shells screaming by, a hail of bullets whistling out of the woods—then suddenly, the men heard music.

The band of the Fourteenth Connecticut went right out into that open space between our new line and the rebels, with shot and shell crashing all about them, and played "The Star Spangled Banner," "The Red, White and Blue" and "Yankee Doodle" and repeated them for fully twenty minutes . . .

Never was American grit more finely illustrated. Its effect upon the men was magical. Imagine the strains of our grand national hymn, "The Star Spangled Banner," suddenly bursting upon your ears out of that horrible pandemonium of panic-born yells, mingled with the roaring of musketry and the crashing of artillery . . . Its strains were clear and thrilling for a moment, then smothered by that fearful din, an instant later sounding bold and clear again, as if it would fearlessly emphasize the refrain, "our flag is still there."[9]

Thousands of men in the 11th Corps had fled through woods and fields, back toward Chancellorsville. Finding an earthwork, a great number from different regiments halted there and rallied, turning to face the enemy. But as the Rebel troops came on inexorably, the 11th Corps men again took flight. They met an oncoming force: the Union 12th Corps swiftly advancing to stem the tide.

In the 12th Corps marched two Connecticut regiments, the 5th and the 20th. Major General Slocum, commanding the corps, threw his troops forward until they could deploy behind a long stone wall. Behind them a battery drew up, and then the jumbled remains of the 11th Corps. By now daylight was nearly gone. As darkness fell, the firing gradually dropped off.

THE FIGHTING 14TH

For the experienced soldiers of the 14th Connecticut, the sun had barely come up when their 2nd Corps faced the Rebels. The 14th charged ahead, driving the rebels for perhaps half a mile, until the Connecticut boys were well in advance of the rest of the Union battle line. Capt. Samuel Fiske went forward with a message for his colonel to pull the men back. After delivering the message, Fiske started back, rounding up Confederate prisoners on the way.

I would disarm, and put them in squads of three or four, in the charge of some one of our slightly wounded men, . . . till I had picked up some twenty or more of the "Butternuts." Had a couple of the fellows on my hands, and none of my own men in sight, and was hurrying them forward by the persuasion of cocked revolver, expecting every moment to come upon our general; when all at once, pressing through a terribly dense portion of undergrowth, I found myself face to face, at not twelve feet distance, with at least a whole regiment of the brownest and ill-looking vagabonds that I ever set eyes on . . .

. . . Here was a big mouthful to swallow for a belligerent patriot, intent on squelching the Rebellion, . . . Here was a capital chance for a man, who had just gotten his hand in at the business of capturing prisoners, to put a thousand or fifteen hundred more in his bag,—if they would only let him. The undersigned is compelled to acknowledge, that . . . he had drawn a mighty big elephant in the lottery, and didn't know what to do with him.

Few soldiers could write like Samuel Fiske. A minister in Madison, Connecticut, Fiske was also a journalist, chronicling his regiment's doings for a newspaper in his home state of Massachusetts. Writing under the byline of "Dunn Browne" (dun being a dull, grayish brown color), Fiske sent the *Springfield Republican* perceptive articles about battle, camp life, and the frustrations of military red tape. His inimitable tongue-in-cheek style made his accounts of army life stand out from the writings of thousands of other soldiers. Fiske was master of the subtle line—"Things *was* different from the way they were, with a vengeance."

One of the impudent wretches he had captured a few minutes before turned round with a grin, and says, "Cap'en, I reckon things is different from the way they was; and you'll have to 'low you're our prisoner now." A very sensible remark of the young man, and timely, though he didn't have a shirt to his back, and only a pair of pantaloons. Things *was* different from the way they were, with a vengeance.

I gracefully lowered my pistol to an officer, who stepped out from the ranks, and presented to him, apologizing for so doing by the remark, that "doubtless it would be more disagreeable for a whole regiment to surrender to one man, than for one man to surrender to a whole regiment."[10]

While Fiske was busy surrendering, the rest of the 14th Connecticut was retreating under heavy fire, "which we did in very good order, carrying our wounded with us and finally coming out of the woods at the identical spot where we had stacked our knap sacks the night before," wrote Elnathan Tyler. "Any other regiment than the Fourteenth might not have stopped to get their knapsacks under the circumstances, but we had had experience in losing knapsacks . . . we hunted up our own as quickly as possible, and then leisurely and in perfect order still, went back and took up a new position some distance to the rear."[11]

OUR BRAVE BOYS: THE 20TH CONNECTICUT

The 14th boys moved off with their knapsacks and characteristic nonchalance, but the men of the 20th Connecticut were fighting for their lives. Horatio Chapman, a thirty-six-year-old school-teacher from East Hampton, chronicled the battle in his diary:

we had but little or no protection from their battery, the shells of which came screeching and tearing and bursting and [gone] were foot, a finger, and perhaps both arms. Others had bullets through their bodies and were wounded in various places, and their shrieks and groans were sad to hear. Some one was falling constantly in our midst.

After shelling us about two hours and not succeeding in driving us from our position, a battalion of rebel infantry with a yell which seemed almost

Daniel Lee Jewett, assistant surgeon, 20th Connecticut

deafening and unearthly, emerged from the woods and with fixed bayonets charged upon us with impetuosity and fury . . . Our fire was reserved until they were within short range. We opened upon them with fearful effect. They recoiled for a moment but again steadily advanced. We poured volley after volley in rapid succession into their ranks. They wavered, then halted and about faced and broke for the cover of the woods.

Their battery again commenced shelling us and it told fearfully on our brave boys . . . They charged a second time and were again repulsed with considerable loss. They massed and charged a third time . . . in the front of the 145th New York of our brigade. This regiment could not stand the onslaught of the massed hordes but gave way and fled . . .

As the rebels poured over the breast-works, our . . . brave Lieutenant-Colonel Wooster . . . ordered a retreat and every man for himself . . . Cousin Fred running by my side as fast as his legs would carry him, was wounded, fell, and taken prisoner.

Casting my eye as I was running, a little over my shoulder, to the right, I saw two or three rebels almost abreast of me, crying, "Halt, Halt you—Yank." But I didn't halt worth a cent for I was quite sure their guns had been discharged as well as my own, and I well knew this was no time to reload . . . I ran as though my very life depended upon it . . .

. . . beyond on a long rise of ground were two batteries of twelve pounder brass pieces, and General Kane was doing his best to hurry us up to get us in the rear of those brass cannon which were double shotted with grape and canister, and as soon as that was accomplished they simultaneously opened upon the rebels . . . literally mowed them down in heaps. They halted and retreated and as it was now dark the battle of the day was ended.[12]

The 20th had nearly 100 casualties. Some of the wounded had been carried to a field hospital in the Chancellor house. Here the regiment's assistant surgeon, twenty-two-year-old Dan Jewett, was doing his best to treat his mangled patients. As Hooker's troops fled, "the rebels opened fire upon this house, literally riddling it, and finally setting it on fire. Assistant Surgeon Jewett had a man killed under his hands upon the operating table, and others were killed by the bursting of shells in the house. Through it all, these brave surgeons stood by their unfortunate comrades, and, finally, when the building took fire, rescued them from the flames by carrying them to places of safety—a piece of heroism worthy of a better fate than that which soon after befell them"—capture and imprisonment.[13]

27th Connecticut Surprised

Early that morning, the men of the 27th Connecticut had hustled into entrenchments that they'd dug two nights earlier. Their first battle experience, at Fredericksburg, had left them wary. Now, peering into the woods, "we could indistinctly see a large body of infantry making a wide circuit to the right, seemingly with a view to attack some remote part of the line. A similar movement took place also to the left. 'Look out on the right!' 'Look out on the left!' passed up and down the line, and every man was on the alert."

"Suddenly, from unseen batteries behind us, comes a deep roar, and the next moment shell after shell shrieks through the trees and bursts almost in the rifle-pits."[14] Was it Union artillery with poor aim? Or had the rebels gotten around *behind* the 27th? Colonel Bostwick, a thirty-one-year-old clerk in his father's saddle and harness shop, sent his major to seek out their general. The major did not return.

In a few moments the shelling ceased, and far up the road in front appeared a rebel officer waving a flag of truce, and slowly advancing, waiting for a recognition. The men stopped firing in the immediate vicinity of the road . . . At length the rebel officer arrived within a few paces of the works . . . he had been sent to inform us that we were entirely surrounded; that there was no possible avenue of escape, and therefore he summoned us to surrender, and thus avoid the loss of life which would inevitably follow any resistance to the overwhelming force in front and rear . . .

Meanwhile Lieutenant-Colonel Merwin went up through the woods in the rear only to find it too true that the rebels were posted in strong force, to bar any escape in that direction. Masses of the enemy pouring in on the right and left, revealed at once the desperate position in which we were placed, while the singing bullets from the woods behind as well as in front, indicated that the foe were closing in upon us.

The first impulse among officers and men was to attempt to force our way through. But it was evident that such a course would result in the destruction of more than half our number, while the remainder would inevitably fall into the hands of the enemy. After a hurried consultation among the officers, a surrender was agreed upon."[15]

As it turned out, General Hancock had ordered a retreat, but word had never reached the 27th Connecticut. While the units around them withdrew, the regiment had remained at its post in a ravine with underbrush that hid the other troops' movements.[16] Now the men of the 27th Connecticut marched off as prisoners.

The Wounded

Far worse was the fate of the wounded left on the battlefield. James McWhinnie, a soldier of the 20th Connecticut with a bullet in his leg, detailed the men's sufferings after the battle ended:

> There is no shouting or crying of the wounded. In quiet tones they speak to each other. The question passes back and forth, "Where are you wounded?" "Through the body." "And you?" "An arm broken." "My knee smashed." "My lungs!"

> So the low replies pass around. Words of cheer are spoken. Prayers are offered, while over the faces of some the strange gray look is coming that betokens the approach of death. One lies near who had raised many a laugh in the ranks, but now jesting is forgotten. An awe struck face reveals his consciousness of the coming change. A few feet away lies a lieutenant, lately promoted, the smile still on his face, so suddenly the bullet had cut the thread of life. Here and there the confederates are hurrying after their regiments, that are following our retreating army. We are in their hands prisoners on the field.

> One of them, a huge North Carolinian stops near me and seeing my efforts to get out of bullet range puts his hands under my arms and gently lifts me over the little brook and behind a log breastwork in safety. In reply to my question whether he had had any coffee lately, he replies, "Not for three months," and glad to accept the bag of coffee and sugar I offered him. He turns to wave it in a parting salute as he disappears in the woods.

> The long day draws to a close. Four of us thrust our guns by the bayonets into the ground and fastening the corners of a blanket in the gunlocks, under this shelter pass the night. In the early dawn, as we begin to distinguish our comrades here and there, we speak to them. Some of them answer us with feebler voices than yesterday; and some are silent forever, having entered their last sleep in the night.

> The sun rises and another day wears on—the living among the dead, wounds are growing sore and painful. Cries begin to be heard, especially from those

whose wounds are in the body and very serious. The rebels come among us in squads and talk freely with us. Four young Mississippians, addressing each other as "Gentlemen" make us coffee from our provisions and at our invitation sit down to drink it with us. Not an unkind word is spoken. Another confederate asks if he can do anything for us, saying, "I would like to do something in return for the kindness I received when a prisoner in the North."

. . . Another night passes and the morning finds us with fewer alive than yesterday . . . the news comes that the woods are on fire behind us and that rebel and union wounded alike are being consumed in the flames . . . getting onto my feet, by aid of a couple of reversed muskets for crutches, [I] slowly make my way out among the unburied dead.

I look into their faces as I hop over them and scarcely realize that they cannot answer when I speak to them. As I approach a pair of bars which I must pass, a company of rebel cavalry come up on the other side. The captain halts there and speaks to me, "Come on, sergeant, we'll wait for you." One of his men dismounts and comes forward to aid me. Going to a pile of muskets he brings me two of a better size, and with a good natured "You's all right now," mounts and moves off with his company.[17]

Still determined and erect, James McWhinnie stood with the help of crutches for his photograph. At Chancellorsville, a bullet had torn through McWhinnie's left leg, but it was days before he received medical care. Luckier than most, he survived a delayed amputation above the knee. (Connecticut Historical Society, Hartford.) More than a year after the battle, James had finally recovered enough to be discharged. (Soldier identification courtesy of Peter Drummey, the Massachusetts Historical Society.)

Abner Smith of the 20th Connecticut wrote, "I helped carry one man on a strecher six or eight miles. I tell you that was a hard job." The next day Smith transported more wounded during a thunderstorm and a night of drenching rain. It was the following day before the miserable wounded soldiers reached Falmouth to be loaded into train cars for the jolting trip to a hospital.[18]

Two weeks after the Battle of Chancellorsville, Abner again wrote home, describing the horrifying conditions of the boys whose wounds had gone untended day after day.

> those of the wounded that I saw had fared rather hard   they did not get much to eat and their wounds had not been taken care of   a good many or the biggar part of them had not been meddled with except to have a rage [rag] wound round them and such a smell was what got me   I helped load a good many that I thought would knock my head off or at least would make me throw up my insides boots and all, but they poor fellows are to be pittyed   some of them the flies had been to work around and they was rather wormy but by this time they are whare they will have good care taken of them, I hope so at any rate.[19]

Though the clear victors at Chancellorsville, the Confederates also had their share of casualties—nearly 13,000. Their costliest loss was Stonewall Jackson. While reconnoitering through the darkness on the evening of May 2, Jackson was accidentally shot in the arm by North Carolina soldiers on picket duty. A surgeon amputated the general's arm. Lee sent a message: "Give General Jackson my affectionate regards, and say to him: he has lost his left arm but I my right." After the amputation, pneumonia set in; on May 10, 1863, Stonewall Jackson died. His death was a terrible blow for Lee and the South.

Hooker and the Army of the Potomac crawled back to Falmouth. Fighting Joe wasn't bragging any more. On June 28, 1863, President Lincoln replaced Hooker with Gen. George Meade.

Port Hudson, Louisiana

While the Army of the Potomac battled Lee in the East, thousands of Union soldiers were marching through areas of the Deep South that often felt to them like a foreign country.

The Mississippi River flowed straight through the Confederacy, dividing it in two. From the war's beginning, both sides had realized that control of the Mississippi River was essential to victory. The South used the river to transport supplies and troops. Northern commanders were intent on shutting down the supply route and splitting the Confederacy's states and territories.

Early in 1862, the Union had taken over New Orleans. The Confederates, worried they would lose control of the river's midsection, strengthened their positions at Port Hudson, Louisiana, and Vicksburg, Mississippi.

To gain control of the river, the Union would need to seize both Confederate strongholds. The plan was for Maj. Gen. Ulysses S. Grant to capture the Rebel fortifications at Vicksburg while 110 miles downriver, Gen. Nathaniel Banks's Army of the Gulf would attack Port Hudson, Louisiana.

Banks's command—approximately 35,000 troops—included seven Connecticut units: the 9th, 12th, 13th, 24th, 25th, 26th, and 28th Regiments. After long, crowded voyages, the Connecticut

It looked like a life of ease for these officers of the 13th Connecticut seated on elegant furniture "requisitioned" from Southern homes. The sofa where Colonel Charles Blinn sat probably once graced a secessionist's parlor; now its shredded upholstery bore the marks of the Union officers' spurs. When Captain Homer Sprague (*second from right*) wrote the 13th's regimental history, he recounted a scene in Louisiana: "That morning a rebel planter requested Col. Birge to furnish a guard to protect his property. 'Certainly,' said the Colonel, 'if you are a loyal citizen of the United States.' 'I'm a loyal citizen of the Confederate States,' he answered with an oath. 'Then I can't furnish a guard,' was the rejoinder. In a few minutes we saw, on looking back, a dense mass of smoke ascending from his dwelling." (Homer B. Sprague, *History of the 13th Infantry Regiment of Connecticut Volunteers during the Great Rebellion*, p. 122.)

Connecticut's 9th Regiment, composed primarily of Irish immigrants or the sons of Irish immigrants, came south in December of 1861. Stationed in Mississippi and Louisiana, the 9th soldiers endured months of deprivations. Men drilled barefoot, sometimes wearing just a soldier's blouse and underdrawers. Though the regiment lost only 10 men in battle, nearly 250 perished from disease. "The swamp reeked with malaria, and the men slept upon the mud. The supply of quinine . . . was exhausted; there was little medicine of any sort . . . Almost the whole of the Ninth regiment was at one time on the sick-list with fever caused by exposure and privation. The poor fellows died sometimes at the fearful rate of a score a week." (Thomas Hamilton Murray, *History of the Ninth Regiment, Connecticut Volunteer Infantry*, p. 109.)

boys found themselves in tropical landscapes that took them by surprise: live oaks hung with moss, elegant plantations, cypress swamps, palm trees, alligators. The air was hot and moist and redolent with the scent of flowers. One of the Nutmeggers wrote in his diary: "The country charms me with its magnificent lemon and orange groves . . . Upon my word, I am in love with the Sunny South!"[20]

While the scenery in the Deep South might be charming, the mosquitoes were relentless. The Northerners had barely arrived before disease—malaria, typhoid, dysentery—sped through their ranks, claiming hundreds and hundreds of lives.

Banks's troops tangled several times with Confederates in Louisiana, in skirmishes and minor engagements, but these were only previews to what would be the longest siege in American history. In March of 1863, Banks marched his troops toward Port Hudson. On the bluffs overlooking the river, the Confederates had erected earthworks and mounted artillery to control the waterway below.

Adm. David Farragut of the Union navy planned to run a fleet of seven ships past the Confederate batteries at Port Hudson. Farragut would then be in a position to cut off the Rebels' supply route. The role of Banks's troops was to engage the Confederates, distracting them from the admiral's fleet. But Farragut jumped the gun, sending his vessels ahead before Banks's troops were in place. Confederate artillery concentrated its force on Farragut's warships, causing great damage, though two Union ships were able to pass by the Rebel entrenchments.

CAMP MISERY

Unengaged, the Army of the Gulf was sent back to Baton Rouge. Homer Sprague of the 13th Connecticut described the disastrous return march:

> A heavy rain commenced falling, and the roads were soon flooded. We waded on mile after mile in the semi-fluid mud, our shoes and boots being filled by the torrents of water . . . All day and for an hour after nightfall we toiled slowly on, till we reached a point about eight miles above Baton Rouge, when we were

"Phelps and Watson's historical and military map of the border & southern states," 1863

marched by the flank out of the road and into a pond of water, and told to pass the night there! It was an old canefield. The water was from an inch to a foot in depth, with occasional mud islands, stumps, logs, and clusters of bushes . . . darkness was upon us, and the rain was yet falling. Such nights are more destructive than battles . . .

A few of our soldiers . . . groping in the darkness, contrived to get a poor supply of wood, and after a time we had two fires blazing; but there was not room to sleep around them. Colonel Warner, with the surgeon and chaplain and several other officers, gathered around one burning stump, and, after a brief discussion, decided that . . . "The only way to keep the water out is to keep the whiskey in." The chaplain hailed every passer by, with, "Halt! Who goes there? Advance, friend, and give the Countersign!" and then imparted spirituous comfort. Doctor C, usually so abstemious, distinguished himself on this occasion equally by his wit, his sound strategic views, and his medical skill. His advice, loudly proclaimed, and enforced by his own example, was: "If you cant take Port Hudson take Baton Rouge; and if you cant take Baton Rouge, take whiskey!"

Many were the uncomfortable nights we passed, but none worse than this. We named the spot, "Camp Misery."[21]

Alden Skinner was sixty-three when he enlisted as surgeon in Connecticut's 25th Regiment. A Vernon physician, Dr. Skinner was old enough to be grandfather to many of his soldiers. The men loved him. "No one exhibited more tender feeling for the suffering and afflicted than he," wrote one man, "and when there was no hope, he wept like a child." ("Biographical Sketch of the Late Alden Skinner, M.D. of Vernon" by K. Gregory Hall, read before the Tolland County Medical Meeting, April 20, 1864, in *The Proceedings and Medical Communications of the Connecticut Medical Society*, second series, vol. 2, 1864–67.)

Tending scores of men sick with fevers, Dr. Skinner himself succumbed to disease, dying in Baton Rouge on March 30, 1863. Nearly fifty years after his death, his patients still remembered him "with reverent tenderness. He was a good man, a kindly man, whose presence in the sick room was a benediction. He carried cheer with him wherever he went. This was part of his medicine." (*Centennial of Vernon [Rockville]*, history compiled by Henry C. Smith, p. 19.)

During that wretched night in the swamp, the men of the 25th Connecticut learned about dedication from one of their own. Their colonel described "the noble act of Quartermaster John S. Ives, who, almost dead himself, rode his almost dead horse into Baton Rouge and brought out to the men coffee and sugar, which they managed to prepare over small fires."[22]

✳ ✳ ✳

HIND SIDE BEFORE

For Samuel K. Ellis of Rockville, a private in the 25th Connecticut, one skirmish with the Confederates remained vivid in his memory. In April of 1863, General Banks led his troops on an exhausting march to Bayou Vermillion, hoping to arrive before Rebels could destroy a bridge there. But as the bone-weary Union troops approached, Confederate cavalry tore across the bridge, then demolished it.

> The next day was Sunday and while we camped there waiting for the construction of a new bridge, about half the advance division took the opportunity to strip and go in bathing. Suddenly, without an instant's warning, a troupe of cavalry dashed down the opposite bank, and opened fire upon us. Such a spectacle never before was seen. The long roll was sounding and naked men, in every direction were making a dash for their guns, trying to dress as they ran. Some with their trousers on hind side before, didn't know whether they were advancing or retreating, and some ran the wrong way, others, with simply a shirt and cap, were trying to adjust their belts.[23]

✳ ✳ ✳

Back to Port Hudson

It was May before General Banks was ready to return to Port Hudson, where Confederate general Franklin Gardner waited with about 7,000 Rebels behind earthworks stretching over four miles around the town.

John DeForest, a captain in Connecticut's 12th regiment, wrote: "Port Hudson, as I saw it, was an immense knoll or bluff, two miles in diameter, with a rolling surface, a forest, a church, a few scattered houses, and two or three encampments of tents or shanties. The edge of the bluff was marked by a zigzag earth-work, rough in construction, and by no means lofty; and from this line the ground sank on all sides into a valley which in some places was a ravine choked with felled trees."[24]

View of the Confederate works at Port Hudson.

General Banks brought some 30,000 to 40,000 troops to envelop the Confederate position. He might have laid siege to Port Hudson until the enemy ran out of supplies. But Banks was eager to take the rebel position quickly, and move north to aid Grant at Vicksburg. He ordered an assault on the rebel works for May 27. Four of his generals would lead simultaneous attacks from different areas. Since Union forces outnumbered Gardner's rebels four to one, victory seemed within reach.

But an attack on any fortification was fraught with difficulties, as Captain DeForest pointed out.

> Look at a wave rushing up a sloping beach against a line of rocks, and you will see the history of an assaulting column directed against fortifications. At a distance the billow seems irresistible; near at hand the under-current has deprived it of half its force; at last merely a little spray dashes upon the final impediment. Just so slaughter, misdirection, dispersion, and skulking enfeeble the column until only hundreds out of thousands reach the point of hand-to-hand fighting . . . The attacking force must do what is very difficult in the open field; it must advance without firing against a line which is firing at it; it must do this in spite of difficulties of ground which inevitably break up its organization; and after long-continued slaughter it must scale defenses fringed with bayonets.[25]

The terrain before the Confederate fortifications was a jumble of obstacles. Homer Sprague, an intelligent and thoughtful captain in the 13th Connecticut, looked despairingly at what lay before them: "standing timber, and then many precipitous, crooked ravines, filled with a tangled mass of felled trees, vines and brambles; and the level ground was scarcely less obstructed; all being in clear view and point-blank range of the enemy's works, from which arose incessant puffs of smoke, as their men fired from safe cover."[26]

MAY 27, 1863

"I think General Banks ordered the assault of May 27 in the hope that some stroke of luck might give him the victory; and perhaps a general is justified in betting lives upon such a chance," wrote John DeForest. "Yet I never think of that bloody day without saying to myself that we had a very small chance of winning."[27]

Among the advancing troops were two African American regiments, the 1st Louisiana and the 3rd Louisiana, in the first major battle in which white soldiers fought alongside black soldiers. It was a sad fact that many whites, both soldiers and civilians, felt African Americans would not have the courage for combat.

Sgt. George Hammond of Connecticut's 26th Regiment wrote:

> The first thing done was to accept 30 volunteers from our regiment & more from others to form an advance storming party. [The Confederate] parapet had a ditch filled with water outside & in order to get over it you must fill it or make a bridge.
>
> Now, with this party went a lot of niggers with poles and boards to make this bridge. We had a battery on our left clear the parapet. Soon came the order, Charge! Bayonets! Forward! Double Quick! We got within a few hundred yards when they opened their musketry & shot & shell.
>
> Our battery dare not fire in our front so we had to contest our way with muskets alone. Balls whistled on either side. Men commenced to be wounded. But we rushed on as best we could and it brought the different regiments together.

We broke our line, which is not military, but in our haste to advance could not be helped.

We fought in this way about an hour & then there was an order to retreat, but most did not & would not. There was a ravine at the right of the line where many men got to. But it was no use. We could not carry the place this day.[28]

Sam Ellis described an adrenaline-pumping experience as the 25th Connecticut charged forward.

We marched on the double-quick down through the woods, when we were ordered by General Grover to advance to the front and carry the earthworks . . . We rushed on through the woods and down a hill, swept by the enemy's artillery. Here we turned to the right and emerged on to a plain. I shall never forget that sight. The valley was filled with felled trees, and heavy underbrush, while thick and black rolled the battle-smoke.

There was a hill on our left, strongly entrenched and from here loomed up a big gun. Just below on a little bridge was planted a stand of the Stars and Stripes, the glorious old banner, and gathered around it stood a handful of brave men firing a stream of bullets upon that piece. For six long hours the gunners did not dare approach to load and that wicked looking gun was kept silent.

John Stanton, forty-four, had been a watchman in Norwich before becoming captain in the 26th Connecticut. "Our Captain was brave, very, but was equally as rash or crazy," wrote George Hammond about Stanton. "He was up the farthest . . . of most any cheering and waving his hands in defiance of the Rebels & was shot through the head and died almost instantly." (Letter of Sgt. George Hammond to his father, June 1, 1863, collection of Lawrence S. Matthew.)

. . . It was here that we had a taste of real war in all its horrors. It was a sort of a floating panorama that passed before me, a hideous dream. There was a roaring and crashing of artillery, bursting of shells and the rattle of muskets, with hissing and whistling of minié balls and battle-smoke lowering down upon us. There were men dropping here and there and all the horrid experiences of war.

Still we kept on; there was a short turn to the right and in single file we commenced ascending through a deep ravine. Wading through water, stumbling over and under fallen trees, we finally came to a pit about six feet deep; when we had gotten out of that we were on the side of the hill where we had to prepare to make a charge.

It was a wicked place to charge. The nature of the ground was such it was impossible to form in battle line, so to make the attack in three columns over felled trees which were cris-crossed in every shape imaginable. We waited here for a few moments with beating hearts, waiting for the forward charge. The word came and with a terrifying yell we rose to our feet and rushed forward. It was a terrible time, when bounding over the last tree and crashing through some brush we came out within a short distance of the enemy's entrenchments, and it seemed as though a thousand rifles were cracking our doom.

This fire was too deadly for men to stand against. Our brave fellows, shot down as fast as they could come up, were beaten back. Then occurred one of those heroic deeds we sometimes read about. The colors of the One Hundred and Fifty-ninth New York were left on the hill, their color sergeant having been killed. Corporal Buckley of our regiment calmly worked back in that terrific fire, picked up the dear old flag and brought it in, turned to pick up his gun and was killed. He was a noble fellow and much beloved in the regiment.

Resting here a short time, we made a second charge with the same deadly results . . . Sharpshooters on the left picking us off; sharpshooters on right giving it to us and the rifle pits in front. Here we had to stay till after 10 o'clock that night when the order came to fall back, which we did, bringing off our wounded. I was so tired I fell asleep and barely woke in time to get away."[29]

Inside the fortifications, the Confederates were spread thin along the 4½-mile perimeter. If the Union attacks had occurred simultaneously, the rebels might have had trouble repulsing them. But Banks had failed to coordinate the battle: while some forces struck early in the morning, others didn't charge until noon. Gardner was able to shift his forces from place to place to meet the assaults separately. The attack failed miserably. The Confederates lost about 250 defenders; for the Union, a sober John DeForest wrote, "nineteen hundred brave men had fallen uselessly."[30]

Capt. Jedediah Randall, twenty-eight, posed in a resolute stance with the flag, before the 26th Connecticut left for the South. Randall's Company K was known as the Groton Company as nearly every man came from there. When the 26th went into battle for the first time on May 27 at Port Hudson, Randall led his Groton boys forward before falling with a bullet in each leg. "Lieut.-Col. Selden tried to help him; but he said, 'Never mind me, colonel; I'm all right: go and take care of the boys.'" (W. A. Croffut and John M. Morris, *The Military and Civil History of Connecticut during the War of 1861–65*, p. 424.) Randall died June 9, 1863.

Trench Duty

And then, said Captain DeForest, "came forty days and nights in the wilderness of death."[31] The siege had begun.

Union soldiers lost no time in digging in, creating a warren of trenches that gave them at least partial shelter from the rebel sharpshooters and artillerymen. Each side kept up artillery and infantry fire, day after day. Crouched in their trenches or huddled behind earthworks, the men never knew when an enemy shell would hurtle toward them. If a soldier lifted his head a fraction of an inch above the parapet, a sharpshooter took off the top of his skull. Every man's nerves were taut.

"The nuisance of trench duty," explained DeForest, "does not consist in the overwhelming amount of danger at any particular moment, but in the fact that danger is perpetually present. The spring is always bent; the nerves never have a chance to recuperate; the elasticity of courage is slowly worn out."[32]

John Crosby, a thirty-eight-year-old lieutenant in the 24th Connecticut, acknowledged the unremitting strain. "I told the Col. Yesterday that if I could only go off somewhere and have a good cry, put on some clean clothes, get a letter from home, that I would be ready to come back and die like a Christian," he wrote to his wife.[33]

For the occupying force, a routine developed:

> the rule was, one day at the parapet and two days off. On duty days we popped away at the enemy, or worked at strengthening our natural rampart. We laid a line of logs along the crest of the knoll, cut notches in them and then put on another tier of logs, thus providing ourselves with port-holes. With the patience of cats watching for mice the men would peer for hours through the port-holes waiting a chance to shoot a rebel; and the faintest show of the crown of a hat above the hostile fortification, not distinguishable to the inexperienced eye, would draw a bullet . . . The garrison gave us full as good as we sent. Several of our men were shot in the face through the port-holes as they were taking aim.[34]

Being off duty brought no respite from the anxiety. "During our relief days we were quite as much shot at, without the comforting excitement of shooting," DeForest wrote.[35] John B. Clark, a Durham man in the 24th Connecticut, was sitting behind the lines eating dinner when an enemy bullet pierced his hand, traveled down his neck and settled into his lung, where it remained for the rest of his life.

For three weeks after the failed assault, the Union troops lived in their trenches, dodging death amidst the punishing heat and a growing stench. Hundreds of men collapsed with heat-stroke, which killed some and left others insane.

Inside Port Hudson, the Rebels' food was dwindling. On June 13, General Banks demanded that Gardner surrender. The Confederate commander refused. Though his supplies were running thin, Gardner knew that as long as he could keep Banks occupied, the Army of the Gulf could not head north to help Grant take Vicksburg. The Rebels, already eating their mules, would soon be cooking dogs and rats.

John B. Clark died at his home in Durham in 1873. An autopsy revealed a shriveled lung, containing the bullet that struck him at Port Hudson a decade earlier.

JUNE 14, 1863

Banks ordered a second assault. The Union artillery began an unrelenting bombardment, and at 4:00 a.m. on June 14, Banks threw his infantry forward.

Homer Sprague remembered his regiment, the 13th Connecticut, marching forth at daylight, "up to a sort of plateau swept by the enemy's guns. We were halted there and ordered to lie down. As we lay there, a large number of wounded were brought past us, and a hospital was hastily established on the slope. The presence of the groaning sufferers, and the rather rough performances of the surgeons, were not calculated to whet the appetite for battle. We looked on in silence."[36]

The Union plan had included lobbing hand grenades into the rebel works. But the grenades, Captain Sprague explained, "proved a failure; some were thrown too soon, others did not explode; some were picked up inside and hurled back at the besiegers."[37]

The Ketchum hand grenade had an iron body containing a powder charge, topped by a wooden shaft with paper fins to stabilize its flight. To explode, it had to land directly on its base. The Union command expected to use the grenades to great effect at Port Hudson, but a Confederate lieutenant described what happened when the Yankees lobbed the grenades into the Rebel works: "When these novel missiles commenced falling among the Arkansas troops, they did not know what to make of them, and the first few which they caught and not having burst, they threw them back upon the enemy in the ditch. This time many of them exploded and their character was at once revealed to our men . . . Spreading blankets behind the parapet, the grenades fell harmlessly into them, whereupon our boys would pick them up and hurling them with much greater force down into the moat they would almost invariably explode." (Lt. Howard C. Wright, *Port Hudson: Its History from an Interior Point of View*, reprinted from the *St. Francisville Democrat*, 1937.)

For Union troops to climb the Confederate parapets, they first had to cross the moat around the fortifications. The orders for the men of the 24th Connecticut were "to swing their muskets on their backs, with an additional load of two 30-pound gunny-bags of cotton to each man with which to bridge the moats, and to advance with the charge."[38] Under fire, of course.

"As the battle was raging in front, and dead and wounded were brought to the rear, the Connecticut regiments advanced . . . into the open ground near the works of the enemy. The first attacking party had recoiled; and . . . the Thirteenth . . . leaped to the front simultaneously with other regiments . . . The Twelfth was deployed as skirmishers to the left. The men of the Twenty-fourth were running forward with their cotton-bags; and the hand-grenade party was also pushing for the rebel works."[39]

As rapidly as they could, the blue-coated soldiers picked their way across the tangled field, dodging behind stumps or into ravines—anywhere to take shelter from the bullets and shells that flew around them. Homer Sprague noticed

> a little breast-work of cotton-bags, which some of our Union soldiers had rolled before them as a protection against rebel bullets. Behind these, some half-a-dozen brave men kept firing on the enemy. One by one they were struck by the shot, which constantly knocked up the dust around them. For a long time this continued, until the cotton took fire, either from a shell or from their own muskets. As it burned we saw it apparently consume the clothing and the bodies of the dead and dying. As it reached their cartridge-boxes, we saw the quick explosions of ammunition.[40]

"The day passed slowly," wrote Homer Sprague; "a long, exciting, mournful day. The fierce sun above us, we were tormented by thirst. We were faint with hunger. Every heart was sad at the loss of comrades."[41]

Though the cause was lost, examples of courage and heroism were everywhere. Nicholas Fox, an Irish immigrant who hadn't yet become an American citizen, undertook a deed that was to earn him the Medal of Honor. A private in the 28th Connecticut, Fox twice crossed the battlefield under fire to bring water to the wounded.

In the 13th Connecticut, a seventeen-year-old drummer named Charlie Merwin, "brave, amiable, patriotic, a favorite with all . . . had voluntarily gone to the bloody front, to assist in carrying off the wounded. At eleven in the morning, while carrying a wounded man on a stretcher, to

In June of 1863, a Middletown mother opened her mail to find a letter from the chaplain of her son's regiment. Rev. J. C. Ketter wrote: "your son Amos G. Miller of Co. A 24 Regt of Conn. Vols. has fallen in battle . . . On the morning of June 14th while fearlessly holding his place in our advance against the enemy his head was hit by a rifle ball and he died without a struggle. Charles Rigby of Cromwell was the first man of our Regt. that fell in this assault and your son was the second. They are buried side by side on an eminence which is shaded by majestic magnolia trees." (J. C. Wightman, Chaplain, June 17, 1863, Buck Zaidel collection.)

The bodies of scores of Connecticut men were laid to rest at Port Hudson, where they fell. But hundreds more gave their lives for their country when they died of disease. In Baton Rouge, the 25th Connecticut established its own graveyard. Sam Ellis of Co. K wrote feelingly of visiting the boys in the hospital: "the thin and wasted sufferers, many of them stretched on the floor with only a blanket and scarce a comfort, let alone a luxury of any kind; many of them stricken down in their strength by swamp fever; and one by one they dropped off. They had not even seen the enemy. Poor fellows!" (*The Twenty-Fifth Regiment Connecticut Volunteers in the War of the Rebellion*, by George P. Bissell, Samuel K. Ellis, Thomas McManus, and Henry Hill Goodell, p. 19.)

get him out of the reach of bullets, a rifle ball shattered his leg. It was amputated on the field. He was taken to New Orleans. A second and a third amputation became necessary, and he sank under the terrible suffering."[42]

"And now came the fearfully depressing realization that all these efforts, all this heroism, and all this appalling carnage, had failed," reflected Captain Sprague. "Yonder still floated the rebel flag . . . From their bands inside, we could hear their jubilant secession music. We were defeated! With bitter anguish we thought of this, and then of the unavailing slaughter of our near and dear friends. Two thousand men, young, gallant, brave, the flower of our army, had fallen . . . And all in vain!"[43]

VICKSBURG

On July 4, 1863, Ulysses S. Grant and his Union forces took the Rebel stronghold of Vicksburg, Mississippi. With Vicksburg gone, Confederate general Gardner no longer had reason to hold out at Port Hudson. On July 9, Gardner surrendered to Banks.

Somewhere in the South, a young mother waited in vain for her soldier husband to return. After the battle of Port Hudson, her appealing portrait ended up as a souvenir in the knapsack of a Yankee who had fought there. Curtis Arnold of the 12th Connecticut brought the mother-and-child picture hundreds of miles north to his home in East Haddam, where he himself died a few months later.

Despite the futility of the Union losses at Port Hudson, the fall of the two rebel forts now put the Union in the enviable position of controlling the Mississippi River. The river became a wedge down the center of the Confederacy, and the Union was a step closer to victory.

✳ ✳ ✳

CAPTURED

Toward the end of June of 1863, while hundreds of Connecticut soldiers were broiling at Port Hudson, the 23rd Regiment was stationed far to the south along Louisiana's Atchafalaya River. Assigned to guard a railroad, the regiment was separated by companies and detached along several miles. Isolated from each other, the units were vulnerable to attack. On June 23, Confederate forces captured several of the 23rd's detachments.

Days later, the Rebels paroled the 23rd's enlisted men, but sent the captured officers to Tyler, Texas, where they were imprisoned in Camp Ford. It would be over a year before they received their freedom.

At Camp Ford, the Union prisoners were fortunate to have shelter, clean water, and adequate food. Still, imprisonment always brought a depression of spirits. William "Billy" May, a captain in the 23rd Connecticut, found a way to keep up morale.

Billy had once operated a small newspaper in his hometown of Bridgeport. Now he created a single-sheet newspaper that included camp news, jokes, serialized stories, and even

Far left: A ragged Billy May left Camp Ford on parole in July of 1864, having secured a pass for his fiddle. He was able to smuggle out his newspapers by folding them tightly and sewing them under his shoulder straps.

Left: Union officers sported long whiskers and battered sombreros when they posed for a group portrait after their release from prisoner of war camp in Texas. Capt. Julius Sanford (*left*) was forty-five, a former hatter from Newtown. Beside him stood Capt. A. Dwight Hopkins of Naugatuck. A Rhode Island cavalry officer, imprisoned with them, sat at right.

The Old Flag, March 1, 1864

Prisoners placed advertisements right (both real and humorous) in *The Old Flag,* touting their skills in making pipes or giving banjo lessons.

Samuel G. Bailey, a Danbury watchmaker, produced exquisitely detailed chess sets like this example which he carved from orangewood.

advertisements. May handwrote each issue (four in all) on a large sheet of paper. Each single issue circulated around the camp, so that the groups of soldiers who formed a "mess" (a small group that drew rations and ate together) could read it before passing it on to the next group.

In tiny, precise printing, Billy recorded war news and prison events, such as the inmates' celebration of Washington's Birthday. He added jokes that ridiculed the hapless rebels. ("Why is the Southern Confederacy like a tea-kettle? Because the Black is at the bottom of it, and hollow within.")

May's tongue-in-cheek wit ("Marriages and deaths inserted free") brought humor to a gloomy situation, and the men avidly devoured each issue of his newspaper. A group of grateful inmates pitched in to buy the "publisher" a fiddle, purchased from a prison guard for one hundred dollars.

✳ ✳ ✳

WINCHESTER, VIRGINIA

Far to the northeast, in Virginia's Shenandoah Valley, Union general R. H. Milroy telegraphed a message he would always regret. On June 12, 1863, Milroy sent the following communication from Winchester: "The enemy are probably approaching in some force. I am entirely ready for them. I can hold this place."[44]

Robert E. Lee had decided to move his army up the Shenandoah Valley to invade the north. The valley's verdant farmland could supply the Confederates with food, and the Blue Ridge Mountains would conceal Lee's movements. It was an ideal "avenue of advance" into Pennsylvania where Lee could take the war to the northerners, crushing Union morale and giving Virginia a respite from fighting and foraging.

Confederate general Richard S. Ewell went ahead with his 2nd Corps to clear the valley of Union troops. On June 12, the Confederates approached Winchester, where Milroy's 7,000 Union soldiers were garrisoned. Milroy boasted that his troops had had "a splendid little skirmish" with the rebel cavalry, and he confidently awaited the arrival of the rest of the Confederate force.

Among Milroy's troops was Connecticut's 18th Regiment. Pvt. Charles H. Lynch jotted in his diary the events that swiftly unfolded around him:

> While near the Colonel's quarters I saw a scout coming, almost flying, down the pike. Jumped his horse over a stone fence that surrounded our camp. Headed straight for the Colonel's tent. Without any ceremony rushed in, informed the Colonel the enemy was almost upon us . . . With a shout the Colonel called out "Fall in, fall in, double quick."
>
> . . . Left our camp on double quick time to meet the enemy. They opened fire on us and our camp with a battery well posted on a high hill . . . We held them in check for a while when orders came for us to fall back . . . In the meantime the enemy had taken possession of our camp with all its equipage and our knapsacks that contained all our belongings, making a great loss to every man.
>
> The sudden appearance of so large a force was a surprise. We were under fire all day and were obliged to change our position at different points to meet the enemy, who were trying to get into Winchester. It was plainly seen that a large force of Confederates were surrounding the town and that we were in a bad fix, as we could see the gray in all directions and knew that we were more than outnumbered.[45]

The situation became more confusing that night. A rebel force was advancing from the northeast. The 18th men were hustled into rifle pits, then shifted to a fort, and finally ordered to retake the part of Winchester occupied by the Confederates. Part of the 18th was sent to protect supplies in the south of town, while other companies skirmished with the Rebels in town, slowly pushing them back.

Nearby, Confederate sharpshooters occupied a large brick house. It had to be cleared, and the duty fell to Companies F and H. Two artillery pieces shelled the house, and then the men of the assaulting party

> sprang out of the pits, and amid the crashing of shot and shell charged upon the house. The work was short and bloody. Several of the enemy were killed and wounded and thirteen prisoners were captured.
>
> "Never shall I forget" says Lieut. Caruthers, who was severely wounded in the abdomen, "the desperate charge, fighting away from our main force, with great odds against us. Our work being accomplished, the next thing was to get back; being nearly surrounded, we cut our way through into the rifle-pits. So gallantly was it done that cheers went up from our commander in the fort who saw it all." Before making the charge the boys said to each other "Let us each do our part well."[46]

Around 6:00 p.m., General Milroy recalled his Union troops, the brigades forming around the largest fort. Combat continued, with first one side, then the other making headway until darkness fell.

General Ewell's Confederates, joined by those of General Jubal Early, now had possession of the majority of Winchester, and were working their forces around the Union position. Shortly after midnight, Milroy's troops began a silent withdrawal through the darkness, heading north. They weren't yet five miles out of Winchester when the leading troops met the enemy. The two sides traded musket fire but the night's darkness made accuracy impossible. Now the Union's 1st Brigade, which was leading the retreat, charged the enemy, pushing the Confederates back far enough that many of the Union soldiers were able to get by and continue their escape north.

The 18th Connecticut was in the second of the three Union brigades, and could not get away. Along with a remnant of soldiers from the 1st Brigade, the 2nd Brigade now fell back, formed into battle lines, and charged the woods where the enemy lay. An 18th soldier wrote:

> in the gray dawn, nothing could be discerned but the flash of their rifles. We could not see a man; and they had every advantage of us, as we charged from light into the darkness, where they quietly awaited our coming. The crack of rifles was for a time terrific but numbers and position finally prevailed, and we were obliged to retreat.
>
> We formed again, in perfect order, in the open field, and prepared for a second charge. By this time, we could form some idea of the rebel position; for we could see quite plainly. Gen. Milroy was behind us on his horse; and he told us to take that battery; that we could do it in ten minutes. Officers and men were cool again, and in good spirits. Well, the order was given, "Forward, Eighteenth! Charge bayonets! Double quick! March!" and away we went into those woods again. We were met with a murderous fire; but forward sprang the line with a yell. Up the cross-road we charged, in point-blank range of the rebel battery.

A long line of fire streamed from thousands of rifles, interrupted now and then by the blaze of the battery . . . We charged up to the battery and silenced it, killing or wounding every man that stood by it; but they had plenty of artillery in reserve . . . After fighting desperately for some time, and losing many valuable men, the order to retreat was given; and we again fell back.[47]

"The 18th Connecticut Regiment made the third and last charge unsupported, all others having left the field," wrote Pvt. Charles Lynch. "We held the enemy in check until the General, his staff, and escort, left the field, guided by scouts through fields, on to Harper's Ferry . . . The cannon and musketry firing was a grand and awful sight to us young fellows, who were getting our first lessons in a real battle, a hard one and against great odds."[48]

During the 18th Connecticut's third charge, General Milroy and his staff had made their escape and the 3rd Brigade had turned and fled. The 18th's major quickly gathered some of his men, and made a run for Harper's Ferry. Now William G. Ely, colonel of the 18th Connecticut, turned around to look for support—and found himself surrounded.

"The Federals numbered but a thousand men, jaded by two days' sleepless service, and now badly cut up. Under the circumstances, Col. Ely surrendered the command. The men were immediately placed under guard."[49]

The 18th Connecticut lost seventy-five either killed or wounded, and hundreds captured with Colonel Ely. But when the Confederates searched for the their battle trophy, the 18th's regimental flag, there was no sign of it among the prisoners.

Two days later, the regiment's colors arrived safely in Pennsylvania. After the last charge, Color Sergeant George Torrey of Woodstock had made his escape through the woods with the flag wrapped around his body.

At Vicksburg and Port Hudson, Union victories had turned the Mississippi River into a corridor for the Union; here at Winchester, the Confederate victory opened a path for Lee into Pennsylvania. But the 18th Connecticut's Colonel Ely pointed out many years later that if Milroy's forces "had not held in check the advance of Lee's army at Winchester for three days, by which the Army of the Potomac gained time, the [upcoming] battle fought at Gettysburg would probably have taken place nearer Philadelphia—and perhaps with different results."[50]

CHAPTER TEN

That Place Long to Be Remembered

GETTYSBURG, SUMMER 1863

President Lincoln's face was lined with anxiety. He knew Lee and his army were heading north—but *where were they?*

"Something of a panic pervades the city," Secretary of the Navy Gideon Welles wrote from Washington on June 15, 1863. Welles continued: "rumors reach us of Rebel advances into Maryland. It is said . . . some of them have penetrated as far as Chambersburg in Pennsylvania . . . There is trouble, confusion, uncertainty, where there should be calm intelligence."[1]

In the field, General Hooker seemed to have no idea of the Confederates' whereabouts. Lincoln was reduced to sending telegrams to Pennsylvania, asking if the Confederates were in sight.

On the morning of June 28, in Frederick, Maryland, Gen. George Meade was awakened by a messenger with the news that Lincoln had relieved Hooker of command, and appointed Meade commander of the Army of the Potomac. Meade quickly found that Hooker had left no plan to deal with the impending threat. The task before the new commander was paralyzing in its complexity: Meade had to ascertain his own troops' strengths and locations, find a way to protect Washington, and thwart Lee's invasion of the North. But there was no time to be paralyzed—already, the Confederates were advancing through an unprotected Pennsylvania, Meade's home state.

For his part, Robert E. Lee had several goals for the invasion. Morale in the North was at its lowest ebb, following appalling Union losses at Fredericksburg and Chancellorsville. Lee believed his army's presence on Northern soil would strengthen the Copperhead movement and erode Northern support for the war. Capturing Harrisburg, Pennsylvania's capital, would be a great coup. Another Confederate victory—this time in the North—might very well garner Great Britain's support for the Confederacy. Finally, Lee planned to have his troops live off the Pennsylvanian countryside, relieving a devastated Virginia.

"I am moving at once against Lee," wrote Meade to his wife; "I am going straight at them, and will settle this thing one way or the other."[2] Meade's army was already in motion: tens of thousands of Union soldiers rapidly marching northward, always staying between the enemy and Washington.

Confederate troops were well in advance, proceeding toward Harrisburg, but Lee was operating without knowledge of Union army whereabouts; his "eyes and ears"—Jeb Stuart and his cavalry—had not been heard from. When Lee learned that Meade was in pursuit, he changed his plan. His troops, strung out over many miles, had to be consolidated. He swung the majority of his forces around to head southeast and gave his corps commanders instructions to avoid engaging the enemy until the Confederate troops could be massed between Cashtown and Gettysburg.

On June 30, Union general John Buford rode into Gettysburg, Pennsylvania, with his cavalry division to reconnoiter the town. The townspeople informed Buford that Rebel troops had just departed to the west. The Confederates, a brigade of North Carolina soldiers under Gen. Johnston Pettigrew, had been scouting for supplies—specifically, shoes—but with orders to avoid the enemy, they had withdrawn as Buford's men approached Gettysburg.

Using the Blue Ridge Mountains as a screen, Lee skirted his Confederate forces (shown here in *red*) north into Pennsylvania. The Army of the Potomac (*blue*) rushed north to meet the rebels, always keeping between them and Washington, D.C. Oddly, when the two armies met at Gettysburg, Lee's Southern forces attacked from the north, while Union troops approached from the south.

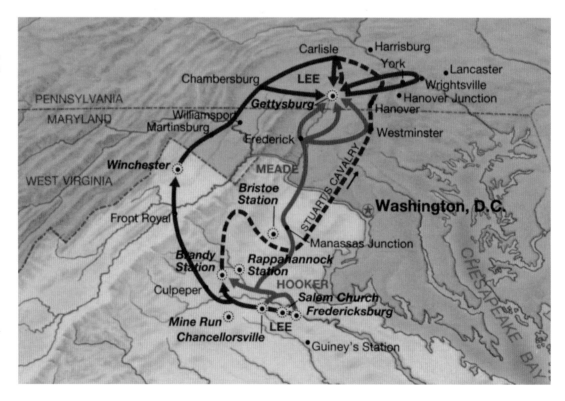

In one of the finest Union infantryman photographs in existence, Henry Cornwall of Portland, a private in the 20th Connecticut, posed in heavy marching order—knapsack with a rolled rubber blanket atop, cartridge box suspended over one hip, canteen and haversack over the other, his trusty Springfield rifle musket and bayonet before him. Each man's trousers, frock coat, and forage cap were made of wool. Suspended over his shoulder was his leather cartridge box containing forty cartridges—paper-wrapped bullets, each weighing one ounce. Slung over his shoulder was his canteen, holding three pints of liquid. The tar-covered linen haversack contained his rations along with personal items like a tin plate, knife, fork and spoon, razor, mirror, coffee, and tobacco. A woolen blanket and often a rubber blanket rode atop the knapsack that may have contained spare clothing and a shelter tent half. His musket weighed nine pounds, bringing the soldier's burden to about forty pounds. Sweat-soaked, exhausted, and thirsty beyond belief, he rushed on toward battle.

When General Pettigrew reported to his Confederate superiors that Union troops were entering Gettysburg, they dismissed his warning, assuring him that the Army of the Potomac was still far to the south; the soldiers he had seen were no doubt only Pennsylvania militia.

On the Union side, the savvy and experienced John Buford foresaw a significant engagement. He sent word of the situation to Gen. John F. Reynolds, commanding the infantry's 1st Corps, and began examining his options. When one of his officers opined that the Rebels would not prove a problem, Buford admonished him: "They will attack you in the morning and they will come booming—skirmishers three deep. You will have to fight like the devil until supports arrive."

Union supports were hurrying north, some brigades covering twenty-five or thirty-five miles a day in the unforgiving heat. Hundreds and hundreds of men fell out on the forced march; "some of the men dropped down dead while marching along in the ranks," said Loren Goodrich of the 14th Connecticut.[3]

But Benjamin Hirst noted the welcome support from civilians, now that they were in the North:

> we pushed along as rapidly as possible the inhabitants along the route helping us all they could. [T]hey handed us water and cheered us on at every step. One old Lady . . . came to her door and I saw she had something in her apron. I stept upon the sidewalk with several others and the old lady showed us her Treasure. She had her apron ful of hot biscuit. She gave us one each while with Tears rolling down her aged cheeks she lamented because she could not make them fast enough.[4]

"Gettysburg and Vicinity," published by Gettysburg Battlefield Memorial Association, 1888, Burk and McFetridge lith., Philadelphia. Gettysburg battlefield encompassed twenty-five square miles, and Connecticut regiments ranged across a vast part of that field. Connecticut troops fought on all three days of the battle, leaving scores of their dead buried beneath Pennsylvania soil.

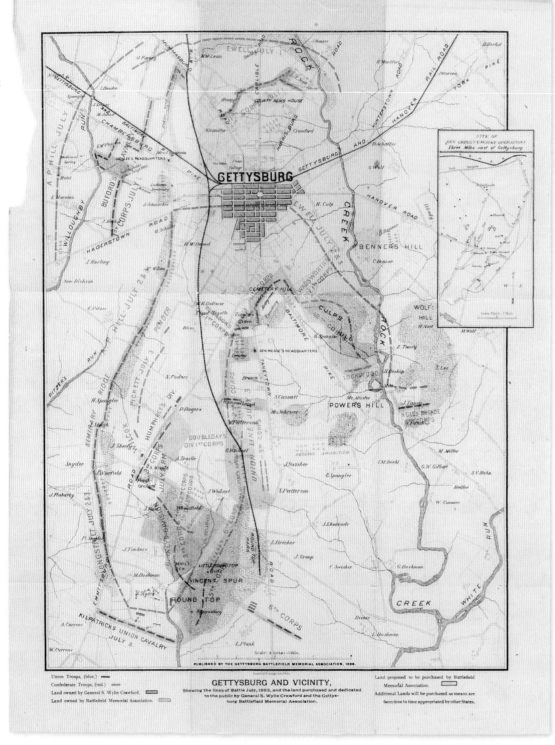

GETTYSBURG AND VICINITY,
Showing the lines of Battle July, 1863, and the land purchased and dedicated to the public by General S. Wylie Crawford and the Gettysburg Battlefield Memorial Association.

Morning of Day One: Union Cavalry Meet Confederate Infantry West of Town

John Buford's aim was to hold up the Rebel troops long enough for Union infantry to reach Gettysburg. Early on the morning of July 1, Buford's cavalrymen, positioned along the Chambersburg Pike west of town, fired on the advancing Confederate column. As the rebels pushed forward, Buford's men fell back and established their battle line on a rise called Herr Ridge about a mile and a half west of town. From behind fence posts, the dismounted cavalry fired their breechloading carbines at a steadily increasing force of Rebels.

As Confederate numbers became overwhelming, Buford's blue coats reluctantly fell back, moving eastward from ridge to ridge toward the town as their lines gave way.

The situation was becoming desperate when Gen. John F. Reynolds's 1st Corps, which included the renowned Iron Brigade, came racing through the cornfields at the double-quick. Their officers rapidly formed them into battle line, with General Reynolds shouting, "Forward men, forward, for God's sake and drive those fellows out of those woods!"

Afternoon of Day One: The 17th Connecticut Enters the Fray North of Town

Connecticut's 17th Regiment had set off from Emmitsburg, Maryland, about five o'clock that morning with the rest of the 11th Corps, and soon crossed into Pennsylvania. Sgt. Maj. Fred Betts knew battle was imminent when "an aide . . . came galloping down the road with orders to hasten forward, and soon afterward I heard heavy firing."[5]

As the 17th advanced into Gettysburg, "citizens lined the streets holding cups of water for the thirsty," said Pvt. Justus Silliman, "but we had no time to stop but passed through almost on the double quick and took our position on the right of the town."[6]

With Confederate troops streaming in from the roads to the north, Union commanders rushed the 11th Corps to the northern edge of Gettysburg near Seminary Ridge; "when we went into the fight which we did without rest," wrote J. Henry Blakeman, a twenty-one-year-old Stratford farmer, "I was almost exhausted."[7] But the men of the 11th Corps, having retreated in chaos at Chancellorsville, knew they had to prove their mettle today. There could be no hesitation.

Up ahead of the 17th Connecticut, the 1st Brigade already was engaging the enemy. The Rebels' numbers swelled as Confederate general Jubal Early's troops joined those of Richard S. Ewell. The Union's 1st Brigade (five regiments) was struggling to hold off the Johnny Rebs.

The 17th advanced under command of its lieutenant colonel, thirty-two-year-old Douglass Fowler, mounted on his white horse. (Colonel Noble, wounded at Chancellorsville, had not yet returned to the regiment.) Fowler sent four of his companies out ahead as skirmishers while the remainder of the regiment briefly supported a Union battery, the men lying uneasily on the ground as shells exploded overhead.

Now Fowler urged his men forward. "Dodge the big ones, boys!" he called jokingly as the rebel shells screamed around them. The men moved toward a pine wood where they could hear the musket fire of the Union's 1st Brigade fighting the Rebels. Suddenly blue-coated soldiers came plunging through their ranks—the 1st Brigade had broken and was in flight.

On the march to Gettysburg, one of the 17th men had slipped out of the ranks to get water. For this transgression, the regiment's lieutenant colonel, Douglass Fowler, was arrested and sent to the rear of his troops. Restored to his position before battle began, Colonel Fowler rode his white horse at the head of his men. Though a conspicuous target for the enemy, Fowler refused to dismount once combat began— maybe feeling a need to redeem his sense of honor.

"We had not gone far when to our horror we saw Colonel Fowler falling from his saddle," wrote Sgt. Maj. Fred Betts. "As his horse galloped away, [Adjutant Whitney] Chatfield . . . hastily dismounted. Poor Fowler was dead . . . we endeavored to lift his corpse upon the adjutant's horse, but we found it impossible to do so, as his weight was beyond our strength, and after several attempts we reluctantly left him." (Account of C. Frederick Betts in William Warren's manuscript, Article 15, Bridgeport History Center, Bridgeport Public Library.) Fowler's body was never recovered.

The fleeing men created havoc in the Connecticut regiment. "All was confusion immediately," wrote the 17th's James Montgomery Bailey,

> our boys, determined to follow the brave Fowler, yelled defiantly, and forced their way through the timid sheep, up, up to the woods . . . The fire had now grown terrific on both sides, but the decidedly superior advantage of the enemy, both in numbers and position, told heavy on us. Although a man is not apt to notice what occurs about him in the midst of leaden hail, yet I could not help but be aware that a fearful avalanche of death was sweeping through my Regiment. It was one continual *hiss* about my ears, and the boys dropped in rapid succession on both sides of me . . . The enemy continued to move slowly up, firing rapidly. The din had reached the standard of a hell, and then the order to retreat was given. Colonel Fowler shouted the command to us, and the next instant he reeled from the saddle, his brains striking the Adjutant, who was by his side.[8]

The 11th Corps was not just outnumbered by the Confederates. Its battle line, stretching along the northern edge of the town of Gettysburg, was weakened when Union general Francis Barlow advanced his division ahead of the rest of the corps. Now the Confederates, moving in on either side of the extended division, created a lethal crossfire on the Union soldiers.

Nineteen-year-old H. Whitney Chatfield, the 17th's adjutant, rode into battle beside Lieutenant Colonel Fowler. When Fowler was hit, his brains spattered on Chatfield's coat. The adjutant dismounted and tried to bring off his colonel's body, but was unable to. With the Confederates nearly upon them, Chatfield swung into his saddle, narrowly escaping. A storm of Rebel musketry and artillery fire killed Chatfield's horse, shredded his haversack, and cut up the Revolutionary War sabre he carried. The old sword may have been a family heirloom: two of Chatfield's great-grandfathers had fought in the Continental army. Chatfield would later give his life in a skirmish in Dunn's Lake, Florida, two months before the war ended.

Confederate general John Gordon, leading a brigade of Georgian troops, assaulted the Union right flank. "You cant concieve [sic] of the destruction in their ranks," wrote Gordon. "It surpassed anything I have seen during the war—We captured a great many prisoners also & routed the Enemy in our front—We drove them before us in perfect confusion."[9]

Many of the 17th Connecticut men were unable to escape. Justus Silliman explained: "My gun would not work so I dropped it and picked up another. This also missed fire . . . Just then a man near me was shot. I seized his gun and had just fired at some rebs advancing on our left when I experienced a curious sensation in the head. On opening my eyes I found myself in a horizontal position and surrounded by Greybacks, our men having been forced back."[10]

For the 17th soldiers not killed or wounded, it was a mad run through Gettysburg's streets and neighborhoods, sometimes just steps ahead of their pursuers. That evening, the ragged vestige of the 17th gathered south of the city on rising ground called Cemetery Hill. They were joined by the battered troops of the Iron Brigade, whose commander, General Reynolds, had been killed that morning at McPherson's Ridge.

Evening of Day One: Union Troops Take "A Very Strong Position" on the Hills South of Town

Union generals Winfield Scott Hancock and Oliver O. Howard met on Cemetery Hill's high ground, and assessed the situation. Hancock, surveying the rise the Army of the Potomac now occupied, declared, "I think this is the strongest position by nature upon which to fight a battle that I ever saw, and if it meets with your approbation I will select this as the battle-field."

Howard agreed. The position's strength was in its height. From their site on Cemetery Hill, the Union generals could look east and see the adjacent Culp's Hill with its rocky slope down toward the town. Turning south, they could look straight down Cemetery Ridge, which extended from Cemetery Hill nearly two miles south to the prominences now known as Little Round Top and Big Round Top.

At Fredericksburg, the Union troops had learned a hard lesson when they attacked an entrenched enemy on the high ground. Here, the Union had the strategic heights.

The Union line began to form the shape of an upside-down fishhook, just south of Gettysburg's downtown. The "hook" portion arched northward across Cemetery Hill and Culp's Hill, with its western leg extending south down Cemetery Ridge. In the next two days, this shape and the Union army's position on the high ground would prove hugely advantageous for Meade and the Army of the Potomac.

July 2, 1863

Morning of Day Two

Mist covered Gettysburg's fields and rolling hills that morning, as thousands of men awoke and realized, with sinking stomachs, what was ahead. More Union troops had come up and

Albert Seeley, a twenty-six-year-old tinworker from Darien, moved out as a skirmisher with his comrades in the 17th Regiment's Company B. Four companies of skirmishers under Maj. Allen G. Brady had orders to take a brick house in the advance. "The enemy, anticipating our movements," wrote Brady, "shelled the house, and set it on fire. We, however, held our ground." (Major Allen G. Brady's official report, July 4, 1863, *The War of the Rebellion: A Compilation of the Official Records of the Union and Confederate Armies* [Washington, DC: Government Printing Office, 1889], ser. 1, vol. 27, part 1, p. 716.) Later, as the tide of battle shifted and the regiment retreated through the town of Gettysburg, Albert Seeley was captured.

Lee had to stretch his battle line around the exterior of the Union's curved line, extending it some seven miles in length. Communication between disparate portions of the army were extremely slow as messengers traveled long distances on horseback along the exterior line. Moving Confederate troops from place to place along the line was cumbersome and time consuming: reinforcements might have to march several miles to their new positions. The Union's defensive line, in contrast, had a shape that was beautifully efficient. If the center of the fishhook's shaft needed reinforcements, Meade could draw them quickly from those positioned at either end of the line. The interior line also allowed Meade and his commanders to communicate quickly. "Map of the battle field of Gettysburg" [July 1, 2, and 3, 1863], J. B. Lippincott Co., 1863.

continued to arrive through the morning. Joining the battered 17th Connecticut in the northernmost arc of the Union line was the 12th Corps, containing Connecticut's 5th and 20th Regiments. The 12th Corps commander was a Connecticut native, Gen. Alpheus Williams.

General Meade, who had reached the town very early, nodded approvingly at the advantageous ground his generals had chosen. Meade selected for his headquarters a small house behind the center of his lines from which he could direct his forces to the right and left.

About ten that morning, the 14th Connecticut came up and took its position with the Second Corps, in the center of the Union line on Cemetery Ridge.

Besides the Fighting 14th, the Second Corps included Connecticut's 27th Regiment, which arrived in Gettysburg "after an excruciating march, almost night and day," in the words of Jim Brand, the regiment's color sergeant.[11]

The 27th had left Connecticut in October of 1862 with 829 men. The new soldiers had met disaster at Fredericksburg; four months later the majority of the regiment had been captured at Chancellorsville. Now the 27th Connecticut was the smallest fighting unit on the battlefield, mustering only 75 men.

The soldiers waited apprehensively on Cemetery Ridge. "You can imagine the strain on our nerves," wrote Pvt. Almond Clark, "while waiting for the order to fall in for the conflict. During the morning the paymaster came around and paid our months wages—but that was a time when we cared little for money."[12]

Leading the jittery 27th soldiers was their lieutenant colonel, Henry Merwin, just twenty-three years old. Back in New Haven, Henry was a bookkeeper in his family's meat packing business. Here in the field, Colonel Merwin's men followed their young commander without hesitation, one

Gen. Alpheus Williams was born in 1810 in what is now Deep River, Connecticut. A Yale graduate, Williams became a lawyer and judge in Detroit, Michigan, and an officer in the militia there. When the war began, Williams quickly rose to be brigadier general, though he was not a West Point graduate. Modest and dedicated, Williams proved a capable general though he was not one to blow his own horn. At Gettysburg, the general rode his sturdy warhorse, Plug Ugly, as he led the 12th Corps on Culp's Hill.

of them writing that "no officer in the regiment attracted to himself such universal and unvarying respect, confidence, and affection among the men of his command."[13]

Merwin surveyed the 27th's diminished ranks. Pvt. Richard Tenner, twenty-five, was a confectioner in New Haven, more used to making desserts than to making war. Tom Yale, a shoemaker, was in his early forties; his brother Merrit was close to fifty. Twenty-two-year-old Marcus Judson had grown up in a New Haven orphanage. John Sanford, nineteen, was the only son of his widowed mother in Milford.

Today, every man of the tiny Connecticut unit would count. Lee intended to make a double-pronged attack, simultaneously striking the northern end of the Union battle line on the hills just south of the town, and the southern end of the line approaching Little Round Top, a prominent rise a mile or so to the south.

But the Confederate movements didn't go according to plan. While Lee had hoped the joint assaults would take place early in the day, Confederate general James Longstreet, commanding the southern attack, was repeatedly frustrated in trying to bring up his thousands of troops without detection by the Union. After marching back and forth in the heat, Longstreet's troops were finally in position about 3:30 p.m. The northern attack was delayed several hours more.

In October of 1862, the two friends joined the 27th Regiment. Henry Merwin (*right*) was a clerk in his family's meatpacking business, while Frank Sloat was a foreman in a factory. Both men lived on Orange Street in New Haven. Only one of them would return home alive. Merwin was already a veteran, having fought with the 2nd Regiment at Bull Run. When he enlisted in the 27th Connecticut, the officers chose him as their lieutenant colonel. Sloat came in as 1st lieutenant and rose to be captain. Henry and Frank were tentmates, as close as brothers. Both were captured by the Rebels at Chancellorsville, but released a few weeks later—in time for Lieutenant Colonel Merwin to take command of the regiment at Gettysburg.

The men of the 27th held Henry Merwin, just twenty-three, in high regard for the courage and empathy they'd seen in him. On July 2, Merwin led his troops into the storm of lead in the wheat field and fell almost immediately, a bullet in his chest. "He was borne back, and after two hours of suffering passed away among soldiers loving and respecting him." (*New Haven Daily Palladium*, July 9, 1863, p. 2.) Merwin's last words were said to be for his men: "My poor regiment is suffering fearfully." (Winthrop D. Sheldon, *The Twenty-Seventh: A Regimental History*, p. 92.) His men did not forget him. After the war, they erected a small stone monument in the wheat field near the site of his mortal wounding.

Afternoon of Day Two: The 27th Connecticut in the Wheat Field

About four o'clock Longstreet launched his assault on the Union left—the southernmost portion of the fishhook's shank, which now extended down Cemetery Ridge to Little Round Top. The battle ranged through a pastoral landscape that included a peach orchard and a field of wheat soon trampled by thousands of men, and filled with flying lead and exploding iron.

Brutal fighting raged for an hour, and the Federal line began to break. Just before five o'clock, Meade sent reinforcements racing to fill the gaps in his battle line. The 27th Connecticut men gripped their rifles and advanced on the double quick. Almond Clark wrote:

> We had gone but a short distance in the field when we received volleys from the rebels, and we gave them the same—it was give and take—we still moving forward.
>
> At this time our Colonel Merwin fell. I was near him at the time, and the last order I heard him give was, "Steady there, men!" Men were falling along the line, but we closed up and kept on the move, firing as fast as we could load; and when about half way of the wheatfield we halted for a minute. The smoke lifted somewhat, and we could see the rebels near a small grove of trees.[14]

Back and forth the combat ranged, control of the wheat field changing hands six times that day. Color Corporal William Boswell, the schoolteacher, went down with a bullet in his lung. A Confederate ball hit Martin Merrill in the face—he would live another thirty-four years with just the remains of a nose. Tom Kilcullen, a fireman who'd been wounded at Fredericksburg, took another bullet. This one he would not survive.

Still the Connecticut men would not yield. Frank Sloat wrote: "The line pressed forward at double time, forcing the enemy from the Wheat Field and into the woods beyond. A ravine, rising into a precipitous ledge on its further side, checked the advancing line. The men with much difficulty clambered up the rocky steep, but as they appeared on the crest of the ledge, the enemy, drawn up in readiness just beyond, within pistol-range, delivered a withering fire."[15]

Jim Brand, the 27th's color sergeant, scrambled up the slope and boldly raised the regimental flag above the rocky ledge. A twenty-nine-year-old Yale student, Brand had a "tall, sinewy frame, high cheek bones, straight hair and piercing eyes."[16] The other color sergeant, nineteen-year-old John Sanford, stood beside him, holding high the national colors.

James Brand, the son of Scottish immigrants, grew up in a large, impoverished family in Canada. As a young man, he came to work in the United States, saving money until he was able to enroll at Yale in his late twenties. He left college in 1862 to join the 27th Connecticut. At Gettysburg, Jim stopped under heavy fire to help Major Coburn, who had been stunned by a shell, leave the battlefield as the 27th retreated. He received a medal for his actions. (Note by Luther Day Harkness in *James Brand, Twenty-Six Years Pastor of the First Congregational Church, Oberlin* [Oberlin, OH: Luther Day Harkness, 1899], p. 53.) After his regiment was mustered out, Brand returned to Yale, and went on to become a minister. In 1885, Rev. James Brand gave the oration at the dedication of the 27th Connecticut's monument at Gettysburg.

Cornelius Jay DuBois lay bleeding on the battlefield, his right arm severely wounded.

The twenty-six-year-old captain, a graduate of Columbia Law School, had rushed forward with his men into the wheat field. But at the end of the day, when the 27th withdrew to Cemetery Ridge, there was no sign of him. Captain DuBois's younger brother, Henry, found him on the field among the dead and wounded. An assistant surgeon in the regular army, Henry used all of his skill and connections to save his brother. Captain DuBois eventually returned to service in the Union army, but never fully recovered from his wound. He went on to graduate from Yale's medical school, but died in his early forties.

Using the summit of the rise as their protection, the 27th men would duck down to reload and then rise and fire on the enemy. "The 27th seemed to be alone," wrote Almond Clark wonderingly; "there were but a few of us—not more than twenty-five, and our position was very critical . . . All we could do was load and fire at them as fast as we could. We had our flags with us, and being held above the elevation we could see the rebel's bullets strike their folds."[17]

While the 27th and others of its brigade held this advanced position, rebel troops began edging toward the ends of the Union battle line, attempting to flank the Federals. With no support in sight, Col. John Brooke, the brigade commander, finally ordered his men to withdraw.

When Henry Merwin fell, command of the 27th had devolved upon its major, James H. Coburn. As the regiment retreated, the twenty-six-year-old Coburn seemed dazed and unable to move. The two color sergeants, Jim Brand and John Sanford, stopped under heavy fire to help him off the field. Gripping the major under each arm, the men pulled him out of the bloody wheat field to safety.

"We found our way back to the main line," said Almond Clark, "nearly exhausted, after about three hours of hard fighting, leaving half our number on the field killed and wounded."[18]

As the handful of 27th men retreated to Cemetery Ridge, new Union troops were advancing as their reserves. Among them were Connecticut's 5th and 20th Regiments, which had marched three miles south and west from their positions at the fishhook's barb, on Culp's Hill. All during the march, "the rebs had a battery playing onto us," wrote Abner Smith, a private in the 20th Regiment. "We had to drop to the ground often to save our heads from the shell."[19]

But when the reserves arrived about 7:00 p.m. and formed in line of battle, they found no enemy to engage. Action at the wheat field had ended. The ferocious Confederate assault had failed to turn the Union left.

Evening of Day Two: The Rebels Take Union Entrenchments on Cemetery Hill

Two miles to the north, on the extreme right of the Union line, Confederate general Richard Ewell had at last organized his part in Lee's two-pronged attack. He had misunderstood Lee's intention for the two assaults to be simultaneous, and it was not until about 7:00 p.m.—just as Longstreet's attack at the wheat field was ending—that the Confederates struck Union lines on Cemetery Hill, where the fishhook curved.

Maj. Allen G. Brady took command of the 17th Connecticut after Col. Douglas Fowler was killed in battle on July 1. A Torrington manufacturer, Brady was in his early forties. He'd served with the 3rd Connecticut in 1861, though much of his ninety-day enlistment was spent under arrest for insubordination for refusing to recognize the governor's appointment of a new colonel over him. On the evening of July 2, Brady's troops were fighting to keep Ewell's Rebels from overrunning their position on East Cemetery Hill. A shell fragment broke Brady's scapula, ending his service with the 17th Regiment.

The men of the 17th Connecticut, exhausted from the previous day's battle and their flight through the streets of Gettysburg, were about to face combat once again. Since the death of their colonel in battle, command rested with Maj. Allen G. Brady. As dusk set in, Brady's men—now about 240 strong—were furiously digging in behind stone walls partway down the eastern slope of Cemetery Hill. On the crest of the hill, Union artillerymen aimed their pieces eastward, while the 5th Maine Battery mounted six cannon on a rise between the 17th Connecticut's position and Culp's Hill, just to the southeast.

About 8:00 p.m., Confederate troops began their approach to Cemetery Hill. Major Brady quickly sent two of his 17th Connecticut companies forward as skirmishers into a grain field, while the enemy—a brigade known as the Louisiana Tigers, which had chased the 17th soldiers out of town the day before—could be seen moving through the woods before them. The 5th Maine Battery opened on the rebels, firing over the heads of the 17th's skirmishers. But, as the 17th's Lt. Milton Daniels noted with dismay, "the lead wadding from one shot killed one of our men, which demoralized us worse than the enemy in our front."[20]

Despite the shelling, the Confederates still came on, and the 17th skirmishers swiftly fell back to join their unit behind the stone walls. "We had not more than time to form behind the wall," wrote Major Brady, "before the enemy were discovered advancing rapidly upon us on our right and a full brigade obliquely toward our left. When within 150 paces of us, we poured a destructive fire upon them."[21]

Artillery thundered and rifles cracked, darkness was falling, officers shouted and wounded shrieked, smoke obscured the soldiers' views, and the enemy was about to flank the 17th Connecticut. In the midst of the pandemonium, Lieutenant Daniels observed two of his privates, George Wood and William Curtis: "While the Tigers were coming across the meadows George and Bill were sitting down behind the stone wall, and you would have supposed they were shooting at a target. I saw George shoot, taking a dead rest, and heard him say, 'He won't come any further, will he, Bill?' Then Bill shot, and said: 'I got that fellow, George.' And they kept it up that way, perfectly oblivious to danger themselves."[22]

Despite telling volleys from the 17th, and destructive cannon fire from the 5th Maine Battery, the Louisiana Tigers came charging up the hill. The Nutmeggers were able to repulse the Rebels, but not for long. Minutes later, a North Carolina

Ironically, the Union Hotchkiss shell that killed a soldier in the 17th Connecticut was probably made in his home state, in the iron-rich town of Sharon. Its lead wadding (the uneven band in the photo) was meant to keep the force of the explosion behind the projectile, instead of allowing it to escape through the rifled channel that gave the shell its spin. As the shell blasted out of the cannon, so too did the lead wadding—in this case, with a fatal result.

brigade forced other Union troops to retreat up the hill toward the cemetery, and Major Brady had to quickly shift the 17th into the gap to the right.

Now another hole opened: the position the 17th had just left behind the stone walls. Through that gap charged the Rebels, and suddenly the enemy was *behind* the 17th men. Now the fighting became hand to hand, with desperate soldiers on both sides lunging with their bayonets, using their rifle stocks as clubs, and officers slashing with their swords. The Federals were able to drive off the Southerners, but the Rebels reformed and charged again, nearly 100 of them making it to the top of Cemetery Hill where they fought the artillerymen for possession of the batteries. But no Rebel reinforcements joined them, and without help they could not hold the position. The Union troops forced the Confederates to retreat back down the hill, peppered with bullets and raking artillery fire.

As darkness set in, the firing decreased. The 17th Connecticut men looked around to find that 62 of their number had been killed or wounded, including their major.

That night, the 17th with grit and courage had made its name, redeeming its reputation after being routed at Chancellorsville, and fleeing through the Gettysburg streets the day before.

Night of Day Two: Returning to Culp's Hill

While the 17th fought on Cemetery Hill, Connecticut's 5th and 20th Regiments were marching about on Cemetery Ridge. Sent to back up the Union troops in the wheat field, the two Connecticut regiments (both in the 1st Brigade, 1st Division) had left the sturdy entrenchments they'd built on Culp's Hill and headed southwest to find the battle with Longstreet's troops just coming to an end. Abner Smith of the 20th Connecticut, wrote: "as soon as it was found that we ware not needed we

On the neighboring Culp's Hill, Rebel soldiers ascended under sparse cover from rocks and trees. Throughout much of the Battle of Gettysburg, Confederate soldiers had to fight their way up rising ground like this to confront entrenched Union troops. Artist Edwin Forbes was at Gettysburg, sketching scenes throughout the battlefield during the three-day fight. (Painting by Edwin Forbes, 1865.)

started back for our intrenchments but when we got nearly back it was found that the rebs had com in and taken possession of our breastworkes whilst we was gone."[23]

Gen. Alpheus Williams surmised that the Confederates held only a small portion of the Union entrenchments, and sent forward a line of skirmishers. "But the heavy musketry fire that greeted our men told plainly that the rebels were there in force and that only a battle would give us possession of the works again."[24]

Culp's Hill was the extreme right of the Union line. Losing it put everything in jeopardy. As the 20th's Philo Buckingham observed, "The foothold [the enemy] had gained on our right promised victory; if Ewell's column could be forced through . . . our right flank would be turned, and our whole position would become untenable. Having gained a portion of our works, it seemed to be almost certain of accomplishment."[25] There was no choice: the Federals had to take the hill back.

The Union soldiers wanted to kick themselves: the day before, they'd spent hours building their entrenchments. They chopped down trees, piled up logs, dug rifle pits, and packed dirt around the fortifications. Now they pictured the enemy sheltered safely in their works.

It was 11:00 p.m., and General Williams knew no assault would be successful in the darkness. He would attack in the morning.

The 221 men of the 5th Connecticut were dog-tired. Upon their arrival in Gettysburg on the night of July 1, they'd been ordered to support an artillery unit, and then sent out as skirmishers. They rejoined their brigade at 4:00 a.m., in time to go to work building fortifications, then waited all afternoon for the battle they knew was coming. They needed sleep badly.

> Such of the men as could threw themselves on to the ground and attempted to get a little rest, but every now and then some watchful sentry would fire his musket at an enemy whose tread he heard in the thick darkness of the woods; the flash revealing his locality would be followed by two or three shots from the opposing pickets; then a half dozen more, until the firing extended all along the right of the line, each opposing picket firing at the flashes from the musket of the other, until, presently, would burst forth a volley.

> Roused by the tumult, our men in the line of battle would seize their muskets and spring into their places, thinking the expected attack had begun, but directly the firing would grow less, and the pattering fire along the picket line gradually slackening would finally die out altogether, and all, except the pickets and the detail at work entrenching, would again stretch themselves out to rest, only to be roused again shortly by a similar alarm.[26]

Day Three: July 3, 1863

Morning of Day Three: The 20th Connecticut Assaults Culp's Hill

"Thus the night passed away," wrote Major Buckingham, "and as the first faint streaks of light became visible in the eastern horizon, the men in the union ranks were roused and ordered to stand to their arms; and the artillery of the 12th Corps began its thunders, sending solid shot, shell and cannister over the heads of the men in our infantry line, into the woods among the rebel masses. This fire was continued for about an hour when the two divisions of infantry belonging to the 12th Corps were ordered to advance and retake the line of works held by the enemy. Then began a contest as fierce and bloody as any that occurred during the three days battle."[27]

Robert E. Lee had ordered General Ewell to push through from Culp's Hill to the Baltimore Pike where they could come in behind the Union's lines.

Alpheus Williams broke up his Union 12th Corps, sending the 5th Connecticut to take up a defensive position near the Baltimore Pike. The 20th Connecticut advanced to push the rebels off Culp's Hill—and found the Confederates coming out to meet them. East Hampton schoolteacher Horatio Chapman, 20th Connecticut, recorded what came next.

> After going through a strip of woods we came to an opening beyond which were our works. About four or five rods from our breastworks the rebels had also a strong line of skirmishers. We poured a volley into them and it was returned vigorously and the firing along the whole line of skirmishers became more and more rapid and incessant.
>
> In about an hour . . . a second line of rebel skirmishers more numerous than the first came over the breastworks and joined their first line and advanced rapidly upon us. We were forced to retreat as fast as possible back through the woods.
>
> We went and met our brigade advancing in line of battle. One volley was poured into them and it checked them instanter and they about faced and retreated, leaving many dead and wounded. We continued to advance . . . until within short range of our works, and from our own breastworks which was now their protection, they poured such a withering fire into our ranks . . . that our brigade was forced to retreat . . . and so it was a continued fight of advance and retreat, advance and retreat.[28]

The men of the 20th Connecticut were in the thick of the firefight, facing Rebel rifle fire and artillery as they scrabbled their way up the slope of Culp's Hill, taking shelter where they could behind trees and rocks. "The sharp and almost continuous reports of the twelve pounders, the screaming, shrieking shell that went crashing through the tree tops; the

Pvt. George W. Warner lost both his arms when the 20th Connecticut fought to take back Culp's Hill on July 3. Warner was beside a tree when a shell burst above him. "One fragment struck the right arm a few inches below the shoulder—entirely severing it from the body and carrying it several feet from him. The shell was from a Federal Battery. Another fragment struck the left unit and forearm lacerating the soft parts badly and breaking the bones. Amputation made an hour after receipt of injury." (Pension records of George W. Warner, 20th Regiment Connecticut, National Archives.) The regiment's historian wrote that "strange to say, he was unaware that he had lost but one limb until coming [to] soon after under the hand of Surgeon Terry, when he coolly remarked, 'Why, surgeon, I've lost my right arm, too! I thought I had only lost my left.'" (John W. Storrs, *The Twentieth Connecticut: A Regimental History*, p. 107.)

deadened thud of the exploding shell; the whizzing sound of the pieces as they flew in different directions; the yells of the rebels when they gained a momentary advantage; the cheers of our men when the surging tide of battle turned in our favor; the groans of the wounded, and the ghastly, disfigured forms and blackened faces of the dead, rendered the scene one that will never be effaced from the memory of those who witnessed it."[29]

By 1:00 in the afternoon, the blue coats had driven the enemy back. "When the rebels turned and fled, such a genuine hearty Yankee cheer went up as was seldom heard before," wrote Philo Buckingham.[30] The stretcher-bearers went to work taking up the wounded, and the boys of the 20th Connecticut collapsed behind the lines.

Culp's Hill was safe.

Morning of Day Three: Bliss Farm between the Lines

The men of the 14th Connecticut woke early on the morning of July 3 on Cemetery Ridge. Before sunrise, their commanding officer, Maj. Theodore G. Ellis, sent two companies out on the skirmish line. Sgt. Elnathan Tyler remembered:

> Those of us detailed to go out on the line crawled out across the wheat field to the fence beyond and lying upon the ground behind the posts and lower rails of the fence, began the sharp-shooters drill of the day. The space between us and the rebel skirmish line was open and clear in the main and the least showing of head, hand or foot was an invitation for a target of the same. One thing we soon learned and that was the puff of smoke from our rifles when we fired made an unpleasantly close target even when we were sure we were unseen ourselves.[31]

About two hours later, the next two 14th companies set out as relief—but now the sun was up, making them visible to the enemy. "The relieving squad would leave the reserve rendezvous moving in any way possible to avoid the observation of the enemy, but when a place was reached where exposure was unavoidable each would take to running at highest speed, and upon reaching the fence would throw himself at once upon the ground. Then must the relieved ones get back to the reserve in a similar manner; and 'relieving' seemed a misnomer."[32]

Benjamin Hirst wrote: "I found one of the men I was to relieve [Corp. Sam Huxham] Dead at his Post. He was shot through the Head and from his position he seemed to be taking aim at a Rebel. I didn't know he was Dead until I put my hand upon his shoulder, and spoke to him."[33]

On a small rise between the Union lines and those of the enemy stood the white farmhouse and sturdy barn of a Gettysburg family named Bliss. The Bliss barn was large, its first story of stone, topped by another story of brick. "The Confederate sharp-shooters were not long in seeing the advantage of this improvised fort," explained the 14th Regiment's historian; "and soon every window, door and crevice showed the protruding muzzles of long range rifles ready to do their deadly work."[34] From the barn, the Rebels could reach

Kneeling behind a wooden fence, Cpl. Sam Huxham steadied his rifle on a cross rail and fired at the Confederate skirmishers across the field. Tall grain concealed Huxham's location, but the Rebels could make out the puff of smoke from each shot. When another 14th soldier came to relieve Sam, he found him kneeling at his post, his rifle resting on the middle fence rail. He seemed just about to fire at the Rebels—but he was dead, a bullet in the head.

not only the Union skirmish line, but also a Federal battery on the ridge, so that the artillerymen could not touch their guns without risking death.

Union general Alexander Hays ordered the barn to be seized, and a series of dangerous missions ensued. Union troops would dart out, under fire, and capture the barn. Once the Federals had driven out the enemy and secured the position, they would withdraw—and more Confederates would sneak back to reoccupy the barn, and continue their deadly task. Finally, on the morning of the third day of battle, General Hays had had it: he ordered the 14th Connecticut to take the position once and for all.

The Bliss barn stood some four-tenths of a mile from the 14th's line. The assignment went to Capt. Samuel A. Moore and a detail of about fifty or sixty soldiers.

Moore led his men down a lane. Ahead lay an open field where the 14th men would be full in the sights of the waiting Confederates, both the sharp-shooters in the barn and the skirmish line.

"Then the desperate character of the sortie was fully revealed," wrote the 14th's chaplain, Henry Stevens; "but no man could recoil though death seemed inevitable. As to advance in any kind of a formation would but furnish a better target to aim at, the order was to . . . scatter and run. Every man was put to his mettle and ran with all his might for the barn."[35]

One man said it was "like dodging ten thousand shafts of lighting."[36] Every few yards a man fell wounded or dead, but enough of Captain Moore's band made it to the Bliss barn that the Confederates "skedaddled," leaving the gasping 14th men in possession. But within minutes it was clear that occupying the barn was not going to solve the problem: the rebels had retreated to the white farmhouse about 150 feet away, and kept firing.

Now it fell to Major Ellis and the regiment's remaining four companies to capture the Bliss house. Their route would be even more exposed than that of Captain Moore's detachment, "subjected to a hot fire from the house and skirmish line, and for the last three hundred yards or more to a still hotter one on the right flank."[37]

"The men never could describe their feelings on those mad runs for life," mused Chaplain Stevens years later. "We have never heard any

Capt. Samuel Moore was, to no one's surprise, the first man to enter the Bliss barn. Leading four companies, the tall, red-bearded Moore set off across the open field. Minutes later, Moore and his men sent the Confederate sharpshooters flying. Samuel Moore's men respected him for his bravery and honesty, his devotion to the Union and to them. Just before the Battle of Fredericksburg, Moore had been sent to Washington on a regimental errand, returning after the battle was over. One of his men wrote: "had he been with us, another noble officer would doubtless have been killed: for all the regiment knows that there never was a fight yet, but what he always took the lead . . . On arriving here and seeing only a little band of us left,—scarcely one hundred fit for duty,—his feelings overpowered him, and for a while he was completely overcome." (Sgt. E. H. Wade, as quoted in Charles D. Page, *History of the Fourteenth Regiment, Connecticut Volunteer Infantry*, p. 107.)

Though he gave his occupation as "butcher" at enlistment, Sam Moore had worked as store clerk, cod fisherman, and carpenter. He had lived in Massachusetts, Minnesota, and Wisconsin before returning to his home in New Britain to run his father's meat business. He was twenty-nine when he joined the 14th Connecticut as a lieutenant. Three months after Gettysburg, Moore was raised to lieutenant colonel. He was suited to army life—his obituary nearly fifty years later noted that "He seemed to enjoy the smell of powder." (*Hartford Daily Courant*, May 13, 1912, p. 13.)

really attempt it. The excitement, the frenzied effort, the terrible sense of imminent, savage danger could not be clearly called up nor could words express them."[38]

Of the many 14th soldiers who fell on the "rush across that bullet swept plain,"[39] one stood out in Chaplain Stevens's memory: young Thomas Jeffrey Brainard.

> Bright little "Jeff" of Co. F. was . . . dashing ahead well to the front, and one of his comrades heard him shouting to some who seemed to be laggard, "Come on, you cowards!" when he was struck near the shoulder by a musket shot, the ball passing down into his chest.
>
> He was the life of his company, full of rollicking fun, and when Capt. Broatch heard him "yell" and saw him leap into the air he thought it was "one of Jeff's antics." Poor, dear boy, when he touched the earth he rose no more unhelped. Sergt. Maj. Hincks as he rushed by heard his shrill cry: "My God! my God, I'm hit!—Oh, how it *hurts* me!"[40]

Companions carried Jeff to the rear, where the chaplain hurried to him and

> dropping upon one knee at his side, took his hand. His frenzied grasp and the contortions of his countenance told the agonies of pain he felt. Dr. Dudley came at once and probed the wound, but quickly withdrew in a manner unperceived by Jeff, giving a significant glance which said, "Fatal—I leave him with you!" . . . still holding his hand and stroking his forehead, [the chaplain] said, "What shall we think of you, Jeff." With a startled expression he looked up, when, seeming to comprehend the significance of the words and tone, he spoke: "Tell my mother—tell—my" and was gone.[41]

Others were dead as well, and many wounded. Major Ellis and his men now had possession of the Bliss farmhouse though the Confederates, sheltered in the family's peach orchard, were blasting bullets through the house's walls. Captain Moore and his detachment were doing their best to hold the barn.

Speaking years later to the 14th's veterans, Chaplain Stevens said in wonder, "The enemy's skirmishers . . . were closing in upon you; the sharpshooters had a bead on every head, hand, or foot that appeared outside of the buildings; and the rebel artillery was dropping shells among you through the roof of the barn, and it seemed to you that you must be annihilated or captured . . . But you had been ordered to 'hold' the buildings, and hold them you must as long as any of you were left there alive."[42]

As the situation began to look bleak indeed, the 14th men became aware of a man on horseback riding pell-mell from Union headquarters, across no-man's land, right toward them. "Erect in his saddle, with his fine horse making mighty leaps, the target of more than fourscore rifles and muskets, the gallant Capt. Postles of the 1st Del[aware] . . . delivered an order to set fire to the buildings and retire . . . then he turned and rode back in the same dashing, fearless manner . . ."[43]

The 14th Connecticut's boyish surgeon, Frederick Dudley, was only twenty-one in July of 1863. A native of Madison, Connecticut, Dudley had graduated from Yale Medical School the previous year. While caring for the regiment's wounded at Gettysburg, Dudley was struck by a shell fragment that lacerated his arm. Nurse Cornelia Hancock praised Dudley for his dedication to the men in his care, declaring him "perfectly reckless in time of battle" when he would go to the front lines to tend the injured soldiers. (Cornelia Hancock, *Letters of a Civil War Nurse*, edited by Henrietta Stratton Jaquette, p. 82.)

The 14th soldiers wasted no time in setting flame to the barn and house. "Then the men, taking up tenderly their wounded and dead and gathering their arms, started on their perilous return, running nearly the same hazard as when advancing."

"In that brilliant sortie," wrote Chaplain Stevens, "some precious lives went out, some cripples were made, and every man that escaped . . . came back panting and wearied and feeling that 'out of the jaws of death' had he come."[44]

Afternoon of Day Three: The 14th Connecticut Faces Pickett's Charge at Cemetery Ridge

Back on Cemetery Ridge, the 14th men caught their collective breath. They were positioned in a long line of Union troops behind a low stone wall running south toward Little Round Top. Just to the left of the 14th soldiers, the stone wall jutted out some eighty yards to the west, towards the far-off Confederate position, then turned at a ninety-degree angle to run south once more. This readily recognizable jog in the stone wall would be called "the Angle" from that day forward, as yet another pastoral landscape—like the wheat field and the peach orchard—entered the national memory with new connotations. The new meanings called up sacrifice and valor, not fruit and grain.

The 14th boys sprawled on the ground behind the wall. Some lit their pipes; others brought out pencil and paper to write home; many found themselves suddenly hungry. The boys in Company A crowded around Cpl. Al DeForest, who had somehow emerged from the raid on Bliss farm with a live chicken under his arm. DeForest got the chicken into a pot and began cooking it over a fire in the rear of the regiment's lines. He had great plans for that chicken, but he was to be disappointed.[45]

At one o'clock, all hell broke loose.

"Who can fitly describe that awful pounding of those two hundred rapid, fierce-firing cannon?" Chaplain Stevens recalled. "The solid earth trembled with the concussion, and the air seemed filled with hurtling, whizzing shot and bursting shell."[46]

Robert E. Lee was going to send his infantry against the center of the Union line—but first, he had ordered his artillery to "soften up" the Federals. And the Union's big guns answered immediately. The deafening artillery duel that resulted was the most intense of the war.

The 14th Connecticut, part of the 2nd Corps that formed the Union's center on Cemetery Ridge, was right in the middle of the terrifying barrage. Benjamin Hirst described

Major Theodore Ellis, thirty-three, was known for his coolness in battle. A civil engineer in private life, Ellis had quickly become adept at military tactics. His regiment knew him as a strict drillmaster. On the morning of July 3, Major Ellis led the second group of four companies of 14th men in a hazardous mission to capture the Bliss farmhouse from Rebel sharpshooters. The raid resulted in thirty-four casualties to the 14th.

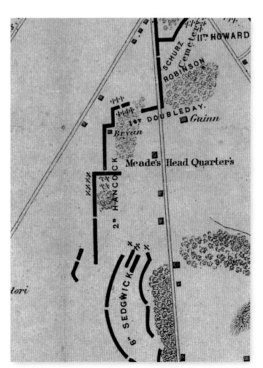

Detail of "Map of the battle field of Gettysburg," J. B. Lippincott Co., 1863. At the center of the Union line was the Angle, near which the 14th Connecticut took its position.

the Fiercest cannonading I ever heard, the shot and shell came from Front and Right and Left. It makes my Blood Tingle in my veins now; to think of . . . it seemed as if all the Demons in Hell were let loose, and were Howling through the Air. Turn your eyes which way you will the whole Heavens were filled with Shot and Shell, Fire and Smoke. The Rebels had concentrated about 120 Pieces of Artilery upon us and for 2 long hours they delivered a Rapid and Destructive fire upon our Lines . . .

To add to all this was our own Batteries in full Blaze, every shot from which seemed to pass over our heads; it was a terrible situation to be in between those two fires; how we did Hug the ground expecting every moment to be our last. And as first one of us got Hit and then another to hear their cries was Awful. And still you dare not move either hand or foot, to do so was Death.[47]

Sgt. Maj. William Hincks wrote:

Without waiting for orders, which could hardly have been heard, we advanced with one impulse for a few paces and lay down just behind the First Delaware men, who had taken our places at the wall . . . the enemy's guns were pointed so that the shot mainly cleared us and went over the crest of the hill into the valley beyond . . .

The battery on our left . . . kept up a steady reply for more than an hour, though I am at a loss to know what they could have seen to fire at, the smoke was so thick. So very thick was it that the sun seemed blotted out. One of the guns was directly behind me and at every discharge, the concussion would throw gravel over me and I could not only see and smell the thick cloud of burning powder, but could taste it also. I lay with my arm thrown over Pearce Hart and so hot was it that the drops of perspiration falling from my face made mud of the dusty soil on which we were stretched.

No one moved or spoke save the gunners behind us and ever and anon I could hear the ringing voice of the sergeant nearest us giving command to aim, fire, (a tremendous crash) load, to be after a brief interval repeated. Then after a time I judged that he was wounded, for his voice was silenced, and out of the cloud came another and different voice, repeating the same command. From time to time, we could hear the wailing of some one wounded, but still their fire did not slacken. When the gunners fell, the drivers took their places.[48]

Amid the constant, thundering roar, about 100 Connecticut artillerymen were blasting away from their position to the left of the 2nd Corps on the ridge. Connecticut's 2nd Light Battery, assigned to the artillery reserve under Gen. Robert O. Tyler, brought two twelve-pounder howitzers and four six-pounder James rifles to the fight.

Soldiers were desperately blocking their ears. "I utterly despair of giving any idea of the various diabolical sounds to which we listened," wrote the 14th's William Hincks, "the howling of the shell as they sped through the air was like the voice of the tornado upon the ocean, and the sound of their bursting like incessant crashes of the heaviest thunder."[49]

The thundering guns, it was said, could be heard for 100 miles—but, incredibly, soldiers in the 17th Connecticut were asleep on Cemetery Hill. The men were so overwhelmed with exhaustion, wrote their sergeant major, that "This day seems like a dream to me . . . I recall but little, and in common with most others in the regiment, I fancy spent most of the day trying to sleep, in spite of the roar of the guns."[50]

After nearly two hours, the Federal artillery deliberately slackened and then stopped its fire. The Confederates, believing they had silenced many of the Union guns, now ordered an end to the barrage and readied their infantry for the climactic charge.

Ben Hirst said, "as the Smoke lifted from the Crest we saw our Guns leaving one after another and soon a terrible stillness prevailed so that you could almost hear your heart thud in your bosom."[51]

"We rose from the ground and stretched our cramped limbs," recalled Hincks, "and in our inexperience, thought the battle was over, but Major Ellis was better posted than we. 'No,' said he, 'They mean to charge with all their infantry.'"[52]

Ellis was right: the Confederates would commence their dramatic infantry assault—forever after known as Pickett's Charge—a few moments later. From the woods far across the grassy plain, the Rebel commanders could clearly see a grove of trees that grew just south of the Angle in the stone wall. General Lee chose that copse of trees as the spot his troops should march toward.

Less than three hundred yards from the copse of trees, the 14th men began strengthening their stone wall. But all the while, they were watching—staring intently down the gently sloping plain to the field beyond, and finally to the woods a mile away, where they knew the enemy was.

Then out of the woods came the Confederate army.

"The spectacle was magnificent," wrote Major Ellis of the twelve thousand Confederates marching toward them.[53]

"As far as eye could reach could be seen the advancing troops, their gay war flags fluttering in the gentle summer breeze, while their sabers and bayonets flashed and glistened in the midday sun. Step by step they came, the music and rhythm of their tread resounding upon the rock-ribbed earth. Every movement expressed determination and resolute defiance, the line moving forward like a victorious giant, confident of power and victory. If one listened, he might hear the voice of the commander, 'Steady men, steady.' There is no swaying of the line, no faltering of the step. The advance seems as resistless as the incoming tide."[54]

The Union infantry had orders to hold its fire until the Rebel lines were closer, but Union artillery fired steadily into the advancing mass. The artillerymen of Connecticut's 2nd Light Battery, commanded by Capt. John Sterling, sent shells hurtling toward the enemy. "Sterling's men made superb firing," wrote a Pennsylvania officer, "their shells bursting in the faces of the advancing host. One of the lieutenants of the battery, a very tall long legged fellow, could not restrain his delight at seeing the excellent work that his battery was doing, and when he would see a good shot and his shells bursting right in the ranks of the Confederates, the arms and legs flying, he would leap up, crack his heels together, and give a great scream of joy."[55]

As the 14th Connecticut men waited tensely at the stone wall, their two companies of skirmishers were ordered in, just ahead of the Confederate advance, and "fell back to the position on

When the Confederates reached the fence at the Emmitsburg road, Union troops began firing as fast as they could. Some of the 14th men had to sacrifice water from their canteens to cool the barrels of their rifles. Lt. William H. Hawley, pictured here, teamed up with his friend William Hincks. Sergeant Major Hincks recalled, "I was firing two Sharp's rifles, which Lieutenant Hawley was loading for me; they belonged to men wounded early in the day." (William Hincks, as quoted in Page, *History of the Fourteenth*, p. 156.) Loading a cartridge into the breech of a Sharps rifle was much faster than going through the many steps required to get a muzzle-loading rifle musket ready to fire.

the ridge," wrote the chaplain, "taking their places among their comrades—and now all the members of the little Fourteenth band were together, shoulder to shoulder ready for the supreme, crucial moment, with tingling nerves and bated breath awaiting the onset."[56]

"It was, indeed, an anxious moment. One you can see is looking at the far off home he will never see again. Another is looking at his little ones, as he mechanically empties his cartridge-box on the ground before him, that he may load more quickly, determined to part with life as dearly as possible. Others are communing with Him before whom so many will shortly have to appear."[57]

With flags flying, the Rebel lines approached inexorably, "and a stillness supervened that made the sound of the enemy's tread audible and the calm orders of the officers: 'Steady men! Guide centre!' to come up as distinctly as though delivered on dress-parade."[58]

Now they were in range of the 14th's rifles, but General Hays had ordered his infantry to hold their fire until the enemy reached the Emmitsburg road. There, the Confederates would arrive at a wooden fence they would need to climb over.

It was all the 14th men could do to hold their fingers still on the triggers. Steadily on came the magnificent Confederate lines, three deep. And now—"the fence was reached, and simultaneously with it rang out at our brigade the order: 'Fire!' 'Fire!!' 'Fire!!!' and our rifles spoke in a volley so full, so well directed that the front line of the enemy mounting the fence seemed wiped away," said Chaplain Stevens.[59]

The 14th's historian wrote that

> the men dropped from the fence as if swept by a gigantic sickle swung by some powerful force of nature. Great gaps were formed in the line, the number of slain and wounded could not be estimated by numbers, but must be measured by yards. Yet on came the second line in full face of the awful carnage. No longer could the measured tread be heard, no longer were the orders of the commanding officers audible for the shrieks of the wounded and groans of the dying filled the air, but on they came, meeting with the same fate as their comrades.[60]

Just to the left of the 14th's position, the Rebels were smashing through the Union line at the Angle. Confederate General Armistead, his hat atop his sword, charged to the front, shouting to his men to follow. They answered with the Rebel yell, and a mob of Virginians leaped the stone wall. Now the fighting became savage, hand-to-hand combat. Some Union troops broke, and others rushed into the fray.

Just yards away, the 14th had to react instantly. Major Ellis shouted, "Fire left oblique!" and his men pivoted left and fired into the melee at the Angle. In the space of a few minutes, the Confederate troops began to fall back.[61]

About fifty yards out in front of the 14th's position, a Tennessee color-bearer had planted his regiment's flag and thrown himself on the ground to avoid the intense fire. Major Ellis called out to the men of the 14th for a volunteer to seize the rebel colors. Three men at once hurdled the stone wall and raced toward the flag: Sgt. Maj. William B. Hincks, Capt. John Broatch, and Sgt. George Brigham: "Brigham was shot down by a retreating rebel, but the other two sped on, Hincks finally outstripping Broatch, ran straight and swift for the color, amid a storm of shot. Swinging his saber over the prostrate Confederates and uttering a terrific yell, he seized the flag and hastily returned to the line. He was the object of all eyes and the men cheered him heartily as he reached the ranks."[62]

The Confederate lines, which moments before had looked invincible, now wavered and began to break, "and seeing this a shout went up from the regiment, which was taken up and echoed and reechoed along the whole Union line. In vain did the Confederate commanders attempt to reform their broken columns, colors were dropped and the men fled in confusion."[63]

"The men now careless of shelter stood erect and with loud shouts continued to fire into the retreating army as long as they were within range. Many of the retreating column lay down behind stones and hillocks, and even the dead bodies of their comrades, to be protected from the Union shots."[64]

Triumphant at last, the 14th boys "would rise and howl, 'How do you like Fredericksburg now?'"[65] In all, the 14th Connecticut captured five regimental flags from Confederate units in their front.

"Presently, as by one common impulse, bits of white cloth and handkerchiefs were waved as signals of surrender," wrote the 14th's historian. "In response to these signals, our men leaped over the wall and advanced toward the retreating foe. When they reached the point where the enemy's advance had halted, rebel wounded and unwounded in large numbers rose up and surrendered themselves."[66]

"One of the lieutenant-colonels taken by our regiment, coming up to our thin line, asked us where all our troops were, and being told that he could see all there were, exclaimed, 'Oh! that I had known it a half hour since.'"[67]

The 14th men were ecstatic with the Union victory. "Oh, it was a glorious day for the old Fourteenth!" exulted Edward Wade of New Britain.[68]

"Well," reflected Chaplain Stevens, "we paid dearly for it. In all, sixty-six out of about one hundred and sixty had been lost to us. Thirteen were killed or mortally wounded, forty-nine wounded and four captured. Some of our wounded received three or four hits."[69]

William Glossinger, a thirty-six-year-old corporal in Company H, later wrote movingly to his friend Thomas Gardner, who'd been hospitalized after taking a bullet in the head during the Bliss farm raid. Glossinger described the death of their friend Thomas Martin Ames: "Martin was clost

William B. Hincks of Bridgeport might not have looked like a daredevil, but in the 14th Connecticut's first battle, his comrades watched him stop in an orchard—under fire—to pick apples. At Gettysburg, Sergeant Major Hincks raced across the battlefield with bullets flying around him, and seized the flag of the 14th Tennessee Regiment. Two of his brothers-in-arms, Elijah W. Bacon and Christopher Flynn, also captured Confederate battle flags that afternoon. The three 14th Connecticut soldiers received Medals of Honor.

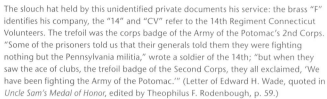

by me but I did not Notice him until the fight was over and looking behind me I saw he had fallen I went to him and saw at wonce[?] that that he was gone. I spoke to him and he opened his eyes and asked me to examin his wounds   after I had looked at them he sead to me am I dieing   I told him he was   he then said all things work to gether for good to them that love the Lord   he lived about, 2 hours."[70]

The 14th soldiers turned to the sad duties that followed battle: "the boys of the regiment went out and brought in the wounded, although under a heavy fire from the skirmish line which the Confederates had been able to reestablish. These Confederate wounded were tenderly treated and cared for, even portions of the precious stone wall being removed so that they could be taken in without jolting. Coffee was made and the meager rations shared."[71]

"Meager rations" was an understatement, as Cpl. Edward H. Wade made clear.

> We had scarcely anything to eat from July 1 to the night of the 3rd, when we crawled out on the battlefield after dark, where the enemy's wounded lay, and took the haversacks from those who had been killed in the fight that day; these haversacks were nearly all full of nice hoe-cakes. Some that we found were stained with blood where it had run into their haversacks from their wounds. But we were so hungry that we didn't stop for that. This may seem a tough story, but it is true.[72]

In Connecticut's 20th Regiment, on Culp's Hill, thirty-eight-year-old Horatio Chapman described their sad duties on the night of July 3.

> We built fires all over the battle field and the dead of the blue and gray were being buried all night, and the wounded carried to the hospital. We made no distinction between our own and the confederate wounded, but treated them both alike, and although we had been engaged in fierce and deadly combat all day and weary and all begrimed with smoke and powder and dust, many of us went around among the wounded and gave cooling water or hot coffee to drink. The confederates were surprised and so expressed themselves that they received such kind treatment at our hands, and some of the slightly wounded were glad they were wounded and our prisoners.
>
> But in front of our breastworks, where the confederates were massed in large numbers, the sight was truly awful and appalling. The shells from our batteries had told with fearful and terrible effect upon them and the dead in some places were piled upon each other, and the groans and moans of the wounded were truly saddening to hear. Some were just alive and gasping, but unconscious. Others were mortally wounded and were conscious of the fact that they could not live long; and there were others wounded, how bad they could not tell, whether mortal or otherwise, and so it was they would linger on some longer and some for a shorter time—without the sight or consolation of wife, mother, sister or friend.[73]

Chapman's wife and toddler were back home in Connecticut. Maybe they were on his mind when he bent over a Rebel soldier on the field. "I saw a letter sticking out of the breast pocket of one of the confederate dead, a young man apparently about twenty-four. Curiosity prompted me to read it. It was from his young wife away down in the state of Louisiana. She was hoping and longing that this cruel war would end and he could come home, and she says, 'Our little boy gets into my lap and says, "Now, Mama, I will give you a kiss for Papa."' But oh how I wish you could come home and kiss me for yourself."[74]

While soldiers were bearing off the wounded, the surgeons had begun their terrible work. They would not sleep that night. "Every dwelling house and barn within reasonable distance (besides numerous hospital tents erected in all directions) were devoted to the bloody, yet merciful, surgical work, outside of which were to be seen heaps of amputated limbs, while within, in long rows, were the wounded on stretchers and on the ground in almost every conceivable form of mortal agony."[75]

James Middlebrook, a Trumbull farmer in the 17th Connecticut, helped care for wounded soldiers in a large barn: "200 on the first floor where I am & under the Barn as many more & lots of them in Tents around outside there are some 80 men in the Barn with legs & arms off."[76] Middlebrook's work seemed never-ending: ten days after the battle ended, he wrote that he still had not been out of sight of the field hospital where he labored.[77]

On the night of July 4, Robert E. Lee stealthily withdrew his Confederate troops and began a rapid march southward. He left a nightmare behind him. Dennis Tuttle, a Connecticut native,

Twenty-one-year-old Charles Fuller of New York's 61st Regiment was wounded in the wheat field in both the ankle and shoulder. After having his leg amputated, Fuller lay in a hospital tent for six days before a surgeon looked in on him. "He took the bandages off," Fuller wrote, "and found that there were a large number of full grown maggots in the wound. The discovery for the moment was horrifying to me. I concluded if all the other things did not take me off the skippers would, but the good doctor assured me that the wigglers didn't amount to much in that place, and he would soon fix them. He diluted some turpentine, took a quantity of it in his mouth and squirted it into the wound, and over the stump. It did the business for the intruders, and I had no more trouble of that sort." (Charles Augustus Fuller, *Personal Recollections of the War of 1861*, p. 69.)

described it for his wife: "You can have no idea of how the field looked . . . I think I could have walked from a ¼ to a ½ mile on dead rebels without once even stepping on the ground. Horses and men, the living and dead were mingled together on the field. Oh! But it was horrid and it made my heart sick to see it."[78]

Though the men of the 14th Connecticut had buried hundreds and hundreds of soldiers in the last year, "The sight of some of the dead was moving to the sternest hearts. Some were in attitudes indicating that life went out in agony, and others holding likenesses of home loved ones they had spent their last moments in gazing upon."[79]

✶ ✶ ✶

Loren Goodrich, a private in the 14th Connecticut, described the battle and its aftermath in a letter to friends at home.

[Day Three] . . . everything went along quietly until 2 oclock in the afternoon when the enemy opened 75 pieces of canon on to us   it was one of the hardest artillery fight that we have ever had   it kept up for 2 hours when the enemy having smashed one of our batteries all to pieces made an advance on us with 3 battle lines a mile long

they came up in beautiful style with their beautiful battle flags flying open to the breeze   it was a splendid sight to see but alas how many there were of those brave men that were launched into eternity during the terrible struggle   onward they came cheering till within 200 yards when we opened a terrible fire upon them which staggered them for a moment

they then rallied and tried to flank us but were again repulsed   the other lines then advanced but were repulsed in the same way with great slaughter   they scattered in every direction a great many of them laying down and waving their white handkerchiefs in token of their surrender   our men then ceased firing and our regiment succeeded in capturing over 400 prisoners 4 stands of colors and 8 swords which are to be sent home   it was a scene of the wildest confusion our men were cheering and our division General General Hayes was riding up and down the lines dragging a secesh flag after him and cheering up the men

by the time that the excitement was over the shades of evening closed over the scene   the men were hungry their rations having run out the night before   one supply train was ordered to the rear on account of the cannon-ading that night I went down onto the battle field to see if I could find any grub in the rebs haversacks   I am ashamed to own it but then the pangs of hunger will do most anything   I went around and felt in the dead rebs haversacks in nearly every one of them I found a plenty of fresh meat and wheat bread which I took up and distributed amongst the boys   they were glad to get it

it was a horrible sight to see those poor fellows lying there who a few hours before were in the full bloom of manhood   one man who lived 2 hours after the battle was holding in his hand the picture of his wife and children   there he died with no loving hand or kind friend to soothe or cheer him with kind words grasping in his death clutch the picture of those innocent ones who will be left fatherless

I passed on to another man   touched him to see if he was alive he looked up the stamp of death was marked on his features   says he young freind give me a drink of water   he could not raise his head to drink   one of my compan-ions being with me raised his head for him which was covered with blood   I had a canteen which holds 3 pints of water that I gave to him he drank the whole of it and he wanted more.

the night was still and dark   I could hear the groans of the wounded that lay between the two skirmish lines nearly a half a mile calling for water . . .

the next morning we looked down on to the field in front of us   there you could see the poor fellows that we thought were dead dragging themselves out of the mud.[80]

✳ ✳ ✳

The Union army's victory at Gettysburg was a turning point of the war. The following day, July 4, 1863, another victory bolstered the Union's position when the Confederates surrendered Vicksburg, Mississippi, to Ulysses S. Grant. The fall of Vicksburg effactually tore the Confederacy in two, and gave the Union army and navy control of the Mississippi River.

Four months later would come another milestone in the Civil War, when President Lincoln accepted an invitation to say "a few appropriate remarks" at the dedication of the Soldiers' National Cemetery in Gettysburg. Lincoln's remarks—just 273 words—paid deep, heartfelt homage to the valiant soldiers who battled there. They also broadened the war's aims, giving the Union army and the people of the North a new cause to fight for—freedom.

The Gettysburg Address

Four score and seven years ago our fathers brought forth on this continent a new nation, conceived in liberty, and dedicated to the proposition that all men are created equal.

Now we are engaged in a great civil war, testing whether that nation, or any nation, so conceived and so dedicated, can long endure. We are met on a great battle-field of that war. We have come to dedicate a portion of that field, as a final resting place for those who here gave their lives that that nation might live. It is altogether fitting and proper that we should do this.

But, in a larger sense, we can not dedicate, we can not consecrate, we can not hallow this ground. The brave men, living and dead, who struggled here, have consecrated it, far above our poor power to add or detract. The world will little note, nor long remember what we say here, but it can never forget what they did here. It is for us the living, rather, to be dedicated here to the unfinished work which they who fought here have thus far so nobly advanced. It is rather for us to be here dedicated to the great task remaining before us—that from these honored dead we take increased devotion to that cause for which they gave the last full measure of devotion—that we here highly resolve that these dead shall not have died in vain—that this nation, under God, shall have a new birth of freedom—and that government of the people, by the people, for the people, shall not perish from the earth.

In July of 1865, as his Civil War service was ending, a 17th Connecticut soldier wrote to his wife about the future before them, and the past behind. "Make up you[r] mind to travel some when we get Home," said James Middlebrook. "I think of going to that place long to be remembered—Gettysburg—"[81]

Thousands and thousands of soldiers felt the same pull. To them, the battlefield was a sacred place. For decades to come, Union and Confederate veterans would return to Gettysburg, drawn back again and again, "to that place long to be remembered."

In 1888, Professor Joshua Lawrence Chamberlain, who as colonel of the 20th Maine had defended Little Round Top, voiced the significance of Gettysburg for the nation:

> In great deeds, something abides. On great fields, something stays. Forms change and pass; bodies disappear; but spirits linger, to consecrate ground for the vision-place of souls. And reverent men and women from afar, and generations that know us not and that we know not of, heart-drawn to see where and by whom great things were suffered and done for them, shall come to this deathless field, to ponder and dream; and lo! the shadow of a mighty presence shall wrap them in its bosom, and the power of the vision pass into their souls.[82]

CHAPTER ELEVEN

There Will Be No Turning Back

STUBBORN FIGHTING, JULY 1863 TO JUNE 1864

MORRIS ISLAND, SOUTH CAROLINA

The Connecticut men waited tensely on the beach as dusk descended. "[J]ust at dark we wer ordered to the front," wrote Martin Eddy of New Britain; "we knew what was coming next   a charge."[1] At the head of Martin's regiment stood their colonel, John Lyman Chatfield, his sword raised, waiting for the order to advance.

Chatfield and his regiment had been here on South Carolina's Morris Island for over a week. The recent victories at Gettysburg and Vicksburg had given the Union the momentum it had desperately needed. Now the North had a chance to push on toward the final victory by taking Charleston, the birthplace of the Confederacy. To do that, Union brigadier general Quincy Gillmore planned to capture Morris Island, then use it as a base for Union artillery to smash Fort Sumter. With these Rebel strongholds gone, Union forces could sweep into Charleston.

On July 11, Gillmore had ordered an assault on Fort Wagner, a Confederate battery that protected Charleston's harbor from nearby Morris Island.

But Fort Wagner was well fortified, and Gillmore's assaulting troops were repulsed. Now, a week later, Gillmore had ordered his artillery and Union navy gunboats to pound the Rebel fort all day, hoping to weaken Wagner before his infantry made another assault. Gillmore planned to send 5,000 infantry troops against Wagner, where some 1,620 Confederates waited with plenty of artillery.

John Lyman Chatfield of Waterbury "was born a soldier," according to one of his men. (Charles K. Cadwell, *The Old Sixth Regiment: Its War Record, 1861–5* [New Haven, CT: Tuttle, Morehouse & Taylor, 1875], p. 77.) By trade, the thirty-six-year-old Chatfield was a carpenter, but the military drew him like a magnet. Before the war he'd led men in two militia units: the Derby Blues and the Waterbury City Guard. At Lincoln's first call for troops, Chatfield had enlisted, bringing with him a company from the City Guard. He quickly advanced to become colonel of Connecticut's 3rd Regiment, which he commanded at the Battle of Bull Run.

Now Colonel of the 6th Connecticut, John Chatfield inspired intense loyalty and respect from his soldiers. He was known for his "calm self-possession" in battle, his skill in military movements, and his insistence on strict, but fair, discipline. His men loved him. On July 18th, the regiment was ordered to storm Fort Wagner at dark. "Never was an order more cheerfully obeyed," wrote Sgt. Charlie Cadwell, "especially as the word passed around that Col. Chatfield was to lead us into action, the Colonel declaring his preference 'to stand or fall with the men of the Sixth,' and refusing the honor of commanding our brigade, which belonged to him as the ranking officer." (Cadwell, *The Old Sixth Regiment*, p. 70.)

The Union gunboats, reported one soldier, poured "shell enough into Wagner to start several first class iron foundries . . . Before night came, hardly a gun boomed from Wagner, and many seemed to think an easy victory was within reach. As twilight approached the whole command lay under cover of the sand hills, waiting for the order to advance."[2]

Leading the assault was an African American regiment, the 54th Massachusetts. Their colonel, Robert Gould Shaw, seized the chance to show what his men could do.

Behind them would be Colonel Chatfield and his 6th Connecticut. "The command formed silently on the beach; the men seemed impatient to move," wrote Charlie Cadwell, then a twenty-two-year-old sergeant.[3]

At nightfall, the advance began. With the 54th Massachusetts in the lead, eight Union regiments marched up the thin strip of beach toward the fort. The navy's guns fell silent, and for a moment the men could hear the waves lapping on the sand. Then came the order to charge. About three hundred yards from the fortifications, "they opened on us," wrote Martin Eddy of the 6th, "and then they give us a little of every

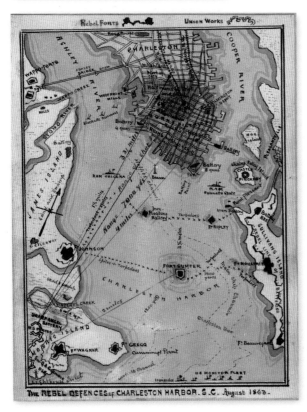

"The Rebel Defences of Charleston Harbor S.C.," drawn by Robert Knox Sneden. Fort Wagner (*lower left corner*) was one of a swath of Confederate batteries guarding Charleston (*upper right*).

thing grape and canister Shell and musketry and hand gronades."[4]

In the devastating fire, "The Fifty-fourth wavered for a moment," recalled Charlie Cadwell. But Colonel Chatfield bounded ahead, waving his sword and encouraging the men of the 6th Connecticut, who "picked our way through the abatis, descended the ditch and climbed up the steep sides of the fort, and gaining the parapet, was among the rebels. The flash of a thousand rifles poured into us, followed in quick succession by hand grenades. Shrapnel, canister and grape were freely showered into the ranks, while we leaped down to the casemates and bomb-proofs, driving the enemy before us in great confusion."[5]

As Chatfield lay bleeding from two wounds, a young private from New Britain demonstrated the devotion the men felt for their colonel. Bernard Haffey reportedly lay down beside Chatfield to shield him from further harm. (Fred W. Chesson, "Colonel Chatfield's Courage or a Share of 'Glory,'" online at http://pages.cthome.net/fwc/GLORY.HTM.) Two other soldiers, putting themselves at great risk, carried the wounded colonel to the rear. Haffey received a special medal that Gen. Quincy Gillmore presented to 400 soldiers for bravery in the operations to take Charleston.

"[O]ur Col was the first man in," recounted Eddy; "we drove them out of the first part of the fort   it is a large fort all partishioned of[f]   we got on to the Second paripet but the fire was So hot and our numbers So small we could [not] get over."[6] As Chatfield led his men up the second parapet, Confederate grapeshot shattered his left leg below the knee. Unable to rise, Chatfield nevertheless continued to guide and encourage his men.

For close to three hours, the 6th Connecticut attempted to hold its position, waiting for support that never came. Finally, Chatfield gave the word to withdraw and his men began to pick their way through the darkness toward the rear. As the colonel attempted to drag himself off the parapet, an enemy bullet shattered his hand and sent spinning the sword he held.

In the frantic retreat, "the ded and wounded was pilled [piled] up too and 3 deep all around me," said a horrified Martin Eddy, "So I could not Step without Stepping on them."[7] Union soldiers who reached the beach found it crowded with wounded "and as the salt water surged over their bodies and in their wounds, their groans and cries were terrible to hear. Men begged piteously to others more fortunate, to remove them out of reach of the incoming tide."[8]

The attack was over. In those few hours, Union losses reached over 1,500 while the Confederates claimed just 174 casualties. A chastened General Gillmore would soon move to a siege operation. On September 7, the Rebels abandoned Wagner.

Col. John Chatfield survived long enough to reach his home in Waterbury, dying there a few weeks after the fruitless battle. The men of his regiment never forgot him, one writing that "His name was synonymous with all that was good, noble, brave, and kind."[9]

Moving On: Fall and Winter 1863

The Union's loss at Fort Wagner was the summer's last major engagement. September brought the brutal Battle of Chickamauga, Georgia, in which both armies sustained heavy losses, though no Connecticut troops were engaged. Minor engagements in Tennessee, Missouri, North Carolina, Virginia, and Louisiana filled the rest of the autumn.

The tattered remains of the regimental flag told the story of the 6th Connecticut's desperate fight at Battery Wagner. The regiment's flags were the first Union colors to reach the Confederate fort, but the color-bearer, "a German named Gustave DeBouge, was shot through the fore head while carrying the colors in the assault, and fell dead upon the flag, his life blood staining them through. Several brave ones who were near seized them, but they also fell either dead or wounded." (Cadwell, *The Old Sixth Regiment*, p. 73.) Capt. Frederick B. Osborn, determined to save the colors, "attempted to pull them from under the bodies; but, in so doing, the flag, which had become very much shattered by shots, was torn through the center, and the part attached to the staff only was saved." (Croffut and Morris, *Military and Civil History*, p. 445, quoting Redfield Duryee in presenting the regimental flag to Governor Buckingham.) The regiment itself was equally damaged: "our regt went with about 250 and came out less than 100," wrote Martin Eddy; "loss 163 killed wounded and prisoners most of them killed or wounded." (Letter of Martin Eddy to his brother, August 1, 1863, printed with permission of the Pearce Museum, Navarro College.)

Out west, Gen. Ulysses S. Grant, who had orchestrated the Union victory at Vicksburg, received a promotion to commander of the Union Military Division of the Mississippi. His new position would be a stepping-stone to greater things.

Morton's Ford, February 6–7, 1864

In Virginia, the Army of the Potomac settled into winter camp. The men had built their huts; some of the officers had even sent for their wives. But unbeknownst to the troops, Union commanders had planned a surprise strike against Richmond.

As a diversion, part of the Army of the Potomac would cross the Rapidan River in several places, forcing the Confederates to shift forces to meet it. On the morning of February 6, the men of the 14th Connecticut found themselves wading through the chilly waters of the Rapidan, nearly

In March of 1863, Farmington native James Halsted had journeyed north to Massachusetts to enlist in the Union army. It would be months before Connecticut would approve its own African American units, so eighteen-year-old James and a handful of other Connecticut residents joined the 54th Massachusetts Regiment. Many white Americans maintained that black men did not have the courage to fight. On the night of July 18, 1863, James Halsted and his brothers-in-arms prepared to lead the assault on Fort Wagner. The Confederates had vowed that they would kill all black prisoners. The 54th's colonel, Robert Gould Shaw, spoke quietly to his soldiers: "'Now I want you to prove yourselves men,' and reminded them that the eyes of thousands would look upon the night's work." (Luis Fenollosa Emilio, *History of the 54th Regiment of Massachusetts Volunteer Infantry, 1863–1865* [Boston: The Boston Book Co., 1894], p. 78.) In the three hours that followed, Colonel Shaw would be shot dead with many of his men. The 54th lost 42 percent of its troops in casualties. James Halsted was one of the survivors, but he did not come away from his service unscathed. Heatstroke suffered in South Carolina brought on epileptic seizures that returned regularly for the rest of Halsted's life.

waist-deep at a crossing called Morton's Ford. Wet and shivering, the men moved behind a small hill where they could build a few fires.

Near dark, Confederate shells came streaking toward them: Gen. Richard Ewell's troops were answering the perceived threat. Rebel infantry followed up, and the Connecticut men scrambled into a battle line.

"The darkness was intense, the artillery had ceased to play and the sharp flashes of the musketry were the only indications of the whereabouts of the enemy," wrote the regiment's historian. "Above the shouts and clatter of the musketry could be heard the sharp tenor voice of Lieutenant-Colonel Moore, directing his men and encouraging them to proceed."[10]

Pvt. Charlie Pollard wrote: "we had heavy skirmishing till near midnight bullets flying from all directions being so dark we could not see 15 rods having to fire where we saw the flash of the musket."[11]

Ahead in the darkness, Rebel soldiers were firing from behind a house and outbuildings. The 14th boys moved in to dislodge the enemy, "and in many cases it was a hand to hand fight with bayonets in the darkness."[12]

Some of the Connecticut soldiers later accused their division commander, Gen. Alexander Hays, of being drunk, claiming that Hays had ordered Union reinforcements to fire on their position; "and how many of the brave Fourteenth fell by that stupid drunken order will never be known."[13]

Later that night, the Union troops were withdrawn, slogging back across the river before dawn. Of the Federals' 262 casualties, 252 came from General Hays's division—and 115 of those were in the 14th Connecticut. The rebels lost fewer than 60 men.

The plan to strike Richmond was dropped. Once again, the men of the 14th Connecticut reflected that their regiment's sacrifice had been futile.

CAN THIS BE HELL?

Long before the spring of 1864, the 16th Connecticut Regiment had faced misfortune: at Antietam, the new soldiers—just learning how to load their muskets—had been slaughtered. Things couldn't get any worse. Could they?

On April 20, Confederate troops captured the Union-held town of Plymouth, North Carolina, taking prisoner about 400 members of the 16th Connecticut. The 16th's officers went to various Confederate prisons, while the enlisted men and noncommissioned officers were sent to Georgia.

The rebel guards marched the 16th Connecticut men through the gate of a large stockade. "As we entered the place a spectacle met our eyes that almost froze our blood with horror, and made our hearts fail within us," remembered Robert Kellogg, a twenty-year-old from Wethersfield. "Before us were forms that had once been active and erect;—stalwart men, now nothing but mere walking skeletons, covered with filth and vermin."[14]

"Captain Broatch, senior captain of the regiment, while advancing sword in hand was struck by a bullet which shattered his fingers and threw his sword twenty feet into the air. Picking it up and grasping it in his left hand he swung it over his head, at the same time guiding his men with his voice until his wound proved so painful that he was obliged to retire from the field." (Page, *History of the Fourteenth*, p. 220.) Its tip severed by a bullet, John Broatch's sword also bears a gash on the grip, from a shot that took off a finger on his right hand.

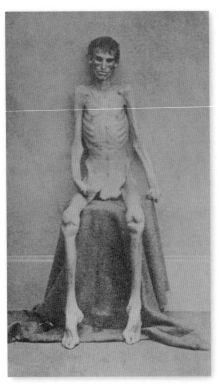

Staring blankly at the camera, this skeletal soldier represented thousands and thousands of Union prisoners of war. Disease, starvation and exposure ruled the prisoners' lives in camps at Andersonville and Belle Isle, Virginia. "I have seen men lying with their hip and back bones protruding through the skin," wrote a Connecticut soldier who survived Andersonville. (*Hartford Daily Courant,* June 27, 1865, quoting June 23, 1865, letter from Dorence Atwater.) Some days, over 100 gaunt corpses would be carried out to the mass graves outside the Andersonville stockade.

Andersonville.

Thousands of ragged, emaciated men were crowded in here, without shelters or sanitary facilities. The 16th men looked around them in horror. Their Confederate captors divided the regiment into groups of 90 men each, and assigned them areas to live. Robert Kellogg wrote in despair: "In the center of the whole was a swamp, occupying about three or four acres of the narrowed limits, and a part of this marshy place had been used by the prisoners as a sink, and excrement covered the ground, the scent arising from which was suffocating. The ground allotted to our ninety was near the edge of this plague-spot, and how we were to live through the warm summer weather in the midst of such fearful surroundings, was more than we cared to think of just then."[15]

Though thousands slept on the bare ground with no shelter, some prisoners were fortunate to own a rubber blanket, or tent half. Others had managed to hold on to a little money or perhaps a watch they could trade with the guards. These lucky prisoners could erect at least a small shelter from the rain and the southern sun. Kellogg's group bought saplings from the guards, and built a frame that they draped with their remaining blankets.

Dorence Atwater, a Terryville soldier, wrote, "My shelter with eight others was a scant fly and the earth our bed. My comrades all died, and

"Can this be hell?" asked the men of the 16th Connecticut in revulsion. (Robert H. Kellogg, *Life and Death in Rebel Prisons* (Hartford, CT: L. Stebbins, 1865), p. 56.) When a Georgian photographer captured this image of the prison in August 1864, Robert Kellogg noted in his diary that the Southerner was "taking pictures of our misery." (Letter of Robert H. Kellogg to George Godard, February 23, 1922, State Archives, Connecticut State Library, Hartford.) The stockade, built to hold about 10,000 prisoners, at one time contained over 32,000 men and boys. An estimated 45,000 prisoners passed through Andersonville's gates in all. Nearly a third of them died in the camp; many others expired soon after being released.

twenty more that came to the tent afterwards. It was nothing strange to awake from a sleep and find a dead man by my side."[16]

As fast as prisoners were dying, more arrived. Earlier in the war, the Union and Confederate armies had had regular prisoner exchanges, but General Grant ordered a halt to the exchanges. Andersonville's population reached 32,000 that summer.

Rations, already in short supply, dwindled to almost nothing: mostly tiny amounts of corn-meal so coarse it was nearly indigestible. The men got dysentery, with fever, chills, and terrible diarrhea. Scurvy made their feet swell and their teeth fall out. They became skeletons.

James Haggerty of Willimantic was fifteen or sixteen when he arrived at Andersonville with 12 others from the 18th Connecticut. His pal, Gilbert Gott, was even younger. "Poor Gott," wrote James Haggerty; "One morning In August we awoke and Gott complained of his feet. We examined them and sure enough, Scurvy had taken hold of him. His feet were swollen and looked bad. He stood it a few days and then was brought outside where he died four days after."[17] Of the 13 prisoners from the 18th Connecticut, Haggerty was the only to survive. He wrote: "When a man died he lay as he died . . . At 10 oclock every morning the Reb's sent in the ration wagons and Into them the bodies were dumped one on top of another and so were carried out and buried in a long trench near the prison. At four oclock the same wagons came In loaded with rations for the Camp . . . There was no medicine for the sick. There was no nothing."[18]

James himself was finally paroled in December of 1864. After lying near death for some time, he was at last "sent home as a hopeless Case . . . helped along by kind strangers I reached Willimantic four day's after . . . a good Subject for an Undertaker to practice on."[19]

What did it mean to die as a prisoner of war? Homer Sprague of the 13th Connecticut tried to express it:

> It is comparatively easy to face death in battle. No great courage or merit in that. The soldier is swept along with the mass . . . There is a consciousness of irresistible strength as he beholds the gleaming lines, the dense columns, the smoking batteries, the dancing flags, the cavalry with flying feet . . . Our soldier in battle imagined the world looking on, that for him there was fame undying; should he fall wounded, his comrades would gently care for him; if slain, his country's flag would be his shroud.
>
> By no such considerations were our imprisoned comrades cheered. Not in the glorious rush and shock of battle; not in hope of victory or fade-less laurels; no angel charities, or parting kiss, or sympathetic voice bidding the soul look heaven ward while the eye was growing dim; no

Prisoners had to be vigilant to protect their few belongings. The Raiders, a band of vicious prisoners who robbed and beat their fellow soldiers, stole food, watches, shoes—even wooden spoons. "Thieving was the order of the day," wrote Sylvester O. Lord of the 11th Connecticut. "When we lay down at night we would tie our cup and spoon to our arms and I have often felt a pull at my string. None but an old prisoner can realize that value of a cup and spoon to our boys in prison." (Lord memoir, typescript, NPS/Andersonville National Historic Site.)

William and Christopher Johnson of Simsbury were among the scores of 16th Connecticut soldiers who suffered and died at Andersonville. The two hearty young men photographed in 1862 became feeble skeletons. Christopher died on November 12, 1864. William took his last breath on Christmas day. The Johnsons' graves stand in Andersonville National Cemetery, with those of many of their comrades in the 16th Connecticut.

dear star-spangled banner for a winding sheet. But wrapped in rags; unseen, unnoticed, dying by inches, in the cold, in the darkness, often in rain or sleet, houseless, homeless, friendless, on the hard floor or the bare ground, starving, freezing, broken-hearted.[20]

In September of 1864, Confederate authorities worried that Union troops were getting too close to the prison. They began shifting prisoners to other camps, drastically reducing the population. Finally, at the end of February 1865, thousands of Union soldiers were released from Andersonville and other prisons. They were transported to Wilmington, North Carolina where a Connecticut nurse, Harriet Hawley, took on their care. She wrote to relatives at home:

> You know that over nine thousand of our prisoners were delivered to us here, and no human tongue or pen can describe the horrible condition which they were in. Starving to death, covered with vermin, with no clothing but the filthy rags they had worn during their whole imprisonment—a period of from five to twenty months; cramped by long sitting in one position so that they could not straighten their limbs—their feet rotted off—oh, God! I cannot endure to speak of it! . . .

> You at the North will never be able to conceive of our prisoners . . . More than forty men, whose feet or portions of them had rotted off, left on the steamer yesterday . . . Think of it, feet so rotted away that the surgeon cut them off with scissors above the ankle! Has God any retribution for those who inflicted such suffering? Has their country any rewards for the men who suffered thus?[21]

The Beginning of the End

The spring of 1864 would be perhaps the most crucial period of the war. After three years of fighting, the Union seemed no closer to victory. And the presidential election was months away.

Chaplain Jacob Eaton was sick and exhausted. He should have been in bed. Eaton's regiment, the 7th Connecticut, was stationed in the newly captured city of Wilmington, North Carolina, in early 1865. Over 8,000 emaciated Union soldiers had just arrived from Rebel prison camps, transforming the city into a giant hospital roiling with typhoid fever.

Though ill and weak himself, Chaplain Eaton insisted on tending the sick: he couldn't bear to see the suffering of the skeletal soldiers that were dying by the score each day. "Warned by a friend not to sacrifice himself, he said, 'They ought to be and must be cared for by some one; and I will do all that lies in my power for the poor, emaciated, and helpless creatures'" (Croffut and Morris, p. 764).

When the war began, Jacob Eaton had been a Congregational minister in Meriden. After the Union loss at Bull Run, Rev. Eaton wrote in the church records: "The darkest hour has come . . . After mature reflection, I have asked of my people leave of absence for one year, that I may enlist in the grand army of freedom" (Croffut and Morris, p. 763–64). Eaton joined the 8th Connecticut as a private, rising to be lieutenant. Wounded at Antietam, he came home to recover, but didn't stay. In the spring of 1864, Eaton became the 7th Connecticut's chaplain.

In the midst of tending the pitiful men in Wilmington, Eaton wrote, "'Early and late we stand, ministering to once healthy, hopeful men, now mere skeletons, their eyes sunken, glassy, vacant, and wild in expression—men literally covered with reeking filth and crawling vermin—men with long matted locks—with deep lines furrowing their every feature—men reduced to almost idiocy or second childhood by protracted hunger, neglect of body and mind; night and day we pass amid the dying, or burying the dead'" (Letter of Jacob Eaton, March 12, 1865, as quoted in *The Western Recorder*, April 5, 1865).

Eight days later, Eaton died among the men he was striving to save. A friend wrote that the chaplain "gave his life joyfully in exchange for the life of the republic" (Croffut and Morris, p. 764).

Lincoln knew that his reelection hinged upon the Union army's success: "Upon the progress of our arms . . . all else chiefly depends."

Many Northerners had become disillusioned with the war. Northern Democrats were holding out the promise of peace if their candidate were elected. If the Union army did not make significant headway—*soon*—the Republicans could lose the election.

The president turned to Ulysses Grant. On March 1, 1864, Lincoln nominated Grant to command the entire Union army. Congress confirmed him the next day. Quiet, reflective, and determined, Grant developed a coordinated plan that would transform the war, and lead to its conclusion. He realized that though the Confederates had far fewer troops, Lee thus far had been able to move his forces around to confront Union threats. Now, Grant decided, the Union would go on the attack, simultaneously striking at multiple locations so that Lee wouldn't be able to mass his troops in one location. His strategy became known as the Overland Campaign.

Grant's aim was to demolish the Confederate army. In battle, he planned to fight Lee on open ground where the Union's superior numbers would overwhelm the Confederates. But combat was not Grant's only weapon. Union troops would destroy southern railroads, making it harder for Lee to move troops and supplies; they would devastate farming areas, so the Rebels would run out of food. They would also strike the South's industries to damage its already shaky economy.

From now on, Grant would be relentless. And hundreds of families in Connecticut would pay the price—soon.

The Wilderness: "A Tangle of Battles and Skirmishes"[22]

With his plans in place, Grant now moved swiftly. The Army of the Potomac began a rapid march toward Spotsylvania County, Virginia.

Grant had hoped his infantry would reach Spotsylvania Court House, where the open topography would favor his plan to attack Lee. But the Confederate general, ever the wily strategist, rushed his troops forward, confronting the Union army at a place aptly called The Wilderness, thick with nearly impenetrable underbrush and low, shrubby trees like scrub oak and scrub pine. Here, visibility would be constricted, and narrow roads and thick woods would make it impossible for Grant to maneuver his artillery and cavalry.

On the afternoon of May 5, the veterans of the 14th Connecticut Infantry were in the forefront, crashing through the undergrowth and crouching behind trees to load their rifles. In the tangled terrain, it was impossible to know exactly what was happening.

Charlie Blatchley of Company I described a terrifying moment:

> The deadly fire which we had kept up in front of us had held back the enemy . . . till they had driven our troops back on both sides of us, leaving our little regiment sticking out . . . The dense woods prevented us from discovering this until the break reached our own flanks. I was awakened from my absorption in the business of saving my country by looking up, as I did occasionally, to see if the flag was still there, to find it gone. In another second I realized the fact that I was almost alone, and that the flag was rapidly making its way to the rear. I followed it.[23]

Lucius Bidwell, a painter from Middletown, had posed with his trusty Sharp's rifle after joining the 14th Regiment. In 1862, Bidwell was wounded at Fredericksburg. He recovered to fight in eight more engagements before falling at the Wilderness, on the first day of battle.

Though outnumbered, the Confederates fought doggedly. Gen. James Longstreet ordered his men to charge the bluecoats. Elnathan Tyler of the 14th remembered:

> How defiantly and continuously that rebel yell of the oncoming foe held its own even above the volleys of musketry . . . Still onward they come . . . And now they had come so near we began to distinguish the brown and butternut colored uniforms among the trees and our rifles had distinct targets and the increasing closeness of their shots showed they too were having the same advantage. Now we could see them still more plainly. They were not coming fast, simply moving forward slowly, steadily and oh, so obstinately and surely! We could not check them.[24]

For two days the battle raged. In the midst of the bloodshed, the soldiers smelled smoke—but it wasn't the smoke from their rifles. The Wilderness had caught fire. From tree to tree and through the underbrush the flames swept, moving so fast in some places that there was no time to get the wounded out, and they were burned to death.

The carnage for the two-day battle was devastating. The Union had lost roughly 18,000 men; the Confederates totaled only about 11,000 casualties. The wounded and dying were everywhere.

Like a Leech

But Grant wasn't stopping. Unlike the Union generals that preceded him, he immediately put his army in motion, moving south to hit Lee again. He sent Lincoln a message: "There will be no turning back."

When Grant's men realized they weren't retreating but going after the Rebels again, spirits rose in the Army of the Potomac. Like a pack of dogs, Union troops darted forward to attack Lee almost daily. On May 8, the 1st Connecticut Cavalry skirmished with the enemy in Spotsylvania. On May 10, the 14th Connecticut formed in line of battle and charged the Confederates; two days later, they attacked again. On May 11, Connecticut's cavalrymen were with Sheridan when his forces succeeded in fatally wounding Confederate general Jeb Stuart.

"Grant is sticking to them like a leech," wrote the 14th's John Hirst gleefully, "and I think we are getting the best of it."[25]

But Grant's dogged offensive had its price.

Nursing the Wounded: "A Little World of Suffering"[26]

"I know no words to describe the amount & intensity of the suffering I see around me every moment," wrote Harriet Hawley. "As I wrote that I stopped to look at the peaceful face of a poor fellow who has just died eight feet from my chair. One leg had been amputated above the knee 10 days ago—& he had suffered terribly . . . You do not dream of what these men undergo."[27]

"Wounded escaping from the burning woods of the Wilderness." (Alfred R. Waud drawing, 1864.)

Few generals were as beloved by their men as John Sedgwick. The soldiers of the 6th Corps, which Sedgwick commanded, fondly referred to him as "Uncle John." Sedgwick's grandfather had served as an officer in the Revolutionary War, and John Sedgwick himself graduated from West Point and became a career army officer. A Connecticut native, Sedgwick loved his home village of Cornwall Hollow. On May 9, 1864, General Sedgwick was positioning his artillery near Spotsylvania Court House. Confederate sharpshooters, some 1,000 yards away, were sending bullets whizzing around him, causing his soldiers to duck. Sedgwick reproved his men, famously declaring that "They couldn't hit an elephant at this distance." The remark was scarcely out of his mouth when he was shot through the head, dying instantly.

Harriet Ward Foote Hawley

Harriet, only five feet tall, and always of "delicate health," had arrived in Washington days earlier to serve as a nurse. She was assigned to Armory Square, a barracks hospital that included eleven buildings, and when needed, countless tents. Now it was crammed to overflowing with the worst cases from the Army of the Potomac. Hawley had charge of a ward with nearly 100 men. With no operating room, surgeons amputated legs and arms in the ward, just a few feet away from other patients.

One of her fellow nurses at Armory Square wrote of the crushing hopelessness the nurses felt as they fought to save the Wilderness wounded.

> I am tired to death . . . I cannot write a connected letter; I lost my senses two weeks ago and haven't known my own name for a week. I cannot begin to tell you of what we are going through . . . Oh! they are piled in on us till one's heart sinks, and I, who am good in emergencies, energetic . . . slink up to the door of my ward and stand there, dreading to go in . . . all say and feel that their burden is greater than they can bear . . . The odor is awful; the cases are all bad . . . there are forty-five dead to-day.[28]

Harriet Hawley looked at the poor soldiers in her ward—writhing in pain, gasping, hemorrhaging, calling for their mothers or wives—and said, "I can't let them die—if they do a piece of my life dies too."[29]

Nurse Amanda Akin's diary recorded the inescapable result of Grant's campaign. (Like most of the nurses, she referred to her patients by the numbers on their cots.)

> May 27, 1864. Fifteen patients were transferred to Philadelphia. Others were brought in to fill their places, with still worse wounds, uncared for and unwashed; they were well-nigh dead from the toils of their journey . . . I managed to write to the wife of No. 45, who died two days since, and to Lieutenant Bly's widow . . .

> May 28, 1864 . . . No. 25 died during the night. No. 44 was bleeding and very weak. I went to market, and on my return found ten more wounded had been brought in . . . Was all day in the ward, and the air was foul and dreadful.[30]

Nurse Akin described "a poor rebel boy, only eighteen, from Louisiana; he looks so pitiful and grateful for every little kindness which he does not expect." Of Armory Square Hospital, she wrote that she "Could scarcely realize before that it held such a little world of suffering."[31]

Poet Walt Whitman came regularly to visit the wounded soldiers in Washington. He tried to soothe and cheer the men, often bringing small gifts such as fruit or books, writing letters to their families, or just sitting and talking to them. On one visit, Whitman stopped at the cot of a young Connecticut soldier named Henry Boardman. "When I first saw him he was very sick, with no appetite," wrote Whitman.

As I was quite anxious to do something, he confess'd that he had a hankering for a good home-made rice pudding—thought he could relish it better than anything. At this time his stomach was very weak . . . I soon procured B. his rice-pudding. A Washington lady, (Mrs. O'C.), hearing his wish, made the pudding herself, and I took it up to him the next day. He subsequently told me he lived upon it for three or four days. This B. is a good sample of the American eastern young man—the typical Yankee. I took a fancy to him, and gave him a nice pipe, for a keepsake. He receiv'd afterwards a box of things from home, and nothing would do but I must take dinner with him, which I did, and a very good one it was.[32]

Inexorable Grant

"I propose to fight it out on this line, if it takes all summer," wrote Ulysses S. Grant days after the Battle of the Wilderness. To hit Lee hard and continually, the Union commander was going to need all his resources. Among these were the 1,800 men of the 2nd Connecticut Heavy Artillery, stationed in the forts protecting Washington. For the last year, the 2nd Heavies had been on garrison duty, drilling in their white gloves and polished boots. Now Grant sent the regiment new orders. Adjutant Theodore Vaill recalled: "It was about one o'clock on the morning of the 17th of May, when an orderly galloped up and dismounted at headquarters near Fort Corcoran, knocked at the door of the room where Colonel Kellogg and the Adjutant lay soundly sleeping, drew from his belt and delivered a package . . . as little conscious that he had brought the message of destiny to hundreds of men as the horse which bore him."[33]

Grant's orders—the "message of destiny"—would forever alter the lives of the 2nd Heavies and hundreds of families in the quiet hill towns of Litchfield County.

As their colonel read the order aloud, the men caught their breaths. General Grant had ordered the regiment to leave its big guns behind, and join the Army of the Potomac in the field near Spotsylvania Court House, Virginia.

Henry D. Boardman was nineteen when Walt Whitman visited him in the hospital, bringing him a rice pudding. The young soldier recovered and returned to his home in Northford, Connecticut.

Whitman also gave Boardman a pipe "for a keepsake"— was it the one Henry was smoking in his portrait?

Far right: Soldiers unfit for the rigors of field service because of wounds or disease could serve in the Invalid Corps, later renamed the Veteran Reserve Corps. VRC soldiers wore distinctive sky blue uniforms, and usually worked in hospitals or guarding prisoners. This VRC private, photographed in Hartford, displayed an unknown object—love letter? military appointment?—whose meaning is lost to history.

"No matter how long a man has been a mere denizen of the unthreatened Camp, drilled, mustered, and rationed,—no matter how much blank cartridge firing he has done,—when at length he realizes that he must go to the front, and hear the ultimate arguments in the great debate of war, he feels a certain sinking of the heart, as though the lead of the enemy had already lodged there," confessed Adjutant Vaill.[34]

Within a week, the 2nd Heavies—who had the reputation of a "band box" regiment from their relatively safe duty inside Union forts—were pounding down dusty southern roads with their rifled muskets slung over their shoulders, on their way to the front.

"Grant needs us," wrote Fred Lucas to his mother in Goshen, "and we are ready & eager to aid him."[35]

On May 20, the 2nd Heavies reached Spotsylvania, where Grant's weary army waited. For the last week, the Army of the Potomac and the 9th Corps (totaling about 100,000 soldiers) had been repeatedly assaulting the four miles of entrenchments that held Lee's Army of Northern Virginia. Though Grant's forces outnumbered Lee's nearly two to one, Union troops had been unable to overwhelm the entrenched rebels. And Union casualties were alarmingly high: about 18,000 as compared to approximately 12,000 for the Confederates.

The 2nd Heavies looked about them at the muddy Union soldiers crouched in their entrenchments, and listened to the shells that screamed overhead. Fred Lucas wrote excitedly, "We . . . are now lying on the battlefield of Spotsylvania, south of the rebel entrenchments and near Grants and Meade's hdqtrs. only a few rods from them. These Generals are living just as we are in shelter tents on the ground. This is action service & real soldiering with no boys play about it."[36]

The regiment reported to its new command, the 6th Corps, whose battered veterans took one look at the 2nd Heavies' uniforms—natty in comparison to their own rags—and immediately began taunting them. "They

From the moment Elisha Kellogg took command, he inspired respect and loyalty in his men. "In the eyes of civilians," said his adjutant, Theodore Vaill, "Colonel Kellogg was nothing but a horrid, strutting, shaggy monster. But request any one of . . . the Second Artillery to name the most perfect soldier he ever saw, and this will surely be the man . . . In every faculty of body, mind, heart and soul, he was built after a large pattern. His virtues were large, and his vices were not small. As Lincoln said of Seward, he could swear magnificently. His nature was versatile and full of contradictions; sometimes exhibiting the tenderest sensibilities, and sometimes none at all.

"Now he would be in the hospital tent, bending with streaming eyes over the victims of fever . . . and an hour later would find him down at the guard house, prying open the jaws of a refractory soldier with a bayonet, in order to insert a gag; or in anger drilling a battalion, for the fault of a single man, to the last point of endurance; or shamefully abusing the most honorable and faithful officers in the regiment . . .

"But notwithstanding his faults, notwithstanding his frequent ill treatment of officers and soldiers, he had a hold upon their affections such as no other commander ever had, or could have. The men who were cursing him one day for the almost intolerable rigors of his discipline, would in twenty-four hours be throwing up their caps for him, or subscribing to buy him a new horse." (Vaill, *History of the Second*, pp. 326–27.) Fred Lucas put it simply: "He is rough and very profane *but has a heart as large as ever beat in man's bosom.*" (Letter of Frederick A. Lucas to his mother, March 3, 1863, in Ernest B. Barker, *Dear Mother from your Dutiful Son*, p. 57.)

thought . . . that we could do nothing & whenever they met us, greeted us with 'Horary Heavies, How are the Washington Pets?'—'White gloves & shiny brasses' etc."[37]

The 1,800 members of the regiment were mostly workingmen and farmers from Litchfield and its surrounding villages. Their imposing colonel, Elisha Kellogg, was known for his toughness and profanity, his temper earning him the admiring description of "a perfect *tiger*" from his men. Now the 2nd Heavies were mortified to be labeled a "band-box" regiment by more seasoned soldiers.

The repeated Union strikes at Spotsylvania had brought no clear outcome. On the night of May 21, General Grant stealthily withdrew his troops and began moving southward. Robert E. Lee would have to interpose his army between the Union forces and Richmond.

Cold Harbor

For the 2nd Heavies, the next ten days would be a "long and terrible series of marches," wrote one man, "continued almost without a breathing spell, until the first of June."[38] It was about noon that day when they reached a small, ramshackle settlement called Cold Harbor where Colonel Kellogg called a halt. The exhausted men dropped to the ground.

"In a few minutes," wrote Adjutant Vaill, "the advance of several other columns, together with batteries of field artillery, and ammunition trains, began to appear . . . but we were so nearly dead with marching and want of sleep, that we hardly heeded these movements, or reflected on their portentous character."[39]

Beyond a small patch of woods and a large open plain, the Confederates were waiting. Lee's troops had arrived the day before; immediately they had gone to work with their shovels and axes. Now the rebels lay in shallow entrenchments protected by banks of earth in front. Across the banks they'd constructed a hasty abatis, laying pine branches and small trees on its slopes to impede the enemy.

Each side's artillery now began hurling shells, and Colonel Kellogg moved his Heavies to a hollow where they waited. "Col. Kellogg wearing his old straw hat walked back and forth in front of the regiment and watched the shells explode around him," remembered Lewis Bissell, a private in Company A.[40]

They would attack at 5:00. Kellogg, trying to prepare his inexperienced troops, "marked out on the ground the shape of the works to be taken—told the officers what disposition to make of the different battalions; how the charge would be made."[41]

Despite their inexperience, the 2nd Heavies would be in the lead. His voice grave, Colonel Kellogg addressed his men, "———spoke of our reputation as 'a band-box regiment.' 'Now we were called on to show what we could do at fighting; he felt confident we would in this, our first fight, establish, and ever afterward maintain, a glorious reputation as a fighting regiment.'"[42]

The colonel went on,

> "Now men, when you have the order to move, go in steady, keep cool, keep still until I give you the order to charge, and then go arms a-port, with a yell. Don't a man of you fire a shot until we are within the enemy's breastworks. I shall be with you."

Even all this, added to a constantly increasing picket fire, and ominous signs on every hand, could not excite the men to any great degree of interest in what was going on. Their stupor was of a kind that none can describe, and none but soldiers can understand. In proof of this, only one incident need be mentioned. Corporal William A. Hosford . . . heard the foregoing instructions given by Colonel Kellogg, and yet was waked out of a *sound sleep* when the moment came to move forward.[43]

Adjutant Vaill described the 2nd Heavies' charge:

> a few tall pine trees, not numerous enough to hide our movements—extended about ten rods to the front, and then came an open field. Colonel Kellogg, having instructed Majors Rice and Ells to follow at intervals of one hundred paces, placed himself in front, and gave the command, "Forward! Guide Center! *March!*"
>
> The first battalion, with the colors in the center, moved directly forward through the scattering woods, crossed the open field at a double-quick, and entered another pine wood . . . where it came upon the first line of rebel rifle pits, which was abandoned at its approach. Passing this line, the Battalion moved on over sloping ground until it reached a small, open hollow, *within fifteen or twenty yards of the enemy's main line of breastworks* . . .
>
> Up to this point there had been no firing sufficient to confuse or check the battalion; but here the rebel musketry opened. The commander of the rebel battalion directly in our front, whoever he was, had his men under excellent control and his fire was held until our line had reached the abbattis, and then systematically delivered—first by his rear rank, and then by his front rank. A sheet of flame, sudden as lightning, red as blood, and so near that it seemed to singe the men's faces, burst along the rebel breastwork . . . The battalion dropped flat on the ground, and the second volley, like the first, nearly all went over. Several of the men were struck, not a large number . . .
>
> But at that moment a long line of rebels on our left . . . having unobstructed range on the battalion, opened a fire which no human valor could withstand, and which no pen can adequately describe . . . It was the work of almost a single minute.
>
> The air was filled with sulphurous smoke, and the shrieks and howls of more than two hundred and fifty mangled men rose above the yells of triumphant rebels and the roar of their musketry.
>
> ABOUT Face! shouted Colonel Kellogg,—but it was his last command. He had already been struck in the arm, and the words had scarcely passed his lips when another shot pierced his head, and he fell dead upon the interlacing pine boughs.[44]

Their colonel was dead. They were taking fire from two directions. Shells were exploding in their midst. "LIE DOWN! said a voice that rang out above the horrible din."[45] It was their brigade commander, twenty-four-year-old Emory Upton.

The Heavies who could move inched their way back into the wooded area that would give them some protection. "[General] Upton stood behind a tree in the extreme front and for a long time fired muskets as fast as the men could load and hand them to him," wrote Theodore Vaill. "Some sudden movement caused a panic and they started to flee, when he cried out with a voice that no man who heard it will ever forget,—'*Men of Connecticut, stand by me! We* MUST *hold this line!*' It brought them back and the line was held."[46]

With continual firing, the Heavies were able to force back the Confederates in many places. Several hundred Rebels fled to the Union lines in surrender. Captain Walter Burnham rushed forward with his men to occupy a section of the Confederate entrenchments. (Burnham reported that in spite of the foot of standing water in the trench and the din of gunfire, most of his men sank into an exhausted sleep.) During the night, more and more of the Nutmeg troops pushed forward; by morning, the 2nd Heavies were well established in the enemy breastworks.

The wounded lay on the battlefield "with shattered bones, or weak with loss of blood, calling vainly for help, or water, or death."[47]

"We could hear our men groan," said Lewis Bissell sadly, "but could not leave our position to attend to their wants."[48] The regiment had taken over 300 casualties.

"The field in front of us after the repulse of the main attack was indeed a sad sight," wrote a 6th Corps general later. He continued:

> I remember at one point a mute and pathetic evidence of sterling valor. The Second Connecticut Heavy Artillery . . . had joined us but a few days before the battle. Its uniform was bright and fresh; therefore its dead were easily distinguished where they lay. They marked in a dotted line an obtuse angle, covering a wide front, with its apex toward the enemy, and there upon his face, still in death, with his head to the works, lay the Colonel, the brave and genial Colonel Elisha S. Kellogg.[49]

No one was using the term "band-box" now.

It was impossible to hold their advanced position for long, and the 2nd Heavies fell back into their own entrenchments on June 2. That day, the remains of the regiment, their eyes red with exhaustion and horror, went looking for their brothers, cousins, sons, and friends.

Lewis Bissell found his cousin and pal, twenty-two-year-old Lyman J. Smith. "He had been shot in the head and breast . . . I wish he could have had a box or some sort of coffin but that is not to be had down here."[50] Lewis carved a wooden marker with Lyman's name to mark the grave. Later he would send Lyman's bible to his parents in Litchfield.

Colonel Kellogg's body, "majestic even in death, was placed upon a rubber blanket and borne with labor from the field; and as it passed along, the men looked down with wonder upon the lifeless clay, half questioning within themselves whether the old lion would not rouse himself and scatter all his and his country's foes."[51]

LITCHFIELD ENQUIRER

EXTRA.

JUNE 10TH, 1864.

...sualities in the 2d Conn. Heavy Artillery, in the battles of June 1st,
...d 4th, at Coal Harbor, Va.
...e gather the following list of casualties in our County Regiment from
...vate letters, and the N. Y. *Tribune* of the 9th inst. We shall issue further
...arns as we receive them.

KILLED.
Col. Elisha S. Kellogg, Derby.
WOUNDED.
Maj. Wm. B. Ells, Plymouth.

Co. A.
KILLED.
Capt. Luman Wadhams, Litchfield.
1st Serg't Jos. P. Paras, New Milford.
Corp. Albert A. Jones, Harwinton.
" Apollos C Morse, Litchfield.
Private Lyman J Smith, "
" John Ifland, "
" Rob't Wait, "
WOUNDED.
Lieut. B H Camp, Harwinton, leg.
Serg't G W Mason, Litchfield, head, slightly
Corp Chas. Adams, Jr., " arm, severely.
" Seth Waiting, " shoulder.
" C P Wedge, " hand.
" John A Sanford, " thigh.
" Apollos C Morse, " chest, died.
Private, Elson Dayton, leg.
Jas. Bradley, Litchfield, arm.
Michael Bray, " hip.
A J Brooker, " both legs.
Truman Matthewy, chest.
B O Wood, both arms.
F W Benshing, leg, reported dead.
Geo. Savage, both arms amputated.
John M Prindle, hand.
John London, buttock.
Edlik, Washington, thigh.

Co. B.
KILLED.
Amos Woodin, Salisbury.
WOUNDED.
Serg't J McGraw, Canaan, abdomen.
Corp Jacob Rapp, Salisbury, side, dead.
" A Tolford, hand.
" E J Carroll, arm.
N W Coggswell,
D Danlaby, hand.
J Snyder, Salisbury, shoulder.
Wm Connell, head and face.
Horace Easl, shoulder.
Chas O Whaples, Litchfield, thigh.
John Funk, Salisbury, neck.
C Salver, shoulder.
L Hunt, face.
Henry Tanner, thigh.
Richard Brown, skull.
D E Taylor, finger.
Chas Warner, hand.
A Adams, Norfolk, thigh.
Amos Whitten, chest.
Ezra Clark, neck.
Thos Moore, hand.
W Beach, arm.
A Ayres, back.

Co. C.
WOUNDED.
H W Richards, arm.
G W Manning, heel.
L B Palmer, shoulder.
B Burts, shoulder.
C Bryonson, ankle.

Co. D.
WOUNDED.
Capt. Jas. Deane, Canaan, head.
Serg't D B Wooster, Plymouth, hip & thigh.
John McMahon, thigh.
S Dreen, leg.
Wm Elbert, shoulder.
J Stoughton, Plymouth, back.
C Carter, shoulder.
J Quinn, leg.
G T Cooke, Plymouth, shoulder.
Thos Mann, Plymouth, leg.

Co. E.
KILLED.
Jas Mooney, Winchester; Albert Comins,
Winchester; John M Teeter, Winchester.
WOUNDED.
Serg't J A Green, Winchester, heel.
E Rieker, elbow.
W J Whitehead, Winchester, hand.
H Wenzel, thigh.

Elizur Maltbie, Norfolk, leg.
J Leroy, shoulder.
S U Brennan, thigh.
C H Stanley, abdomen.
R C Gingell, Norfolk, hand.
Walker Stone, foot.
Geo L Beach, thigh.
David Miller, hand.
Nathan Perry, shoulder.
C A Johnson, thigh.
E Back, hip.
W A Hosford, back and shoulder.
Pat Lynch, arms and hips.
C Cagan, back.

Co. F.
KILLED.
Serg't Sam'l E. Gibbs, Colebrook.
Corp Geo. F. Daniels.
WOUNDED.
Jas O Hotchkiss, arm.
Alex Waters, head.
T F Kelley, arm.
Wm Burke, Burkhamsted, chest.
G N Andrus, Norfolk, heel.

Co. G.
WOUNDED.
H S Dean, thigh.
Charles Keech, leg.
M Curley, Sharon, leg amputated.
John Dougherty, Cornwall, left arm.
W Bonnell, hand.
Wm Kelley, abdomen.
G G Rose, hand.
J Leonard, finger.

Co. H.
WOUNDED.
Lieut H E Tuttle, scalp.
Serg't L W Mosher, New Milford, arm.
U H Sanliker, Kent, neck and side.
H Payne, Kent, heel.
H O Donnell, scalp.
J Johnson, Kent, thigh.
J Harris, foot.
C B Howard, chest.
Henry Denton, Washington, both legs.
L F Morehouse, New Milford, wrist.

Co. I.
WOUNDED.
Corp B Wellman, Woodbury, face.
E Thomas, leg.
C T Tyrell, Roxbury, shoulder.
J L Hotchkiss, Woodbury, hand.
C Wheeler, " knee.
Abner Bennett, wrist and hand.
S Lebdell, thigh and wrist.

Co. K.
KILLED.
Edward Griffin, New Milford.
Charles Read, Watertown.
A Morse.
Anson Jackson.
WOUNDED.
Corp E J Stoats, Kent, back.
E G Warhurst, Torrington, head.
S W Hodge, Sherman, arm.
Wm H Stevens, hip.
S P Harlow, Morris, thigh.
Geo E Taylor, Washington, arm.
Thos Colraine, shoulder.
Patrick Kennedy, abdomen.
Geo A Wood, Washington, arm.
J Monson, New Milford, back.
F Southergill, arm.
Lyman F Cole, left hand.
Geo Brown, shoulder.
C A Hoyt, thigh.

Co. L.
WOUNDED.
Serg't A P Kickham, head.
Wm Day, thigh.
Wm Vrooman, thigh.
John Pollard, scalp.

Co. M.
WOUNDED.
L A Palmer, hand.
S S Osborn, leg.

The majority of the 2nd Heavies came from Litchfield County. After the Battle of Cold Harbor, anxious families in Litchfield and the surrounding villages gathered to scan an extra edition of the *Litchfield Enquirer*, which listed the regiment's dead and wounded. With sinking hearts, mothers, fathers, wives, and grandparents read through scores of familiar names, hoping their soldier wasn't among them. "Cold Harbor!" said a Salisbury, Connecticut man nearly five decades later; "those syllables came to have a dreadful sound in hundreds of Litchfield homes." ("Salisbury in War Time," address given by Thomas Lot Norton, Salisbury, Memorial Day in 1901.)

Grant's troops, including several more Connecticut regiments, continued to arrive at Cold Harbor. So did Lee's. The Confederates quickly threw up some seven miles of earthworks. On June 3, Union troops struck the Rebel lines and were driven back with huge loss. For the next week, both sides engaged in trench warfare.

Ulysses Grant would later write of Cold Harbor: "No advantage whatever was gained to compensate for the heavy loss we sustained."[52]

As for the 2nd Heavies, Lewis Bissell wrote bitterly, "They can never get us to make another such charge. We don't care where they put us the men will not do it."

"Old Litchfield's best sons have laid their lives on the alter of their country," Bissell wrote to his parents.[53] The 2nd Heavies sustained over 300 casualties at Cold Harbor. And each loss had a human face.

Top row, left to right:
Elizur Maltbie of Norfolk, mortally wounded
Cpl. Apollos Morse of Litchfield, killed
Justin O. Stoughton of Plymouth, wounded
George Tatro of Canton, killed
Lucius Palmer of Bridgeport, mortally wounded

Second row, left to right:
Bushrod Camp of Harwinton, wounded
George L. Beach of Plymouth, mortally wounded
Charles Warner of Watertown, wounded
Maj. William B. Ells of Plymouth, wounded
Col. Elisha Kellogg of Derby, killed

✲ ✲ ✲

So Costly a Sacrifice

The story of three brothers from Litchfield County—Henry, Luman, and Edward Wadhams—was the story of Grant's campaign.

Luman Wadhams, twenty-nine, was a captain in the 2nd Heavy Artillery. A native of Goshen, Luman was working in a Waterbury factory when the war broke out; he'd enlisted immediately. One of his men called him "the best line officer in the regiment."[54]

"Capt. Wadhams loved his men, and did all he could to help them. When on duty, he was their officer; at other times, their friend. He seldom punished his men; yet they were seldom in the guard-house. If a man was disorderly, he called him aside, pointed out the offense, and tried to inculcate the duties of a soldier. He governed mainly by strengthening self-respect in his men. They, in turn, felt for him the most enthusiastic affection."[55]

As the 2nd Heavies were marching south to join the Army of the Potomac, they joined scores of other regiments streaming in the same direction. Luman's friend Theodore Vaill wrote:

> The whole army seemed to be close along, and there was considerable Cavalry skirmishing somewhere in the neighborhood. As the Second Corps was moving by to the left, just in front of us, Captain Luman Wadhams came up to head-quarters and asked permission to go and see his brother, Lieutenant Henry W. Wadhams of the Fourteenth Connecticut. "Certainly," said Colonel Kellogg, "but make a short visit, for there's no telling when orders to move will strike us."

> Captain Wadhams returned in about twenty minutes. "Well, did you find him?" inquired the Colonel. "I found that he was killed day before yesterday, in the fight at Hanover Junction, and buried on the field," was the sad reply.

> Four days afterward the Captain followed the Lieutenant,—and both of them died without knowing that their younger brother, Sergeant Edward Wadhams, of the Eighth Connecticut, had preceded them to a soldier's grave, at Fort Dar-ling, on the 16th of the same month.

> Three brothers, in three different Connecticut regiments, in three different army corps, all slain in the approaches to Richmond within the space of fourteen days![56]

The three Wadhams brothers joined thousands of other Union deaths in the early weeks of the campaign. Grant, hitting the enemy at every turn, had made up his mind to accept the resulting casualties.

In the fall of 1864, President Lincoln wrote to a Boston mother about the loss of her sons:

> I have been shown in the files of the War Department a statement of the Adju-tant General of Massachusetts that you are the mother of five sons who have died gloriously on the field of battle. I feel how weak and fruitless must be any words of mine which should attempt to beguile you from the grief of a loss so overwhelming. But I cannot refrain from tendering to you the consolation that

may be found in the thanks of the Republic they died to save. I pray that our Heavenly Father may assuage the anguish of your bereavement, and leave you only the cherished memory of the loved and lost, and the solemn pride that must be yours, to have laid so costly a sacrifice upon the altar of Freedom.[57]

In Litchfield, Connecticut, a middle-aged farm couple was feeling the same grief. Mary and Edwin Wadhams had laid "so costly a sacrifice upon the altar of Freedom"—and their three boys would never return.

 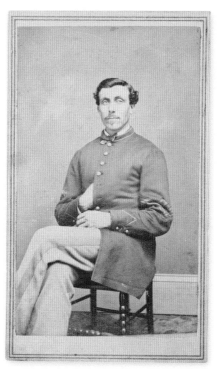 

Left: Captain Luman Wadhams had been married for just three months when his regiment, Connecticut's 2nd Heavy Artillery, entered its first major battle at Cold Harbor, the men so exhausted they could barely stand. Capt. Edward Marsh, whose company followed Wadhams' into combat that day, wrote: "I can never forget his bearing as he led us to the charge. His commanding figure, his determined step, and electric glance, told that he was nerved to his responsible work; and his men emulated his example." As they rushed towards the enemy's works, a Confederate bullet struck Wadhams in the abdomen. His men made a stretcher from their rifles, and carried him a mile and a half to the rear, but there was no hope. He died two days later. "When I heard that our dear captain was dead," wrote one of his soldiers, "I could not keep from crying." (Croffut and Morris, *Military and Civil History*, p. 595.)

Center: The youngest of the three brothers, Edward Wadhams (*center*) was the first to die. The twenty-seven-year-old was a sergeant in Connecticut's 8th Regiment, serving under Gen. Benjamin Butler in the Army of the James. In May of 1864, Butler began to move against Richmond, the Confederate capital. A dense fog on the morning of May 16 hid the movements of Confederate troops that attacked Butler's right flank at Drewry's Bluff. "We held our position on the works for some time with considerable loss, until flanked both right and left, when we fell back . . . the fog and smoke being so dense that it was impossible for officers or men to distinguish each other," wrote Lt. Col. M. B. Smith. (Report to Adjutant General by M. B. Smith, Lt.-Col. commanding,

8th Connecticut Volunteers, May 18, 1864.) The 8th Connecticut "suffered severely," wrote one of its soldiers. "Among the killed were two of the bravest and most efficient soldiers of the regiment—Captain McCall, and Sergeant Edward Wadhams." (J. H. Vaill, "History of the Eighth Regiment C.V. Infantry," in *Record of Service of Connecticut Men in the Army and Navy of the United States During the War of the Rebellion*, compiled by authority of the General Assembly under the direction of the Adjutants-General, pp. 327–28.)

Right: On May 26, 1864, the 14th Connecticut faced entrenched Confederate troops at the North Anna River in Virginia. Near dusk, four companies were ordered to take the Rebel works. Lt. Henry Wadhams led his men in the charge "over the rebel parapet, and fell within the enemy's works, pierced by a bullet." Once darkness fell, two of his men risked their lives to carry their wounded lieutenant back to their lines. "O my poor wife and child!" Henry said over and over. "He lived a few hours, and died, murmuring still of the gentle and patriotic woman who had not opposed his going to the War." (Croffut and Morris, *Military and Civil History*, pp. 591–92.) Henry's daughter, Jessie, had visited the regiment with her mother three months earlier. Born on February 29, 1860, Jessie had celebrated her "first" leap-year birthday in Virginia. After the war, the 14th Connecticut "adopted" thirteen-year-old Jessie as the regiment's daughter.

✳ ✳ ✳

Some time prior to Grant's offensive, sixteen comrades of the 21st Connecticut decided to be photographed together for posterity. (This proved to be a challenge to the cameraman in a small studio; he answered it by photographing the soldiers in two sittings and melding the images into one large group shot.) It was a prescient decision, for in a month's time four of the group were wounded, while Capt. Frank Long (seated, *bottom left*) was dead, killed instantly as an exploding shell gashed his neck while he commanded sharpshooters at Petersburg.

THE MISSIONS

To strike many places simultaneously, Grant had sent off his generals and their troops with specific objectives. From Tennessee, William Tecumseh Sherman would march his troops through Georgia, taking on Confederate general Johnston's army, and destroying Southern resources wherever possible. On the Virginia peninsula, Benjamin Butler would threaten Richmond from the south. Nathaniel Banks and his Army of the Gulf would head for Mobile. Franz Sigel, commanding the new Department of West Virginia, would attack Virginia's breadbasket, the Shenandoah Valley. Phil Sheridan came east to take charge of the Union cavalry. With Union troops threatening throughout the South, Lee would not be able to concentrate his numbers.

In the spring of 1864, Wolcott Wetherill had made it through two and a half years of war. He was just sixteen when he enlisted, leaving a factory job and his parents' crowded home in Killingly to join Connecticut's 6th Regiment. At Fort Wagner, the blue-eyed teenager had won the Gilmore Medal for gallant and meritorious conduct in the assault and siege on Morris Island. Now Wolcott and his regiment were marching through Virginia, just south of Richmond. In a period of six weeks, the 6th would fight the Rebels seven times. On May 20, the 6th Connecticut charged a Confederate line of rifle pits near Bermuda Hundred. Wolcott was wounded during the fight. He died the following February and was buried in Virginia.

The Union offensive claimed its victims indiscriminately: young and old, enlisted men and officers. On June 5, Union forces were pushing through the bountiful Shenandoah Valley with the aim of cutting off supplies to the enemy when the 18th Connecticut and other Union troops encountered Rebel forces near Piedmont, Virginia. In the ensuing battle, young William Albee was wounded, and the 18th's respected lieutenant, John T. Maginnis, was killed.

Earlier in the war, Maginnis had been captured and sent to Libby Prison, where he developed a serious respiratory illness. After his release from Libby, Lieutenant Maginnis went home to Salem, Connecticut, on furlough but still could not recover his health. When his leave elapsed, friends urged him to remain at home, "but his reply was: 'My boys are already in the field; they are on the march; they need me. My country needs the help of every single arm. Of what account is my poor life . . . if thereby our nation is saved.'" (Walker, *History of the Eighteenth*, p. 239.)

William Albee

John T. Maginnis

First Connecticut Cavalry Regiment

"I have been almost constantly in the saddle for the month past," wrote a weary captain of the 1st Connecticut Cavalry on June 6, 1864.[58] Since May 1, the regiment had been galloping through Virginia, fighting almost constantly. In just over eleven months' time, the Connecticut cavalrymen would take on the enemy in *sixty* engagements.

"There had been little rest thus far, and little food. All the sleep the men had was generally snatched while lying at their horses' heads."[59] The horsemen seemed to be everywhere: opening the Wilderness battles with the Army of the Potomac, then dashing with Phil Sheridan toward Richmond, tearing up railroads, skirmishing both mounted and unmounted—and always, losing men and horses.

Joseph Backus of Hebron wrote, "I have had two bullets through my coat, and one of my horses was shot from under me. I have lost a number of my men, and I know not how soon my time may come, but if I fall I die for my country."[60]

It was late in June when over 5,000 Union cavalry troops, including the 1st Connecticut, set out on a raid to destroy the railroad south and west of Petersburg, cutting an important supply line for Lee's troops there. Under Union generals James Wilson and August Kautz, the cavalrymen rode for days, stopping to tear up the tracks, and burn train cars and depots, before moving on to repeat the process. Theodore Holmes, the 1st Connecticut's chaplain, wrote:

After Maginnis fell at Piedmont, his father-in-law, Orramel Whittelsey, created a unique memorial to him. Whittelsey, who ran a music school in Salem, Connecticut, composed a song in Maginnis's honor: "There's a Proud, Noble Flag."

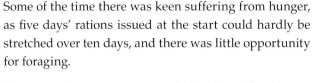

Four days after he wondered "how soon my time may come," twenty-one-year-old Joseph Backus of Hebron was killed in a skirmish at Old Church Tavern, Virginia. When his comrades retrieved his body after the fight, the enemy had taken everything but Backus's shirt.

Some of the time there was keen suffering from hunger, as five days' rations issued at the start could hardly be stretched over ten days, and there was little opportunity for foraging.

Not more than once was permission formally given to unsaddle and to make coffee, though it was possible to nibble at hard tack and salt pork, where any could be got, at odd moments of halting, or while on the march. All suffered, too, very much, from want of rest. During the ten days, not more than two hours out of the twenty-four, on an average, could be afforded for comfortable sleep . . .

Very many of the horses became worn out, having been almost constantly saddled, marching over three hundred miles, kept on short forage or oftener none, going sometimes for forty-eight hours without a drop of water . . . [in] the very hottest of the hot weather for which that summer seemed specially marked.[61]

The Union raiders were in enemy territory, and soon Confederate cavalrymen were in pursuit. The exhausted Union horsemen had to turn and fight again and again. When enemy reinforcements arrived, it became clear that the Union mission—which had done great damage—would now have to be abandoned. General Kautz would retreat with his cavalry, supply wagons, ambulances, and artillery to the town of Ream's Station, supposed to be held by Union troops.

General Wilson, who commanded the division encompassing the 1st Connecticut, would cover the withdrawal. They reached the town to find Rebel forces—infantry, cavalry, and artillery—waiting for them. "The order

In a simple gesture of unit pride, an unidentified private in Connecticut's 1st Cavalry displayed his cap: its brass insignia of crossed sabers denoted the cavalry, and the numeral "1" above it was his regiment's number. He had much to be proud of: by war's end, the regiment would fight in almost ninety engagements, and have the honor of escorting Grant to Lee's surrender at Appomattox.

was given for men to throw off all superfluous baggage. The wagon-trains were parked and set on fire; the ammunition was destroyed; and the ambulances, with the wounded, were abandoned."[62]

The Union riders would have to make a run for it—and the 1st Connecticut would be the rear guard, fighting off the Confederates to cover the retreat.

Uriah Parmelee of Guilford jotted down his impressions of that frantic action:

> Ye big skeedaddle—hot—sandy—fight—tired—horses —change position—what under the heavens are they going to do? Wilson and Col. McIntosh talk together—ordered to burn all the ammunition that the men cannot carry—artillery bury ammunition. We move back—white flag—ambulances—disconsolate wounded—trains half set on fire—caissons and limbers burning—a yell—pressed and hurrying ranks— the rebs rush out with their battle-flag. Why have we no flankers out![63]

"That night's march was the most exhausting and fearful of any of our marchings. The regiment destroyed bridges in rear of the column, and put every obstruction in the way of the enemy," wrote their major.[64] In a day and a night, the 1st Connecticut lost 64 of its members in casualties.

Captain John Morehouse, thirty-seven, was slightly wounded in the fight at Ream's Station. A native of Fairfield, Morehouse had journeyed to California during the gold rush, where he remained for thirteen years. Described as "a sober, solid man, near middle life, and possessed of considerable wealth," Morehouse returned to Connecticut at the beginning of the war "and enlisted in the first company he met, which chanced to be in the cavalry battalion. Attracting attention at once for his promptness and enthusiasm, he was offered a commission, but refused it, conscientiously regarding himself as unqualified. He studied tactics and practiced sword exercise constantly. Through four years of sturdy service, he rose steadily to a major's commission; never better earned by living soldier." (Croffut & Morris, *Military and Civil History*, p. 213.) Always ready to take on a dangerous assignment, Morehouse earned the nickname of "The War Horse" among his comrades. He was wounded twice and taken prisoner twice in his three and a half years of fighting.

"One of the Chief Surgeons of the division remarked, he was surprised at one time to realize that he had not slept at all in seventy-two hours, and his whole nervous system was almost entirely prostrated by fatigue and excitement. It was his opinion that the greater part of the missing had fallen out from mere exhaustion, and been captured."[65]

Losses and Gains

Connecticut's cavalry had lost a quarter of its fighting force on Wilson's raid. The 2nd Heavies, in one battle, had suffered over 300 casualties. In June of 1864, the *Hartford Daily Courant* reported that the state's 8th Regiment, which had begun Grant's Overland Campaign with more than 700 soldiers, could now muster only 192 men.[66]

Besides the increasing casualties, many regiments' three-year terms of enlistment were expiring. Their men would soon be returning home. If the Union army was going to survive General Grant's offensive, it was going to need a substantial infusion of troops.

In March of 1864, the government had called for an additional 200,000 men. In July came a call for 500,000 more. The conscription, or draft, was bringing in thousands of new soldiers, but at a cost. Many conscripts deserted, and those who didn't were untrained and untested. Frank

Soldiers who reenlisted for an additional three years earned service chevrons like those worn on the forearm (below his sergeant's chevrons) by Charlie Beeman of Warren. Beeman had joined the 8th Connecticut in 1861. At Antietam, he was severely wounded in the leg, and discharged shortly afterwards. After recovering at home, Beeman reenlisted, joining the 2nd Heavy Artillery. He served with his new regiment until the end of the war, earning promotions to corporal and sergeant.

Stoughton of the 14th complained, "Their was 100 recruits left New Haven for our Regt and they got here with 82. We did not have them but 3 days when all but 34 Deserted and now we have got 19 left. Them are the men that the folks at home send to us to put down the Rebellion with, but it will be a long time before the Rebellion is put down with such men as them."[67]

It was far better to retain veteran soldiers, and to this end the government began offering enormous bounties and furloughs to soldiers who would reenlist.

"Recruiting-officers were sent to the regiments in the field; and the soldiers having less than one year to serve were offered the veteran bounty of $702 to re-enlist, with a furlough of thirty days before the expiration of their original term of enlistment. The effort was attended with abundant success."[68] In each of Connecticut's three-year regiments, hundreds of men reenlisted despite the hardships they'd endured, and the uncertainty of what lay ahead.

Chapter twelve

Hope Never Dying

From the Siege of Petersburg to the Sea, June to December 1864

Now well into the second month of his offensive, General Grant—despite losing both battles and men at an inordinate rate—moved forward with single-minded purpose.

"Grant keeps making flank movements, and gets nearer Richmond every time he moves," wrote Walter Orton, a Woodbury man in the 2nd Heavy Artillery. "He stops in one place until he gets the whole Rebel forces in the position that he wants them, then starts off in the nights and leaves them behind."[1]

The Union army was getting closer to Richmond, yes—but Grant had a different target in his sights. Engineers constructed a pontoon bridge nearly four-tenths of a mile long across the James River, allowing Union troops to cross and advance on Petersburg, just south of the Confederate capital. A thriving city on the Appomattox River, Petersburg was crucial to Lee's operations: five railroads converged there, making it the supply center for the whole region, including Richmond. If Grant took Petersburg, he could cut the supply line for Lee's army and for the Confederate capital, and starve out the enemy.

The rebels had constructed miles of entrenchments around the strategic city. On June 9, Union troops under Gen. Benjamin Butler made tentative strikes on the fortifications and quickly withdrew. The Army of the Potomac and supporting troops began a second assault on the night of June 15. Despite a huge advantage in troop strength, Union commanders, in repeated assaults over a four-day period, failed to coordinate attacks or follow up advances. The Confederates lost approximately 4,000 soldiers in the four-day battle, while Union losses nearly tripled that number.

The Union army dug in and prepared for a long siege.

By the time Union troops reached Petersburg, a soldier's shovel rivaled his rifle in importance.

Early in the 1864 campaign, the men had learned to construct improvised earthworks that would give them a modicum of protection. Col. Griffin Stedman reported that at Cold Harbor, his 11th Connecticut soldiers "threw up, with cup, plate, and bayonet, an infantry parapet of considerable strength." (Official Report of Colonel Griffin A. Stedman, Jr., 11th Connecticut Infantry, June 10, 1864, *The War of the Rebellion: A Compilation of the Official Records of the Union and Confederate Armies*, ser. 1, vol. 51, part 1, p. 1264.) At Petersburg, both sides took the digging to a new level, constructing miles of zigzagging, connected trenches in which they would live for months to come.

Among the thousands of Union troops at Petersburg, Connecticut was well represented, its 1st Heavy Artillery Regiment joining the state's 6th, 8th, 10th, 11th, 14th, 21st, and 29th infantry regiments. The 2nd Heavies also made a brief appearance in Petersburg.

THE 1ST HEAVIES

The men of Connecticut's 1st Heavy Artillery Regiment had left the forts around Washington in May of 1864 (like the 2nd Heavies), when General Grant summoned thousands of artillerymen to bolster his offensive. The 1st Heavies arrived in Petersburg in June, and Grant put their colonel, Henry Abbot, in charge of siege artillery. Abbot created a line of batteries seventeen miles long, and assigned his 1st Heavies to man over half of the 73 mortars and 127 cannon in his siege train.[2]

"It will really be hard work for me to open fire in the beautiful city of Petersburg, but we shall have to do it, and in such a way that the enemy cannot live in it," wrote Thomas S. Trumbull, major of the 1st Heavies. "I believe that the enemy will be forced to make a big fight at Petersburg, or evacuate Richmond. They must get hungry soon."[3]

Field officers like Trumbull each commanded a group of batteries. Trumbull had been in Petersburg a week when he wrote to his mother:

Detail from "Investment of Petersburg by Genl. Grant 1865," by Robert Knox Sneden.

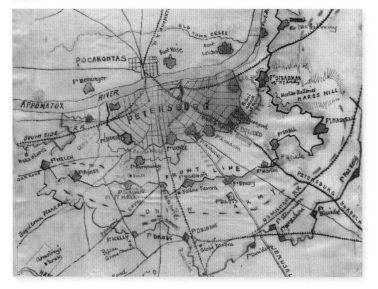

> I have been at work night & day almost constantly since my arrival. I think I have never slept two hours at a time . . . Most of my work too has been done under fire, and such a fire. Daily I crawl along our lines, from battery to battery (I have nine in my charge) popped at almost every step. On Thursday behind a tree examining the reb lines, within

150 yds., when more than a dozen bullets struck the tree, coming, too, with that terrible velocity that means death, fired as they were by the heavy sharpshooters rifle.

Our Regt. is not losing its reputation here. We receive compliments from all sides . . . Gen Grant has shaken hands with me . . . In the night Gen. Smith sent for me & directed me to take a very intelligent deserter from the enemy around the lines so that he could point out different buildings of importance in Petersburg & show me vulnerable points on the enemy part. I did so & have already profited by the information gained . . . Oh Mother, I wish some of my friends who get impatient because our "Army doesn't move," could . . . see our men & line officers lying behind the little breastworks in the broiling hot sun day after day, where it is impossible to lift their heads for a breath of air without getting shot.[4]

"[I]n the 38 days that I was in the trenches with my battery," wrote a lieutenant in the 1st Heavy Artillery, "I fired twenty four hundred and eighty five (2485) 8 inch shell. each shell weighs forty six pounds. making over 56 tons of iron from my battery alone. If every shell has killed a Johnie [Reb] I am glad of it." (Letter of Lt. Lewis W. Jackson to his sister, Mrs. Barzilla Thresher of Hartford, August 19, 1864, typescript by Dean Nelson, Connecticut State Archives, Hartford.) Here, Capt. John H. Burton tempted fate (and Rebel sharpshooters) by standing on the parapet of one of the Petersburg batteries, directing the fire of three 30-pound Parrott rifles manned by his 1st Heavies.

In addition to manning batteries, the 1st Heavies operated a massive 13-inch mortar that weighed over 17,000 pounds. The mortar had its own railroad car, strengthened with iron rods to bear the recoil of firing. An engine ran the mortar out to different locations on a specially laid track in a ravine hidden by woods from the distant Rebels.

The great mortar was "Cast Iron" Jackson's pride and joy. He wrote to his sister back in Hartford:

> we are over two miles from the nearest rebel works that we fire at twelve and a half pounds of Powder is the smallest charge we use . . . but we can use twenty pounds if it is necessary. that will give us a range of over four thousand yards. this is a gay style of fighting.
>
> we have got a large platform car that is all iron clad to keep off the bullets of the Sharp shooters. On this we haul our 13 inch mortar . . . behind this we have another iron clad car for the ammunition, and one for my 26 men to live in. we also have a Locomotive which with the engineer is under my command.
>
> we run up the railroad towards the city [Petersburg] as near as we want and blaze away at the rebel batteries turned on us till we can't stand it any longer then we hitch on the engine and run down the road a couple of miles or so out of range of the Johnies rifled guns and be off and rest a spell and watch the Grey Backed devils through a glass from the signal station until they get their guns trained on some other points then we run up and give them Rats again. so goes the Siege of Petersburg. day after day the same old story . . .
>
> The shell that I am firing now are 13 inches in diameter and weigh one hundred and ninety four pounds each. we put 7½ pounds of powder in the Shell and ten pounds of lead bullets so you can judge what kind of projectile it

The huge mortar threw shells that weighed over 200 pounds, with a range of approximately two miles.

Lead gunner on the great mortar was Lt. Lewis Jackson, *far right*, a Hartford machinist. Known as "Cast Iron" Jackson, the lieutenant may have drawn his nickname from the weapon he manned, or from his own tough demeanor.

would be to hit a man in the head with. It behooves all Johnies to look out for their Gopher Holes when we get to work at them . . .

We have not fired a shot yet this morning, neither do I want to for a day or two for we are all deaf we can scarcely hear anything.[5]

Company G of the 1st Heavies was drawn from students at Wesleyan University. One student noted that they were able to "use Prof. Van Vleck's mathematics," explaining: "The rebels had a couple of Whitworth guns enfilading our line from the opposite bank of the river . . . The mortar used a 200 lb. unloaded, or 225 when loaded with bullets. A mile of woods intervened to prevent aim. So we made a topographical map, and ran the [mortar] car back . . . By using the shell loaded and unloaded, we calculated the height of the bluff, and . . . blew up one of the guns, platform and some fourteen men many feet in the air."[6]

In the Trenches

Infantry soldiers sheltered in miles of intersecting trenches, but even there they were constantly vulnerable to enemy artillery shells and sharpshooters' bullets. "It is not pleasant to feel never safe," wrote a Connecticut man. "Bullets are whistling past us during most of the time. Rebel shells explode above us, or tear up the ground in our camp on their bounding way . . . When we lie down at night it is with the understanding that we may be shot before we rise."[7]

Siege work was mostly waiting, but a soldier's duties varied somewhat. "The rule now is, one day on picket, two days in the trenches, one day in camp, one day on fatigue. This gives us one day in five for rest, but that in a place of considerable peril."[8]

After weeks in the trenches, Moses Smith, the 8th Connecticut's chaplain, wrote wearily:

> A month of siege-work; lying in the trenches; eyeing the rebels; digging by moonlight; broiling in the sun; shooting through a knot-hole; shot at if a head is lifted; artillery compliments passing and repassing; our lives endangered by shells from both sides; officers falling; comrades dying; everybody wearied by the monotony, and exhausted by heat . . . numbers growing less, but hope never dying . . .[9]

The Crater

In Petersburg, the men's nerves were becoming frayed. Morale was terrible. When a Pennsylvania officer, Lt. Col. Henry Pleasants, proposed an extraordinary plan to end the siege, General Grant listened.

A mining engineer, Pleasant envisioned digging a secret tunnel under the Rebel works and placing an exploding mine at the end. The explosion would create a breach in the Confederate works, through which Union troops would pour, taking the enemy by surprise.

Early on the morning of July 30, 1864, Union forces detonated the mine beneath the Confederate works. When Union troops charged forward they found a massive crater, thirty feet deep. Then, chaos ensued.

Regiment after regiment reached the vast hole with no instructions on how to proceed. Soldiers charged down into the crater, then were unable to scale its sheer walls to get out. Others poured in behind. Thousands of men and officers were now milling around with no clear idea of what to do. Meanwhile, the Confederates were rapidly rallying after the shock of the explosion.

Col. Henry Goddard Thomas, twenty-seven, commanded a brigade of African American soldiers that included the brand new 31st United States Colored Troops, which had arrived in Petersburg late the night before. Several hundred of the 31st U.S.C.T. had enlisted in Connecticut. The green troops waited with their colonel for the order to move, but it was over an hour before the word came, and the brigade moved forward through the Union trenches known as the "covered way."

Now they waited again, listening to the artillery fire and the sharp musketry. Before long came a steady stream of wounded men by them; some walking, others carried on stretchers. "We stood there over an hour with this endless procession of wounded men passing," Colonel Thomas wrote. "There could be no greater strain on the nerves."

> Finally . . . we got the order for the colored division to charge . . . The crater was already too full; that I could easily see. I swung my column to the right and charged over the enemy's rifle-pits . . . —a labyrinth of bomb-proofs and magazines, with passages between . . . My brigade moved gallantly on right over the bomb-proofs . . . As we mounted the pits, a deadly enfilade from eight guns on our right and a murderous cross-fire of musketry met us.[10]

By now the Confederates were mounting a furious counterattack, hitting the Federals with both infantry and artillery fire. The colored troops were ordered to make a charge over the entrenchments to a rise ahead of them. A sergeant from a Pennsylvania regiment watched as "a division of Colored soldiers rushed into the jaws of death with no prospect of success; but they went in cheering as though they didn't mind it, and a great many of them never came back."[11]

Officer after officer was shot down and "hundreds of heroes 'carved in ebony' fell," wrote Colonel Thomas.[12] The inexperienced 31st Regiment found itself with scarcely an officer left to direct it. One of Colonel Thomas's staff, a twenty-one-year-old lieutenant named Christopher Pinnell, seized the brigade's green and white guidon. "With his sword uplifted in his

Richard K. Woodruff, a Yale student, had joined the 15th Connecticut as a corporal in 1862. When the Union army established African American units, white enlisted men could apply to become regimental officers. Hundreds of white soldiers—some seeking officers' pay, some choosing to support the cause of emancipation—applied for the posts. Woodruff became a captain in the 31st United States Colored Troops, leading a company of Connecticut men. As Captain Woodruff led his men out of the entrenchments in a charge, a Rebel bullet shattered his elbow. Twelve days later, the twenty-three-year-old minister's son died of tetanus.

Isaac B. Truitt was one of the lucky survivors of the 31st U.S.C.T. At the Battle of the Crater, his company, under Captain Woodruff, had a casualty rate of approximately 25 percent; other companies lost more. That day, Truitt received a promotion from private to corporal. He later rose to be sergeant. A sailor, Truitt had been forty-three when he left his wife and children and enlisted for the Union. After the war, he lived in Middletown, Connecticut, where this photograph was taken about 1870.

right hand and the banner in his left, he sought to call out the men along the whole line of the parapet. In a moment, a musketry fire was focused upon him, whirling him round and round several times before he fell."[13]

The enemy fire was devastating, unendurable. "The men of the 31st making the charge were being mowed down like grass, with no hope of any one reaching the crest, so I ordered them to scatter and run back," Thomas wrote.[14]

The Union's uncoordinated attack had catastrophic consequences for thousands of blue-coated soldiers. Men trapped in the crater were shot like fish in a barrel. Captured African American soldiers were massacred by their captors. Union casualties reached almost 4,000 while the Confederates lost only 1,500 or so. Grant called the assault "the saddest affair I have witnessed in the war."

The 31st's major, Thomas Wright, wrote of his soldiers: "More bravery and enthusiasm I never witnessed. Besides their patriotic ardor, they went into that action with a determination to command the respect of white troops; which we knew could only be obtained by hard fighting."[15]

Colonel Thomas reported: "The 31st had but two officers for duty that night."[16]

I WOULD DIE TO HAVE THE DAY COME

The day after the Battle of the Crater, hundreds of black soldiers lay dead or dying. Among them was Leonard Percy from the small farming community of Granby, Connecticut. Born about 1807, Len Percy was in his mid-fifties when he joined Connecticut's 30th Regiment. Three of his sons, Earl, Alfred, and Sylvester, had enlisted already in the 29th Connecticut.

"Once let the black man get upon his person the brass letters U.S.; let him get an eagle on his button, and a musket on his shoulder, and bullets in his pocket, and there is no power on earth . . . which can deny that he has earned the right of citizenship in the United States," said Frederick Douglass. ("Should the Negro Enlist in the Union Army?" July 6, 1863, at National Hall, Philadelphia, published in *Douglass' Monthly*, August 1863.) This unidentified first sergeant from the 29th Connecticut, with gold-accented eagle buttons and an expression of solemn dignity, personified the black soldier that Douglass described.

After the war, a white resident of Granby named William Case was giving a speech at the town's Civil War monument. Carved into the stone marker were the names of the Granby soldiers who had given their lives, including that of Leonard Percy.

Prior to Percy's enlistment, Case declared, Granby's white residents considered him "poor and ignorant and black, so worthless in his life . . . hovering on the outskirts of the village, . . . his sole business to own the worst horse and the most dogs."

But, Case went on, their vision of Percy changed. Before the war, a group of white men from Granby were having a conversation—"talking politics—about slavery, and about the negro—for those were the stirring subjects of those days—and one of us expressed the belief . . . that the day would come when the negro would vote. At this, 'Len' who crouched hard by taking in the talk stood up and said, 'Do you believe that? I would die to have the day come.'"[17]

Len Percy did exactly that.

Every Nerve Was Kept on Tension

After the disaster at the crater, the siege, with all its dangers, resumed. Henry Ward Camp, adjutant of the 10th Connecticut, wrote: "casualties came to be so frequent, that officers and men moved about with an ever-present consciousness that they might fall the next minute. Frequently, one on stepping from his tent would ask his friend to forward an open letter, . . . in case he did not come in again; and every nerve was kept on tension by this sense of personal peril."[18]

Soldiers on picket duty were in the trenches (called "vidette pits") closest to enemy lines, sometimes a mere fifty yards from the Johnnies. Rebel sharpshooters watched them constantly. "Men on duty there could be relieved only by night, and then as quietly as possible," said the 10th Connecticut's chaplain. "If a soldier raised head or hand above the low earth bank by day, 'chew' came a bullet past him, or 'chug' came a bullet into him."[19]

Chaplain Trumbull told a tragic story of two friends in the 10th Regiment, on picket duty together:

> One day in September an enlisted man of our regiment, in one of those pits, showed his head above the mound [of dirt]

Griffin A. Stedman Jr., a Hartford native and Trinity College graduate, became colonel of Connecticut's 11th Regiment when he was only twenty-four years old. His regiment took part in the siege at Petersburg. Stedman's friend, Thomas S. Trumbull, wrote sadly on August 5: "I am sitting by Grif. Stedman, who is, I fear, dying . . . there was a demonstration made on our lines by the enemy. Griffin was in the very front, & was hit in the chest by a musket bullet . . . I have talked but little with him, of course, for he cannot talk much. He says, 'Major, its in a bad place.' . . . I shall stay with him as long as I can . . . My heart grows sick when I think of him. I find myself totally unmanned before I know it . . . I fear that he has fought his last battle." (Courtesy of Cowan's Auctions, Inc., Cincinnati, Ohio.) Colonel Stedman received a hurried promotion to brigadier general, and died the following day.

A portrait of Col. Griffin Stedman hung behind this unidentified sitter, almost certainly Stedman's sweetheart, Julia Beach. When soldiers did not return from the war—as was the case for Stedman—their pictures were lasting memorials. Julia Beach created an additional memorial to the colonel when she gave his regiment a national flag in 1865. On the flagstaff, she had affixed a silver plate engraved, "To the Eleventh Regt. Conn. Vol. This flag is presented by Julia A. Beach in memory of their pure and valorous commander, Colonel and Brigadier General Griffin A. Steadman, Jr. fallen before Petersburg, Aug. 6, 1864 and in memory of the officers and soldiers of the regiment who have nobly dared and died in its defense."

for a moment. A bullet crashed through his forehead, and he fell back unconscious.

His sole comrade in the pit, who was as brave and daring a soldier as could be found in the regiment, knew that an attempt to get his wounded comrade to the rear would be certain death. No stretcher corps could come to his relief before dark. There was nothing left for the lonely watcher but to *wait* . . . nine weary, dreary hours, until the night came with its welcome cover.

Cramped in that close clay pit, by the side of his bleeding, moaning, dying fellow; unable to lift himself for a full change of posture; helpless to give, or to seek, relief for the speechless sufferer; in the heat of a burning sun, and again in the drenching of a pouring rain; now brushing the flies from the upturned, disfigured face; now giving scanty drops of water to moisten the parching lips of the wounded and dying veteran; now shielding that face from the force of the beating shower,—he passed the long hours of the dragging day, longing for darkness . . .

That night, in camp, when the bleeding form was laid in a low splinter-proof before headquarters . . . we watched his heavy breathing, and looked in to his familiar, now unresponsive, face, while kind yet unheeded words were spoken to him, until just past the midnight hour, when . . . he gave his last labored, low sob, and all was still.[20]

"I stood one bright September day during the siege on the slope of a hill, by a fresh made grave," wrote David Torrance of Norwich, an officer in the 29th Connecticut. "Of its occupant I knew nothing save that he had passed from the thunder of the guns and the roar of battle around Fort Hell, to the great peace beyond, and in some lull after the fight had been laid there to rest. At the head of the grave stood a rough board with a brief memorial of the name, company and regiment of the sleeper, rudely carved thereon and beneath all the simple words 'We miss him much.'" ("Reminiscences of the War," memoir by David Torrance, courtesy of descendants of David Torrance.)

While sharpshooters and artillery shells were taking hundreds of Union lives at Petersburg, another enemy was killing Connecticut soldiers in Newbern, North Carolina—"an enemy against whom watchfulness and personal bravery were of no avail"—yellow fever. The men of Connecticut's 15th Infantry were on provost duty in Newbern when the disease began to move through the city. "In a short time, more than half the regiment were down with the disease. A little later the muffled drums of the burial parties were sounding constantly from sunrise till dark. A few more days and all burial ceremony was dispensed with, and the bodies of the victims were hurried under ground in the quickest manner possible . . . not until frost came in November was there any relief." (Colonel George M. White, "History of the 15th Regiment C.V. Infantry," in *Record of Service of Connecticut Men*, p. 588.) Of the approximately 3,000 people who caught yellow fever in Newbern, over 40 percent died. Sgt. J. Henri Burwell of Danbury looked to be a well-armed warrior in his portrait, with rifle musket, bayonet, and NCO sword at his hip, but his weapons were no match for the invasive enemy he faced. Burwell died in October and was buried outside Newbern with his brothers-in-arms.

Casualties at Petersburg continued to mount every day. On August 17, Lincoln telegraphed Grant: "I have seen your despatch expressing your unwillingness to break your hold where you are. Neither am I willing. Hold on with a bull-dog grip, and chew and choke, as much as possible." The siege would continue for seven more months.

ON THE OFFENSIVE

True to his plan, General Grant did not let anything stop him from taking the fight to Lee. In mid-August, he sent part of the Army of the Potomac out to wrestle control of the Weldon Railroad, one of the Confederacy's most important supply lines.

The 14th Connecticut left Petersburg on August 22, marching south, and reached Ream's Station two days later. Here the men went to work destroying train track and burning railroad buildings. The plumes of smoke were clear signals, and the following afternoon the Rebels attacked.

The 14th's assistant surgeon, Levi Jewett, wrote:

A jagged gash in Dr. Levi Jewett's slouch hat bears witness to his part in the battle: "at this time I was struck down by a fragment of shell and was taken a short distance to the rear just in time to escape being run over by the enemy." (Page, *History of the Fourteenth*, p. 295, quoting Dr. Levi Jewett.)

> The woods were thick in our front so that the enemy could not be seen, and we only learned of their approach by . . . the frightened birds flying toward us and the startled squirrels, rabbits and small game scurrying in our direction, showing that the line of battle was sweeping all before it.
>
> Soon the battle was on with the suddenness of a clap of thunder. The crackling of the musketry was continuous mingled with the heavier sound of the cannon, the shouts of the officers and above all was the shrill and continuous "rebel yell" punctuated by their rapid footsteps, showing that they came into the fight on the run. It was a time of terror and it seemed

Capt. James R. Nichols of Norwich was barely twenty-one when he was shot in the leg at the Battle of Ream's Station. That night, two 14th soldiers who had been captured by the enemy snuck away in the darkness. Crossing the battlefield in search of their command, "we heard a voice calling for assistance; stopping to investigate we found it came from Captain Nickels, Company D, laying there wounded," wrote Sgt. Henry Lydall. "[T]he rebel cavalry had been there and robbed him of hat, coat, watch, money and other valuables, and only desisted from taking his boots on discovering that in trying to move them from his wounded limb, they caused him such intolerable suffering as to touch the heart of even a rebel cavalryman: and as if to add still more to the poor Captain's suffering the rain just then began to pour down in torrents, and we not being able to carry him, made him as comfortable as possible with our rubber blankets." Lydall returned with several comrades, and carried the wounded Captain Nichols to an ambulance. But the ambulance had to drive "over stumps, stones and uneven ground, making such thumping and jostling that Captain Nickels was unable to endure the pain it caused, and I was compelled to procure a stretcher and with such help as I could procure from stragglers I tramped along through that whole night, sometimes I would be without help and would be compelled to wait, accosting the weary stragglers as they passed, imploring them to give the Captain a little assistance . . . Fourteen weary miles we tramped carrying the wounded man that night, through woods and swamps and over rocks until just as day dawned upon us, we reached the hospital tent more dead than alive, and left the brave man to the tender mercies of the surgeons." (Page, *History of the Fourteenth*, pp. 306–7, quoting Sgt. Henry Lydall.) Nichols suffered for nearly seven months before he died of the effects of his wound.

impossible for our men to hold their line against such a fierce assault. They fought well till they saw the rebel line extending around their flank and to their rear when they had to fall back slowly and in good order, firing as they went.[21]

Union troops were forced to retreat, and their casualties far outnumbered the Confederates' losses. Nevertheless, the Rebels withdrew that night, leaving the Union in control of the railroad.

On the Move with Sherman

After the Battle of Gettysburg in July of 1863, the 5th and 20th Connecticut Infantry Regiments had found themselves shifted from the Army of the Potomac west to join the Army of the Cumberland under Gen. William Tecumseh Sherman. In March 1864, Sherman took command of the Military Division of the Mississippi, which combined three armies: the Cumberland, the Tennessee, and the Ohio.

From Chattanooga, Tennessee, General Sherman set his sights on Atlanta, a manufacturing and rail center crucial to the South. In early May of 1864, he marched his armies south to invade Georgia.

Horatio Chapman of the 20th Connecticut wrote of the devastation that Sherman's army brought as it moved through Georgia: "where the army goes everything is taken, wheat and corn-fields destroyed, mills burned, horses, cattle and mules taken, etc. But their cows and gardens . . . are generally left or they would starve . . ."[22]

Before heading off to Atlanta, four officers of the 20th Connecticut Infantry posed at Pulpit Rock on Lookout Mountain, near Chattanooga, Tennessee. With blankets rolled and slung, haversacks on the hip, tin cups at the ready, they gave a rare glimpse of Union line officers at war in the field. Identified, *from left to right*: Lt. William Spencer of Cheshire, Capt. John Doolittle of Derby, Lt. Theodore Jepson of Hartford, and Lt. Ezra Sprague of Derby.

Southern women brought their garden produce to trade with the soldiers for food for their families.

> They will not take money for their produce for it is of no use to them for they cannot buy anything with money . . . Just at night a sad looking woman with two little children came into my tent with produce . . . blackberries, new fresh butter and beets and green peas . . . "And what do you want in exchange?" "Oh, I want something that I and my children can eat." Says I, "Hard-tack?" "Yes." "Pork?" "Yes, sir . . . my children are hungry" . . . "How far have you come today with your children and load?" "Seven miles . . ."

> I took all she had and gave in exchange all my pork, hard-tack, coffee, salt, and sugar. Cousin Fred and Smith also gave her some of their provisions . . . some we had saved from time to time over and above our regular rations. She was much pleased, thanked us and left. This is only one case in a thousand.[23]

Wherever Sherman moved, Confederate troops were there to confront him. The armies battled at Resaca, Cassville, Peach Tree Creek, and in smaller actions and skirmishes almost without respite. Sherman called it "a continuous battle of 120 days."

Abner Smith of Moodus, fighting with the 20th Connecticut, informed his wife: "we have drove the Rebs right straight along all of the time there may have been one or two points where they got the advantage for a short time, but as a whole we have drove them right along as you can plainly see for we are now one hundred & thirty five and a half miles from Chattanooga and we have had to fight them most of the way."[24]

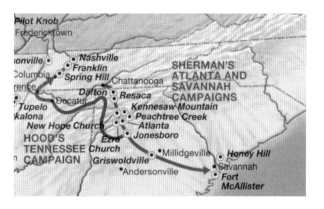

From southern Tennessee, Sherman's troops marched southeast to Atlanta before beginning their vaunted March to the Sea.

With agile flanking movements, Sherman got his armies to the gates of Atlanta in mid-July. His shrewd maneuvering had not brought about the horrific casualties Grant's offensive caused; nevertheless, the names of 172 men of the 5th and 20th Connecticut were added to the casualty rolls.

Not Moving

Just outside of Atlanta, Sherman's army floundered, sweltering week after week with seemingly no progress in taking Atlanta from the Rebels whose entrenchments protected the pivotal city. Outside of Petersburg, Grant was likewise stymied.

Morale in the North began to plummet. Growing casualty lists and a lack of military successes caused Union supporters to question the cause. At the White House, President Lincoln considered his prospects for reelection dismal. "I am going to be beaten," Lincoln said, "and unless some change takes place, badly beaten."[25]

Capt. Oliver R. Post of Hartford fell mortally wounded at the Battle of Peach Tree Creek on July 20. His friend Ezra Sprague, also of the 20th Connecticut, wrote: "Our regiment, after some skirmishing, became heavily engaged just before 3 o'clock, p. m., and so continued for more than four hours, in open field, suffering much. The 139th N. Y., of our brigade, was ordered up to our relief, and we, exhausted, fell back a few yards . . . Capt. Post returned to the old line to get a roll of blankets he had left there, was struck by a musket ball which, nearly severing his sword belt, passed completely through his body and out at his back. I heard a person cry, 'Oh, Capt. Post!' and turning, saw him sinking to the ground. I immediately ran to him, but a step or two, and asking him where he was wounded, opened his clothing. With a calm smile upon his features, he looked up at me, and as the crimson stream of life oozed out, said, 'I have got my furlough—I have tried to do my duty.' Then, addressing himself to his 2d Lieut., said, 'Lt. Abbott, take good care of the boys.' Some shelter tents were brought, upon which he was placed and borne to the rear. I clasped his hand at parting, but could not say, 'good-bye.'" (Storrs, *The Twentieth Connecticut*, p. 244, quoting letter to Mrs. Post from Capt. Ezra Sprague, July 22, 1864.) Oliver Post had been a newspaper editor before the war. He left a wife and four small children.

In Connecticut, the *Hartford Daily Courant* called it a "season of public depression . . . there was a strong current of popular feeling against the administration. The democratic leaders were sharp enough to see it. They became jubilant over it. It again promised success to their cherished scheme."[26]

It looked likely that at the Democratic Convention in Chicago at the end of August, the peace faction would dominate. The *Courant* admitted grimly, "Here in Connecticut the peace element is stronger than in any other State, yet it has a powerful organization throughout the country."[27] In Connecticut cities and towns, Copperheads attracted thousands to their meetings.

SOME CHANGE TAKES PLACE

Several miles south of Atlanta, explosions rocked the night air on September 1. The 20th Connecticut soldiers jumped to their feet to see "mountains of flames . . . vividly flashing up in the heavens and shot and shell in quick . . . succession going up with great velocity and bursting in the air." Atlanta seemed to be on fire, wrote Cpl. Horatio Chapman, but the soldiers "could not in the least understand its import."[28]

The next morning the troops exulted to find that the besieged city had fallen to the Union. With thousands of other Union troops, the 20th Connecticut soldiers marched into the city to find devastation. Union artillery had damaged parts of the city, and before the Rebels fled, they tried to destroy anything their enemy could use.

A jubilant Sherman telegraphed to Washington, "Atlanta is ours, and fairly won."

Walking about the abandoned city, the Connecticut soldiers saw how determined the Rebels had been to hold them off.

> There is a fort on every little eminence . . . and they are very strong, the embra-sures all being made with bags of sand . . . Their forts all have mounted cannon bearing on every approachable spot. There were deep ditches to be got over and row after row of sharpened stakes, innumerable secret wires stretched along about a foot from the ground and an obstruction still more formidable, the *cheval-de-frise*, which is impossible to get over without a pocket ladder and then there were ten and twelve-pounders brass, bearing on the *cheval-de-frise* at short range—and we all would have been killed before we could scale these . . .
>
> But they were outgeneraled, outwitted and flanked, and before they were aware of it their railroad destroyed and their communications cut . . . and they had to . . . retreat as fast as possible, and we are in the city.[29]

"This is the heaviest blow that could befall the rebels," the *Hartford Daily Courant* crowed.[30] In Norwalk, a 100-gun salute celebrated the victory, while bells tolled throughout New Haven.

The fall of Atlanta was a significant victory not just for the Union, but also for Abraham Lincoln. Sherman's success erased much of the Northern pessimism. Republicans united again behind Lincoln. And more Union victories quickly followed.

Sheridan in the Shenandoah

In the Shenandoah Valley, Ulysses Grant had placed thirty-three-year-old Philip Sheridan in command of about 40,000 Union troops called the Army of the Shenandoah. Grant had two goals for Sheridan: to pursue Confederate general Jubal Early "to the death," and to destroy the bountiful valley's crops, livestock, and farms.

For a month, Sheridan proceeded warily through the valley, skirmishing several times with Rebel forces. Jubal Early, noting Sheridan's cautiousness, assumed his enemy to be tentative. He was wrong. In mid-September, Grant met with an eager Sheridan, who pulled out a map and demonstrated how, if Grant approved, he would "whip them."[31]

A Connecticut soldier wrote: "Capt. Gordon has just told me he [General Grant] never said a word yesterday but held his cigar in his hand, head bowed while Sheridan was telling what [he] would do if he give permission. All he said, Go in, Phil, my boy—jumped on his horse and away he went."[32]

On September 19, at Opequon Creek in Winchester, Virginia, Sheridan's Army of the Shenandoah made a frontal assault on Jubal Early's Rebels. Sheridan's force included the men of five Connecticut regiments—the 1st Cavalry, 2nd Heavy Artillery, and 9th, 12th, and 13th Infantry.

The cavalrymen of the 1st Connecticut would open and close the battle, dashing across the Opequon Creek at sunrise and "driving the enemy at a gallop until the first line of rebel earthworks was in sight. Then the whole brigade in line, the First Connecticut in the center, charged magnificently up the slope, and with a yell went over the breastwork, man and horse together, capturing 100 prisoners . . . The brigade held this position till our infantry came up."[33]

It was nearly noon when Sheridan's infantry began the attack, moving under heavy musketry and artillery fire. When the 13th Connecticut joined the fight, Lt. Col. Homer Sprague wrote, "Our advance commenced with steadiness and in a beautiful line, but gradually quickened into a rapid charge."[34] They seemed to be pushing back the Confederates, but abruptly, the tide of battle turned: a gap had developed in the Union line, and the Rebels swiftly advanced into that breach. Suddenly thousands of Union soldiers were retreating, running in panic.

John DeForest, a captain in the 12th Connecticut, witnessed "a state of confusion which threatened wide-spread disaster. Sixth Corps men and Nineteenth Corps men were . . . rushing towards the cover of the forest . . . Early's veterans advanced steadily with yells of triumph and constant volleys of musketry, threatening to sweep away our centre, and render our struggle a defeat."[35]

In the midst of the chaos, Union general Emory Upton pushed forward his brigade to plug the gap and drive back the Rebel attackers. Connecticut's 2nd Heavies constituted roughly half of Upton's brigade, and "It was this movement of our brigade that checked the enemy until the lines were restored and the two or three thousand fugitives brought back," wrote the regiment's adjutant.[36]

At the head of the 2nd Heavies rode their new colonel, Ranald Mackenzie, who had replaced the regiment's beloved colonel, Elisha Kellogg. Mackenzie was only twenty-four, but had graduated first in his class at West Point, and Grant felt he was the Union's "most promising young officer."

Union officers had shepherded many of their fleeing men back to the lines, and with his command somewhat restored, Sheridan didn't wait but ordered an advance. The 2nd Heavies "charged across the field, Mackenzie riding some ten rods ahead, holding his hat aloft on the point of his

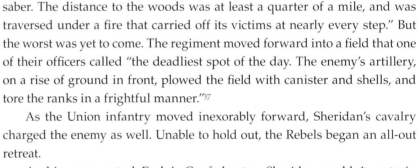

Seymour Eldridge of Goshen was advancing with the 2nd Heavies when "the musket in his hands was struck by a shell, cutting it in two and leaving the barrel in his hands, then cutting a large hole in Sergeant Homer W. Griswold's pants, cutting off both legs of Peter Burke at the ankles, crushing a foot for Anson F. Balcom, reaching the ground and exploding, throwing the dirt and gravel-stones into the face of Lieut. D. C. Kilbourne, cutting and bruising the skin badly, and the concussion paralyzing both arms for a time. Burke and Balcom died, as the result. Eldridge coolly held up the part of his musket that was left, and asked his captain if he could 'turn it in and draw another.'" (Rev. A. G. Hibbard, *History of the Town of Goshen, Connecticut*, pp. 383–84.)

saber. The distance to the woods was at least a quarter of a mile, and was traversed under a fire that carried off its victims at nearly every step." But the worst was yet to come. The regiment moved forward into a field that one of their officers called "the deadliest spot of the day. The enemy's artillery, on a rise of ground in front, plowed the field with canister and shells, and tore the ranks in a frightful manner."[37]

As the Union infantry moved inexorably forward, Sheridan's cavalry charged the enemy as well. Unable to hold out, the Rebels began an all-out retreat.

As his men routed Early's Confederates, Sheridan couldn't restrain himself. Michael Kelly of the 2nd Heavy Artillery described Sheridan "like a meteor, a flash of lightning in the sky all a blaze, reins thrown across a silver hook attached to his uniform coat, hat in one hand, sword in the other, guiding his horse with his feet & going like lightning speed, crying out, Give them Hail Columbia, boys, whack it into them, drive them."[38]

Connecticut's 1st Cavalry charged around Early's left flank, completing the rout. At the end of the day, the Union had sent Early's forces "whirling through Winchester," according to Sheridan, "and we are after them to-morrow."[39] The Union had taken 2,000 prisoners. The price for Sheridan's triumph was substantial. In one division (usually ten to twelve regiments), the casualties included every single regimental commander. The 2nd Heavies had 136 dead and wounded—but, as one officer put it, "unlike Cold Harbor or Petersburg, there was victory to show for this fearful outlay." He reflected that the Shenandoah had become

> the valley of decision. If Sheridan had been routed at Winchester, Early would have been across the Potomac at once, marching unopposed upon Washington . . . and

Major of the 2nd Heavy Artillery, Jeffrey Skinner of Winchester "was struck on top of his head by a shell, knocked nearly a rod, with his face to the earth, and was carried to the rear insensible." (Vaill, *History of the Second*, p. 96.) Skinner recovered and later became the regiment's lieutenant colonel.

In the 2nd Heavy Artillery's charge, Horace Hubbard, a thirty-two-year-old 2nd lieutenant from Plymouth, fell mortally wounded. "His back was fearfully torn by a shell, and he lived but a short time. He sent dying messages to his friends at home, and said he believed it was all for the best. 'Tell the boys of Company D, (in which he was formerly First Sergeant,) that I always meant to do right by them, and to forgive me if I have not.'" (Vaill, *History of the Second*, p. 196.)

the war would have been what the Chicago Democratic Convention had just declared it to be—a failure. That is, it would have been a failure for the government of the United States, and a complete triumph for the domineering lords of the South, who would have established their Confederacy upon the ruins of the Republic.[40]

Three days later, Sheridan struck Early again. The Rebels, said to be holding an "impregnable" position on Fisher's Hill, were soon in a headlong retreat, with the Army of the Shenandoah in pursuit.

The Confederates fled south, leaving the rich Shenandoah Valley to the mercy of the Yankees. And Sheridan set his army to work on Grant's order to turn the valley into "a barren waste so that crows flying over it for the balance of this season will have to carry their provender with them."

A soldier in the 2nd Heavies described the Union cavalry "burning grain, barns, mills, and in fact all property which could be of any service to the enemy." He added, "This act was a military necessity, from the fact that Early subsisted entirely upon the productions of the Valley . . . The destruction of grain and forage alone will in a great degree hinder future raids north by this route."[41]

CEDAR CREEK

In their camp near Cedar Creek, Sheridan's army was enjoying the fine fall weather. The men were relaxed, in spite of the fact that Jubal Early had marched his Rebels back into the valley, and lay close by. "[Early] was known to be receiving reinforcements, and his signal flags on Threetop Mountain . . . were continually in motion," wrote a man in the 2nd Heavy Artillery. "Nevertheless, it seemed the most improbable thing in the world that he could be meditating either an open attack or a surprise."[42]

Over six feet tall, George Bates of Plymouth stood out among the 2nd Heavies not only for his height, but also for his religious ardor. The Terryville soldier regularly held prayer meetings that earned the scorn of some of his less pious comrades. At Winchester, Private Bates fell severely wounded by a shell in his back and side, but survived, living into his mid-eighties.

Union casualties totaled only 528 at Fisher's Hill, while the Confederates had well over twice that number. In the 2nd Heavy Artillery, 5 men were killed outright, including thirty-six-year-old David B. Wooster, a Plymouth farmer. The regiment's adjutant called Wooster, a quartermaster sergeant, "one of the best men that ever entered the service." (Vaill, *History of the Second*, p. 105.)

On the evening of October 18, the Union soldiers went to sleep in their tents as usual. That night, a thick fog rolled in. Very early the next morning, before sunrise, some of Connecticut's 2nd Heavies became aware of crackling noises far off to the right of their lines. It was musketry, to be sure; but far away, and probably just pickets. Most soldiers were still asleep. Now the distant gunfire on the right increased, with artillery joining in. "But suddenly every man seemed to lose interest in the right, and turned his enquiring eyes and ears toward the *left*. Rapid volleys and a vague tumult told that there was *trouble* there. 'Fall in!' said [Colonel] Mackenzie."

There was no time. Snatching up their guns, they ran to their places, and the colonel rushed the regiment to the left. Hundreds, thousands of Union soldiers were fleeing before the Rebel advance.

General Sheridan was miles away, in Winchester; "General Wright, the temporary commander of the army, bareheaded, and with blood trickling from his beard, sat on his horse near by, as if bewildered."[43]

The 2nd Heavies with the other regiments of the 6th Corps formed in a line to make a stand against the enemy coming from the east. Their adjutant described

> The newly risen sun, huge and bloody . . . we could see nothing but that enormous disc, rising out of the fog, while they could see every man in our line, and could take good aim. The battalion lay down, and part of the men began to fire,—but the shape of the ground afforded little protection . . . Four-fifths of our loss for the entire day occurred during the time we lay here—which could not have been over five minutes.[44]

A lieutenant rode up with orders to fall back, but Colonel Mackenzie cried, "My God! I cannot! This line will break if I do."[45] The lieutenant gestured toward the Union troops around them, rapidly retreating.

The fog was thinning, and with sinking hearts the 2nd Heavy men watched as the "firm rebel line, with colors full high advanced, came rolling over a knoll just in front of our left, not more than three hundred yards distant. 'Rise up! Retreat!' said Mackenzie."

With Early's Rebels at their heels, the Union retreat devolved into bedlam: "the whole corps was scattered over acres and acres, with no more organization than a herd of buffaloes. Some of the wounded were carried for a distance by their comrades who were at length compelled to leave them to their fate in order to escape being shot."

The blue-coated soldiers ran "until a halt was made upon high ground, from which we could plainly see the Johnnies sauntering around on the very ground where we had slept."[46]

Jubal Early had been entirely successful. The night before, he'd sent two columns of troops in different directions: one command stealthily approached the Union right while the other column silently snuck up on the Union left and looped around it.

"The surprise was complete. The Eighth corps was unable to form a line of battle, and in five minutes was a herd of fugitives. Many of the men awoke only to find themselves prisoners."[47]

At the center of the Union line was the 19th Corps, which included Connecticut's 9th and 12th Regiments. As the rebels rushed upon them, the 12th Connecticut "was one of the first regiments to rally," wrote a soldier from another regiment. "They fired three volleys; but the far superior weight of the enemy crushed them, as an elephant would trample down a bull-dog."[48]

The Rebels captured some 1,500 Union soldiers, along with artillery pieces, ammunition, and supplies—but this last would be their downfall. Instead of following up the rout, the hungry Confederates fell to eating Union rations, and plundering the dead and wounded.

Meanwhile, several miles away, Union officers were gathering their commands and reestablishing order. "The cavalry formed a long line across the field, stopped all stragglers, and compelled them to fall in with the nearest organization."[49] And then—"Gen. Sheridan came up with a rush," wrote Capt. Leonard Dickinson of the 12th Connecticut. "He was received with thundering cheers, and his appearance was as good as a re-enforcement of ten thousand men. We began to rally our men, and soon had a strong line of battle formed. Gen. Sheridan . . . rode along the lines telling the boys that they would sleep in their old camp that night."[50]

By midafternoon, Sheridan's men were poised for a counterattack. With a tremendous yell, the Union troops charged forward. "Oh! How the boys did fight! The enemy fell back, slowly at first, then faster, then on a run—then a rout with our forces after them. By sundown we were back in the old camp sure enough, and our cavalry were riding the rebels down by scores."[51]

As the Union troops charged over the same ground they'd ceded earlier that day, they came across their own dead and wounded. Theodore Vaill wrote:

> the severely wounded had lain all day on the ground, near where they were hit, while the tide of battle ebbed and flowed over them. Some of the mortally wounded were just able to greet their returning comrades, hear the news of victory, and send a last message to their friends, before expiring.

> Corporal Charles M. Burr . . . was shot above the ankle, just after the battalion had risen up and started to retreat. Both bones of his leg were shattered, and he had to be left. In a few minutes the rebel battalion . . . came directly over him in pursuit, and was soon out of his sight. Then, being alone for a short time, he pulled off the boot from his sound leg, put his watch and money into it, and put it on again. Next, a merciful rebel lieutenant came and tied a handkerchief around his leg, stanching the blood.

> Next came the noble army of stragglers and bummers, with the question, "Hello, Yank, have you got any yankee notions about you?" At the same time thrusting their hands into every pocket. They captured a little money and small traps, but seeing one boot was spoiled, they did not meddle with the other. Next came wagons picking up muskets and accoutrements, which lay thick all over the ground. Then came ambulances and picked up the rebel wounded, but left ours . . .

In the early part of the battle, Capt. Benjamin F. Hosford of Winchester was shot in the head, and died immediately. "His brother and other men of Company D carried the body about half a mile on the retreat, and were compelled to leave it there," wrote a comrade. "At night it was found that the rebels had taken a ring from his finger, the straps from his coat, and the shoes from his feet." (Vaill, *History of the Second*, p. 130.)

And thus the day wore along until the middle of the afternoon, when the tide of travel began to turn . . . the roar of battle grew nearer and louder and more general,—then came galloping officers and all kinds of wagons,—then a brass 12-pounder swung round close to him, unlimbered, fired one shot and whipped off again,—then came the routed infantry, artillery and cavalry, all mixed together, all on a full run, and strewing the ground with muskets and equipments.

Then came the shouting "boys in blue,"—and in a few minutes Pat. Birmingham came up said, "Well, Charley, I'm glad to find you alive. I didn't expect it. We're back again in the old camp, and the Johnnies are whipped all to pieces."[52]

His tibia and fibula shattered, Charley Burr underwent an amputation of his lower leg. The Norfolk native would live for another sixty-eight years, dying in California at the age of 89.

As the men of the 2nd Heavy Artillery combed the battlefield for their dead and wounded, they came across the bodies of Cpl. Charles J. Reed and Cpl. George W. Page. The two friends had their arms around each other. Reed, shot in the chest, and Page in the neck, had "crawled quite a distance to each other from where they were hit to die in embraced Arms," wrote Michael Kelly.[53] Tears rolled down the faces of their brothers-in-arms. They buried the two soldiers together on the field.

REELECTION

Less than three weeks after Sheridan's victory, President Lincoln won his second term. Theodore Vaill claimed that "Sheridan's three victories in the Shenandoah . . . were at that time universally regarded as pre-cursors, if not procurers, of Lincoln's re-election, and the overthrow of rebellion."[54] As part of the Army of the Shenandoah, Vaill may be forgiven for forgetting that Sherman's success in Georgia also had an impact on the election.

The *Hartford Evening Press* proclaimed the news on the day after the election: "Victory Won, The Union Saved" (*Hartford Evening Press*, November 9, 1864.)

TO THE SEA

A week after the election, Sherman's troops left Atlanta and began their famous March to the Sea. In their wake, the Union soldiers left a path of devastation sixty miles wide, destroying farms, mills, bridges, and businesses. Abner Smith of the 20th Connecticut wrote, "we tore up and burned the Rail Roads all through the State where the army came, burned all the Cotton & Cotton Gins on the way and all public buildings in the cities and towns that we passed through."[55]

Union troops seized thousands of horses, mules, and livestock of all kinds. Their rations came from foraging, wrote Abner Smith: "In marching through the State of Georgia . . . we lived on the country and generaly had all that we could eat and more   to we lived on fresh pork sweate potatoes hens Turkeys Gees and ducks. we had all the Molasses & Honey that we wanted for every house had barrels of Molasses and what the army could not use they would destroy."[56]

While Abner seemed to enjoy the fruits of the land, his good friend and tentmate, Horatio Chapman, wrote sadly, "I did feel sorry for the women and innocent children . . . the corn, pork, poultry, etc., taken from them . . . what they will do to get a living is more than I can tell. But it is of no use for me to moralize. How little the people of the north know to what straits the women and children are brought. But our army is here and must be fed."[57]

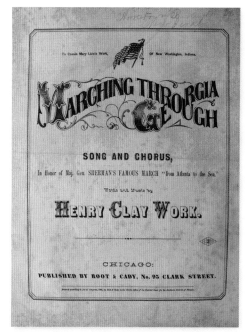

Henry Clay Work, a Middletown native, composed the jaunty "Marching through Georgia," in celebration of Sherman's advance.

> So we made a thoroughfare for Freedom and her train,
> Sixty miles in latitude—three hundred to the main;
> Treason fled before us, for resistance was in vain,
> While we were marching through Georgia.

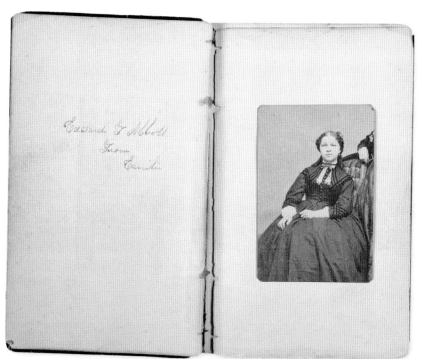

In mid-December, Edward Abbott of New Haven was hunkered down with his regiment, the 20th Connecticut, outside of Savannah. The men were living in "gopher holes" they'd dug for protection, and subsisting on a meager diet of rice and mustard. Even here, the mail reached the troops, and Edward received a package from his sweetheart, Emilie Doolittle. He opened it to find a small testament that Emilie had personalized: she had Edward's name and regiment letter-pressed on the book's cover in gilt, and tipped in her own earnest image. Edward prized the little volume, jotting on an inside page, "In line of battle before Savannah Dec 18 1864, just received 4 p.m." He survived the war, and in 1866 married the girl in the picture.

This piece of bunting is presented
to my school-mate
Addison G. McKee
for the Cabinet at Mansfield Post.
It was part of Genl. Sherman's
Head-Quarters Flag, The first U.S. Flag
which waved over the Capitols of
Georgia, South-Carolina and North Carolina after Secession.
I was Signal Officer on the dome
of the Capitol at Raleigh during its oc-
cupancy by Shermans Army. I saw the
flag raised, by a Captain from Army
Head-quarters, on the Capitol of N.C.
and the Captain informed me at the
time concerning its previous history.
The Flag was very large and when
at rest touched the roof of the building.
During a storm some pieces were torn
off, which I preserved. This fragment
is from one of said pieces.
Middletown Ci.   Geo. C. Round
June 13. 1894   Late Lieut. & Signal Officer

This worn scrap of red cloth once flew over Sherman's headquarters in
Savannah. "It was part of Genl. Sherman's Head Quarters Flag, the First U.S.
Flag which waved over the Capitols of Georgia, South Carolina and North
Carolina after Secession." George C. Round *(left)*, a former Wesleyan student
who became an officer in the Signal Corps, preserved the red fabric as a
memento of his war experiences.

Confederate forces skirmished and battled with Sherman's army all along the way, but on December 10, the Union troops arrived in Savannah. Within the city, Confederate general Hardee's troops were entrenched.

Capt. Horace G. H. Tarr of the 20th Connecticut described his part in what came next:

> I was permitted to conduct two flags of truce through our lines, conveying despatches to Gen. Hardee demanding a surrender of the city. It was a novel and pleasant thing to meet, socially, the men we had been fighting so many months and laugh over with them some of the incidents of our campaigns together. 'Tis strange how little feeling exists between men who have fought to the death! And it is a curious phase in human nature, that there is no one you have more respect for than for the man who has given you a manly fight.[58]

Days later, Confederate forces fled the city, and Savannah surrendered. On December 21, Sherman sent President Lincoln a telegraph: "I beg to present you as a Christmas gift the City of Savannah."

As 1864 drew to a close, the Union found itself in a far better situation than it had been a year earlier. Grant, Sherman, and Sheridan were finding success across the South. Lincoln would soon begin his second term. And the Confederacy was every day showing more signs of strain and breakdown.

Surely, the end of the war could not be far away.

CHAPTER THIRTEEN

Our Army Perfectly Crazy

ON TO APPOMATTOX, 1865

As 1865 opened, the *Hartford Daily Courant* declared, "The future is bright with promise." The war was on a different footing now, the editor asserted: "For several months, hardly a week has passed without bringing tidings of fresh triumphs."[1] In eastern Connecticut, the *Willimantic Journal* agreed: "A few more vigorous blows and the rebellion which is tottering falls to rise no more."[2]

In a tent hospital for the wounded in Virginia, a Connecticut farm boy named George Meech started the year by joking with President Lincoln. Meech, a private in the 21st Regiment, was stationed at Point of Rocks when he learned that the president would be visiting wounded soldiers there on New Year's Day.

> We knew that in order to get to the hospital Lincoln would have to pass by the building where I was working so a group of us thought that we would have some fun with him. For some time we had been keeping an immense pair of shoes . . . so we put these out in front with a large placard underneath them reading: "Shoes with which Abraham Lincoln is to crush the Rebellion."
>
> President Lincoln himself came in sight, walking slowly toward us alone, rather sad and melancholy-looking. He was wearing a silk hat and a Prince Albert coat and had his hands behind his back as if he were pondering the outcome of the war. We were all peering through a shutter to see what he would do. On he came and then stopped right in front of our office to read our placard. He smiled and passed on . . .

At the hospital later Lincoln spoke with the sufferers, expressing his sympathy. "Comrades," he said to one group of them in my own hearing, "I'm very sorry to see you here in this condition but no matter what happens the war must be won." They cheered him to the echo.[3]

Just a few weeks later, there was more cheering—this time, in Washington. On January 31, the House of Representatives passed the 13th Amendment, prohibiting slavery in the United States. When the vote was announced, "the tumult of joy that broke out was vast, thundering and uncontrollable," the *Hartford Daily Courant* reported.[4]

At last, Abraham Lincoln had momentum. And in the field, Grant was setting his commands in motion, planning to intensify the pressure on all fronts, and drive the war to a conclusion.

Sherman and his army had left Savannah and were marching north through the Carolinas, foraging and burning as they came. "In South Carolina, they [Union troops] . . . resolved to collect principal and interest of the debt long due to justice. The pestilent State was swept with a besom of flame; little was left that could be used; and tall blackened chimneys [marked] where plantation-houses had been."[5] Their march was interrupted by numerous skirmishes with the enemy; Lt. Col. Philo Buckingham of Connecticut's 20th Regiment commented on "the obstinacy with which the rebels fought" though their cause seemed lost.[6] Approaching from the south, Sherman's forces would harass the diminishing Rebel army in Virginia.

Meanwhile, Grant kept goading Lee. In early February he pulled troops from the trenches at Petersburg, sending them on an offensive to the west to shut down more of the rebel supply route. In a skirmish near Hatcher's Run, five men of 14th Connecticut were wounded, and the regiment lost its youngest officer, nineteen-year-old lieutenant Franklin Bartlett, to a Confederate bullet in the chest.

Hundreds of miles to the south, Connecticut men were fighting for their lives near St. Augustine, Florida. Lt. Col. Albert H. Wilcoxson of the 17th Regiment had led a foray to seize a supply of cotton from a Rebel farm. Returning with their supply carts full, they were attacked by Florida cavalry under Capt. J. J. Dickison. Wilcoxson, in the rear with two of his 17th officers, galloped toward the sound of the gunfire to find that the Confederates had captured nearly all of his men.

The wife of Confederate captain Dickison later reported the skirmish as her husband described it, praising Wilcoxson's courage:

> He fought fearlessly; after firing his last shot, he threw his pistol at one of our soldiers, then drew his sword and started down the road, where two or three men were guarding the prisoners. There was but one way for him to make his escape, between this guard and Captain Dickison . . . Driven to desperation, [Wilcoxson] drew his sword and made a furious charge at the captain, who fired, the shot taking effect in his left side.
>
> As their horses were moving rapidly, they passed each other. Captain Dickison quickly turned and soon gained upon his adversary, whose glittering sword flashed defiance. Again the Captain fired . . . One more shot, and his antagonist fell."[7]

Lieutenant Colonel Wilcoxson, who ran a hardware store in Norwalk, died several days later in Confederate custody. One of his men later wrote from Florida: "We have found Col Wilcoxson's grave and have fixed it up and we keep a vase of flowers on it all the while. it is in the Cemetery there. He had good care taken of him while laying in hospital there. He was a Mason "Free" and most all the Reb officers are here the Captain that shot Col. is one and he feels awful about it now."[8]

In March, while the fighting continued in multiple locations, Abraham Lincoln once again took the oath of office in Washington. In his brief inaugural address, Lincoln anticipated the close of the war, and made it clear that as soon as the Confederacy was defeated, Southerners would be welcomed back to the Union. As the sun broke through the clouds of a gray, rainy morning, the president said: "With malice toward none, with charity for all, with firmness in the right as God gives us to see the right, let us strive on to finish the work we are in, to bind up the nation's wounds, to care for him who shall have borne the battle and for his widow and his orphan, to do all which may achieve and cherish a just and lasting peace among ourselves and with all nations."

THE 15TH REGIMENT AT KINSTON

But "malice toward none" was not yet achieved. Five more weeks of hard fighting lay ahead. Connecticut's 15th Regiment, decimated by yellow fever a few months earlier, was about to meet another deadly foe.

On March 7, Union troops encountered Braxton Bragg's Confederates well entrenched near Kinston, North Carolina. The Union force drew up, and the 15th Connecticut's brigade took an advanced post close to the enemy's lines. Col. Charles Upham of Meriden commanded the advanced brigade of about 1,500 men, which held the left of the Union line. The bulk of the Federal troops remained more than a mile in the rear.

Capt. Julius Bassett (*center*) posed with his two lieutenants, Marshall C. Augur (*left*) and George C. Merriam—all three Meriden men. Captain Bassett, forty-seven, had been a blacksmith in his youth; later he went west in the gold rush, returning to Connecticut in the 1850s. At the onset of war, Bassett joined a ninety-day regiment and fought at Bull Run. In 1862, when President Lincoln asked for more troops, Julius Bassett raised Company A of the 15th Connecticut, and became its captain. He was an experienced leader in 1865 when his regiment fought the Rebels at Kinston. One of his men recalled that during the battle, "Captain Bassett of Co. A, always brave as the bravest, was brave to rashness here, repeatedly exposing himself by passing along the line almost within pistol shot of the enemy, and was finally mortally wounded by a rebel musket ball at short range." (Thorpe, *History of the Fifteenth*, p.112.)

Confederate soldiers removed Bassett's sash and sword, and presented them to their own captain, Robert Allen Carter of North Carolina's 42nd Infantry. Impressed by Captain Basset's courage, Carter always honored the memory of the Union officer. In 1886, Robert Allen Carter contacted the governor of Connecticut, seeking to return the sword to Bassett's family. Upon receiving their father's sword, Bassett's children sent Captain Carter an ebony walking stick, its gilt head engraved "Captain Robert A. Carter from the family of Captain Julius Bassett." In 1888, twenty-three years after Julius Bassett's death, Carter honored the Union officer once again, naming his newborn daughter Lilly Bassett Carter.

The next morning, the Rebels began trading shots with Upham's skirmish line. Suddenly, the Confederates "burst through like a torrent on Upham's flank."[9] Upham's men changed front and desperately tried to hold off the Rebels, as "the heaviest fire was coming from what was but a few moments before our rear, it was evident that the enemy had got between us and the main column and that we were isolated."[10]

A Rebel detachment had silently slipped around behind Upham's brigade, cutting it off from the main body of Union troops. "A flight of less than a thousand yards and the entire force ran plump into the net waiting to receive them," one soldier put it. With Bragg's Confederate force of roughly 9,000, versus Upham's 1,500—"Surrender followed as a matter of course."[11]

The fighting had left the 15th Connecticut with 25 dead and 47 wounded, while over 450 marched off as prisoners of war. Hundreds of the 15th's captured men ended up at Libby Prison in Richmond. Most would receive their paroles before the end of the war.[12]

✯✯✯

Henry C. Baldwin, a sergeant from Naugatuck, recorded his experiences as the Rebels closed in around his regiment. "I crossed the road on the right with a dozen others and attempted to make a stand in a clump of pine trees; of the twelve men, seven were shot down in less time than I write this paragraph." He continued:

> I fired once holding my rifle by the side of a tree. One ball pierced my hat and another stopped in the tree not far from my nose. I was so frightened that I think my hair had elevated my hat . . . Harmon Johnson of Co. G was standing near and raised his gun, but his forehead was that instant pierced by a minnie ball. Sergt. Smith of Co. H fell with a ball in his right knee.
>
> Before I could load my piece after taking that last shot, two Enfield rifles with a "gray back" behind each were thrust in my face, with the command, "you d——d Yank, surrender." I remarked, gracefully as I could in the circumstances, "I think I will." I was soon started with two guards toward the mill, but slipped away suddenly, resolving to get through to our lines again, and with that in mind went directly back to that very clump of trees, and as I was passing, Sergt. Smith said, "Hen, for God's sake don't leave me." I stopped and examined his wound when up came another Confederate, and took me prisoner again.[13]

All around him, Henry could see wounded men, some of them his own friends; many in great pain. As Confederate general Bragg rode by, Henry boldly stopped him and asked if he could stay on the field to help his wounded comrades. Bragg agreed. Henry approached a Confederate surgeon and proposed a trade: his fine penknife for some of the surgeon's morphine.

With morphine in hand, Henry made his way over the battlefield.

> One little Frenchman, of Co. E, I found with both hips shattered, and he had endured the agony for four long hours, and as he saw me he exclaimed, "Oh,

Sergeant, do shoot me, do shoot me." I gave him a dose of the blessed pain destroyer, and his way to death was made easy. Two hours later I looked into his face; the agonized expression was gone, and the poor boy had entered upon his last long sleep.

Elias Andrews I found was shot through the abdomen and Charley Patterson through the stomach. I administered a liberal dose of morphine to each, and before I left the field, at midnight, both had fallen asleep. The hours that day seemed longer than days.[14]

That night, Sergeant Baldwin helped load the wounded men into farm wagons, then climbed into the last wagon to accompany them to an old storehouse where he assisted a Confederate surgeon in operating on the wounded.

Hours later, their Confederate captors ordered the wounded to be loaded into railroad cars. "There was no light in the cars, and before the train reached Goldsboro, it stopped and started at least twenty times, and at every start a jerk was given that sent a thrill of agony from one end of the train to the other," Baldwin lamented. "I could distinctly hear the broken bones grate at such times."[15]

Henry was left alone to care for perhaps 100 men lying on the bare floor in varying degrees of agony. Some didn't suffer long. "Burke of Co. G died from lock-jaw as I held his head on my arm trying to pry open his teeth, to force some brandy down his throat. His arm had been amputated at the shoulder."[16]

For the next two weeks, Henry Baldwin scarcely slept. "Some of the wounded required attention every hour, and bandages were so scarce I had to wash them out and use them over and over again," he remembered. At night he lit a strip of rag stuck in a pot of grease, and made his rounds by the faint flame. One night, he found he was too exhausted to stand; crawling, he made his way around the room to tend his patients. At last he collapsed from exhaustion. When he awoke two weeks later, the war was over.

✻ ✻ ✻

Lieutenant Edwin W. Bishop, a New Haven bookkeeper, was shot down during the Battle of Kinston. One of the men explained, "When Col. Tolles found it necessary to move his skirmish line . . . it necessarily devolved on Lieut. Bishop to convey the order. To do this he had to pass over open ground which had all day been mercilessly swept by the rebel infantry fire at short range . . . Bishop went with all the alacrity and cheerfulness he would on an errand of pleasure, and even when the rebel bullet pierced his spine and laid him helpless where no aid could reach him, his cheerfulness did not desert him.

"All that afternoon, until his captured comrades carried him to the old mill within the rebel lines, and until two days afterward they were compelled to leave him lying on the floor of the Fair Ground Hospital, in Goldsboro . . . he conversed as cheerfully as if he was unharmed, although he well knew that he had but a few days, probably but a few hours, to live. In those fearful hours of misery he won the admiration of every one of his comrades, who were permitted to grasp his hand in a last farewell by the calm cheerfulness with which he faced the death he knew was inevitable." Bishop lingered for ten days before dying in the rebel prison in Salisbury, age thirty. (Thorpe, *History of the Fifteenth*, pp. 115–16.)

PECK BROS. Photographers, New Haven, Conn.

William H. H. Johnson, wounded in the right arm at Averysboro, was one of thirty-four casualties in the 20th Connecticut that day. Johnson had enlisted as a musician and became 2nd lieutenant. He survived his wound and was mustered out with his regiment in June of 1865. Soldiers with wounds to their extremities accounted for over 60 percent of the wounded that surgeons treated, since battle wounds to the head, abdomen, and chest often brought death before the victim reached a hospital. It's estimated that Union surgeons performed some 30,000 amputations. When a doctor was able to amputate within forty-eight hours of the injury, the survival rate approached 75 percent. Soldiers whose amputations were performed later were more likely to develop gangrene and die.

Averysboro and Silver Run, North Carolina, March 16, 1865

As Grant and Sherman drew the noose tighter around the neck of the South, the two sides were battling almost daily. On the morning of March 16, Connecticut's 5th and 20th Regiments clashed with the Confederate troops of Gen. Joseph Johnston at Averysboro, North Carolina.

That afternoon, the 5th Connecticut fought again in a swamp near Silver Run in what was to be the regiment's last fight. The blue coats succeeded in driving the Rebels from their works, but Capt. Ed Marvin wrote sadly:

> Lieutenant James P. Henderson was the only officer killed in this battle. He had fought his way up from a private soldier of Company F to the position he held, by faithful service alone, and it was a sad sequel to all his deservings that he should fall in the last encounter of the regiment with the enemy, and by almost the last bullet that was fired towards the regiment. He had been worth his weight in gold to the regiment. His good stories, his good spirits, his mimicry, and his practical jokes had made "Jack" Henderson the life of his company on many a dismal day, and there were tears on the cheeks of many a comrade that came to see for themselves that poor "Jack," too, was dead.[17]

✯ ✯ ✯

John Taylor Finds the 5th Connecticut

John Taylor was born enslaved on a cotton plantation in Bear Creek, North Carolina, about 1849, one of eleven children of parents "owned" by two separate planters. In March of 1865, when General Sherman and his troops came to nearby Goldsboro, fifteen-year-old Johnnie joined thousands of other African Americans seeking shelter with the Union troops.[18]

Connecticut's 5th Regiment took him in, and Johnnie probably earned his keep by working as a servant to one or more of the Yankees. One of the 5th soldiers, Cpl. Charles Hallock, took a special interest in him. When Hallock decided to have his photograph taken, he asked the teenager if he'd like to join him. Though he "didn't know what it was all about," John agreed, posing uncertainly next to the corporal.

Corporal Charles Hallock of Connecticut's 5th Regiment took John Taylor under his wing when the teenager fled to the Union lines in 1865. When the war ended, the fifteen-year-old accompanied Hallock to his hometown of Norwalk.

Hallock acted as a mentor, but some Union soldiers subjected African Americans to inhumane treatment. In one brutal "game" arranged by the whites, two African-American men ran at each other, ramming heads until one knocked the other unconscious. As an old man, Mr. Taylor "remembered full well how he was knocked out several times and he used to say 'Yes, and I knocked out quite a few of them, too.'"[19]

When the war ended, Hallock brought John Taylor home with him to Norwalk. Over the next decade, John hired himself out to local men, worked as a servant and in a hat factory. He married three times, bought a house, had children and grandchildren, and was an active church supporter. When he died in his eighties, Deacon John Taylor was so beloved in the community that the Norwalk newspaper ran his obituary and photograph on the front page.[20]

✯ ✯ ✯

Bentonville, North Carolina, March 19–21, 1865

A few days later, Sherman's troops faced the Johnnies again in nearby Bentonville. The battle had been raging for some time when the 20th Connecticut was hurried forward to relieve a brigade in the thick of combat. The Nutmeggers advanced through a swamp and into some woods, straight into "a tremendous volley from the enemy (whose lines lay concealed not more than a dozen rods from us, behind the underbrush), which we immediately returned."[21]

The battle raged until darkness fell. The 20th Regiment's lieutenant colonel reported proudly that his veteran troops "stood as firm as a rock," in the face of the enemy's onslaughts.[22]

But Cpl. Horatio Chapman wrote in anguish:

> my dear comrade, Abner Smith, than whom there was no better or [more] courageous soldier, who had marched by my side from the commencement of our enlistment in '62, almost three years, and had been in every general engagement in which the regiment had been engaged, and had been my tent-mate all the time—just as the battle closed, was wounded.
>
> I received permission to help carry him to the rear about one and a half miles to our field hospital. A minnie ball had entered his right leg just above the knee, and shattering the bone all to pieces. His leg was immediately amputated and he was laid in a tent on some straw. I . . . stayed there until the effects

of the ether passed off, and returned to the regiment . . . feeling very sad at the loss of my tent-mate and brave comrade.[23]

Abner, a poor farmer and sometime shoemaker from East Haddam, dictated a letter to his family a few days later.

> My dear wife
>
> it is under rather peculiar circumstances I cause this letter to be wrote but while some has been cut down I am still living minus one leg   feeling thank-full that I am so well as I am . . . the right leg is cut off above the knee and the wound is doing first rate   you need not worry about me
>
> I will write you again soon   I think with care I may be permited to come home before long . . . Dear children I would say a word to you   I am thankfull to god that I am so well as I am I would have you be good children till I see you again of which I hope wont be long   may god in his mercy spare us all to meet again once more in the flesh."[24]

Five days later, Abner died. After nearly three years of soldiering, the uncomplaining corporal fell with just weeks left in the conflict. He was forty years old.

HATCHER'S RUN, VIRGINIA, MARCH 25, 1865

On March 25, the 14th Connecticut men were back at Hatcher's Run, Virginia, wading through chest-deep water to attack the Confederate entrenchments on the opposite side. Here twenty-one-year-old Russell Glenn suffered a severe chest wound—the *fourth* time he'd been wounded in battle with the 14th. (Glenn somehow survived; less than a year later he married, and went on to become a Bridgeport police officer. He would live for another fifty-four years.)

PETERSBURG, VIRGINIA, MARCH 25, 1865

At Petersburg, Lee's army was steadily weakening. Theodore Vaill of the 2nd Heavies reflected on "the tattered and cadaverous [Confederate] deserters who now came over to us not only in the night but also in broad daylight."[25]

Lee knew that Sheridan, marching north, would arrive in Virginia soon to bolster Grant's forces. On March 25, the Confederate general ordered a desperate assault on the far right of the Union lines.

Just after four in the morning, hundreds of Confederate soldiers began pouring over the Union parapets, striking Fort Stedman and the adjacent batteries. In two of these batteries were stationed Connecticut's 1st Heavies.

> It was so dark that a man could hardly distinguish friend from foe, and the enemy had nearly gained possession of the batteries before the men knew of the movement. At one time, the rebels were firing part of the mortars in Battery No. 10, and our men firing the rest. The enemy made a spirited charge

on Batteries 8 and 9; but Lieut. Drown [Azro Drown of East Haddam] used his mortars with such effect, that they had to retreat, losing heavily.[26]

The 1st Heavies suffered scores of casualties in the early moments of the attack. But the Confederate success was brief. "The heavy guns which could be brought to bear from batteries 4, 5, 8, 9, and Fort Haskell (all served by the 1st Connecticut Artillery) . . . delivered so heavy a fire upon the captured works that the enemy was driven into the bombproofs, and was finally captured about 8 A.M."[27]

Grant, realizing that Lee must have drawn his assaulting troops from somewhere along the Rebel line, sent troops in a counterattack. Connecticut's 2nd Heavies charged at sunset, "across a swampy run, then over ascending ground, among stumps and scrub oaks, for twenty or thirty rods." They ran through both musketry and artillery fire that wounded twenty of them; seven fatally. The end of the day "found miles of the rebel picket lines in our possession, thousands of prisoners in our hands, and the grip of the Union armies upon Petersburg greatly tightened," wrote Adjutant Vaill.[28] Lee's promising attack had failed.

FIVE FORKS, APRIL 1, 1865

Southwest of Petersburg, Confederate general George E. Pickett's command—one infantry division and three cavalry divisions—had entrenched at an important crossroads called Five Forks. Lee had sent Picket a message: "Hold Five Forks at all hazards. Protect road to Ford's Depot and prevent Union forces from striking the Southside Railroad." Sheridan had to be prevented from reaching the railroad, the Confederates' supply route. But on April 1, Pickett and several of his officers rode off to enjoy a dinner of spring shad several miles away—leaving the rebel troops without a commander as Sheridan brought up his army.

The men of Connecticut's 1st Cavalry–without food for the last day and a half—would fight dismounted that day at Five Forks. Their colonel, Brayton Ives, advanced his soldiers in line of battle to the edge of a wooded area. Looking out before them toward the enemy, the men saw an open field with a peach orchard in full bloom beyond it. A Union officer rode up, shouting that the orchard hid an unsupported Rebel battery. Colonel Ives remembered:

> Officers and men entreated me by looks and words to allow them to go forward; and I think I was persuaded by Capt. Parmelee. I sat on my horse near him; and I never shall forget his eagerness to advance, nor the appealing look he gave me.

Uriah N. Parmelee

Brayton Ives

> Unable to resist longer, I cried, "Forward!" and with a yell the First Connecticut charged "on the run." But no sooner had we reached the outer edge of the woods than the peaceful-looking peach-orchard assumed a different character. The bright pink blossoms were blown into the air by bullets, shells, canister, and grapeshot. Every man who had gone into the open field was shot down. Fortunately, another staff-officer rode up with an order for the line to retire. Just at this moment, a shell struck Capt. Pamelee in the breast, killing him instantly.[29]

General Sheridan himself came forward to lead a successful charge on Pickett's left flank; later, Union cavalry swept around the right of the Rebel line as well. Thousands of Pickett's men were forced to flee or surrender—and with the rout went General Lee's last chance of protecting his supply line on the Southside Railroad.

Petersburg, Virginia, April 2, 1865

With the Confederacy on the verge of disintegration, Grant moved to cement the Union's success. He ordered an assault on the Rebel works at Petersburg to begin at dawn.

Connecticut's 2nd Heavy Artillery, acting as infantry at the left of the Union line, charged "with a great rush and a yell," racing toward the Confederate breastworks.

> There was but little firing on our side,—but with bayonets fixed, the boys went in—not in a very mathematical right line, but strongly and surely.—on, on,

until the first line was carried. Then, invigorated and greatly encouraged by success, they pressed on,—the opposing fire slackening every moment,—on, on, through the abbattis and ditch, up the steep bank, over the parapet, into the rebel camp that had but just been deserted. Then, and there, the long tried and ever faithful soldiers of the Republic saw DAYLIGHT!—and such a shout as tore the concave of that morning sky, it were worth dying to hear.[30]

Was it possible? For nine months, the Union army had been holding Petersburg in siege—now, Yankee soldiers were standing in the enemy's entrenchments. As the 2nd Heavies continued to push forward toward the city, they were raked by artillery fire from Rebel defenders in the inner lines. But "suddenly, hurrah!" wrote Theodore Vaill; "a column of reinforcements comes over the hill by Fort Fisher! The rebels turn their guns in that direction, but to no purpose;—for the Twenty-Fourth Corps marches steadily forward, . . . one of the most magnificent sights our soldiers ever saw."[31]

Marching with the 24th Corps were the men of Connecticut's 10th Regiment, veterans of over a score of battles. Their orders were to take Fort Gregg, a stockaded fort surrounded by a moat, and armed with two pieces of artillery. Only about 330 Confederates held Fort Gregg, with another 200 or so in the adjacent fort (alternately called Fort Whitworth and Fort Baldwin). But these Rebel soldiers would fight with terrible determination: upon them rested the future of Lee's army. If they could hold off the 4,400 Union attackers long enough, Lee could evacuate Petersburg and get his soldiers to safety.

Inside Fort Gregg and Fort Whitworth, the rebels had grimly prepared for the onslaught, gathering extra muskets and ammunition. While some soldiers would fire through the stockade's loopholes, others would quickly reload the extra weapons, ensuring a continual small-arms fire.

As Union general John Gibbon readied his troops for the charge, the 10th Connecticut soldiers surveyed the two forts in the distance. They would have to cross over five hundred yards of open ground, pass through a moat, and then scale the walls—some fifteen feet high—to fight their way in. All of this would be under fire from both artillery and musketry.

In the assaulting force were thousands of veteran soldiers who had experienced the worst of war over the last four years—yet for many, this battle was to remain in their memories as the most brutal. Soldier after soldier, both blue and gray, described the fight for Fort Gregg as "desperate."

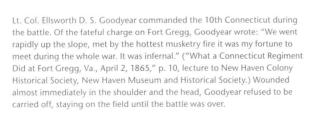

Lt. Col. Ellsworth D. S. Goodyear commanded the 10th Connecticut during the battle. Of the fateful charge on Fort Gregg, Goodyear wrote: "We went rapidly up the slope, met by the hottest musketry fire it was my fortune to meet during the whole war. It was infernal." ("What a Connecticut Regiment Did at Fort Gregg, Va., April 2, 1865," p. 10, lecture to New Haven Colony Historical Society, New Haven Museum and Historical Society.) Wounded almost immediately in the shoulder and the head, Goodyear refused to be carried off, staying on the field until the battle was over.

The 10th's chaplain, Henry Clay Trumbull, set out with the men on the charge.

It was impossible to keep up an unbroken line in crossing the fire-swept plain of death, but the orders were for every man to make, at any cost, for that fort, and for all to rally on the face of its embankment. The colors were, of course, to be the rallying-point, and to get those colors there was the duty and pride of their devoted bearers and guard. At the word, our men started on the run. Both the national and the state flags were in the race; but they were a special target for the enemy . . . Officers and men dropped by the way, but others pushed on, and the colors were quickly taken up by new bearers as often as they went down.

A color-sergeant bearing our state flag had dropped just before this charge was ordered. Corporal Northrop took the colors in his place. He fell wounded before the ditch was reached. Corporal Phillips and Corporal Parmalee of the colorguard caught at the falling flag, in the storm of grape and bullets, saying cheerily: "Let's take hold of it together, and run for the fort. Maybe one of us will get there."

In the charge across the plain to the fort, flag bearers fell one after another. Still, every time the flag went down, another soldier picked it up and raced on. Sgt. Allen Tucker earned the Medal of Honor that day for "gallantry as color bearer in the assault on Fort Gregg." A teamster from the town of Sprague, Tucker had fought at Bull Run before enlisting in the 10th Regiment.

Both of them got there. Through the ditch, up the slope toward the parapet, they carried the blue flag of Connecticut . . . There they held it as a rallying-point for the irregular besieging line struggling across the death-swept plain . . .

Corporal Phillips was barely nineteen at that time, yet he had been already three years in service. As he held up that flag above the parapet, his life was nothing to him in its comparison . . . Reporting his service afterwards to his commander, he said drily: "I worried 'em with the flag. I'd shake it in their faces and when they'd grab it, Parmalee would shoot 'em."[32]

For perhaps thirty minutes, the two sides fought hand to hand; the enlisted men using bayonets and clubbed muskets, the officers striking with their swords. It was one thing to shoot an enemy who was two hundred yards away; it was quite another to plunge a bayonet into his chest when you could see his face.

"Union and Rebel soldiers were found dead in each other's grasp, thirteen Rebels were found inside the Fort killed by bayonet thrusts, and scores were wounded by the same weapon."[33]

At last, Union troops overwhelmed those on the parapet and surged into the fort. With scarcely a man left unwounded, the Confederates surrendered. Capt. Francis Hickerson of the 10th, with three companies, assaulted the adjacent Fort Baldwin, which fell as well.

At battle's end, the men of the 10th had paid a high price: of the 193 engaged that day, 126 of them were wounded or killed.[34]

And the Confederate soldiers in the two forts, with unwavering courage, had offered themselves up in order to buy General Lee the time he needed. His forces withdrew from both Petersburg and Richmond, and began a rapid march to the west.

"Lee ordered his troops to assemble at Amelia Court House," said Grant, "his object being to get away, join Johnston if possible, and try to crush Sherman before I could get there."[35]

RICHMOND

General Lee sent word to evacuate the Confederate capital. On the night of April 2, Union troops outside of Richmond could hear multiple explosions. Early on the morning of April 3, soldiers of the 29th Connecticut Regiment hurried into the city.

Richmond was in ruins. Smoke drifted through shells of buildings—houses, factories, shops—destroyed by Union artillery fire. Before the government fled, officials had destroyed much of what they couldn't take with them. Hundreds of Union soldiers moved through the devastation in wonder.

The men of Connecticut's 29th Regiment were among the first to enter Richmond after the capital city fell. The following day they were elated to see Abraham Lincoln arrive with his son Tad, and walk through the city surrounded by cheering African Americans. ("Union Troops Entering Richmond," *Frank Leslie's Illustrated News*, April 25, 1865.)

The following day, April 4, a boat approached on the river. President Lincoln stepped ashore with his son Tad, and they began walking. Alexander Newton, sergeant in the 29th Connecticut, wrote:

> It was a sight never to be forgotten. He passed through the main street. There were multitudes of Colored people to greet him on every hand. They received him with many demonstrations that came from the heart, thanking God that they had seen the day of their salvation, that freedom was theirs, that now they could live in this country, like men and women . . .
>
> I noticed one white lady in a window, who turned away from the whole scene as if in utter disgust. There were still two sides to the question, then and there are two sides to it today. How long will these two sides remain, is the question.
>
> As the President looked out upon the poor Colored people and remembered how many lives had been lost in working out their salvation, he was not able to keep the tears from his eyes. They were tears of gladness and sorrow, of regret and delight; but the tears of my own people were the tears of the greatest joy.
>
> The President went to the state capitol where he made a short address in which he said: "Now you Colored people are free, as free as I am. God has made you free and if those who are your superiors are not able to recognize that you are free, we will have to take the sword and musket and again teach them that you are free. You are as free as I am, having the same rights of liberty, life and the pursuit of happiness."[36]

THE RETREAT

As Lee pushed his army toward North Carolina, Union troops were right at his heels. The Confederates were suffering from hunger; supply wagons were unable to connect with the army. Lee aimed for Appomattox Station to meet a supply train.

On April 6, Sheridan's cavalry was able to cut off almost a quarter of Lee's army from the main body. Here Connecticut's 2nd Heavies once more took the field, advancing across Sailor's Creek and into a hot fire from the desperate Rebels. By late afternoon, the Heavies had the Confederates on the run.

The next day, the 1st Connecticut Cavalry was in the lead. "It attacked Lee's wagon train near Harper's Farm, and routing the guard, separated; Colonel Ives with the right battalion charged a battery in the woods defended by infantry, and captured five guns with caissons, men, and horses, and two battle-flags; Major Moorehouse with the left battalion went towards the head of the train, capturing men, horses, and mules, and burning wagons."[37] As dusk gathered, the Union force charged once again on the enemy, taking thousands of Rebel prisoners.

"On the 9th Sheridan saw that the end was near. He had cut off the enemy's way of retreat and was just advancing to a grand final charge."[38]

Confederate forces fought their way through the Union cavalry, only to find that the Union's 24th Corps was waiting in line of battle, and the 5th Corps ready beside it. General Lee said wretchedly, "Then there is nothing left me but to go and see General Grant and I would rather die a thousand deaths."[39]

Lt. Col. E. W. Whitaker of the 1st Cavalry, now acting as chief of staff to General Custer, wrote of the rapidly evolving events:

> After passing the artillery as General Custer was about to order a charge, a rebel officer, named Capt. Sims of Gen. Longstreet's staff met us (I was riding by General Custer's side at head of the column) and said General Lee asks a suspension of hostilities. General Custer (as quick as lightning) said Whitaker take the flag go with this officer to General Lee with my compliments and tell him I can not stop this charge unless he announces an unconditional surrender as I am not sole in command on this field.

> Capt. Sims guided me to where he left Generals Lee, Gordon and Longstreet. I found there only Generals Gordon and Longstreet who explained that they were in command as General Lee had galloped off to the rear to find General Grant immediately after authorizing a request for a suspension of hostilities.

Whitaker recalled that "by good luck [Confederate Captain Robert M.] Sims found a white towel in his saddle bag." Hanging it from the tip of his sword, he approached the Union lines to urge a cessation of the attack. (Letter of Edward Washburn Whitaker, April 29, 1901, to General Joshua Lawrence Chamberlain, Edward W. Whitaker Collection, State Archives, Connecticut State Library, Hartford.)

> These Generals both assured me of an absolute surrender and that they were personally satisfied of the result the night before, but that General Lee still had hope of being able to get through to Lynchburg and with that expectation ordered the charge by Gordon's command which had been repulsed by infantry. I was suspicious of their good faith as all firing had not stopped and artillery with smoking guns was passing us, and while hesitating about my report to General Custer they very impatiently begged me to hurry and to first stop that infantry line with the announcement. I consented to do so only stipulating that a rebel officer go with me.

> I galloped out to the infantry line and steered for what appeared to be the Commander's flag and announced the surrender of Lee's Army . . .

> The moment the surrender was announced the greatest, loudest cheers I ever heard went up from right to left along your line . . . I at once galloped across the field to General Custer to whom I repeated the announcement of an unconditional surrender of the rebel army, and then was repeated that shout of joy all along the cavalry line.[40]

Connecticut's cavalrymen escorted Ulysses Grant to a brick house in Appomattox Courthouse where Robert E. Lee waited. The two generals finalized the surrender documents about four o'clock that afternoon.

GLORIOUS NEWS !

SURRENDER OF LEE AND HIS WHOLE ARMY!

THE LAST PROP OF THE RE-BELLION BROKEN !

Correspondence Between Generals Grant and Lee !

THE END OF THE WAR!

PEACE ! UNION ! HAPPINESS !

"Peace! Union! Happiness!" proclaimed the *Hartford Daily Courant* on April 10, 1865. A frenzy of rejoicing swept through Hartford when the good news arrived by telegraph on the night of the surrender. At ten p.m., church bells were ringing across the city, and thousands of residents poured into the streets. "Around the telegraph office an immense crowd collected, and cheered and re-cheered amid the wildest enthusiasm." Revelers lit bonfires, and an impromptu parade formed, with marchers carrying lanterns and flags, and blowing horns. "Many buildings were illuminated . . . and ladies appeared at windows waving flags and handkerchiefs . . . The enthusiasm . . . was beyond anything this people have witnessed before." (*Hartford Daily Courant*, April 10, 1865.) In the following days, celebrations erupted throughout Connecticut: fireworks in West Hartford, a concert by Colt's band in New Britain, cannons firing in Southington, and in Glastonbury, men and women singing patriotic songs in the streets.

As the momentous day unfolded, Nelson Stowe of the 14th Regiment recorded events in his diary: "Packed up and left camp at 7 A M. Moved out on the Lynchburg Road. Heavy firing ahead at 7:30. Sheridan has them cut off. Lee attacks in three different places, but repulsed each time and sends in a Flag of Truce for forms of capitulation and at 3 PM surrenders . . . Salutes fired, bands playing, troops cheering, hats flying and in fact our army perfectly crazy."[41]

As General Meade rode through the Army of the Potomac with news of Lee's surrender, a glorious chaos ensued.

> Men were completely beside themselves; they flunk [flung] their caps into the air, threw their knapsacks under his horse's feet; danced and laughed and shouted and rolled on the ground and cried all at the same time. Men who declared when they went into that field in the morning that they were so foot-sore that another step was impossible went out of that field that afternoon to the tune of Yankee Doodle, with steps as light as boys just out of school.[42]

Joy Turned to Sorrow

Just days later, a young corporal from Connecticut recorded the devastating news in his diary:

> Reported the assassination of our beloved President. At first it could not be believed . . . It was a great shock and cast a great gloom over our camp. How sudden the change. Joy turned to sorrow, when we were rejoicing over the prospects of peace and the end of the cruel war. At first it was reported that he might recover. Later report he was dead.
>
> We could not do anything but talk over the sad event. We all became angry and hated the South worse than ever. Thought all the leaders should be condemned to death. Indignation and rage was expressed alike by citizens and the soldiers.[43]

Soldiers showed their grief for Lincoln by wearing mourning bands, as this unidentified sergeant displayed on his right arm. I. J. Hill, of Connecticut's 29th Regiment, was stricken. "This good and God-fearing President . . . bore to heaven the fetters of four millions of slaves, and I think I can hear him say to the Father of all good spirits, 'These are they that came up through great tribulation.' . . . No class of people feel his death as the colored people do, for we have lost the best friend we had on earth, our great deliverer." (I. J. Hill, *A Sketch of the 29th Regiment of Connecticut Colored Troops*, p. 28.)

The people of the North fell into a stunned sorrow in the midst of their celebrations. In the town of Windham, Connecticut, a six-year-old boy named Allen Bennett Lincoln observed the shocking turn of events, which he never forgot.

> First came the joyous news of the fall of Richmond, when bells rang and cannons boomed. Young and old displayed the national colors. My own special delight was in a tiny flag worn proudly in the hat or carried running in the breeze—we little folks had them, we knew not really why, but we knew and felt that some great joy was at hand.

> Then came the sudden plunging into deepest grief, our little flags were trimmed with crepe, and the church bells tolled, and solemn services were held, men and women wept like children. The great grief hangs even now like a heavy pall over my childhood's memory . . . They said the President was dead, shot by the hand of a traitor."[44]

In cities and towns across Connecticut, church bells tolled as somber citizens made their way to funeral ceremonies held at the same time as the president's funeral in Washington. Public buildings were draped in black; schools and businesses were closed. American flags trimmed in black crepe hung from shops and homes. It was "a sad, sad day, not soon to be forgotten," the *Hartford Daily Courant* affirmed.[45]

Peace

As the reality of Lee's surrender set in, many Confederate soldiers, hungry and far from home, came forward to turn themselves in. In the 14th Connecticut, "the men mingled freely with the Confederates and all were mutually glad the war was at last over."[46] On April 26, Gen. Joseph E. Johnston surrendered his forces, and the remaining Confederate units laid down their arms soon thereafter.

The government planned a Grand Review of the Union forces, to be held in Washington on May 23 and 24, and some Connecticut regiments soon began their journeys to the capital city. The 14th Regiment set out from Virginia with some 200 miles ahead of them, "but every mile covered brought the men nearer to their homes, there was little complaint and the route was enlivened by songs and jests and joyousness . . . Every step of the men grew firmer, the eye brighter and the musket grasped with more loving grip than ever."[47] Still, their jubilation faded as the regiment "approached the land overlooking Fredericksburg. Here they found many tokens of the fight for the possession of the city. The men marched on quietly without noise, as if conscious of moving over ground sanctified by the suffering and death of their comrades."[48]

On the day the 18th Connecticut began their march toward home, Charles Lynch wrote in his diary:

> Taps sounded later than usual last night. When the lights were put out we could not sleep for joy, as we were all so happy over the prospect of going home. I cannot write and do justice to those happy hours. Will remain with me as long as memory lasts. The hymns heard mostly last night were "Oh Happy Day" and "We are going home, to die no more." Everybody can sing at this time if they never can again.
>
> Reveille sounded very early this morning, for the last time at Martinsburg. Broke camp . . . In line, waiting for orders to march. This is a fine morning.
>
> We shall soon be homeward bound. When orders were given to march great excitement prevailed. Cheers and shouting as we marched along.[49]

On the twenty-third of May, the 14th Connecticut took part in the Grand Review through the streets of Washington, parading before President Andrew Johnson and the cabinet members, to the cheers of thousands. The procession of the 14th's ragged veterans—numbering fewer than 250 now—was a far cry from the 1862 review when the jaunty new regiment, a thousand strong, had burst into song before President Lincoln.

HOMECOMINGS

In Windham, Connecticut, six-year-old Allen B. Lincoln witnessed the soldier boys reaching home at war's end: "boys in faded blue, with garments war-worn, flags tattered and faces haggard. I can see them now, as though it were but yesterday, standing there on Union Street, in front of the Baptist Church . . . and though the spectacle was to our childish minds simply one of awe and wonder, we felt that somehow those men had suffered."[50]

In the Fairfield County village of Georgetown, Wilbur F. Thompson gave a touching image of a company of local men coming home:

> Those who are still living who saw the soldiers on the train that morning will never forget the sight . . . bearded, ragged and bronzed men, some shaking with fever and ague, others weak from sickness. The company formed and marched up the street past the old armory . . . Wives were marching with husbands; sons and daughters were carrying fathers' knapsacks and muskets. At the head of the company marched two great negroes, George Washington and Ed Lewis (who had come from the south with the soldiers,) loaded down with knapsacks and muskets of men who were too weak to carry them. This was the home-coming of Company E.[51]

Hundreds of Connecticut men arrived home as damaged as the tattered, bullet-torn flags they carried. Orsamus R. Fyler had been a strong and hearty twenty-two-year-old when he enlisted in 1862. He returned to Torrington in 1865, feeble, suffering, and permanently disabled. As his regiment, the 2nd Heavy Artillery, had charged the Rebels at Winchester, Fyler fell with a bullet in his leg. The shot shattered his tibia, but instead of amputating his leg, a surgeon cut out the three-inch section of bone that was damaged. As the wound healed, Fyler's leg became twisted and shortened, as the engraving showed. He was never able to bear weight on the injured leg, and had to wear a seven-pound brace. For the rest of his life, he walked with a crutch, and was never without pain. His physician wrote, thirteen years after the injury: "I consider his present condition worse than if he had amputation above the knee; locomotion is very painful indeed" (Pension document written by Dr. H. E. Gates of Litchfield, Connecticut, in 1877, in *Medical and Surgical History of the War of the Rebellion*, part 3, vol. 2, p. 446.). Fyler preserved the bullet that changed his life, but he never let his battle wound hold him back. He married Mary Vaill (pictured here) and went on to become a wealthy and prominent public figure. Today his home is the headquarters of the Torrington Historical Society, whose collection includes the Rebel bullet from Fyler's leg.

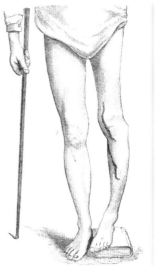

Charles Lynch recorded the welcome that awaited his regiment, the 18th, in Norwich: "A great parade and reception to our regiment . . . on the parade, many people were in tears, and we knew the reason why. Their husbands and boys did not come home. While we were happy we did not forget the good fellows and the homes that contained a vacant chair."[52]

When the 14th Regiment returned to Hartford, after fighting in twenty-four engagements, the *Courant* reported its arrival in somber tones. Worn and ragged, the 14th men were but a remnant of the proud regiment that set forth in 1862.

> The first of our Connecticut three years' regiments to return is the Fourteenth; it reached here Saturday forenoon shortly after ten o'clock, on the steamer Granite State, from New York, and it comes bearing evidence of its heroism.
>
> In the fall of 1862, it left Hartford with over one thousand men; since then it has received over one thousand recruits, and now the rank and file step from the boat upon the wharf, and the hundreds of men, women and children who throng the landing to catch sight of the brave veterans count one, two, three— *two hundred and twenty-six!*
>
> The story is told. Yet sad as it is, there is glory in it. The nation is saved; freedom has triumphed; and this band of brave men are heroes for all time.[53]

Soldiers of the Union Mustered Out

THE AFTERMATH

Charlie Upham came home to Meriden with a bullet in his shoulder. In 1862, serving as a captain in Connecticut's 8th Regiment, he'd been wounded in the Battle of New Bern, North Carolina. He would carry the bullet in his flesh for eighteen years without complaint. Upham's doctor described his condition in 1871:

> a rifle ball entered the left shoulder at the top, breaking the bone [and] passing under the clavicle where it now remains. The present effect of the wound is constant lameness of the shoulder and two running sores, one on the top of shoulder and one on the back . . . it is with great difficulty that he can do any labor with the left arm . . . Sometimes the arm is so lame that it hangs by his side for a month . . . at such times he can only use the left arm by taking hold of it with the right hand.[1]

For his disability, Upham received a pension of $6.66 a month. Eventually a doctor was able to remove the bullet, which Charlie would keep.

Upham's other war injury was less evident. In 1863, while home on furlough, Charlie had married his sweetheart, Emma Clark. Just a few days later, he had to leave his bride and return to his regiment in the South. Within the year, Emma gave birth to their daughter. Charles could not, of course, come home for the birth, nor was he home when his young wife died from complications ten days later.

The uniform that Capt. Charles Upham wore in the Battle of Newbern, North Carolina, bears a gash from the bullet that struck his shoulder. For almost two decades the rifle ball remained lodged under his collarbone, causing pain, stiffness, and running sores. When it was finally removed, Upham preserved the lead bullet, striated from the trim of the shoulder strap it passed through.

At Gettysburg, Union artillery fire blew off one of George Warner's arms, and shattered the other, forcing his surgeon into a double amputation. A New Haven resident, Warner lived to be ninety-one years old.

"We are not the same people that we were, and never can be again," Rev. Horace Bushnell acknowledged soon after the close of the war.[2]

George W. Warner had lost both his arms at Gettysburg. A teacher before the war, Warner now faced a dilemma: How was he to support his large family? In addition to his pension of seventy-two dollars a month, Warner sold photographs of himself (sometimes with his family), exposing the "empty sleeves" that made clear his sacrifice for the nation.

In 1885, when the 20th Connecticut dedicated its monument at Gettysburg, George Warner had the honor of unveiling the memorial, which was draped in a large American flag. A rope ran from the flag to a pulley in a nearby tree, and then was fastened to Warner's waist. At a signal, Warner walked away from the monument, raising the flag and the spirits of his comrades.

For Oliver Dart of South Windsor, the Battle of Fredericksburg would change his life forever. When a shell exploded in the midst of his regiment, a "fragment tore off most of the face of Dart, frightfully disfiguring him for life," wrote the 14th's chaplain, Henry Stevens.[3]

"The reality of war," wrote one amputee, "is largely obscured by descriptions that tell of movements and maneuvers of armies, of the attack and repulse, of the victory and defeat, and then pass on to new operations. All of this leaves out of sight the fellows stretched out with holes through them, or with legs and arms off."[4]

Disfigured soldiers even faced hostility. One veteran wrote bitterly that at the beginning of the war, "every soldier was a hero . . . it was not until they began to lose their arms, and legs, and heads, and were thus rendered proportionately helpless and homely, that they depreciated in value; it was not until several years after the war, that people became educated up to that standard of patriotism and humanity that they could drive the crippled veteran from their streets, because he sought to earn an honest, though humble living, with a hand-organ."[5]

Not all war wounds were visible. Artillerymen suffered hearing loss. Insanity, alcoholism, and drug addiction afflicted many survivors. Sanford Perkins, the 14th's lieutenant colonel, never fully recovered from a severe neck wound; a decade later, "insanity followed a series of epileptic fits and he was removed to the state insane asylum where he died," wrote Henry P. Goddard, one of his officers.[6]

On a farm in Windham, an elderly couple kept their veteran son, Cornelius Dayton, locked in a cage. In 1863, Cornelius had suffered hyperthermia while his regiment, the 28th Connecticut, lay in the trenches at Port Hudson, Louisiana. Hundreds of other Union soldiers were experiencing the same condition, which they called "sunstroke." Many died, but Cornelius had survived with brain damage.

"Bereft of all senses and violently mad a good share of the time, Cornelius S. Dayton . . . since his return from the battlefields has lived in a one-room building ten by ten feet, the interior of which is a lattice work of iron," wrote the *New York Tribune* in 1910. "At times he carries spoons as he did a gun in the war, believing he is on guard duty."[7] Dayton was seventy-three when he died. He had lived nearly half a century in the enclosure on his family's farm.

Even more pitiful were the damaged veterans with no one to care for them. In Darien, a retired merchant named Benjamin Fitch anticipated their need. Before the war ended, he opened a home for disabled soldiers in the Noroton section of Darien. "Fitch's Home for Soldiers" provided a home and medical care for disabled or penniless Connecticut veterans. The complex grew to include a chapel, library, hospital, art gallery, and cemetery.

After Benjamin Fitch's death, the state assumed control of the home. By 1910, over 500 veterans were living there. They woke to the sound of reveille, and turned in at taps. The drum's "long roll" announced each death.

Surely She Gave Her Life for Her Country

Decades after the war ended, a small, frail woman on crutches would make her laborious way up the steps of the Bureau of Pensions in Washington. It was a familiar trip for Guilford native Harriet Hawley.

During the war, Harriet had worked as a nurse, caring for wounded soldiers at Armory Square Hospital in Washington. Now, a few blocks away and many years later, she volunteered for disabled veterans who needed help obtaining their pensions from the government.

Amputations, open wounds, deafness, frostbite, chronic diarrhea, sunstroke, insanity— many disabilities left men unable to hold regular jobs, or to work at all. A pension promised a veteran a frugal living, or a much-needed subsidy to what he earned.

But it was no easy task for a soldier to document his infirmity and prove that it originated with his war service. For many Connecticut veterans who couldn't manage it for themselves, Harriet Hawley tracked down old comrades and officers who could corroborate a man's story— often writing fifteen letters a day—and kept careful records of each soldier's case.

A veteran from Connecticut's 1st Light Battery remembered:

> For twenty years of her life after the war, while suffering from injuries . . .
> she manifested an intense interest in the crippled and disabled soldiers . . .
> Well do I remember her at the State encampment in Niantic, in the year 1885, a
> few months before her death, supported on crutches, going among the veteran
> soldiers and making inquiries as to their welfare, and being especially anxious

about those whose claims upon the Government she was doing her best to have adjusted. Many a crippled and disabled soldier has to thank her for her loving interest and persistent efforts on his behalf. Surely she gave her life for her country as much as anyone.[8]

When Harriet died in 1886, old soldiers crowded into her funeral in Hartford, and veterans of her husband's 7th Regiment carried her coffin to the hearse. They remembered her devotion to the wounded, her selflessness, her sense of duty, calling her "one of the bravest and most heroic of women." Harriet Hawley "had earned the love of every soldier."[9] Every year on Decoration Day (now known as Memorial Day), her sister Kate noted, the veterans "always mark her grave in the cemetery with a little flag and flowers just as they do those of the other soldiers."[10]

COMRADES FOREVER

In the weeks and months and years after peace was declared, many former soldiers found it difficult to reenter civilian life and live once more with their families. For years, the men had been looking forward to going home. But now, a bleak emptiness pervaded many of them.

Back in their home communities, the men found they needed each other. They'd fought at each other's sides, slept in the same tents, shared meals, and marched hundreds of miles together. Now they drew together, socializing or just offering the silent support of another soldier who understood his comrade's feelings.

The bond of shared experience united entire regiments for annual reunions and banquets where the men could reminisce. Veterans of the 14th Connecticut observed the anniversary of the Battle of Antietam together, and planned to continue the annual gathering "as long as there are any of us left who can walk, talk, or shake hands."[11]

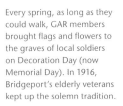

Every spring, as long as they could walk, GAR members brought flags and flowers to the graves of local soldiers on Decoration Day (now Memorial Day). In 1916, Bridgeport's elderly veterans kept up the solemn tradition.

While veterans often remained connected to their own regiments, thousands also joined a national organization of Union veterans called the Grand Army of the Republic. The G.A.R. had local chapters in cities and towns across the North. By 1890, the G.A.R. claimed nearly half a million members, who wore military-style uniforms for their meetings, outings, and parades. The group became a political force, using its influence to elect five former soldiers as presidents, and pressuring the government to provide military pensions.

The G.A.R. offered Civil War veterans camaraderie, support, and respect, decade after decade. World War I came and went; but the old soldiers still gathered. In Cheshire, the Edward A. Doolittle Post was still meeting in 1937—more than three-quarters of a century after the Civil War began.

COMMEMORATING

[A]fter monuments have grown old and time has effaced their inscriptions, the names will still be remembered, all of them,—written on the hearts of grateful countrymen.[12]

Now that the Union had finally won, Connecticut's people felt a need to commemorate the great struggle and those who had fought in it. Towns and cities across the state, eager to honor their own soldiers, commissioned scores of monuments, from Portland's soldier statue carved of local brownstone, to the yellow brick Memorial Hall in Madison. The townspeople of Kensington had erected a stone obelisk to their soldiers even before the war ended.

Old soldiers of the 14th Connecticut stood proudly before their regimental monument at Antietam. At battlefield reunions, they once again sat beside the campfire, sharing stories and singing the old songs together.

After Eben Hall was killed by a Rebel sharpshooter at Petersburg, two remembrances of him endured—one of stone and one of paper. In 1888, the town of Suffield erected a granite monument to honor its Civil War soldiers. Eben Hall's name begins the engraved list of those who gave their lives for the Union. Eben had enlisted as a private just after the war began, rising to become corporal and then sergeant in the 1st Heavy Artillery. In April of 1864, he received a promotion to second lieutenant. The regiment had only a few short weeks before it was sent to man the big guns at Petersburg, but in that time Eben made it into Washington to have the renowned Brady Studio photograph him in his officer's uniform. Less than three months later, he was killed.

Veterans often found the most meaning in battlefield monuments that honored their own regiments. Stone memorials—some stately, others simple—marked the places where they had fought, and where their friends and comrades had fallen. At Gettysburg, for instance, where six Connecticut regiments fought, all six erected monuments—some more than one.

Gettysburg continued to have a powerful pull on the old soldiers. Over 53,000 Union and Confederate veterans encamped there in 1913 to observe the battle's fiftieth anniversary. In 1938, seventy-five years after the battle, 1,800 Civil War veterans came to Gettysburg. They walked the battlefield under a blazing hot sun, and slept in tents at night. Their average age was ninety-four.

At Gettysburg's famous stone wall, a veteran sat and reflected. Here, in July of 1863, the men of the 14th Connecticut had watched Pickett's charge approaching. That afternoon would become the turning point of the war.

The 14th's chaplain, Henry S. Stevens, captured the feelings of the old soldiers as they visited that wall decades later. "Gettysburg has lived in your memories and conversation all the intervening years . . . You once more look on the fields and positions that have been pictured in your memories, upon this wall that has almost a *sacred* significance to you, and the old *thrill* comes back to you; and you will carry away that thrill with you and keep it—aye, forever!" (Henry S. Stevens, *Address Delivered at the Dedication of the Monument of the 14th Connecticut Volunteers at Gettysburg*, p. 25.)

Robert Kellogg, who'd survived imprisonment at Andersonville, spoke:

> We stand here as citizens of a great, powerful and prosperous country, the hope of the oppressed of all the world, thankful that in its day of direful need there was a great army of those who willingly gave life itself in its defense.
>
> Andersonville becomes an object lesson in patriotism. To this retired and beautiful spot will thousands resort in the long years to come, to learn again and again the lessons of heroic sacrifice made by those who quietly sleep in these long rows of graves. Erecting this beautiful monument to their memory, we will leave them where they died, to sleep in the shadow of these friendly oaks, with the song of the wood-thrush and the mocking-bird for requiem. We who still remain will again take up the active duties of life, glad to be able to still lend a hand and striving to so acquit ourselves as to be worthy of those who lives we here commemorate.[13]

CALLING UP THE PAST

Soldiers brought back all kinds of things from the war: trophies of battle (a captured Confederate sword, for instance) held places of honor beside more personal items (a battered tin cup that brought back the familiar taste of coffee cooked over the camp fire). Veterans preserved bullets picked up from the battlefield, photographs of buddies who didn't return home, even the army's reviled hardtack.

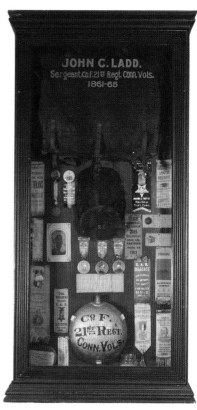

John Ladd's carefully arranged collection of army gear and veteran memorabilia showed that he still strongly identified himself as a soldier many years after the war had ended. Sergeant Ladd's knapsack, forage cap, and canteen hang alongside a tintype of him in uniform, and a Confederate button kept as a souvenir. Ribbons and badges represent reunions of his regiment, the 21st Connecticut, and local veterans' groups.

Some soldiers opted for elaborate memorials of their Civil War service. George Meech brought home handfuls of Southern cotton (*right*) that subtly represented the root cause of the conflict.

For rarity, no one could top the trophy Maj. Albert Brooker took home to Torrington: a Rebel hat (*far right*) of butternut felt with a rattlesnake band. The hat's story is lost to history, making it impossible for us to know if Brooker considered it merely a curious artifact, or if it recalled to him an exploit of the Rebel soldier who wore it. When the hat was passed down to a Torrington youth, it always enlivened show-and-tell at school.

Such mementoes directly linked an old soldier to his war experiences and his comrades. But the objects also served to tell his stories to others: many a veteran proudly displayed war souvenirs at home, subtly informing visitors of his courage and sacrifices. And while a faded infantry cap always reminded a veteran of his past, it could also create a link to the future, allowing an old man to connect with his grandson, and retell the war stories that might carry through the generations.

BATTLE FLAG DAY

Only soldiers who have watched and defended a flag in the hours of battle can realize how much the flag was to those who gave their lives for it, or who were ready to die.[14]

It was no wonder the 8th Regiment's flag was in shreds. The veterans couldn't help reflecting that it was exactly seventeen years ago that their color-bearers had fallen at Antietam, one after another—until eleven of them had been killed or mortally wounded, and the flags themselves were riddled with holes. Other regiments' banners were equally tattered. If anything, the men loved their flags even more reverently because of the bullet holes and wear.

Now they could honor the flags once again: September 17, 1879, was Battle-Flag Day in Hartford. Connecticut's veterans, along with scores of bands, would march with their national and regimental flags to the Capitol, where each regiment would present its banners to be carefully preserved in special cases.

By early afternoon, when the parade stepped off, over 8,000 veterans were in the ranks. A crowd estimated at 100,000 people cheered the old soldiers who marched with their regiments, or rode in carriages. Rev. Thomas Brown, the 21st Regiment's chaplain, marched with his "boys" though he was eighty-one years old. In the 12th Connecticut marched Jonathan Reynolds, who'd lost a leg at Winchester, Virginia, and now wore a wooden one. Englebert Sauter, wounded as color-bearer in the 13th Regiment, once more carried the flag. Many of the men were limping, or had an empty sleeve pinned up.

A committee of women had tried to stabilize the flags for the parade, but their efforts met with varying success. As Harriet Hawley bent over the flags of her husband Joe's regiment, her eyes filled with tears. In 1863, while visiting Joe in the field, Hattie had seen that the flags needed patching. "It was Sunday but we hunted up the one or two silk dresses we had ventured to bring, took pieces from them, sent around to the wives of the other officers to know if they could not also contribute (they did—what they could), and we worked all day on the piazza patching the eagle, and the stripes, and stars."[15]

The flag of the hard-luck 16th Connecticut was completely transformed. When the regiment had been captured at Plymouth in 1864, its colonel had ordered the regimental flag torn from its staff to keep the rebels from seizing it. Tearing the flag into strips, the men hid the blue silk pieces inside their uniforms. Some of the soldiers who survived the hellish imprisonment at Andersonville still had the scraps of the original flag. On Battle-Flag Day, the 16th Regiment had "a new flag of white silk, the central device on which is composed of pieces of the national flag torn up to prevent capture, and carried through Andersonville by the survivors."[16]

The parade included eighty flags, many kept furled because of their frail conditions. The crowd didn't seem to mind. The *Hartford Daily Courant* noted: "It was a brilliant parade as a military affair but that was the least of it. It was when the ten thousand veterans went by, regiment after regiment, bringing each its colors, faded, shot, torn, fluttering in rags or tied to the staff . . . that the cheers went up and tears dimmed the admiring eyes that looked."[17]

Joseph Hawley, newspaper editor, general, and former governor, directed the day's ceremonies. When the last flag had been presented, he spoke to the onlookers: "Let the flags rest. In a few years these men will no longer be able to bear arms for the land they love, but these weather-worn and battle-torn folds shall remain through the centuries, testifying that Connecticut was true to free government."[18]

There would be other reunions and dedications and ceremonies, but Battle-Flag Day seemed to bring a sense of glad closure to the veterans. The flags they held sacred would be safe in a place of honor, fragile touchstones for other generations.

MEMORIES

Looking back on their war experiences wasn't always easy. "The memories of the war are one of the saddest features thereof," wrote Alexander H. Newton. "These memories can never be blotted out; for as we grow older they seem to become more vivid."[19] Recalling the death of a brother or close friend, or calling up a battle's images of horror could bring on tears fifty years later.

Still, for many men—perhaps for most—the Civil War was the defining period of their lives. Despite the sacrifices and suffering, veterans valued the ordeals they had endured. Charles Fuller, who left a leg at Gettysburg, was clear that "it was well worth hardship, wounds, loss of limbs, or life even, to have a hand in preserving in its integrity such a country as ours."[20]

The shreds of blue silk that returned home with the 7th Connecticut bore little resemblance to the glossy regimental flag the color-bearers carried four years earlier when they left Connecticut for the South.

Joseph Hawley, an old soldier himself, spoke of the war in terms of sacrifice and debt. "I think of the men in the ranks, the private soldiers, who never wished to be any thing but private soldiers, who died private soldiers, and whose thousands of graves scattered over the hillsides of the South give the highest and deepest proof of their devotion to their country," Hawley said. "To such men, the country owes its success . . . theirs is the only debt we can never pay,—the debt we owe to the men who in the darkest hours have cheerfully laid down their lives for liberty and their country."[21]

In 1862, the new soldiers of the 14th Connecticut had rushed into their first battle without any idea of what it meant. Nearly three decades later, the survivors returned to Antietam as middle-aged and elderly men who'd had years to reflect. Still, as they dedicated their regimental monument there, they seemed to need to hear the reassurances of one of their comrades: "the warm light of every September moon will awaken in this New England stone, a soul, that will go out and testify to the unmarked dead, o'er all these fields, that a grateful people has not forgotten, and never will forget the sufferings or the valor of those who stood by the Union in those days."[22]

John Lyman Wilcox (*left*), a Wolcottville blacksmith, was one of the private soldiers that Joe Hawley spoke of. Wilcox was thirty-six when he enlisted in the Union army. He never rose above the rank of corporal in Connecticut's 2nd Heavy Artillery. At the Battle of Cedar Creek, John was wounded in the back and the side; "the shot was not found until the third day: when it was removed he bled anew" and died on the way to a hospital. (Vaill, *History of the Second*, p. 171.)

For good and for bad, the war never left the old soldiers. In Canton, Lewis Sprague Mills photographed his elderly father, Archibald, (*right*) proudly wearing the uniform he had first donned in 1862.

Was it worth it—all that agony and death? Henry Goddard reminded his brothers-in-arms that the cause they had fought for had been a noble one. In four years of war, the suffering had been terrible and the losses immense, but

> at last those who wore the blue and those who wore the grey carry the same old banner of the Union . . . while each tenderly cherish the memories and decorate the graves of their own loved ones who fell on either side, whether the graves be in the South land or in the North land, under the palmetto or under the pine, both now acknowledge a common country, a common government, "of the people, by the people, for the people."[23]

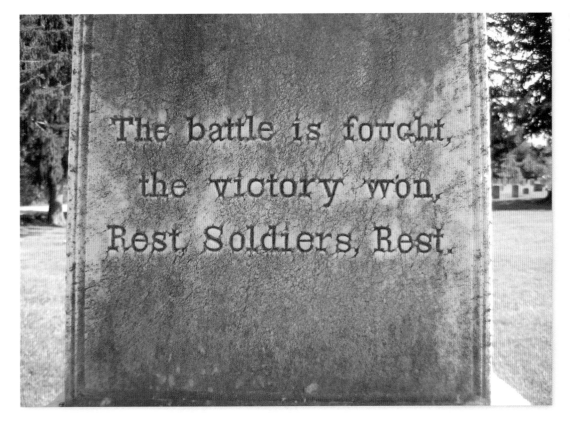

Gravestone to Henry, Luman, and Edward Wadhams, West Cemetery, Litchfield.

Preface

1. Letter of George E. Stannard to his mother, September 20, 1862, Buck Zaidel collection.
2. Diary of George Meech, Thanksgiving 1862, courtesy of the Middlesex County Historical Society, Middletown.
3. Manuscript of William Relyea, p. 1, Connecticut Historical Society, Hartford.
4. Henry Ward Camp, as quoted in *The Knightly Soldier: A Biography of Major Henry Ward Camp, Tenth Connecticut Volunteers*, by Henry Clay Trumbull (Boston: Nichols and Noyes, 1865), p. 150.
5. Letter of Lucien R. Dunham, February 3, 1863, Connecticut Historical Society, Hartford.
6. Samual Proal Hatfield Civil War photograph album, Special Collections and Archives, Wesleyan University, Middletown.

1. Men of Connecticut!

1. *Hartford Daily Courant*, April 13, 1861.
2. Ibid., April 15, 1861, p. 2.
3. John Boyd, *Annals and Family Records of Winchester, Connecticut* (Hartford, CT: Case, Lockwood & Brainard, 1873), pp. 462, 463.
4. *Hartford Daily Courant*, April 13, 1861.
5. Ibid., April 18, 1861.
6. Ibid.
7. W. A. Croffut and John M. Morris, *The Military and Civil History of Connecticut during the War of 1861–65* (New York: Ledyard Bill, 1869), p. 41.
8. Typescript of letter from Theodosia Knapp, April 22, 1861, courtesy of the Middlesex County Historical Society, Middletown.
9. *Hartford Daily Courant*, March 6, 1860.
10. Jon Grinspan, "'Young Men for War': The Wide Awakes and Lincoln's 1860 Presidential Campaign," *Journal of American History* 96, no. 2 (September 2009); Major Julius G. Rathbun, "'The Wide Awakes': The Great Political Organization of 1860," *The Connecticut Quarterly* 1 (January/February/March 1895), pp. 327–35.
11. *Hartford Daily Courant*, January 26, 1860.
12. Harold Holzer, *Lincoln at Cooper Union: The Speech That Made Abraham Lincoln President* (New York: Simon and Schuster, 2004), p. 202.
13. *Hartford Daily Courant*, March 6, 1860.
14. *New Haven Palladium*, March 7, 1860.
15. John Niven, *Connecticut for the Union* (New Haven, CT: Yale University Press, 1965), pp. 3–5.
16. "Republican Wide-Awakes of Hartford," printed form letter, 1860–61, Connecticut Historical Society, Hartford.
17. *Hartford Times*, November 7, 1860.
18. *Hartford Daily Courant*, April 20, 1861.
19. The *Middletown Constitution*, April 24, 1861.
20. Diary of William North Rice, April 21, 1861, William North Rice Papers, Special Collections and Archives, Wesleyan University, Middletown.
21. Croffut and Morris, *Military and Civil History*, p. 55.
22. Ibid., pp. 43–44.
23. Letter of George Clary, April 24, 1861, Connecticut Historical Society, Hartford.
24. Diary of Horace Purdy, April 17, 1861, family of Horace Purdy.
25. *Hartford Daily Courant*, April 19, 1861.
26. Gustavus Sullivan Dana, as quoted in Lester L. Swift, "Bully for the First Connecticut: The Recollections of a Three-Month Volunteer," in *Lincoln Herald* 67, no. 2 (June 1965): 73.
27. Elnathan B. Tyler [Frinkle Fry], *"Wooden Nutmegs" at Bull Run: A Humorous Account of Some of the Exploits and Experiences of the Three Months Connecticut Brigade and the Part They Bore in the National Stampede* (Hartford, CT: George L. Coburn Steam Print, 1872), pp. 27–28.
28. Letter of Andrew Knox to his wife, April 21, 1861, The Connecticut Historical Society, Hartford. Andrew Knox's grandfather served in the War of 1812, and his great-grandfather fought in the Revolutionary War.
29. Diary of Horace Purdy, April 30, 1861, family of Horace Purdy.
30. Forrest Morgan, ed., *Connecticut as a Colony and as a State* (Hartford, CT: The Publishing Society of Connecticut, 1904), p. 52.
31. Tyler, *"Wooden Nutmegs,"* p. 13.
32. Thomas L. Snead, *The Fight for Missouri from the Election of Lincoln to the Death of Lyon* (New York: Charles Scribner's

Sons, 1886), pp. 199–200.

33. *Hartford Daily Courant*, May 9, 1861.

2. No One Dreamed of Anything but Victory

1. Tyler, *"Wooden Nutmegs,"* pp. 32–33.
2. Letter of Joseph R. Hawley to Charles Dudley Warner, May 24, 1861, as quoted in *Major General Joseph R. Hawley, Soldier and Editor (1826–1905)*, edited by Albert D. Putnam (Hartford, CT: Connecticut Civil War Centennial Commission, June 1964), p. 9.
3. Tyler, *"Wooden Nutmegs,"* pp. 39–42.
4. Diary of Horace Purdy, June 18, 1861, family of Horace Purdy.
5. Letter from John C. Comstock to R. S. Ely, June 23, 1861, as quoted in the *Hartford Daily Courant*, July 1, 1861, p. 2.
6. Dana, as quoted in Swift, "Bully for the First Connecticut," p. 78.
7. Typescript of letter from Eli Walter Osborn to his mother, May 16, 1861, private collection.
8. Andrew Knox to Sarah Knox, July 14, 1861, GLC03523.20.02, courtesy of the Gilder Lehrman Institute of American History.
9. Tyler, *"Wooden Nutmegs,"* p. 60.
10. Testimony of Gen. Irvin McDowell, *Report of the Joint Committee on the Conduct of the War in Three Parts* (Washington, DC: Government Printing Office, 1863), part 2, p. 39.
11. Dana as quoted in Swift, "Bully for the First Connecticut," p. 77.
12. Diary of Horace Purdy, July 17, 1861, family of Horace Purdy.
13. Dana, as quoted in Swift, "Bully for the First Connecticut," p. 77.
14. Tyler, *"Wooden Nutmegs,"* p. 67.
15. Diary of Rev. Hiram Eddy, collection of Linda Lyles Goodyear, Eddy's great-granddaughter.
16. Tyler , *"Wooden Nutmegs,"* p. 66.
17. Dana, as quoted in Swift, "Bully for the First Connecticut," p. 78.
18. Ibid., pp. 78–79, 80.
19. Tyler, *"Wooden Nutmegs,"* p. 67.
20. Diary of Hiram Eddy, collection of Linda Lyles Goodyear.
21. Tyler, *"Wooden Nutmegs,"* pp. 67–68.
22. Official report of Col. Erasmus D. Keyes, July 25, 1861, Eleventh U.S. Infantry, commanding First Brigade, First Division in *The War of the Rebellion: A Compilation of the Official Records of the Union and Confederate Armies* (Washington, DC: Government Printing Office, 1880), ser. 1, vol. 2, chap. 9.

23. Tyler, *"Wooden Nutmegs,"* pp. 70–71.
24. Diary of Horace Purdy, July 21, 1861, family of Horace Purdy.
25. Dana, as quoted in Swift, "Bully for the First Connecticut," p. 79.
26. Diary of Hiram Eddy, collection of Linda Lyles Goodyear.
27. Tyler, *"Wooden Nutmegs,"* pp. 76–77.
28. Letter from GWB [probably George W. Barnett], Rifle Co. C, 3rd Connecticut Regiment, dated July 24, 1861, printed in the *New Haven Daily Morning News*, July 26, 1861.
29. Diary of Hiram Eddy, collection of Linda Lyles Goodyear.
30. Dana, as quoted in Swift, "Bully for the First Connecticut," p. 80.
31. Tyler, *"Wooden Nutmegs,"* p. 78.
32. *Hartford Daily Courant*, August 18, 1861, quoting the *New York World*.
33. *New York Times*, as quoted in Croffut and Morris, *Military and Civil History*, p. 99.
34. Croffut and Morris, *Military and Civil History*, p. 101.
35. Tyler, *"Wooden Nutmegs,"* p. 82.
36. Horace Bushnell, "Reverses Needed: A Sermon Delivered on the Sunday after the Disaster at Bull Run, in the North Church, Hartford, July 1861," in *The Spirit in Man* (New York: Charles Scribner's Sons, 1910), p. 161.
37. Croffut and Morris, *Military and Civil History*, p. 101.

3. The Voice of Duty

1. Stephen Walkley, *History of the Seventh Connecticut Volunteer Infantry* (n.p.: 1905), pp. 7–8.
2. Letter of Horace Garrigus to his father, September 1861, Civil War letters of Horace Garrigus, Garrigus Family website: www.garrigus-family.com/horaceletters.html.
3. Proclamation of Gov. William A. Buckingham, July 3, 1862, in Croffut and Morris, *Military and Civil History*, p. 223.
4. Charles D. Page, *History of the Fourteenth Regiment, Connecticut Volunteer Infantry* (Meriden, CT: Horton Printing Co., 1906), p. 16.
5. Herbert W. Beecher, *History of the First Light Battery Connecticut Volunteers, 1861–1865* (New York: A. T. De La Mare, 1901), vol. 1, pp. 27–28.
6. *Bridgeport Advertiser and Farmer,* August 5, 1861, as quoted in Croffut and Morris, *Military and Civil History*, p. 106.
7. Croffut and Morris, *Military and Civil History*, p. 104.
8. John E. Talmadge, "A Peace Movement in Civil War Connecticut," *New England Quarterly* 37, no. 3 (September 1964): 310.
9. Ibid., pp. 311–12.
10. Croffut and Morris, *Military and Civil History*, p. 108.
11. *New Haven Palladium*, as quoted in *The Rebellion Record: A*

Diary of American Events; Documents and Narratives, vol. 3, edited by Frank Moore (New York: G. P. Putnam, 1862), p. 3.

12. Journal of James Sawyer, August 1862, Connecticut Historical Society, Hartford.

13. Ibid.

14. *The Story of the Twenty-first Regiment, Connecticut Volunteer Infantry*, by members of the regiment (Middletown, CT: Stewart Printing Co., 1900), pp. 25–26.

15. Sheldon Brainerd Thorpe, *The History of the Fifteenth Connecticut Volunteers in the War for the Defense of the Union, 1861–1865* (New Haven, CT: Price, Lee and Adkins, 1893), p. 13.

16. Diary of Michael Kelly, 2nd Connecticut Heavy Artillery, August 15, 1862, Connecticut Historical Society, Hartford.

17. Journal of James H. Sawyer, p. 2, Connecticut Historical Society, Hartford.

18. William Carey Walker, *History of the Eighteenth Regiment Connecticut Volunteers in the War for the Union* (Norwich, CT: Published by the Committee, 1885), p. 21.

19. Theodore F. Vaill, *History of the Second Connecticut Volunteer Heavy Artillery* (Winsted, CT: Winsted Printing Co., 1868), p. 13.

20. *Hartford Daily Courant*, August 7, 1862.

21. Journal of James H. Sawyer, p. 4, Connecticut Historical Society, Hartford.

22. *Hartford Daily Courant*, quoting Mayor Henry C. Deming, April 22, 1861.

23. Charles M. Coit to his family, September 18–19, 1862, GLC03603.144, courtesy of the Gilder Lehrman Institute of American History.

24. Henry P. Goddard, *14th C.V. Regimental Reminiscences of the War of the Rebellion* (Middletown, CT: C. W. Church, 1877), p. 6.

25. Levi Jewett, as quoted in Page, *History of the Fourteenth*, p. 19.

26. Goddard, *14th C.V. Regimental Reminiscences*, p. 6.

27. Samuel Fiske, as quoted in Page, *History of the Fourteenth*, p. 23.

28. Stephen Walkley, *History of the Seventh Connecticut Volunteer Infantry* (Hartford, CT: no publisher, 1905), pp. 20–21.

29. Albert R. Crittenden, as quoted in Page, *History of the Fourteenth*, p. 23.

30. *The Story of the Twenty-first Regiment*, pp. 26–27.

31. Charles M. Coit to his family, May 12, 1862, GLC03603.104, courtesy of the Gilder Lehrman Institute of American History.

32. *Allen's Compendium of Hardee's Tactics* (New York: M. Doolady, 1861), p. 128.

33. Letter from Frederick A. Lucas, December 17, 1862, as quoted in *Dear Mother from your Dutiful Son*, by Ernest B. Barker (Goshen, CT: Purple Door Gallery Press, 2003), pp. 28–29.

34. Diary of Michael Kelly, October 22, 1862, Connecticut Historical Society, Hartford.

35. Frederick Burr Hawley journal, Buck Zaidel collection.

36. Edward Ashley Walker, *Our First Year of Army Life* (New Haven, CT: Thomas H. Pease, 1862), pp. 23–24.

37. Ibid., p. 49.

38. John W. DeForest, *A Volunteer's Adventures* (New Haven, CT: Yale University Press, 1946), p. 7.

39. *Hartford Daily Courant*, October 18, 1861.

40. Letter of Charles Squires to his sister, September 1861, Connecticut Historical Society, Hartford.

41. Letter of Private Cyrus B. Harrington, Co. C, 8th Connecticut, March 15, 1862, as quoted online in *Civil War Gazette*, March 15, 2007, http://civilwargazette.wordpress.com.

42. Letter of Joseph H. Converse in the *Hartford Press*, as quoted in Croffut and Morris, *Military and Civil History*, p. 173.

43. Croffut and Morris, *Military and Civil History*, p. 208.

44. Walker, *Our First Year*, pp. 72–73.

45. Edwin E. Marvin, *The Fifth Regiment, Connecticut Volunteers* (Hartford, CT: Press of Wiley, Waterman & Eaton, 1889), pp. 158–59.

46. Ibid., p. 160.

47. Ibid., p. 162.

48. Official report of Brigadier General S. W. Crawford, August 14, 1862, as quoted in Marvin, *The Fifth Regiment*, p. 182.

49. Croffut and Morris, *Military and Civil History*, p. 221.

50. William P. Bacon, *Fourth Biographical Record of the Class of Fifty-eight, Yale University* (New Britain, CT: Adkins Printing Co., 1897), p. 74.

51. S.E.B., in *The Connecticut War Record*, August 1865, pp. 511–12.

52. Letter of George A. Blake to Leslie Robison, February 5, 1864, Connecticut Historical Society, Hartford.

53. Croffut and Morris, *Military and Civil History*, p. 213.

54. *Connecticut War Record*, August 1865, p. 512.

55. Ellsworth Eliot, Jr., *Yale in the Civil War* (New Haven, CT: Yale University Press, 1932), p. 42.

56. Letter of William C. Bennett to George A. Blake, October 1862, Blake Collection, Connecticut Historical Society, Hartford.

57. Letter of George A. Blake to Leslie Robison, February 5, 1864, Blake Collection, Connecticut Historical Society, Hartford.

58. Goddard, *14th C.V. Regimental Reminiscences*, p. 7.

59. Page, *History of the Fourteenth*, p. 27.

60. Ibid.

61. Benjamin Hirst, as quoted in ibid., pp. 27–28.

62. Nelson Bailey as quoted in ibid., pp. 24–25.

4. War by Citizen Soldiers

1. Letter of Dr. George Clary, May 7, 1861, Connecticut Historical Society, Hartford.

2. Beecher, *History of the First*, vol. 1, p. 25.

3. Ibid.

4. Carl F. Price, *Postscripts to Yankee Township* (East Hampton, CT: East Hampton Bicentennial Committee, 1975), p. 354.

5. Ibid., 355.

6. *The Story of the Twenty-first Regiment*, pp. 190–91.

7. Ibid., p. 356.

8. Vaill, *History of the Second*, p. 325.

9. Surgeon Nathan Mayer, as quoted in Croffut and Morris, *Military and Civil History*, pp. 280–81.

10. "Address of Henry R. Jones," from *Souvenir of Excursion to Antietam and Dedication of Monuments of the 8th, 11th, 14th and 16th Regiments of Connecticut Volunteers*, edited by Walter J. Yates (New London, CT: E. E. Darrow, 1894), p. 23.

11. Cogswell, a Schaghticoke Indian, died from wounds on October 7, 1864, giving his life for a country that did not allow him to vote. The United States did not grant citizenship to Native Americans until 1924.

12. Letter of Lt. Benjamin Wright to his wife, April 20, 1864, online at soldierstudies.org.

13. Letter from Henry H. J. Thompson to his wife, December 21, 1862, David M. Rubenstein Rare Book & Manuscript Library, Duke University.

14. Letter of William W. VanDeursen, December 26, 1862, courtesy of the Middlesex County Historical Society, Middletown.

15. *Statistical Pocket Manual of the Army, Navy, and Census of the United States of America* (Boston: D. P. Butler, 1862), pp. 12–14.

16. Croffut and Morris, *Military and Civil History*, p. 242.

17. Letter of Henry Perkins Goddard to his mother, September 23, 1863, courtesy of Calvin Goddard Zon.

18. Letter of George Gilbert Smith, January 8, 1863, Stamford Historical Society.

19. Edward Brewer as quoted in *The Sacrifice Consumed*, by Jeremiah Taylor (Boston: Henry Hoyt, 1863), pp. 91–92.

20. Letter of Lucius E. Bidwell, November 26, 1863, collection of Cathy Branch Stebbins.

21. Letter of John G. Pelton, as quoted in the *Middletown Constitution*, December 24, 1862.

22. Capt. J. H. Harpster, "The Ambulance Officer's Story," in *The Story of Our Regiment: A History of he 148th Pennsylvania Volunteers*, edited by Joseph Wendell Muffly (Des Moines, IA: The Kenyan Printing and Mfg. Co., 1904), p. 290.

23. Draft of report from John G. Pelton, Chief of Ambulance, 2nd Army Corps, to Surgeon A. N. Dougherty, Medical Director, 2nd Army Corps, October 31, 1864, papers of John G. Pelton, courtesy of the Middlesex County Historical Society, Middletown.

24. Harpster, "The Ambulance Officer's Story," pp. 294–95.

25. H. Clay Trumbull, *War Memories of an Army Chaplain* (New York: Charles Scribner's Sons, 1898), p. 8.

26. Letter from Henry Camp, 10th CV, to his family, August 1864, as quoted in *The Knightly Soldier: A Biography of Major Henry Ward Camp, Tenth Connecticut Volunteers*, by Henry Clay Trumbull (Boston: Nichols and Noyes, 1865), pp. 272–73.

5. I Never Knew What War Meant till Today

1. Croffut and Morris, *Military and Civil History*, p. 260.

2. B. F. Blakeslee, *History of the Sixteenth Connecticut Volunteers* (Hartford, CT: Case, Lockwood & Brainard Co., 1875), pp. 11–12.

3. Manuscript of William H. Relyea, p. 22, Connecticut Historical Society, Hartford.

4. Official Report of Gen. Joseph Hooker, November 8, 1862, in *The War of the Rebellion: A Compilation of the Official Records of the Union and Confederate Armies* (Washington, DC: Government Printing Office, 1887), series 1, vol. 19, part 1, p. 218.

5. John Pope, "War Reminiscences, XV," *National Tribune*, March 19, 1891.

6. John Mead Gould, *Joseph K. F. Mansfield, Brigadier General of the U.S. Army* (Portland, ME: Stephen Berry, 1895), p. 29.

7. Ibid., p. 15.

8. Letter of P. H. Flood, transcript courtesy of the Middlesex County Historical Society, Middletown.

9. Gould, *Joseph K. F. Mansfield*, p. 15.

10. Frederick Burr Hawley journal, September 17, 1862, Buck Zaidel collection.

11. Page, *History of the Fourteenth*, pp. 35–36.

12. Samuel Willard, as quoted in Samuel Irenaeus Prime, *The Power of Prayer* (New York: Scribner, Armstrong & Co, 1873), p. 409.

13. *Shoreline Times* (New Haven), June 15, 1961.

14. Page, *History of the Fourteenth*, p. 36.

15. Lt. Colonel Sanford H. Perkins's official report, September 19, 1862, as quoted in Page, *History of the Fourteenth*, p. 57.

16. Frederick Burr Hawley journal, September 17, 1862, Buck Zaidel collection.

17. Letter from Benjamin Hirst to Luther Morse, September 20, 1862, collection of the New England Civil War Museum,

as quoted in *The Boys from Rockville*, ed. Robert L. Bee (Knoxville: University of Tennessee Press, 1998), pp. 20–21.

18. Page, *History of the Fourteenth*, pp. 37–38.

19. Henry S. Stevens, *Souvenir of Excursion to Battlefields by the Society of the Fourteenth Connecticut Regiment and Reunion at Antietam, September 1891* (Washington, DC: Gibson Brothers, 1893), p. 52.

20. Frederick Burr Hawley journal, Buck Zaidel collection.

21. Letter of Benjamin Hirst to Luther Morse, September 20, 1862, as quoted in Bee, *The Boys from Rockville*, p. 21.

22. Letter of Robert Hubbard to Josiah M. Hubbard, August 13, 1862, as quoted in the *Middletown Penny Press*, April 13, 1898, p. 5.

23. Frederick Burr Hawley journal, Buck Zaidel collection.

24. Elnathan B. Tyler, "History of Co. B," manuscript transcribed and annotated by Henry S. Stevens, p. 9, as quoted in Thomas E. LaLancette, *A Noble and Glorious Cause* (Middletown, CT: Godfrey Memorial Library, 2005), p. 65.

25. Letter of Robert Hubbard to his mother, August 25, 1862, as quoted in the *Middletown Penny Press*, April 13, 1898, p. 5.

26. William Hincks, as quoted in Page, *History of the Fourteenth*, pp. 45–46.

27. Frederick Burr Hawley journal, September 17, 1862, Buck Zaidel collection.

28. Rev. Henry S. Stevens, as quoted in Page, *History of the Fourteenth*, p. 45.

29. George E. Stannard letter, Buck Zaidel collection.

30. Lt. J. H. Converse, 11th Connecticut, as quoted in Croffut and Morris, *Military and Civil History*, p. 265.

31. Nathan Mayer, as quoted in ibid., p. 280.

32. Letter of Nathan Mayer, September 26, 1862, as quoted in the *Hartford Daily Courant*, October 7, 1862.

33. Croffut and Morris, *Military and Civil History*, pp. 280–81.

34. Ibid., pp. 266–67.

35. Letter of Nathan Mayer, September 29, 1862, as quoted in the *Hartford Daily Courant*, October 7, 1862.

36. Nathan Mayer, as quoted in Croffut and Morris, *Military and Civil History*, p. 279.

37. Diary of Roger M. Ford, September 17, 1862, copy at Antietam National Battlefield.

38. Croffut and Morris, *Military and Civil History*, p. 276.

39. Letter of Wolcott P. Marsh to his wife, September 24, 1862, as quoted in *Letters to a Civil War Bride: The Civil War Letters of Captain Wolcott Pascal Marsh*, compiled by Sandra Marsh Mercer and Jerry Mercer (Westminster, MD: Heritage Books, 2006), p. 468.

40. *New York Tribune,* October 3, 1862.

41. Letter of Wolcott P. Marsh to his wife, September 24, 1862, in Mercer and Mercer, *Letters to a Civil War Bride*, p. 470.

42. Croffut and Morris, *Military and Civil History*, pp. 271–72. John Morris, who doubtless wrote this description, was the 8th Regiment's chaplain at Antietam.

43. Jacob Eaton, *Memorial of Marvin Wait* (New Haven, CT: T. J. Stafford, 1863), pp. 4–5.

44. Ibid., pp. 7–9.

45. Charles Coit, as quoted in Eaton, *Memorial of Marvin Wait*, p. 10.

46. Eaton, *Memorial of Marvin Wait*, pp. 11–12.

47. Letter of Wolcott P. Marsh, September 24, 1862, in Mercer and Mercer, *Letters to a Civil War Bride*, pp. 470–71.

48. Diary of Roger M. Ford, September 17, 1862, copy at Antietam National Battlefield.

49. "Address of Capt. Henry R. Jones" in Yates, *Souvenir of Excursion to Antietam*, p. 25.

50. After being paroled and discharged because of disability, Jones returned to the Union army, serving in the Veterans Reserve Corps through the war, and afterwards for many years as an officer in the regular army. The bullet remained in his shoulder all this time, causing constant pain. In 1903, forty-one years after Antietam, the ball loosened from the open wound, and Jones was able to draw it out of his shoulder. *New York Times*, July 20, 1903.

51. Letter of Wolcott P. Marsh, September. 24, 1862, in Mercer and Mercer, *Letters to a Civil War Bride,* p. 472.

52. "Address of Capt. Henry R. Jones" in Yates, *Souvenir of Excursion to Antietam*, p. 26.

53. Nathan Mayer, "Reminiscences of the Civil War," typescript, Connecticut Historical Society, Hartford.

54. Manuscript of William Relyea, p. 20, Connecticut Historical Society, Hartford.

55. Letter of Austin D. Thompson to Electa Churchill, September 21, 1862, Connecticut Historical Society, Hartford.

56. Ibid.

57. Manuscript of William Relyea, pp. 23–24, Connecticut Historical Society, Hartford.

58. Ibid., pp. 24–25.

59. Blakeslee, *History of the Sixteenth*, p. 15.

60. Ibid.

61. Ibid.

62. Diary of B. F. Blakeslee, as quoted in Croffut and Morris, *Military and Civil History*, p. 271.

63. Manuscript of William Relyea, p. 26, Connecticut Historical Society, Hartford.

64. Croffut and Morris, *Military and Civil History*, p. 271.

65. Letter of William H. Drake to his cousin, September 29, 1862, Connecticut Historical Society, Hartford.

66. Diary of Elizur Belden, September 19, 1862, Connecticut

Historical Society, Hartford.

67. Letter of John B. Cuzner to Ellen Van Dorn, September 21, 1862, Connecticut Historical Society, Hartford.

68. Letter of Adjutant John H. Burnham to his mother and family, October 4, 1862, State Archives, Connecticut State Library, Hartford.

69. Manuscript of William Relyea, p. 27, Connecticut Historical Society, Hartford.

70. Letter of Henry C. Hall, 8th Connecticut, October 5, 1862, to his sister, David M. Rubenstein Rare Book & Manuscript Library, Duke University.

71. Croffut and Morris, *Military and Civil History*, p. 271.

72. *The Connecticut War Record*, March 1865, p. 373.

73. Military and Biographical Data of the 16th Connecticut Volunteers, George Q. Whitney Papers, box 8, State Archives, Connecticut State Library, Hartford.

74. Croffut and Morris, *Military and Civil History*, p. 283.

75. *The Connecticut War Record*, March 1865, p. 373.

76. Manuscript of William Relyea, pp. 44–45, Connecticut Historical Society, Hartford.

77. Ibid., p. 28.

78. Blakeslee, *History of the Sixteenth*, p. 17.

79. Ibid., p. 19.

80. Mayer, "Reminiscences of the Civil War," typescript, p. 5, Connecticut Historical Society, Hartford.

81. Manuscript of William Relyea, p. 29, Connecticut Historical Society, Hartford.

82. Ibid., pp. 43–44.

83. Ibid., p. 29.

84. Ibid.

85. Ibid., p. 38.

86. Goddard, *14th C.V. Regimental Reminiscences*, p. 9.

87. Manuscript of William Relyea, pp. 29–30, Connecticut Historical Society, Hartford.

88. Letter of Austin Thompson to Electa Churchill, September 21, 1862, Connecticut Historical Society, Hartford.

89. Letter of William H. Relyea to his wife, September 26, 1862, Connecticut Historical Society, Hartford.

90. Letter of Charles Henry Greenleaf of Hartford, 2nd Lt., 5th New York Cavalry, September 20, 1862, Connecticut Historical Society, Hartford.

91. Manuscript of William Relyea, pp. 39–40, Connecticut Historical Society, Hartford.

6. Emancipation Is a Mighty Word

1. Abraham Lincoln, "Emancipation Proclamation," September 22, 1862.

2. James Lindsay Smith, *Autobiography of James L. Smith* (Norwich, CT: Press of the Bulletin Co., 1881), p. 82.

3. Letter of Abraham Lincoln to Horace Greeley, August 22, 1862, as quoted in the *New York Times*, August 24, 1862.

4. Gideon Welles, *Diary of Gideon Welles* (Boston and New York: Houghton Mifflin, 1911), vol. 1, p. 70.

5. [Maria Huntington and Kate Foote], *Harriet Ward Foote Hawley* (privately printed, no place, no date), pp. 30–35.

6. Letter of Charles Greenleaf, January 31, 1863, Connecticut Historical Society, Hartford.

7. Letter of William H. Relyea, December 2, 1862, Connecticut Historical Society, Hartford.

8. Letter from unidentified soldier in the 7th Regiment Connecticut Infantry, quoted in the *Hartford Daily Courant*, November 23, 1861.

9. Homer B. Sprague, *History of the 13th Infantry Regiment of Connecticut Volunteers, During the Great Rebellion* (Hartford, CT: Case, Lockwood & Co., 1867), pp. 62–63.

10. Letter of Uriah Parmelee to his brother, Samuel S. Parmelee, April 23, 1862, David M. Rubenstein Rare Book & Manuscript Library, Duke University.

11. Letter of Uriah Parmelee to his mother, September 8, 1862, David M. Rubenstein Rare Book & Manuscript Library, Duke University.

12. Letter of Uriah Parmelee to his father, March 29, 1863, David M. Rubenstein Rare Book & Manuscript Library, Duke University.

13. Randall C. Jimerson, *The Private Civil War: Popular Thought during the Sectional Conflict* (Baton Rouge: Louisiana State University Press, 1994), p. 39.

14. Unnamed officer of the 9th Connecticut, as quoted in the *Hartford Daily Courant*, August 26, 1863.

15. Letter of Charles A. Boyle, November 4, 1863, Connecticut Historical Society, Hartford.

16. Horatio Dana Chapman, *Civil War Diary of a Forty-Niner* (Hartford, CT: Allis, 1929), p. 101.

17. Letters of Frederick A. Lucas, May 12, 1865 and February 18, 1865, in Barker, *Dear Mother*, pp. 383, 359.

18. Letter of Andrew Upson to his sister-in-law, Mrs. Bingham, November 23, 1863, Southington Library and Museum, Barnes Museum.

19. Letter of Charles A. Boyle, November 4, 1863, Connecticut Historical Society, Hartford.

20. Trumbull, *War Memories of an Army Chaplain*, p. 383.

21. Thorpe, *History of the Fifteenth*, pp. 149–50.

22. John W. Storrs, *The Twentieth Connecticut: A Regimental History* (Ansonia, CT: Press of the Naugatuck Valley Sentinel, 1886), p. 261.

23. Lt. Solomon R. Hinsdale, 12th CV, letter to his mother, August 2, 1862, as quoted online in *The Civil War Gazette,* November 16, 2008, http://civilwargazette.wordpress.com.

24. Letter of John G. Crosby, January 24, 1863, courtesy of the Middlesex County Historical Society, Middletown.

25. Letter from Menominee L. Maimi to his wife, March 1863, as quoted in the *Weekly Anglo-African* (New York), April 18, 1863.

26. Jeremiah Asher, *Incidents in the Life of the Rev. J. Asher, Pastor of Shiloh (Coloured) Baptist Church, Philadelphia, U.S.* (London: Charles Gilpin, 1850), pp. 15–20.

27. Ibid., pp. 50, 52–53.

28. "An Act for Enrolling and Calling out the National Forces, and for Other Purposes," *Congressional Record,* 37th Cong. 3d. Sess. Ch. 74, 75. 1863. March 3, 1863.

29. *The Hartford Daily Courant,* November 14, 1863.

30. Letter of Abraham Lincoln to James Conkling, August 26, 1863, as quoted in *Abraham Lincoln: His Speeches and Writings,* edited by Roy P. Basler (Cleveland, OH: World Publishing Co., 1946), pp. 722–24.

31. Letter of Joseph Orrin Cross to his wife, December 31, 1864, Connecticut Historical Society, Hartford.

32. Alexander H. Newton, *Out of the Briars* (Philadelphia, PA: The A.M.E. Book Concern, 1910), p. 37.

33. *New Haven Daily Palladium,* March 21, 1864.

34. I. J. Hill, *A Sketch of the 29th Regiment of Connecticut Colored Troops* (Baltimore, MD: Daugherty, Maguire & Co., 1867), p. 8.

35. Newton, *Out of the Briars,* p. 38.

36. Letter of Abner Mitchell to his parents, February 2, 1864, collection of the Gunn Memorial Museum, Washington, CT.

37. Hill, *Sketch of the 29th,* pp. 7–8.

38. Ibid., pp. 12–13.

39. Vaill, *History of the Second,* p. 72.

40. Newton, *Out of the Briars,* pp. 47–48.

7. No Men on Earth Can Be Braver

1. Frederick Burr Hawley journal, September 27, 1862, Buck Zaidel collection.

2. Ibid., December 12, 1862.

3. Letter of Benjamin Hirst to his wife, Thanksgiving, 1862, Collection of the New England Civil War Museum, as quoted in Bee, *The Boys From Rockville,* p. 42.

4. Winthrop D. Sheldon, *The Twenty-Seventh: A Regimental History* (New Haven, CT: Morris and Benham, 1866), p. 26.

5. Ibid., p. 21.

6. Josiah M. Favill, *The Diary of a Young Officer* (Chicago, IL: R. R. Donnelley & Sons, 1909), p. 206.

7. Ida M. Tarbell, *A Reporter for Lincoln: Story of Henry E. Wing, Soldier and Newspaperman* (New York: Book League of America, 1929), p. 36.

8. Sheldon, *The Twenty-Seventh,* pp. 22–23.

9. Page, *History of the Fourteenth,* p. 80.

10. Favill, *Diary of a Young Officer,* p. 210.

11. Ibid.

12. Letter of Henry P. Goddard to his mother, December 14, 1862, courtesy of Calvin Goddard Zon.

13. Tarbell, *A Reporter for Lincoln,* p. 37.

14. Henry P. Goddard, as quoted in Page, *History of the Fourteenth,* p. 100.

15. Frederick Burr Hawley journal, December 13, 1862, Buck Zaidel collection.

16. Letter of Henry P. Goddard to his mother, December 14, 1862; courtesy of Calvin Goddard Zon.

17. Frederick Burr Hawley journal, December 13, 1862, Buck Zaidel collection.

18. Official Report of Major General Darius N. Couch, January 1863, *The War of the Rebellion: A Compilation of the Official Records of the Union and Confederate Armies* (Washington, DC: Government Printing Office, 1888), vol. 21, pp. 222–23.

19. Samuel Fiske [Dunn Browne, pseud.], *Mr. Dunn Browne's Experiences in the Army* (Boston: Nickels & Noyes, 1866), p. 106.

20. Frederick Burr Hawley journal, December 13, 1862, Buck Zaidel collection.

21. Charles Lyman, as quoted in Page, *History of the Fourteenth,* p. 89. Symonds and Dart were brothers-in-law. Both survived the war. Symonds never regained his sight.

22. Benjamin Hirst, "War Papers: History of Co. D, 14th Regt. Conn. Vols," in *Rockville Journal,* March 24, 1887, as quoted in Bee, *The Boys from Rockville,* p. 74.

23. Frederick Burr Hawley journal, December 13, 1862, Buck Zaidel collection.

24. Letter of Henry P. Goddard to his mother, December 14, 1862, courtesy of Calvin Goddard Zon.

25. Months later, Davis was dishonorably discharged.

26. Chaplain Henry Stevens, as quoted in Page, *History of the Fourteenth,* p. 86.

27. Henry P. Goddard, *Memorial of Deceased Officers of the 14th Regiment Connecticut Volunteers* (Hartford, CT: Case, Lockwood & Brainard, 1872), p. 36.

28. Letter of Uriah Parmelee to his mother, December 26, 1862, David M. Rubenstein Rare Book & Manuscript Library, Duke University.

29. Goddard, *Memorial,* pp. 36–38.

30. Ibid., p. 38.

31. Favill, *Diary of a Young Officer,* p. 210.

32. Sheldon, *The Twenty-Seventh*, pp. 25–26.

33. Thorpe, *History of the Fifteenth*, p. 35.

34. Favill, *Diary of a Young Officer*, p. 211.

35. Tarbell, *A Reporter for Lincoln*, p. 38.

36. Favill, *Diary of a Young Officer*, p. 211.

37. Tarbell, *A Reporter for Lincoln*, p. 38.

38. *Charleston Daily Courier*, December 30, 1862, as quoted in Francis Augustin O'Reilly, *The Fredericksburg Campaign—Winter War on the Rappahannock* (Baton Rouge: Louisiana State University Press, 2003), p. 304.

39. Tarbell, *A Reporter for Lincoln*, p. 38.

40. Samuel C. Waldron reminiscence, New Haven Museum.

41. Favill, *Diary of a Young Officer*, p. 211.

42. Sheldon, *The Twenty-Seventh*, pp. 29–30.

43. Favill, *Diary of a Young Officer*, p. 212.

44. Goddard, *14th C.V. Reminiscences*, p. 12.

45. Frederick Burr Hawley journal, December 13, 1862, Buck Zaidel collection.

46. Sheldon, *The Twenty-Seventh*, p. 30.

47. Letter of Assistant Surgeon Thomas Morton Hills, 27th Connecticut, December 15, 1862, Cal Packard at mqamericana.com.

48. Charles Lyman, as quoted in Page, *History of the Fourteenth*, pp. 94–95.

49. Fiske, *Mr. Dunn Browne's Experiences*, p. 107.

50. Charles Lyman, as quoted in Page, *History of the Fourteenth*, pp. 89–92.

51. Frederick Burr Hawley journal, December 14, 1862, Buck Zaidel collection.

52. Tarbell, *A Reporter for Lincoln*, p. 39.

53. Ibid., pp. 39–40.

54. Henry Wing lived until 1925; Jerry Grady (or Gready) died in Vernon in 1897; Frederick Burr Hawley died in 1917 in Bridgeport.

55. Goddard, *Memorial*, p. 13.

56. Page, *History of the Fourteenth*, p. 107.

57. Sheldon, *The Twenty-Seventh*, p. 31.

58. Letter of Samuel K. Zook to E. I. Wade, December 16, 1862, as quoted in Ezra J. Warner, *Generals in Blue: Lives of the Union Commanders* (Baton Rouge: Louisiana State University Press, 1964.

59. Letter of Frederick A. Lucas, December 16, 1862, as quoted in Barker, *Dear Mother*, pp. 26–27.

60. *Meriden Weekly Republican*, June 3, 1897, p. 3.

61. Sheldon, *The Twenty-Seventh*, p. 30.

62. Samuel C. Waldron reminiscences, New Haven Museum.

63. Fiske, *Mr. Dunn Browne's Experiences*, p. 106.

64. Samuel C. Waldron reminiscences, New Haven Museum.

65. Letter of Henry P. Goddard to his mother, December 17, 1862, courtesy of Calvin Goddard Zon.

66. Page, *History of the Fourteenth*, p. 104.

67. Thorpe, *History of the Fifteenth*, pp. 40–41.

68. Letter of George Hubbard, December 31, 1862, courtesy of the Middlesex County Historical Society, Middletown.

8. Who Wouldn't Be a Soldier?

1. Page, *History of the Fourteenth*, p. 110.

2. Letter of Sgt. Charles G. Blake, 34th Massachusetts Regiment, April 12, 1863, Buck Zaidel collection.

3. Vaill, *History of the Second*, pp. 134–35.

4. Unidentified Wesleyan alumnus (probably Wilbur Fisk Osborne), "Wesleyan in the Army, or Every Man His Own Roswell," in *The College Argus*, April 27, 1880, p. 139.

5. Augustus Bronson's letter to the *Danbury Times*, September 12, 1862.

6. Vaill, *History of the Second*, pp. 18–19.

7. Thorpe, *History of the Fifteenth*, p. 41.

8. Ibid., pp. 42.

9. Page, *History of the Fourteenth*, p. 108.

10. Ibid.

11. Thorpe, *History of the Fifteenth*, pp. 42–43.

12. Letter of Fred Doten to Georgia Welles, August 10, 1864, courtesy of K. C. Owings.

13. Journal of James Sawyer, Connecticut Historical Society, Hartford.

14. Sheldon, *The Twenty-Seventh*, pp. 36–37.

15. Ibid., pp. 35, 37.

16. Letter from Charles L. Upham, August 26, 1862, Buck Zaidel collection.

17. Letter of Andrew Upson to his wife, November 11, 1863, Southington Library and Museum, Barnes Museum.

18. Fiske, *Mr. Dunn Browne's Experiences*, p. 71.

19. Letter from Titus Moss, December 6, 1862, Cheshire (CT) Historical Society.

20. Letter from Titus Moss, December 22, 1862, Cheshire (CT) Historical Society.

21. Whitaker diary (typescript), January 17, 1864, NPS/Andersonville National Historic Site.

22. "We've Drunk from the Same Canteen," words by Major Charles G. Halpine, [Miles O'Reilly], music by James C. Clark (New York: William A. Pond & Co., 1865).

23. Page, *History of the Fourteenth*, p. 178, quoting William Hincks' 1879 address.

24. Journal of Reese B. Gwillim, November 18, 1862, Connecticut Historical Society, Hartford.

25. Fiske, *Mr. Dunn Browne's Experiences*, p. 73.

26. Letter of Daniel P. Dewey, January 14, 1863, as quoted in *A Memorial of Lt. Daniel Perkins Dewey of the 25th Regiment Connecticut Volunteers* (Hartford, CT: Case, Lockwood & Co., 1864), p. 51.

27. Letter of Titus Moss, March 11, 1863, Cheshire (CT) Historical Society.

28. Sheldon, *The Twenty-Seventh*, pp. 40–41.

29. Diary entry, October 22, 1863, in Chapman, *Civil War Diary*, p. 42.

30. Charles K. Cadwell, *The Old Sixth Regiment, Its War Record* (New Haven, CT: Tuttle, Morehouse & Taylor, 1875), pp. 44–45.

31. Charles H. Lynch, *The Civil War Diary 1862–1865 of Charles H. Lynch, 18th Conn. Vol's* (Hartford, CT: Case, Lockwood & Brainard, 1915), p. 37.

32. Letter of Frederick A. Lucas to his mother, January 10, 1863, in Barker, *Dear Mother*, p. 34.

33. Diary entry, September 18, 1863, in Chapman, *Civil War Diary*, p. 95.

34. Diary of Alfred P. Hanks, February 9, 1864, Mansfield (CT) Historical Society.

35. Letter of Abner C. Smith, October 5, 1862, online at dbappdev.com/Acs/20thconn/ct20/acs/ltrs/AS_3.013.html.

36. Letter of Charles S. Dudley, October 1, 1862, Edith B. Nettleton Historical Room, Guilford Free Library.

37. Letter of Augustus E. Bronson, November 13, 1862, to the *Danbury Times*.

38. Letter of Frederick Lucas to his mother, September 7, 1864, in Barker, *Dear Mother*, p. 318.

39. Letter of Frederick A. Lucas, February 26, 1864, as quoted in ibid., p. 290.

40. Benjamin Hirst, February 5, 1863, as quoted in Page, *History of the Fourteenth*, p. 111.

41. Vaill, *History of the Second*, p. 79.

42. Thorpe, *History of the Fifteenth*, pp. 49–50.

43. Diary of Captain Horace G. H. Tarr, November 16, 1864, as quoted in Storrs, *The Twentieth Connecticut*, p. 150.

44. Lynch, *Civil War Diary*, p. 64.

45. Sprague, *History of the 13th*, p. 77.

46. Walker, *History of the Eighteenth*, p. 326.

47. Letter of Charles A. Boyle, October 5, 1863, Connecticut Historical Society, Hartford.

48. Edward Ashley Walker, *Our First Year of Army Life*, p. 49.

49. Letter of Frederick A. Lucas, February 23, 1865, Connecticut Historical Society, Hartford.

50. 2nd Heavy Artillery, Homer Sackett, letter of August 3, 1864, Connecticut Historical Society, Hartford.

51. Mary A. Livermore, *My Story of the War: A Woman's Narrative of Four Years Personal Experience* (Hartford, CT: A. D. Worthington and Co., 1888), p. 129.

52. Croffut and Morris, *Military and Civil History*, p. 464.

53. Letter of Robert Fisk, September 18, 1864, as quoted in *Lizzie: The Letters of Elizabeth Chester Fisk, 1864–1893*, edited by Rex C. Myers (Missoula, MT: Mountain Press, 1989), p. 11.

54. Annie Hanshew, *Border to Border: Historic Quilts and Quiltmakers of Montana* (Helena, MT: Montana Historical Society Press, 2009), pp. 18–20.

55. Fiske, *Mr. Dunn Browne's Experiences*, p. 73.

56. Letter of Frederick Lucas to his mother, February 20, 1863, in Barker, *Dear Mother*, pp. 51–52.

57. Letter of Frederick Lucas to his mother, May 11, 1863, in ibid., p. 90.

58. Journal of James H. Sawyer, Connecticut Historical Society, Hartford.

59. Letter of Frederick Lucas to his mother, May 13, 1863, in Barker, *Dear Mother*, pp. 94–95.

60. Walker, *Our First Year*, pp. 84–85.

61. Ibid.

62. Thomas Hamilton Murray, *History of the 9th Connecticut, Connecticut Volunteer Infantry* (New Haven, CT: Price, Lee & Adkins Co., 1903), p. 71.

63. Charles M. Coit to his mother and sister, April 6, 1864, GLC03603.266, courtesy of the Gilder Lehrman Institute of American History.

64. *The Connecticut War Record*, February 1865, p. 358.

65. Letter of Frederick Lucas to his mother, February 22, 1863, in Barker, *Dear Mother*, p. 53.

66. Diary of Nelson Stowe, January 4, 1865, Connecticut Historical Society, Hartford.

67. Whitaker diary (typescript), February 22, 1864, NPS/Andersonville National Historic Site.

68. Goddard, *14th C.V. Regimental Reminiscences*, p. 12.

69. Letter of Andrew Upson, Aug. 12, 1863, Southington Library and Museum, Barnes Museum.

70. Trumbull, *War Memories of an Army Chaplain*, pp. 4–5.

71. Civil War reminiscences of Van Buren Kinney, Connecticut Historical Society, Hartford.

72. Letter of Dr. George Clary, April 5, 1863, Connecticut Historical Society, Hartford.

73. Typescript of letter of Joseph R. Hawley, December, 1861, Connecticut Historical Society, Hartford.

74. Charles M. Coit to his sister, April 12, 1864, GLC03603.267, courtesy of the Gilder Lehrman Institute of American History.

75. Thorpe, *History of the Fifteenth*, p. 77.

76. Letter of Captain Isaac H. Bromley to the *Norwich Bulletin*, September 30, 1862, as quoted in Walker, *History of the Eighteenth*, pp. 41–42.

77. Theodore J. Holmes, *A Memorial of John S. Jameson, Sergeant in the 1st Connecticut Cavalry* (no place, no date, no publisher), p. 14.

78. Raphael Ward Benton letter to his wife, September 7, 1862,

Edith B. Nettleton Historical Room, Guilford (CT) Free Library.

79. Goddard, *Fourteenth Connecticut Volunteers*, p. 15.

80. Ibid.

81. Letter of Frederick A. Lucas to his mother, October 8, 1862, in Barker, *Dear Mother*, p. 23.

82. Letter of Lewis Bissell, as quoted in *The Civil War Letters of Lewis Bissell* (Washington, DC: The Field School Educational Foundation Press, 1981), p. 257.

83. Sprague, *History of the 13th*, pp. 96–97.

84. Letter of Austin Thompson to Electa Churchill, December 27, 1862, Connecticut Historical Society, Hartford.

85. Holmes, *Memorial of John S. Jameson*, pp. 27–28.

9. All This Heroism, and All This Appalling Carnage

1. Page, *History of the Fourteenth*, p. 110.

2. Ibid., p. 116.

3. William H. Warren, manuscript, "Seventeenth Connecticut: The Record of a Yankee Regiment in the War for the Union," Article 11; Bridgeport History Center, Bridgeport Public Library.

4. Ibid.

5. Ibid.

6. Ibid.

7. Charles H. Morgan, as quoted in Francis A. Walker's *History of the Second Army Corps in the Army of the Potomac* (New York: Charles Scribner's Sons, 1886), p. 228.

8. Colonel William H. Noble, "History of the Seventeenth Connecticut," in *The History of Fairfield County, Connecticut,* by D. Hamilton Hurd (Philadelphia, PA: J. W. Lewis & Co., 1881), p. 59.

9. Frederick I. Hitchcock, *War from the Inside* (Philadelphia, PA: J. B. Lippincott Co., 1904), pp. 218–19.

10. Fiske, *Mr. Dunn Browne's Experiences*, pp. 146–48.

11. Elnathan B. Tyler, as quoted in Page, *History of the Fourteenth*, p. 122.

12. Chapman, *Civil War Diary*, pp. 10–12.

13. Storrs, *The Twentieth Connecticut*, p. 53.

14. Sheldon, *The Twenty-Seventh*, p. 52.

15. Ibid., pp. 53–54.

16. Ibid, p. 54.

17. Sgt. James McWhinnie as quoted in *The 20th Connecticut, A Regimental History*, pp. 58–60.

18. Letter of Abner C. Smith, May 7, 1863, online at dbappdev.com/acs/20thconn/ct20/acs/ltrs/AS_1_030.html.

19. Letter of Abner C. Smith, May 16, 1863, online at dbappdev.com/acs/20thconn/ct20/acs/ltrs/AS_1_030.html.

20. Samuel K. Ellis, December 30, 1862, in *The Twenty-Fifth Regiment Connecticut Volunteers in the War of the Rebellion*, by George P. Bissell, Samuel K. Ellis, Thomas McManus, and Henry Hill Goodell (Rockville, CT: Press of the Rockville Journal, 1913), p. 15.

21. Sprague, *History of the 13th*, pp. 104–6.

22. George P. Bissell, "History of the Twenty-Fifth Regiment C.V. Infantry," in *Record of Service of Connecticut Men in the Army and Navy of the Unites States during the War of the Rebellion*, compiled by Authority of the General Assembly under the Direction of the Adjutants-General (Hartford, CT: Case, Lockwood & Brainard, 1889), p. 791.

23. Samuel K. Ellis, "Experiences and Reminiscences of Samuel K. Ellis of Rockville," in *The Twenty-Fifth Regiment Connecticut Volunteers in the War of the Rebellion*, by by George P. Bissell, Samuel K. Ellis, Thomas McManus, and Henry Hill Goodell (Rockville, CT: Press of the Rockville Journal, 1913) p. 61.

24. DeForest, *A Volunteer's Adventures*, p. 112.

25. John W. DeForest, "Port Hudson," in *Harper's New Monthly Magazine*, August, 1867, p. 335.

26. Sprague, *History of the 13th*, p. 149.

27. DeForest, *A Volunteer's Adventures*, p. 105.

28. Letter of Sgt. George Hammond to Cousin Bingham, June 12, 1863, collection of Lawrence S. Matthew.

29. Ellis, *The Twenty-Fifth Regiment Connecticut Volunteers*, pp. 46–47.

30. DeForest, *A Volunteer's Adventures*, p. 114.

31. Ibid., p. 116.

32. Ibid.

33. Letter of John G. Crosby, June 4, 1863, Connecticut Historical Society, Hartford.

34. DeForest, "Port Hudson," p. 337.

35. DeForest, *A Volunteer's Adventures*, p. 119.

36. Sprague, *History of the 13th*, p. 149.

37. Ibid., p. 150.

38. Croffut and Morris, *Military and Civil History*, p. 412.

39. Ibid., p. 413.

40. Sprague, *History of the 13th*, pp. 158–59.

41. Ibid., p. 159.

42. Ibid.

43. Ibid., pp. 160–61.

44. Croffut and Morris, *Military and Civil History*, p. 350.

45. Lynch, *Civil War Diary*, p. 19.

46. Walker, *History of the Eighteenth*, p. 110.

47. Letter of unidentified soldier of the 13th Connecticut, as quoted in Croffut and Morris, *Military and Civil History*, p. 353.

48. Lynch, *Civil War Diary*, pp. 21–22.

49. Croffut and Morris, *Military and Civil History*, p. 354.

50. William G. Ely, "History of the Eighteenth Regiment C.V. Infantry," in *Record of Service of Connecticut Men in the Army and Navy of the United States During the War of the Rebellion*, compiled by Authority of the General Assembly under the Direction of the Adjutants-General (Hartford, CT: Case, Lockwood & Brainard, 1889), p. 665.

10. That Place Long to Be Remembered

1. Entry of Gideon Welles, June 15, 1863, in *Diary of Gideon Welles* (Boston & New York: Houghton Mifflin Co., 1911), vol. 1, pp. 329–30.

2. George Meade, *The Life and Letters of George Gordon Meade* (New York: Charles Scribner's Sons, 1913), vol. 2, pp. 12, 14.

3. Letter of Loren Goodrich, July 17, 1863, Connecticut Historical Society, Hartford.

4. Letter of Benjamin Hirst to his wife Sarah, July 5, 1863, New England Civil War Museum, as quoted in Bee, *The Boys from Rockville*, p. 147.

5. C. Frederick Betts, as quoted in William Warren manuscript, Article 15.

6. Letter of Justus M. Silliman to his mother, July 3, 1863, as quoted in *A New Canaan Private in the Civil War: Letters of Justus M. Silliman, 17th Connecticut Volunteers*, edited by Edward Marcus (New Canaan, CT: New Canaan Historical Society, 1984) pp. 39–41.

7. Letter of J. Henry Blakeman, July 21, 1863, United States Army Military History Institute, Carlisle Barracks, PA.

8. James Montgomery Bailey [H. P. Manton], "Slice Second" in the *Danbury Times*, September 24, 1863, as quoted on the 17th Connecticut Volunteer Infantry Website: www.17thcvi.org.

9. Letter of John Gordon, July 7, 1863, Gordon Family Papers, University of Georgia, as quoted in Edwin B. Coddington, *The Gettysburg Campaign, A Study in Command* (New York: Charles Scribner's Sons, 1968), p. 291.

10. Letter of Justus M. Silliman to his mother, July 3, 1863, as quoted in *A New Canaan Private in the Civil War, Letters of Justus M. Silliman, 17th Connecticut Volunteers*, edited by Edward Marcus (New Canaan, CT: New Canaan Historical Society, 1984), p. 41.

11. James Brand, *Twenty-Six Years Pastor of the First Congregational Church, Oberlin* (Oberlin, OH: Luther Day Harkness, 1899), p. 45.

12. Almond Clark, typescript essay, "The 27th Regiment Connecticut Volunteers—from the Time It Started on the March to Gettysburg—from My Diary," Connecticut Historical Society, Hartford.

13. Sheldon, *The Twenty-Seventh*, p. 91.

14. Clark, "The 27th Regiment," Connecticut Historical Society, Hartford.

15. Frank D. Sloat, in *Record of Service of Connecticut Men in the Army and Navy of the United States during War of the Rebellion*, compiled by Authority of the General Assembly under the Direction of the Adjutants-General (Hartford, CT: Case, Lockwood & Brainard, 1889), pp. 827–28.

16. *Hartford Courant*, April 17, 1899, p. 8.

17. Clark, "The 27th Regiment," Connecticut Historical Society, Hartford.

18. Ibid.

19. Letter of Abner C. Smith, July 4, 1863, online at dbappdev.com/acs/20thconn/ct20/acs/ltrs/AS_1_006.html.

20. Lieutenant M. H. Daniels, as quoted in Warren, Article 15.

21. Major Allen G. Brady's official report, July 4, 1863, *The War of the Rebellion: A Compilation of the Official Records of the Union and Confederate Armies* (Washington, DC: Government Printing Office, 1889), ser. 1, vol. 27, part 1, p. 716.

22. Lieutenant M. H. Daniels, as quoted in Warren, Article 15.

23. Letter from Abner C. Smith, July 4, 1863, online at dbappdev.com/acs/20thconn/ct20/acs/ltrs/AS_1_050.html.

24. Storrs, *The Twentieth Connecticut*, p. 88.

25. Philo Buckingham, as quoted in ibid., p. 90.

26. Ibid., p. 91.

27. Ibid., pp. 91–92.

28. Chapman, *Civil War Diary*, pp. 22–23.

29. Philo B. Buckingham, as quoted in Storrs, *The Twentieth Connecticut*, p. 93.

30. Ibid.

31. Elnathan B. Tyler, as quoted in Page, *History of the Fourteenth*, p. 142.

32. Henry S. Stevens, *Souvenir of Excursions to Battlefields* (Washington, DC: Gibson Brothers, 1893), p. 16.

33. Letter of Benjamin Hirst to his wife, Sarah, July 5, 1863, as quoted in Bee, *The Boys From Rockville*, pp. 148–49.

34. Page, *History of the Fourteenth*, p. 144.

35. Stevens, *Souvenir*, p. 18.

36. Page, *History of the Fourteenth*, p. 146.

37. Stevens, *Souvenir*, p. 18.

38. Ibid., p. 19.

39. Ibid., p. 18.

40. Ibid., p. 19.

41. Ibid.

42. Henry S. Stevens, *Address Delivered at the Dedication of Monument of the 14th Connecticut Volunteers at Gettysburg, Penn., July 3d, 1884* (Middletown, CT: Pelton & King, 1884), p. 18.

43. Ibid.

44. Stevens, *Souvenir*, pp. 21, 22.

45. Ibid., p. 22.

46. Stevens, *Address*, p. 20.

47. Letter of Benjamin Hirst to his wife, Sarah, July 5, 1863, New England Civil War Museum, as quoted in Bee, *The Boys from Rockville*, p. 149.

48. William Hincks, as quoted in Page, *History of the Fourteenth*, p. 149.

49. Ibid., p. 150.

50. C. Frederick Betts, as quoted in Warren, Article 15.

51. Letter of Benjamin Hirst to his wife Sarah, July 5, 1863, New England Civil War Museum, as quoted in Bee, *The Boys from Rockville*, p. 149.

52. William Hincks, as quoted in Page, *History of the Fourteenth*, p. 150.

53. Major Theodore G. Ellis, 14th Connecticut Infantry, Official Report, July 6, 1863, *The War of the Rebellion: A Compilation of the Official Records of the Union and Confederate Armies* (Washington, DC: Government Printing Office, 1889), ser. 1, vol. 27, part 1, p. 467.

54. Page, *History of the Fourteenth*, p. 151.

55. *The Story of the 116th Regiment, Pennsylvania Infantry* by St. Clair Augustin Mulholland (Philadelphia, PA: F. McManus, Jr. & Co., 1899), p. 140.

56. Stevens, *Souvenir*, p. 29.

57. Page, *History of the Fourteenth*, pp. 151–52.

58. Stevens, *Souvenir*, p. 29.

59. Ibid.

60. Page, *History of the Fourteenth*, 152.

61. Ibid., p. 153.

62. Ibid., p. 154.

63. Ibid., p. 153.

64. Ibid., p. 156.

65. Letter from Henry P. Goddard, July 8, 1863, courtesy of Calvin Goddard Zon.

66. Page, *History of the Fourteenth*, p. 156.

67. Edward H. Wade, as quoted in *Uncle Sam's Medal of Honor*, edited by Theophilus F. Rodenbough (New York and London: G. P. Putnam's Sons, 1886), pp. 58–59.

68. Edward H. Wade, as quoted in Page, *History of the Fourteenth*, p. 58.

69. Stevens, *Souvenir*, p. 33.

70. Letter of William Glossinger to Thomas W. Gardner, July 28, 1863, printed with permission of the Pearce Museum, Navarro College.

71. Page, *History of the Fourteenth*, p. 158.

72. Edward H. Wade, as quoted in *Uncle Sam's Medal of Honor*, p. 64.

73. Chapman, *Civil War Diary*, pp. 23–24.

74. Ibid., p. 24.

75. Storrs, *The Twentieth Connecticut*, p. 102.

76. Letter of James Robert Middlebrook, July 9, 1863, Connecticut Historical Society, Hartford.

77. Letter of James Robert Middlebrook, July 13, 1863, Connecticut Historical Society, Hartford.

78. Letter of Dennis Tuttle to his wife, July 5, 1863, printed with permission of the Pearce Museum, Navarro College.

79. Stevens, *Souvenir*, pp. 36–37.

80. Letter of Loren Goodrich to "Friends," July 17, 1863, Connecticut Historical Society, Hartford.

81. Letter of James Robert Middlebrook to his wife, Fanny, July 12, 1865, Connecticut Historical Society, Hartford.

82. Joshua Lawrence Chamberlain, "General Chamberlain's Address" at the dedication of the Maine monuments at Gettysburg, October 3, 1889, as quoted in *Maine at Gettysburg*, report of Maine Commissioners (Portland, ME: Lakeside Press, 1898), pp. 558–59.

11. There Will Be No Turning Back

1. Letter of Martin Eddy to his brother, August 1, 1863, printed with permission of the Pearce Museum, Navarro College.

2. Cadwell, *The Old Sixth Regiment*, p. 71.

3. Ibid., p. 72.

4. Letter of Martin Eddy to his brother, August 1, 1863, printed with permission of the Pearce Museum, Navarro College.

5. Cadwell, *The Old Sixth Regiment*, p. 72.

6. Letter of Martin Eddy to his brother, August 1, 1863, printed with permission of the Pearce Museum, Navarro College.

7. Ibid.

8. Cadwell, *The Old Sixth Regiment*, p. 74.

9. Croffut and Morris, *Military and Civil History*, p. 507.

10. Page, *History of the Fourteenth*, p. 220.

11. Letter of Charles E. Pollard to his mother, February 9, 1864, Buck Zaidel collection.

12. Page, *History of the Fourteenth*, p. 221.

13. Ibid., p. 223.

14. Robert H. Kellogg, *Life and Death in Rebel Prisons* (Hartford, CT: L. Stebbins, 1865), p. 56.

15. Ibid., pp. 57–58.

16. *Hartford Daily Courant*, June 27, 1865, quoting June 23, 1865, letter from Dorence Atwater.

17. Diary of James Haggerty, HM 70395, p. 22, Huntington Library, San Marino, CA.

18. Ibid., pp. 57–58.

19. Ibid., p. 21.

20. Homer B. Sprague, *Lights and Shadows in Confederate Prisons* (New York and London: G. P. Putnam's Sons, 1915), pp. 135–36.

21. Letter written by Harriet Foote Hawley from Wilmington, NC, April 7, 1865 to a cousin, quoted in Huntington and Foote, *Harriet Ward Foote Hawley*, p. 75.
22. Page, *History of the Fourteenth*, p. 233.
23. Charles Blatchley, as quoted in ibid., p. 243.
24. Elnathan B. Tyler, as quoted in ibid., pp. 242–43.
25. John Hirst, as quoted in ibid., p. 245.
26. Diary entry of Amanda Akin, June 7, 1864, at Armory Square Hospital in Washington, as quoted in *The Lady Nurse of Ward E*, by Amanda Akin Stearns (New York: The Baker & Taylor Co., 1909), p. 275.
27. Letter of Harriet Hawley to Cousin Belle, May 31, 1864, Library of Congress.
28. Letter written by nurse Helen Griggs, May 30, 1864, as quoted in Amanda Akin Stearns, *The Lady Nurse of Ward E*, pp. 263–65.
29. Letter of Harriet Hawley to Cousin Belle, May 31, 1864, Library of Congress.
30. Diary entries of nurse Amanda Akin at Armory Square Hospital, quoted in Amanda Akin Stearns, *The Lady Nurse of Ward E*, pp. 261–62.
31. Ibid., pp. 254, 275.
32. Walt Whitman, "A Connecticut Case," in *Walt Whitman: Poetry and Prose*, edited by Justin Kaplan (New York: Library of America, 1982) pp. 719–20.
33. Vaill, *History of the Second*, pp. 48–49.
34. Ibid., p. 49.
35. Letter of Frederick A. Lucas, May 18, 1864, in Barker, *Dear Mother*, p. 267.
36. Letter of Frederick A. Lucas to his mother, May 21, 1864, in ibid.
37. Letter of Frederick A. Lucas to his mother, June 9, 1864, in ibid., p. 277.
38. Vaill, *History of the Second*, p. 51.
39. Ibid., p. 58.
40. Letter of Lewis Bissell, June 6, 1864, as quoted in *The Civil War Letters of Lewis Bissell*, p. 254.
41. Vaill, *History of the Second*, p. 329.
42. Ibid.
43. Ibid., pp. 60–61.
44. Ibid., pp. 62–63.
45. Ibid., p. 63.
46. Ibid., pp. 65–66.
47. Ibid., p. 66.
48. Letter of Lewis Bissell, June 6, 1864, as quoted in *The Civil War Letters of Lewis Bissell*, p. 254.
49. Martin T. McMahon, Brevet Major General, U.S. Volunteers, of the Sixth Corps, "Cold Harbor," in *Battles and Leaders of the Civil War* (New York: The Century Co., 1884), vol. 4, pp. 218–19.
50. Letter of Lewis Bissell to "Aunt," June 10, 1864, as quoted in *The Civil War Letters of Lewis Bissell*, pp. 255, 256.
51. Vaill, *History of the Second*, pp. 327–28.
52. Ulysses S. Grant, *Personal Memoirs of U. S. Grant* (New York: Charles L. Webster, 1885), p. 373.
53. Letter of Lewis Bissell letter, June 6, 1864, as quoted in *The Civil War Letters of Lewis Bissell*, p. 255.
54. Letter of Lewis Bissell to his mother, undated (October 8–12, 1862), as quoted in *The Civil War Letters of Lewis Bissell*, p. 16.
55. Croffut and Morris, *Military and Civil History*, p. 594.
56. Vaill, *History of the Second*, p. 55.
57. Abraham Lincoln's letter to Mrs. Bixby, November 21, 1864, printed in the *Boston Evening Transcript* on November 25, 1864.
58. *Hartford Daily Courant*, June 15, 1864, p. 2, quoting June 6 letter of Joseph Bachus [*sic*].
59. Croffut and Morris, *Military and Civil History*, p. 613.
60. *Hartford Daily Courant*, June 15, 1864, p. 2, quoting June 6 letter of Joseph Bachus [*sic*].
61. Holmes, "Memorial of John S. Jameson," pp. 21–23.
62. Official Report of Major George O. Marcy, First Connecticut Cavalry, July 24, 1864, in *The War of the Rebellion: A Compilation of the Official Records of the Union and Confederate Armies* (Washington, DC: Government Printing Office, 1892), ser. 1, vol. 40, part 1, p. 638.
63. Diary entry for June 29, 1864, in *The Civil War Diary of Captain Uriah Nelson Parmelee, A Son of Guilford*, edited by Charles Lewis Biggs (Guilford, CT: no publisher, 1940), p. 6.
64. Marcy, Official Report, p. 638.
65. Holmes, "Memorial of John S. Jameson," p. 22.
66. *Hartford Daily Courant*, June 15, 1864, p. 2.
67. Letter of Frank Stoughton, August 29, 1864, Mansfield (CT) Historical Society.
68. Croffut and Morris, *Military and Civil History*, pp. 461–62.

12. Hope Never Dying

1. Letter from W. J. Orton, June 15, 1864, as quoted in *History of Ancient Woodbury, Connecticut*, by William Cothren (Woodbury, CT: William Cothren, 1872), vol. 2, p. 1265.
2. Walter L. Powell, "'Let His Big Guns Shoot!' Colonel Henry L. Abbot and the 1st and 2nd Connecticut Heavy Artillery at Petersburg, 1864–1865," in *Connecticut History* 50, no. 1 (Spring 2011): 5.
3. Letter of Thomas Swan Trumbull, 1st Connecticut Heavy Artillery, June 26, 1864, courtesy of Cowan's Auctions, Inc., Cincinnati, OH.

4. Letter of Thomas Swan Trumbull, July 1864, courtesy of Cowan's Auctions, Inc., Cincinnati, OH.

5. Letter of Lt. Lewis W. Jackson to his sister, Mrs. Barzilla Thresher of Hartford, August 19, 1864, typescript by Dean Nelson, Connecticut State Archives, Hartford.

6. "Wesleyan in the Army" (probably written by Wilbur Fisk Osborne) in *The College Argus*, April 27, 1880.

7. Unidentified writer from the 10th Connecticut, in *Hartford Daily Courant*, September 14, 1864, p. 2.

8. Ibid.

9. Moses Smith, July 20, 1864, as quoted in Croffut and Morris, *Military and Civil History*, p. 618.

10. Henry Goddard Thomas, "The Colored Troops at Petersburg," in *Battles and Leaders of the Civil War*, vol. 4, edited by Robert Underwood Johnson and Clarence Clough Buell (New York: The Century Co., 1888), p. 564.

11. Sgt. Harry Reese of the 48th Pennsylvania, as quoted in Richard Slotkin, *No Quarter* (New York: Random House, 2009), p. 240.

12. Thomas, "The Colored Troops," p. 564.

13. Ibid., p. 565.

14. Ibid.

15. Report of Major Thomas Wright, 31st United States Colored Troops, of operations June 4–November 6, 1864 in *Annual Report of the Adjutant-General of the State of Connecticut, for the Year Ending March 31, 1866* (Hartford, CT: A. N. Clark & Co., 1866), pp. 224–25.

16. Thomas, "The Colored Troops," p. 567.

17. Mark Williams, *Tempest in a Small Town* (Granby, CT: Salmon Brook Historical Society, 1996), pp. 369–71; quoting William Case's speech in unidentified, undated newspaper clipping.

18. Trumbull, *The Knightly Soldier*, quoting Henry Ward Camp letter, p. 287.

19. Trumbull, *War Memories of an Army Chaplain*, p. 222.

20. Ibid., pp. 222–24.

21. Page, *History of the Fourteenth*, p. 295, quoting Dr. Levi Jewett.

22. Chapman, *Civil War Diary*, p. 70.

23. Ibid., pp. 70-71.

24. Letter of Abner C. Smith, July 27, 1864, online at dbappdev.com/acs/20thconn/ct20/acs/ltrs/AS_2_051.html.

25. John G. Nicolay and John Hay, *Abraham Lincoln: A History*, 10 vols. (New York: The Century Co., 1890), vol. 9, p. 221.

26. *Hartford Daily Courant*, October 8, 1864, writing about the previous six weeks.

27. Ibid., August 8, 1864.

28. Chapman, *Civil War Diary*, pp. 92–93.

29. Ibid., pp. 93–94.

30. *Hartford Daily Courant*, September 3, 1864, p. 2.

31. Grant, *Personal Memoirs*, p. 490.

32. Diary of Michael Kelly, September 17, 1864, Connecticut Historical Society, Hartford.

33. Erastus Blaskeslee, "History of the First Regiment Connecticut Volunteer Cavalry," in *Record of Service of Connecticut Men in the Army and Navy of the United States during the War of the Rebellion*, compiled by Authority of the General Assembly under the Direction of the Adjutants-General (Hartford, CT: Case, Lockwood & Brainard, 1889), pp. 58–59.

34. Sprague, *History of the 13th*, p. 228.

35. J. W. DeForest, "Sheridan's Battle of Winchester," in *Harpers New Monthly Magazine*, January 1865.

36. Vaill, *History of the Second*, p. 95.

37. Ibid., p. 96.

38. Diary of Michael Kelly, September 19, 1864, Connecticut Historical Society, Hartford.

39. Maj.-Gen. Philip H. Sheridan, Official Dispatch, September 20, 1864, as quoted in correspondence of Brig.-Gen. J. D. Stevenson to E. M. Stanton, September 20, 1864, in *The War of the Rebellion: A Compilation of the Official Records of the Union and Confederate Armies* (Washington, DC: Government Printing Office, 1893), ser. 1, vol. 43, part 2, p. 124.

40. Vaill, *History of the Second*, pp. 98–99.

41. Ibid., p. 109, quoting letters written by Alfred G. Bliss to the *Winsted Herald*.

42. Ibid., p. 113.

43. Ibid., p. 121.

44. Ibid., p. 122.

45. Ibid.

46. Ibid., 123.

47. Edward Albert Pollard, *The Lost Cause* (New York: E. B. Treat & Co., 1867), p. 599.

48. Sprague, *History of the 13th*, p. 239.

49. Ibid., p. 241.

50. Letter from Capt. L. A. Dickinson, 12th CV, Oct. 21, 1864, quoted in *Hartford Daily Courant*, October 29, 1864, p. 2.

51. Ibid.

52. Vaill, *History of the Second*, pp. 129–30.

53. Papers of Michael Kelly, Connecticut Historical Society, Hartford.

54. Vaill, *History of the Second*, p. 99.

55. Letter of Abner C. Smith, December 18, 1864, online at dbappdev.com/acs/20thconn/ct20/acs/ltrs/AS_1_092.html.

56. Ibid.

57. Chapman, *Civil War Diary*, p. 95.

58. Diary of Capt. Horace G. H. Tarr, quoted in Storrs, *The Twentieth Connecticut*, pp. 155–56.

13. Our Army Perfectly Crazy

1. *Hartford Daily Courant*, January 2, 1865.
2. *Willimantic Journal*, January 5, 1865.
3. George T. Meech, "At Ninety-one" (Privately printed, no place, 1935).
4. *Hartford Daily Courant*, February 2, 1865.
5. Croffut and Morris, *Military and Civil History*, p. 767.
6. Official Report of Lt. Col. Philo B. Buckingham, March 28, 1865, in Croffut and Morris, *Military and Civil History*, p. 771.
7. Mary Elizabeth Dickison, *Dickison and His Men* (Louisville, KY: Courier-Journal Job Printing Co., 1890), p. 122.
8. Letter of Willis McDonald, May 27, 1865, quoting an unidentified member of Co. F, 17th Connecticut, Buck Zaidel collection.
9. Thorpe, *History of the Fifteenth*, p. 91.
10. Ibid., p. 112.
11. Ibid., p. 96.
12. Ibid., p. 114.
13. Henry C. Baldwin, in ibid., pp. 247–48.
14. Ibid., p. 248.
15. Ibid., p. 251.
16. Ibid., pp. 251–52.
17. Edwin E. Marvin, *The 5th Regiment Connecticut Volunteers, A History* (Hartford, CT: Press of Wiley, Waterman Eaton, 1889), pp. 371–72.
18. *Norwalk Hour*, September 22, 1930, p. 10.
19. Ibid.
20. Ibid., p. 1.
21. Official Report of Lt. Col. Philo B. Buckingham, as quoted in Croffut and Morris, *Military and Civil History*, p. 770.
22. Official Report of Philo B. Buckingham, as quoted in Thorpe, *History of the Fifteenth*, p. 165.
23. Chapman, *Civil War Diary*, p. 113.
24. Letter of Abner C. Smith, March 23, 1865, online at dbappdev.com/acs/20thconn/ct20/acs/ltrs/AS_2_081.html.
25. Vaill, *History of the Second*, p. 148.
26. Croffut and Morris, *Military and Civil History*, p. 776.
27. Henry L. Abbot, "History of the First Regiment C.V. Heavy Artillery," in *Record of Service of Connecticut Men in the Army and Navy of the United States During the War of the Rebellion*, compiled by Authority of the General Assembly under the Direction of the Adjutants-General (Hartford, CT: Case, Lockwood & Brainard, 1889), p. 119.
28. Vaill, *History of the Second*, p. 153.
29. Brayton Ives, as quoted in Croffut and Morris, *Military and Civil History*, p. 784.
30. Vaill, *History of the Second*, p. 159.
31. Ibid., p. 160.
32. Trumbull, *War Memories of an Army Chaplain*, pp. 164–66.
33. Colonel Edwin S. Greeley, Report to Adjutant General of Connecticut, May 10, 1865, in *Annual Report of the Adjutant General of the State of Connecticut for the Year Ending March 31, 1866* (Hartford, CT: A. N. Clark & Co., 1866), pp. 109–10.
34. John L. Otis, "History of the Tenth Regiment Connecticut Volunteer Infantry," in *Record of Service of Connecticut Men in the Army and Navy of the United States during the War of the Rebellion*, compiled by Authority of the General Assembly under the Direction of the Adjutants-General (Hartford, CT: Case, Lockwood & Brainard, 1889), p. 397.
35. Grant, *Personal Memoirs*, p. 559.
36. Newton, *Out of the Briars*, pp. 66–67.
37. Erastus Blakeslee, "History of the First Regiment Connecticut Volunteer Cavalry," in *Record of Service*, p. 59.
38. Ibid., p. 60.
39. C. S. Venable, address at the Lee Memorial Meeting in Richmond, November 3, 1870, as quoted in *Personal Reminiscences of General Robert E. Lee*, compiled by Rev. J. William Jones (New York: Tom Dougherty Associates, 2004), p. 131.
40. Letter of Edward Washburn Whitaker, April 29, 1901, to General Joshua Lawrence Chamberlain, Edward W. Whitaker Collection, State Archives, Connecticut State Library, Hartford.
41. Diary of Nelson Stowe, April 9, 1865, Connecticut Historical Society, Hartford.
42. Charles G. Blatchley, as quoted in Page, *History of the Fourteenth*, p. 335.
43. Lynch, *Civil War Diary*, pp. 148–49.
44. Allen Bennett Lincoln in *A Memorial Volume of the Bi-centennial Celebration of the Town of Windham, Connecticut* (Hartford, CT: The New England Home Printing Co., 1893), pp. 65–66.
45. *Hartford Daily Courant*, April 19, 1865, p. 2.
46. Page, *History of the Fourteenth*, p. 338.
47. Ibid.
48. Ibid., p. 339.
49. Lynch, *Civil War Diary*, p. 156.
50. Allen Bennett Lincoln in *A Memorial Volume of the Bi-centennial Celebration of the Town of Windham, Connecticut*, published by the Committee (Hartford, CT: The New England Home Printing Co., 1893), p. 66.
51. Description of the return of Co. E of the 23rd Connecticut Volunteers to Georgetown, Connecticut, in September of 1863, from Wilbur F. Thompson, "Georgetown, Connecticut, in the Civil War Times." http://www.historyofredding.com/HRGeorgetown.htm.

52. Lynch, *Civil War Diary*, p. 160.

53. *Hartford Daily Courant*, June 5, 1865, p. 2.

14. Soldiers of the Union
Mustered Out

1. Petition seeking increase in pension for Charles L. Upham, September 27, 1871, Buck Zaidel collection.

2. Horace Bushnell, "Our Obligation to the Dead," an address honoring Yale men fallen in the war, July, 1865, in *Building Eras in Religion* (New York: Charles Scribner's Sons, 1881), p. 331.

3. Stevens, *Souvenir*, p. 83.

4. Charles A. Fuller, *Personal Recollections of the War of 1861* (reprint; Hamilton, NY: Edmonston Publishing, 1990), p. 70.

5. Tyler, "*Wooden Nutmegs*," p. 13.

6. Henry Perkins Goddard, as quoted in Page, *History of the Fourteenth*, pp. 25–26.

7. *New York Tribune*, December 27, 1910, p. 1.

8. Edward Griswold in *First Light Battery Connecticut Volunteers*, vol. 2, pp. 727–28.

9. *The National Baptist*, as quoted in *Hartford Daily Courant*, March 12, 1886, p. 2.

10. Huntington and Foote, *Harriet Ward Foote Hawley*, p. 104.

11. Goddard, *14th C.V. Regimental Reminiscences*, p. 9.

12. Chaplain Theodore Holmes, 1st Cavalry, *Memorial of John S. Jameson*, p. 30.

13. Robert H. Kellogg, address in *Dedication to the Monument at Andersonville, Georgia* (Hartford, CT: State of Connecticut, 1908), pp. 36–37.

14. Chaplain Henry Clay Trumbull, *10th Connecticut, War Memories of an Army Chaplain*, p. 166.

15. Huntington and Foote, *Harriet Ward Foote Hawley*, p. 48.

16. *History of Battle-Flag Day, September 17, 1879* (Hartford, CT: Lockwood and Merrit, 1880), p. 30.

17. *Hartford Daily Courant*, September 18, 1879, as quoted in *The History of Battle-Flag Day*, p. 238.

18. *History of Battle-Flag Day*, p. 62.

19. Newton, *Out of the Briars*, p. 71.

20. Fuller, *Personal Recollections*, p. 107.

21. Croffut and Morris, *Military and Civil History*, p. 809, quoting Joseph R. Hawley's speech on receiving a ceremonial sword presented to him after the war by the people of Hartford.

22. "Address by J. W. Knowlton," at the dedication of the 14th Connecticut's monument at Antietam, in Yates, *Souvenir of Excursion to Antietam and Dedication of Monuments*, p. 16.

23. Henry Goddard's address to veterans of the 14th Connecticut, at their annual reunion, September 17, 1877, courtesy of Calvin Goddard Zon.

Illustration Credits

Unless otherwise noted in the credits below, all of the images in this text are from the following five sources.

Key:

BZC = Buck Zaidel Collection
MCH = Museum of Connecticut History at the Connecticut State Library, Hartford, CT
HDC = *Hartford Daily Courant*, now the *Hartford Courant*, Hartford, CT
MCHS = Middlesex County Historical Society, Middletown, CT
LOC = Library of Congress

The authors wish to thank these sources and all of the private collectors, families, historical societies and museums who generously gave their permission to use illustrations and in many instances also provided important information about the people and places in the images. Due to the scarcity of Civil War images, the identification of a photograph may come down to a single source. The potential of a misidentification of a portrait over generations exists. We apologize for any inaccuracies and welcome additional information from readers.

Frontispiece

Page ii: *Hartford Daily Courant*, June 5, 1865, p. 2

1. Men of Connecticut!

Page 1: Buck Zaidel Collection
Page 2, *left*: BZC
Page 2, *right*: Museum of Connecticut History
Page 3: National Portrait Gallery
Page 4: *Connecticut Quarterly* Magazine, vol. 1, #4
Page 6: The Connecticut Historical Society, Hartford, CT
Page 7, *left*: The Connecticut Historical Society, Hartford, CT
Page 7, *right*: BZC
Page 8: BZC
Page 9, *top*: HDC, April 29,1861 and May 8, 1861
Page 9, *bottom*: BZC
Page 10, *left*: BZC
Page 10, *right*: BZC
Page 11: Museum of Connecticut History
Page 12, *top left*: BZC
Page 12, *top right*: Private Collection
Page 12, *bottom*: MCHS

2. No One Dreamed of Anything but Victory

Page 15: BZC
Page 16: LOC
Page 17: *Wooden Nutmegs at Bull Run* by Frinkle Fry (Hartford, CT: G.L. Colburn, 1872)
Page 19, *left*: BZC
Page 19, *right*: Private Collection
Page 20: BZC
Page 21, *top*: Connecticut State Capitol
Page 21, *bottom*: BZC
Page 22: BZC
Page 25: MCHS

3. The Voice of Duty

Page 27: Connecticut Historical Society

Page 28, *top*: HDC, August 20, 1861
Page 28, bottom: MCH
Page 29: BZC
Page 30: Bridgeport History Center of the Bridgeport
    Public Library
Page 31: BZC
Page 33, *left*: MCH
Page 33, *right*: BZC
Page 34, *left*: BZC
Page 34, *right*: BZC
Page 35, *left*: BZC
Page 35, *right*: BZC
Page 36, *left*: The Wilkinson Collection
Page 36, *right*: BZC
Page 37: LOC
Page 38: BZC
Page 40: LOC
Page 41: BZC
Page 42: BZC
Page 44: BZC
Page 46, *top*: BZC
Page 46, *bottom*: BZC

4. War by Citizen Soldiers

Page 49, [location on page]: Connecticut Historical Society;
    James Sawyer journal
Page 50, *left*: BZC
Page 50, *right*: *Story of the 21st Regiment*, by members of the
    regiment (Middletown, CT.: Stewart Printing Co., 1900),
    p. 127
Page 51, *left*: BZC
Page 51, *right*: BZC
Page 52: BZC
Page 53, *left*: MCH
Page 53, *right*: Collection of Michael J. McAfee
Page 54, *top*: MCHS
Page 54, *bottom*: HDC, September 6, 1862
Page 55, *left*: MCHS
Page 55, *right*: The Connecticut Historical Society, Hartford, CT
Page 56, *top*: BZC
Page 56, *bottom*: BZC
Page 57, *top*: BZC
Page 57, *bottom*: BZC
Page 58: BZC
Page 59: BZC

5. I Never Knew What War Meant
till Today

Page 61: The Connecticut Historical Society, Hartford, CT;
    James Sawyer journal

Page 62, *left*: C. Paul Loane Collection
Page 62, *right*: BZC
Page 63: LOC
Page 64: BZC
Page 65, *left*: BZC
Page 65, *right*: MCHS
Page 66, *top*: Scott D. Hann Collection
Page 66, *bottom*: BZC
Page 68: BZC
Page 69: LOC
Page 71: Scott D. Hann Collection
Page 72: *The Military and Civil History of Connecticut during
    the War of 186–65* by William Croffut and John M. Morris
    (New York: Ledyard Bill, 1868), p.755
Page 73: Photograph by author
Page 74: New England Civil War Museum, Rockville, CT.
Page 75: LOC
Page 76: BZC
Page 77: BZC
Page 78, *left*: BZC
Page 78, *right*: BZC
Page 80: BZC
Page 83, *left*: BZC
Page 83, *right*: BZC
Page 84: MCH
Page 85: MCH
Page 86: MCH
Page 88, *top left*: BZC
Page 88, *top right*: BZC
Page 88, *bottom*: LOC
Page 89: LOC

6. Emancipation Is a Mighty Word

Page 91: MCHS
Page 92: LOC
Page 93: LOC
Page 94: *Frank Leslie's Illustrated Newspaper*, January 24, 1863;
    Special Collections and Archives, Wesleyan University,
    Middletown, CT.
Page 95, *top left*: Thomas Harris Collection
Page 95, *top right*: Thomas Harris Collection
Page 95, *bottom*: BZC
Page 96: BZC
Page 97, *left*: BZC
Page 97, *middle*: BZC
Page 97, *right*: BZC
Page 99: Collection of Joyce Werkman
Page 100, *left*: BZC
Page 100, *right*: BZC
Page 102: Yale Collection of American Literature, Beinecke Rare

Book and Manuscript Library, Yale University

Page 103: BZC

7. No Men on Earth Can Be Braver

Page 105: BZC

Page 106, *top*: MCH

Page 106, *bottom*: *Harper's Weekly*, January 3, 1863; Wesleyan University Special Collections and Archives, Middletown, CT.

Page 107: LOC

Page 110: LOC

Page 111: LOC

Page 112: LOC

Page 113, *left*: BZC

Page 113, *right*: BZC

Page 114: Mary Foote Rounsavall

Page 117: BZC

Page 118, *left*: Don Troiani

Page 118, *right*: Don Troiani

Page 121, *top*: *When Lincoln Kissed Me*, by Henry E. Wing (New York: The Abington Press, 1913)

Page 121, *bottom*: BZC

Page 122: Collection of Diane Ulbrich

Page 123: BZC

Page 124: MCH

8. Who Wouldn't Be a Soldier?

Page 127: The Connecticut Historical Society, Hartford, CT; CHS, James Sawyer journal

Page 128, *top*: LOC

Page 128, *bottom*: BZC

Page 129: BZC

Page 130: BZC

Page 131: The Connecticut Historical Society, Hartford, CT

Page 132, *top*: The Connecticut Historical Society, Hartford, CT

Page 132, *bottom*: MCH

Page 133: MCHS

Page 134: BZC

Page 136: BZC

Page 137, *left*: BZC

Page 137, *right*: BZC

Page 138: BZC

Page 139, *top*: The Connecticut Historical Society, Hartford, CT

Page 139, *bottom*: The Connecticut Historical Society, Hartford, CT

Page 140, *top*: MCH

Page 140, *bottom*: BZC

Page 141, *top*: MCHS

Page 141, *bottom*: MCH

Page 142: BZC

Page 143: BZC

Page 145, *top*: Lincoln Memorial Shrine, Redlands, CA

Page 145, *bottom left*: Montana Historical Society Research Center

Page 145, *bottom right*: Montana Historical Society Research Center

Page 146: BZC

Page 148, *top left*: BZC

Page 148, *top right*: MCHS

Page 148, *bottom*: BZC

Page 149, *top*: BZC

Page 149, *bottom*: BZC

Page 150: The Connecticut Historical Society, Hartford, CT

Page 151: BZC

Page 152, *top*: LOC

Page 152, *bottom*: BZC

Page 153, *left*: BZC

Page 153, *right*: BZC

Page 154: BZC

9. All This Heroism, and All This Appalling Carnage

Page 157: BZC

Page 159: BZC

Page 161: BZC

Page 162: Cheshire Historical Society, CT.

Page 163: BZC

Page 165: The Connecticut Historical Society, Hartford, CT

Page 166: BZC

Page 167: MCHS

Page 168: LOC

Page 169: BZC

Page 170: The Connecticut Historical Society, Hartford, CT

Page 171: The Connecticut Historical Society, Hartford, CT

Page 172: BZC

Page 173: BZC

Page 174: BZC

Page 175: MCHS

Page 176, *top*: BZC

Page 176, *middle*: BZC

Page 176, *bottom*: MCHS

Page 177, *left*: BZC

Page 177, *right*: BZC

Page 178, *top left*: *The Old Flag* by Comrade Frank Miller (Bridgeport, CT: "The Old Flag" Publishing Co., 1914)

Page 178, *top right*: BZC

Page 178, *bottom*: MCH

Page 181, *top*: BZC

Page 181, *bottom*: BZC

10. That Place Long to Be Remembered

Page 183: The Connecticut Historical Society, Hartford, CT; James Sawyer Journal
Page 184: LOC
Page 185: MCH
Page 186: BZC
Page 188, *top*: BZC
Page 188, *bottom*: BZC
Page 189: BZC
Page 190: LOC
Page 191, *top*: BZC
Page 191, *bottom*: BZC
Page 192: *Yale Men in the Civil War* by Ellsworth Eliot (New Haven, Yale University Press, 1932)
Page 193: BZC
Page 194, *top*: BZC
Page 194, *bottom*: MCH
Page 195: LOC
Page 197: BZC
Page 198: MCHS
Page 199: BZC
Page 200: BZC
Page 201, *top*: BZC
Page 201, *bottom*: LOC
Page 204: BZC
Page 205: New England Civil War Museum
Page 206, *top*: BZC
Page 206, *bottom*: Jeff Kowalis
Page 208: BZC

11. There Will Be No Turning Back

Page 211: *History of the First Light Battery Connecticut Volunteers, 1861–1865* by Herbert W. Beecher
Page 212, *top*: BZC
Page 212, *bottom*: Property of Virginia Historical Society, through the Library of Congress
Page 213: BZC
Page 214, *top*: BZC
Page 214, *bottom*: Gary O'Neil
Page 215: MCHS
Page 216, *top*: LOC
Page 216, *bottom*: MCH
Page 217: BZC
Page 218: BZC
Page 219: BZC
Page 220: MCHS
Page 221, *top*: LOC
Page 221, *bottom*: BZC

Page 222: Harriet Beecher Stowe Center, Hartford, CT.
Page 223, *left*: Private collection
Page 223, *right*: BZC
Page 224: BZC
Page 228: MCH
Page 229, *top* Maltbie: BZC
Page 229, *top* Morse: BZC
Page 229, *top* Stoughton: BZC
Page 229, *top* Tatro: BZC
Page 229, *top* Palmer: BZC
Page 229, *bottom* Camp: BZC
Page 229, *bottom* Beach: BZC
Page 229, *bottom* Warner: BZC
Page 229, *bottom* Ells: BZC
Page 229, *bottom* Kellogg: BZC
Page 231, *left*: BZC
Page 231, *middle*: BZC
Page 231, *right*: BZC
Page 232, *top*: BZC
Page 232, *bottom*: BZC
Page 233, *top left*: BZC
Page 233, *top right*: BZC
Page 233, *bottom*: BZC
Page 234, *top*: BZC
Page 234, *bottom*: BZC
Page 235, *top*: BZC
Page 235, *bottom*: BZC
Page 236, *top*: BZC
Page 236, *bottom*: BZC

12. Hope Never Dying

Page 239: *History of the 1st Light Battery Connecticut Volunteers*
Page 240, *top*: BZC
Page 240, *bottom*: Property of the Virginia Historical Society, through LOC
Page 241, *top*: Ronald S. Coddington
Page 241, *bottom*: LOC
Page 242, *left*: LOC
Page 242, *right*: MCH
Page 244: BZC
Page 245, *top*: Special Collections and Archives, Wesleyan University, Middletown, CT.
Page 245, *bottom*: BZC
Page 246: BZC
Page 247, *top*: BZC
Page 247, *bottom*: Descendants of David Torrance
Page 248, *top*: BZC
Page 248, *bottom*: MCHS
Page 249: BZC

Page 250: BZC
Page 251, *top*: LOC
Page 251, *bottom*: BZC
Page 254, *top*: BZC
Page 254, *bottom*: BZC
Page 255, *top*: BZC
Page 255, *bottom*: BZC
Page 256: BZC
Page 258, *top*: BZC
Page 258, *bottom*: HDC, November 9, 1864, p. 2
Page 259, *top*: BZC
Page 259, *bottom*: BZC
Page 260, *top*: MCHS
Page 260, *bottom*: BZC

13. Our Army Perfectly Crazy

Page 263: BZC
Page 265: BZC
Page 267: BZC
Page 268: BZC
Page 269: BZC
Page 271: BZC
Page 272, *left*: BZC
Page 272, *right*: BZC
Page 273: BZC
Page 274, *left*: With permission from the family of Evelyn E. Packard (great-granddaughter)
Page 274, *right*: With permission from the family of Evelyn E. Packard (great-granddaughter
Page 275: *Frank Leslie's Illustrated News*, April 25, 1865; Special Collections and Archives, Wesleyan University, Middletown, CT.

Page 277: National Museum of American History, Smithsonian
Page 278: HDC, April 10, 1865
Page 279: LOC
Page 281, *left*: BZC
Page 281, *right*: *Medical and Surgical History of the War of the Rebellion* (Washington: United States Surgeon General's Office, 1870), part 3, vol. 2, p. Courtesy of the Watkinson Library, Trinity College, Hartford, Connecticut.

14. Soldiers of the Union Mustered Out

Page 283: BZC
Page 284, *top*: Private Collection
Page 284, *middle*: Private Collection
Page 284, *bottom*: BZC
Page 286: Bridgeport History Center, Bridgeport Public Library
Page 287: BZC
Page 288, *top left*: BZC
Page 288, *top right*: BZC
Page 288, *bottom*: BZC
Page 289, *top*: National Parks Service/ Andersonville National Historic Site
Page 289, *bottom*: MCHS
Page 290, *left*: MCHS
Page 290, *right*: Torrington Historical Society Collection; Torrington, CT.
Page 291: BZC
Page 292, *left*: BZC
Page 292, *right*: MCH
Page 293: Photograph by the author

INDEX

Page numbers for illustrations appear in *italics*.

Griswold, Homer W., *254*

Griswold, John, 52, 71–73, *72*, *73*

Gross, August, 68

Gwillim, Reese, 135

Haffey, Bernard, *213*

Haggerty, James, 217

Hall, Eben, *288*

Hallock, Charles, 268–69, *269*

Hammond, George, 171–72, *172*

Hammond Hospital, 120–21

Hancock, Winfield Scott, 109, 116, 164, 189

Handy, Bill, 147

Hanks, Alfred, 139

Hardee, General, 261

hardtack, 18, 36, 140, *140*

Harland, Edward, 74, 75–77, 79, 84

Harper's Weekly, 95

Harpster, J. H., 58, *59*

Harrington, Cyrus, 41

Harris, Jasper S., *83*

Hartford Daily Courant, *73*; Bull Run, 40; Civil War concluding events, 263, 264, *278*, 281; Civil War legacy, 291; on early photography, 33; enlistment, 1, 8; fall of Atlanta, 252; Fort Sumter events, 1, 2–3; Overland Campaign, 236; slavery, 3

Hartford Daily Times, *54*

Hartford Evening Press, 6, *258*

Hartford Times, 5, 29

Haskell, George, 2

Hatcher's Run, Virginia, 270

Hawley, Charles H., *235*

Hawley, Frederick Burr, 38–39; Battle of Antietam, 65, 66, 68, 69, 70; Battle of Fredericksburg, 105, 106, 108, 109, 110, 111–13, 117–18, 120, 121

Hawley, Harriet Ward Foote, 92–94, 95, *114*, 218, 285–86, 291

Hawley, Joseph R., *12*, 17, 23–24, 27, *28*, 92, 151, 291, *292*

Hawley, William H., *204*

Hays, Alexander, 199, 204, 215

Heath, George, 131

Henderson, James P., 268

Herman, Jacob, 52

Hewison, James, 43

Hibbard, Albert, 147

Hickerson, Francis, 275

Higginson, Colonel, 93

Hill, A. P., 44, 76, 83

Hill, Isaac J., 102, 103, *279*

Hilliard, Henry B., 124

Hills, Thomas Morton, 118, *118*

Hincks, William B., 66, 134, 202–3, *204*, 205, *205*

Hinsdale, Solomon R., 98

Hirst, Benjamin, 47, 66, 68, 107, 141, 185, 198, 201–2, 203

Holbrook, Lowell, *181*

Hollister, Francis, 127

Hollister, Frederick, 127

homesickness, of soldiers, *154*, 154–55

Hooker, Joseph "Fighting Joe," 63, 157–66, 183

Hopkins, A. Dwight, *177*

Hosford, Benjamin F., *258*

Hosford, William A., 226

Hotchkiss, Franklin A., 133

"housewives," *143*, 143–44

Howard, Oliver O., 158, 189

Hoyt, Henry, 79

Hubbard, George, 125

Hubbard, Horace, *255*

Hubbard, Josiah, 68, 69

Hubbard, Robert, *68*, 68–69

Hubbard, Robert (nephew), 69

Hull, Ezra M., 154

huts, as camp dwellings, 131–33, *132*, *133*, *134*

Huxham, Sam, 198, *198*

income, of soldiers, *28*, 49, 53–54, 103, 283, 284

Investment of Petersburg by Genl. Grant (Sneden), *240*

"Irish Regiment," 9th Connecticut Regiment as, 41, 52, *53*, 167

Irwin, Sergeant, 122–23

Ives, Brayton, 271–72, *272*

Ives, George E., 152

Ives, John S., 169

Ives, Sarah, *152*

Jackson, Lewis W. "Cast Iron," *241*, *242*, 242–43

Jackson, Stonewall, 40, 43–47, 63, 107, 158–66

Jameson, Colonel, 22

Jewett, Daniel Lee, 162, *162*

Jewett, Levi, 35, *248*, 248–49

Johnson, Andrew, 280

Johnson, Christopher, *218*

Johnson, Frank, 124

Johnson, Harmon, 266

Johnson, William, *218*

Johnson, William H., *38*

Johnson, William H. H., *268*

Johnston, Joseph, 22, 268

Jones, Henry, 52, 80–81

Jones, Ira D., 43

Jordan, Captain, 64

Judson, Marcus, 191

Kanaka, Friday, 52, 102

Kane, General, 162

Kautz, August, 233, 234

Kellogg, Elisha A., 32, 38, 138, 146, 223, 225–29, *229*

Kellogg, Robert H., *84*, *141*, 215–16, 289

Kelly, Michael, 32, 38, 254, 258

Ketter, Rev. J. C., *176*

Keyes, Erasmus, 20, 22

Kilbourne, D. C., *254*

Kilcullen, Tom, 192

Kingsbury, Henry Walter, 71, *71*, 73

Kinney, Van Buren, 151

Kinston, Battle of, 265–67

Klein, Daniel, 9

Knox, Andrew, 10, 18

Knox, Sarah, 10

Lacy-house (hospital), 115

Ladd, John, *289*

Lee, Robert E., 46–47, 62–64; Battle of Chancellorsville and, 157–66; Battle of Fredericksburg and, 106–7, 117; Battle of Winchester (second) and, 179–82; fall of Richmond and, 275–76; Gettysburg strategy of, 183–84, 191, 193, 197, 201, 207 (*see also* Gettysburg, Battle of); surrender at Appomattox, 276–78, *278*, 279–80. *See also* Overland Campaign

Letters to a Civil War Bride (Mercer, Mercer), *16*

women's roles, in Civil War: food bartering with soldiers, 250; as nurses, 218, 221–22, *222*; soldiers' aid societies formed by, 144; substitute soldiers hired by, *56*; uniforms sewed by, *7*; Union support by, *7*. *See also individual names*

Wood, George, 194

"Wooden Nutmegs" of Bull Run (Tyler), *17*

Woodruff, Richard K., *244*

Wooster, David B., *256*

Wooster, Lieutenant-Colonel, 162

Wooster Guard, 8

Work, Henry Clay, 259

Wright, Benjamin, 53

Wright, General, 256

Wright, Horatio, 56

Yale, Merrit, 191

Yale, Tom, 191

Yergason, Edgar, 3–4

Zimmerman, Caspar, 9

Zook, Samuel K., 107–8, 122

Garnet Books

Garnet Poems:
An Anthology of Connecticut Poetry
Since 1776
Edited by Dennis Barone

Food for the Dead:
On the Trail of New England's Vampires
by Michael E. Bell

Early Connecticut Silver, 1700–1840
by Peter Bohan and Philip
Hammerslough
Introduction and Notes by Erin
Eisenbarth

The Connecticut River:
A Photographic Journey through the
Heart of New England
by Al Braden

Tempest-Tossed:
The Spirit of Isabella Beecher Hooker
by Susan Campbell

Connecticut's Fife & Drum Tradition
by James Clark

Sunken Garden Poetry, 1992–2011
Edited by Brad Davis

The Old Leather Man:
Historical Accounts of a Connecticut and
New York Legend
Edited by Dan W. DeLuca

Post Roads & Iron Horses:
Transportation in Connecticut from
Colonial Times to the Age of Steam
by Richard DeLuca

The Log Books:
Connecticut's Slave Trade and Human
Memory
by Anne Farrow

Dr. Mel's Connecticut Climate Book
by Dr. Mel Goldstein

Hidden in Plain Sight:
A Deep Traveler Explores Connecticut
by David K. Leff

Becoming Tom Thumb:
Charles Stratton, P.T. Barnum, and the
Dawn of American Celebrity
by Eric D. Lehman

Homegrown Terror:
Benedict Arnold and the Burning of New
London
by Eric D. Lehman

Westover School:
Giving Girls a Place of Their Own
by Laurie Lisle

Heroes for All Time:
Connecticut Civil War Soldiers Tell
Their Stories
by Dione Longley and Buck Zaidel

Crowbar Governor:
The Life and Times of Morgan Gardner
Bulkeley
by Kevin Murphy

Fly Fishing in Connecticut:
A Guide for Beginners
by Kevin Murphy

About the Authors

DIONE LONGLEY is an independent historian and writer. For two decades, she served as director of the Middlesex County Historical Society; she also annotated *The Old Leather Man* by Dan DeLuca.

BUCK ZAIDEL, a dentist and longtime Civil War enthusiast, collects objects and images related to Union soldiers' daily lives. He has exhibited at Civil War and antique arms shows across the country, and contributed items to museum exhibitions, including *Photography and the American Civil War* at the Metropolitan Museum of Art.

ABOUT THE DRIFTLESS CONNECTICUT SERIES

The Driftless Connecticut Series is a publication award program established
in 2010 to recognize excellent books with a Connecticut focus or written by
a Connecticut author. To be eligible, the book must have a Connecticut
topic or setting or an author must have been born in Connecticut or have
been a legal resident of Connecticut for at least three years.

The Driftless Connecticut Series is funded by the
Beatrice Fox Auerbach Foundation Fund
at the Hartford Foundation for Public Giving.
For more information and a complete list
of books in the Driftless Connecticut Series,
please visit us online at
http://www.wesleyan.edu/wespress/driftless.